The Geopolitics of American Insecurity

This edited volume examines the political, social, and cultural insecurities that the United States is faced with in the aftermath of its post-9/11 foreign policy and military ventures. The contributors critically detail the new strategies and ideologies of control, governance, and hegemony that America has devised as a response to these new security threats.

The essays explore three primary areas. First, they interrogate the responses to 9/11 that resulted in an attempt at geopolitical mastery by the United States. Second, they examine how the US response to 9/11 led to attempts to secure and control populations inside and outside the United States, resulting in situations that quickly started to escape its control, such as Abu Ghraib and Hurricane Katrina. Lastly, the chapters investigate links between contemporary regimes of state control and recently recognized threats, arguing that the conduct of everyday life is increasingly conditioned by state-mobilized discourses of security. These discourses are, it is argued, ushering in a geopolitical future characterized by new insecurities and inevitable measures of biopolitical control and governance.

This edited volume will be of much interest to students of critical security studies, US foreign policy, critical geopolitics and international relations theory.

François Debrix is Associate Professor of International Relations at Florida International University in Miami. He is the author and editor of several books, including *Tabloid Terror* (2007).

Mark J. Lacy is Lecturer of International Relations at Lancaster University. His publications include *Security and Climate Change: International Relations and the Limits of Realism* (2006).

PRIO New Security Studies
Edited by J. Peter Burgess
PRIO, Oslo

The aim of this book series is to gather state-of-the-art theoretical reflexion and empirical research into a core set of volumes that respond vigorously and dynamically to the new challenges to security scholarship.

1 **The Geopolitics of American Insecurity**
   Terror, power and foreign policy
   Edited by François Debrix and Mark J. Lacy

The Geopolitics of American Insecurity

Terror, power and foreign policy

Edited by François Debrix and Mark J. Lacy

LONDON AND NEW YORK

First published 2009
by Routledge
2 Park Square, Milton Park, Abingdon, Oxon, OX14 4RN

Simultaneously published in the USA and Canada
by Routledge
270 Madison Avenue, New York, NY 10016

Routledge is an imprint of the Taylor & Francis Group, an informa business

© 2009 François Debrix and Mark J. Lacy for selection and editorial matter; individual chapters, the contributors

Typeset in Baskerville by Pindar NZ, Auckland, New Zealand
Printed and bound in Great Britain by CPI Antony Rowe, Chippenham, Wiltshire

All rights reserved. No part of this book may be reprinted or reproduced or utilised in any form or by any electronic, mechanical, or other means, now known or hereafter invented, including photocopying and recording, or in any information storage or retrieval system, without permission in writing from the publishers.

British Library Cataloguing in Publication Data
A catalogue record for this book is available from the British Library

Library of Congress Cataloging in Publication Data
The geopolitics of American insecurity : terror, power, and foreign policy / edited by François Debrix and Mark J. Lacy.
  p. cm. — (PRIO new security studies)
  1. United States—Foreign relations—2001- 2. September 11 Terrorist Attacks, 2001—Influence. 3. War on Terrorism, 2001- 4. National security—United States—History—21st century. 5. World politics—1995–2005.
6. Security, International. I. Debrix, François. II. Lacy, Mark J.
  E902.G44 2009
  355'.033573—dc22   2008028831

ISBN10: 0-415-46042-5 (hbk)
ISBN10: 0-203-88421-3 (ebk)

ISBN13: 978-0-415-46042-2 (hbk)
ISBN13: 978-0-203-88421-8 (ebk)

Contents

List of figures	vii
List of contributors	viii
Acknowledgments	ix
Introduction: US foreign policy after hype(r)-power FRANÇOIS DEBRIX AND MARK J. LACY	1
1 Hyper-power or hype-power? The USA after Kandahar, Karbala, and Katrina TIMOTHY W. LUKE	18
2 American insecurities and the ontopolitics of US pharmacotic wars LARRY N. GEORGE	34
3 Power, violence, and torture: making sense of insurgency and legitimacy crises in past and present wars of attrition ALEXANDER D. BARDER	54
4 *Torturefest* and the passage to pedagogy of tortured pasts MARIE THORSTEN	71
5 Designing security: control society and MoMA's *SAFE: Design Takes on Risk* MARK J. LACY	88
6 Deserting sovereignty? The securitization of undocumented migration in the United States MATHEW COLEMAN	107
7 The biopolitics of American security policy in the twenty-first century JULIAN REID	126

8	Human security, governmentality, and sovereignty: a critical examination of contemporary discourses on universalizing humanity KOSUKE SHIMIZU	143
9	The aesthetic emergency of the avian flu affect GEOFFREY WHITEHALL	161
10	Over a barrel: cultural political economy and oil imperialism SIMON DALBY AND MATTHEW PATERSON	181
11	Zombie democracy PATRICIA MOLLOY	197
	Index	215

Figures

6.1 Interior immigration apprehensions vs. interior apprehensions as a percentage of border patrol apprehensions, 1992–2006.   116
6.2 Interior immigration enforcement in the United States, 1992–2003.   117

Contributors

Alexander D. Barder is completing his Ph.D. in the Department of Political Science at Johns Hopkins University, Baltimore, USA.

Mathew Coleman is Assistant Professor of Geography at Ohio State University, Columbus, USA.

Simon Dalby is Professor of Geography and Political Economy at Carleton University, Ottawa, Canada.

François Debrix is Associate Professor in the Department of Politics and International Relations at Florida International University, Miami, USA.

Larry N. George is Professor of Political Science at California State University-Long Beach, USA.

Mark J. Lacy is Lecturer in the Department of Politics and International Relations at Lancaster University, United Kingdom.

Timothy W. Luke is University Distinguished Professor of Political Science at Virginia Polytechnic Institute and State University, Blacksburg, USA.

Patricia Molloy teaches in the Department of Communication Studies at Wilfrid Laurier University, Waterloo, Canada.

Matthew Paterson is Professor of Political Science in the School of Political Studies at the University of Ottawa, Canada.

Julian Reid is Lecturer in the Department of War Studies at King's College, London, United Kingdom.

Kosuke Shimizu is Associate Professor of International Relations in the Faculty of Intercultural Studies at Ryukoku University, Seta, Japan.

Marie Thorsten is Associate Professor in the Faculty of Social Studies at Doshisha University, Kyoto, Japan.

Geoffrey Whitehall is Assistant Professor in the Department of Political Science at Acadia University in Nova Scotia, Canada.

Acknowledgments

This book would not have been possible without the support and dedication of its contributors. As editors, we owe an enormous debt of gratitude to all of the book's contributors who accommodated our repeated requests for revisions, patiently complied with editorial and formatting requirements, and generously accepted to provide critical input on each other's chapters. The project as a whole benefited greatly from comments and suggestions offered by a number of people, including Clair Apodaca, Kyle Grayson, Nicholas Kiersey, Debbie Lisle, Cindy Weber, and Jeremy White. Three anonymous reviewers for Routledge also provided us with important insights that strengthened the manuscript. Early versions of several of the chapters were presented as conference papers at various British International Studies Association and International Studies Association annual meetings. Finally, our gratitude goes to Andrew Humphrys and Emily Kindleysides at Routledge who were supportive of the project from the very beginning and provided useful advice throughout the writing, revising, editing, and production stages.

Introduction
US foreign policy after hype(r)-power

François Debrix and Mark J. Lacy

Contemporary American cinema has no shortage of images of future disasters that, consciously or not, contribute to the debate over the future of American politics and foreign policy. Blockbuster movies such as *I am Legend*, *Cloverfield*, or *The Day After Tomorrow*, along with hit television shows such as *Heroes*, *Jericho*, or *24*, do not only imagine different catastrophic scenarios; they also obsess over the dangers of the state's response to terror and disaster.[1] In Richard Kelly's *Southland Tales*, for example, a nuclear attack on Texas results in World War III, the creation of a radical all-seeing surveillance system, and a beefed-up version of the Patriot Act (called US-Ident). This film's narrative involves a complex intertwining of events related to the apocalypse and the development of wave fuel (called "Fluid Karma") as a response to dwindling oil supplies; the activities of a neo-Marxist revolutionary group in Los Angeles (based in Venice Beach); and the kidnapping of a republican politician's movie star son-in-law. But what stays in the minds of viewers after watching the frenetic and farcical onslaught of surreal scenes in this movie are images that resonate with the contemporary US public sphere and its anxieties: the pop star Justin Timberlake playing an Iraq veteran who surveys a beach in Los Angeles from an armed defensive post that protects the Fluid Karma installation in the ocean; Republican politicians in a medicalized room full of surveillance cameras spying upon the population of the city and aided by staff in transparent raincoats; and a motorized toy solider crawling across the sidewalk. In the end, both critics and audiences did not really know what to make of the film, perhaps because its surreal journey is too much like American everyday life where anything seems possible in this post-9/11 age of hype(r)-power.[2]

New insecurities

In the introduction to New York's Museum of Modern Arts' 2008 exhibition, *Design and the Elastic Mind*, curator Barry Bergdoll comments:

> As in the Cold War era, in today's political and scientific climate huge technological and scientific advances are underway and new behaviors are projected and celebrated. As then, we are gripped by the anxiety that accompanies rapid change, from the internet's profound restructuring of our everyday lives to our capacity to map the human genome, while we simultaneously engage in astoundingly hopeful explorations of both aesthetics and technology. It is the *elastic mind*—with the

flexibility and strength to embrace progress and harness it—that is best suited to confront this world of seemingly limitless challenges and possibilities.[3]

Reality today often feels like what it appears to be in *Southland Tales*, and a common political response is to provide our "elastic minds" with spectacles of control and protection from all sorts of dangerous strangers. Critical social theorist Zygmunt Bauman has noted that the German term *Unsicherheit*—a word that "blends together experiences that three English terms—uncertainty, insecurity and unsafety" convey—is condensed into a focus on safety in the context of contemporary European and North American politics. Safety, it appears, is the "only field in which something can be done and seen to be done."[4] But, Bauman suggests, there is also "a well-understandable inclination of political elites to divert the deepest causes of anxiety—that is, the experience of individual insecurity and uncertainty—to the popular concern with (already misplaced) threats to safety."[5] Al Gore chooses to examine the politics of fear and anxiety through an analysis that combines neuroscience research on trauma and fear, and political theory inspired by, among other figures, Jürgen Habermas' work on the public sphere. In Gore's own contribution to the debate on the problems with Bush's America, *The Assault on Reason*, the former Vice-President writes that television can create memories that have the same control over the emotional system as real ones: "the visual imagery on television can activate parts of the brain involved in emotions in a way that reading about the same event cannot."[6] The "quasi-hypnotic" state created by television and the systematic "exposure to fear" can manipulate the public sphere in a manner that bypasses "reason and logic."[7] While there are many examples of powerful images and stories producing a "vicarious traumatization" (drawing on past traumas and tragedies that create powerful reactions) that can be mobilized to press for social causes, the use of fear through visceral imagery and rhetoric can "ratchet up public anxieties and fears, distorting public discourse and reason."[8] What is more, Gore suggests, this state of fear creates an "addiction to the constant stimulation of two areas of the brain."[9] Gore contends that we need to understand the Bush administration's use of a "fear campaign" in contemporary democracy if we are to challenge a political culture where the security politics of leaders who demonstrate "dogmatic faith in ideological viewpoints" and offer "comfort to a fearful society" continues to shape responses to geopolitical anxiety.[10]

An entire academic/intellectual industry has capitalized on American unsafety since 9/11. Often, this academic/intellectual domain has involved scholars from the field of International Relations (IR) (Stephen Walt and John Mearsheimer, for example[11]). Popular reads, like Naomi Klein's bestseller *The Shock Doctrine: The Rise of Disaster Capitalism* (marketed with "trailers" made by the director of *Children of Men*, Alfonso Cuarón), have also partaken of this intellectual insecurity milieu. Michael Hardt and Antonio Negri, the authors of the hugely successful *Empire*, have boldly declared that the "world is at war again, but things are different this time."[12] On the back cover of the stylish paperback version of their 2004 book *Multitude: War and Democracy in the Age of Empire*, one reads: "MULTITUDE: the resistance of the many against the elite who benefit from empire. We are the multitude. Join Us."[13] And then we have the many intellectuals and pundits of "tabloid geopolitics" who, for more than a decade now, have explored the geopolitical anxieties that American hyper-power is supposed to be able to deal with.[14] Here we find (among the most recently published texts) books such as Thomas Barnett's *Blueprint for Action: A Future Worth Creating*; Tony Blankley's *The West's Last Chance: Will We Win the Clash of Civilizations?*; Ted Galen Carpenter's *America's Coming War with China*; Tom Tancredo's *In Mortal Danger: The Battle for America's Border and Security*; Jed Babbin and Edward Timperlake's *Showdown: Why China Wants War with the United States*; Patrick Buchanan's *State of Emergency: the Third World Invasion of the United States*; and Kenneth Timmerman's *Countdown to Crisis: The Coming Nuclear Showdown with Iran*.[15] Many of these sensationalistic and fear-inducing texts on the allegedly new geopolitical realities of the post-9/11 world could have been written at any time since the end of the Cold War, often with similar concerns (the weakness of liberals, the damaging impact of academic culture in the United States, the dangerous economic consequences of ecological concerns, and the many threats posed by immigration and demographic change to the future of the American nation). Still, some of the less "tabloid" books may turn out to be more revealing about the changes that seem to emerge in the landscape of American security politics.

One of these supposedly less sensationalistic or more sedate forums for discussion on the future of American security has been the journal *The American Interest*. After declaring that we are now "after the neocons," Francis Fukuyama edited a volume (based on one of the journal's conferences) that brought together people "who think about discrete uncertainties and who have also considered the very nature of uncertainty itself."[16] The aim of this book, *Blindside: How To Anticipate Forcing Events and Wild Cards in Global Politics*, was to address the "challenge of uncertainty" and what Fukuyama calls the "wild cards" of low probability but high impact contingencies in global politics. Of course, the discipline of IR has always been intimately concerned with the issue of uncertainty. Stanley Hoffmann famously wrote that IR is "the science of uncertainty."[17] In the introduction to *Blindside* Fukuyama is concerned with institutional constraints and contemporary failings in security thinking, and he suggests that those who "deal professionally with global politics, foreign policy, and national security affairs have particular biases when it comes to thinking about the future."[18] Critics of mainstream approaches to security studies in IR have been making this point for a long time, at least since Richard Falk published *This Endangered Planet* in 1971,[19] and, later, through the critiques of realism developed in the 1980s that eventually led to the work of "critical geopolitics" scholars,[20] or to more recent concerns with "biopolitics."[21] Fukuyama's *Blindside* does include interdisciplinary perspectives that address issues such as why, in cases when it is cost-effective to hedge against a low probability event, policymakers are unwilling to allocate money for prevention (often because of their inability to imagine "a contingency becoming real"[22]). For Fukuyama, the idea behind a volume like *Blindside* (and, by extension, the journal *The American Interest*) is to create a space where creative thinking about security, uncertainty, and the future can take place through a variety of conceptual frameworks or methodologies (in order to select hedges that are "robust over the largest number of possible futures"[23]). To be sure, many discussions in Fukuyama's collection seem to cover topics known to people familiar with the broader literature on risk and uncertainty. Yet Fukuyama's *Blindside* also introduces ideas and thinkers that would be alien to most scholars working on conventional or mainstream security politics (for example, "geo-engineering" as a response to human-generated climate change; Ray Kurzweil's "singularity" argument; or even some of the debates over the desire for "an omniscient, panopticon, Benthamite government that can see the future"[24]). But despite the inclusion of some of these novel notions and analytical perspectives, very little in-depth analysis of non-traditional security problems and their connections to the phenomenon of the production of insecurity (and to the political economy that produces insecurity and the everyday experience of *Unsicherheit* for many inside and outside the United States) in a context of US hype(r)-power is provided. Instead, Fukuyama's project often leaves the reader with a shop-window approach to new security concerns and, as such, it remains to be seen whether these broader perspectives on uncertainty will be more than a "talking shop," unable to provide serious alternatives to more militaristic and conventional approaches to hyper-power and geopolitics (perpetuated by the fear campaigns outlined by Gore and by an insistence on "sensational" visceral future threats).

One of the important points that emerged from the works of critical IR and non-mainstream security studies scholars in the early 1990s (in writings by Simon Dalby, Timothy W. Luke, James Der Derian, or David Campbell, for example[25]) was the way assemblages of moral positions, identity politics, economic interests, official geopolitical knowledge, and popular cultural representations took shape in a manner that normalized certain risks and sought to present some alleged "mortal threats" to the nation or state as given. These constructions were often linked to realist conceptions of danger attached to the nation-state, its central claim to power and force, and its sovereignty. In the process, as these critical scholars showed, other dangers, often more meaningful or material for people's everyday lives, were rendered illegitimate or meaningless. One such threat often presented as irrational or irrelevant in mainstream security literatures was the problem of human-generated climate change.

Of late, and no doubt thanks in part to the critical work of the above scholars in the 1990s, a transformation has occurred in the way human-generated climate change has been constructed as a security threat (along with a more general popular discussion about global uncertainty made possible with the publication of books such as Nassim Nicholas Taleb's *The Black Swan: The Impact of the Highly Improbable*[26]). While there are still many people who wish to contest the scientific evidence about climate change and, just as importantly, there are still some IR/security studies scholars who believe that climate change is only a secondary form of insecurity for the nation-state (the United States, above all), the possibility of environmental disasters resulting from human-generated ecological transformations is much easier to grasp after Hurricane Katrina devastated parts of the US Gulf Coast in 2005 (and perhaps after the popularity of Al Gore's film, *An Inconvenient Truth*, too). Today, to discuss the possibility of human-generated climate change as a pressing security issue for the United States does not involve the same degree of distant uncertainty or far removed political risk as it did only a decade or so ago. As a result, towards the end of the first decade of the new millennium, we are encountering political, social, cultural, economic, and even military anxieties that were traditionally reserved to the domains of "high power politics" (war, deterrence, ideological struggles between superpowers, the Cold War, and the specter of nuclear annihilation) in areas directly or indirectly tied to the climate change debate (but conventionally not associated with power politics). Thus, anxieties over peak oil, energy security, global competition for resources, or food supplies (even in the West) are becoming as relevant as, if not more than, typical geopolitical fears and risks. Whether this apparently new agenda is only media hype or political spin (particularly when US politicians struggle to define the contours of the post-Bush world) remains to be seen. But there are signs that a number of anxieties and insecurities are converging to form a new assemblage of geopolitical, geo-economic, and geocultural discourses loosely arranged around the future of energy, the climate, and the sustenance of life on the planet. At the same time though, one should not perceive the apparent emergence of this new multi-layered security agenda as the result of a "molecular revolution" that would lead to new types of freedoms or to the development of new forms of transnational justice (as Simon Dalby and Matthew Paterson are sure to remind us in their chapter in the present volume). In fact, one should not discount the possibility that such a revised global geopolitics of (in)security (with the United States still seeking to provide a leading role) may be part of a broader reorganization of the (post)modern society of security that is now able to deploy "smart" materials and technologies or "soft" powers and management techniques in order to create new forms of control and surveillance (as Mark J. Lacy argues in his chapter in this volume).

Another major development in the (broadly understood) field of security or, better yet, of uncertainty/unsafety management (as Bauman puts it) since 9/11 and the beginning of the war on terror has been the contestation of the war in Iraq by mainstream IR scholars and theorists who would normally be thought of as supporters of war/military intervention, if only on the grounds that war/intervention solidifies national security or establishes global hegemony. Yet, since 2002, realist intellectuals have been some of the most vocal opponents of the Bush administration's foreign policy strategies (or visions). While it is not surprising to find leftist or liberal critics of the war on terror subjected to various disciplinary or scare tactics by the Bush administration and its supporters, the decision (championed by neo-conservative policy-makers, intellectuals, and pundits) to simply ignore realist voices was less expected. Perhaps the fear that acknowledging realist objections to both the war on terror and the war in Iraq would break the illusion of a consensus in the conservative security establishment supportive of the Bush administration goes a long way in explaining this apparently odd neglect (all the more so since realist security perspectives have always been close to US power and US foreign policy-making).

Two of the most forceful realist critics of the Bush administration, John Mearsheimer and Stephen Walt, became embroiled in a huge controversy in 2006 when they began to publish works on the danger that the Israel lobby represented to US security politics (culminating with the release of *The Israel Lobby and US Foreign Policy* in 2007).[27] While much of their critical assessment of the US security strategy that led to the war on terror has now been sidelined as a result of the Israel Lobby controversy, some of the reservations offered by Mearsheimer and Walt are worth considering as, in many ways, they set up the terms of the debate for future (mostly realist still) investigations of US security and foreign policy in the mainstream of IR. In *Taming American Power*, Walt argues that, while American global primacy provides many advantages, "what others do will still determine whether US foreign policy succeeds or fails."[28] He goes on to suggest that even "an unrivalled superpower" like the United States "cannot defeat the shadowy forces of global terrorism without active, enthusiastic, 24/7 cooperation from foreign intelligence services and law enforcement agencies."[29] In the conclusion of the book, Walt begins to sketch out important areas of security politics that need to be improved if the United States is to develop what he calls a "mature foreign policy." Walt's intervention appears to be a response to the view that power politics and US wars go hand in hand, a view exemplified by self-proclaimed "tabloid" realist public intellectuals like Robert D. Kaplan, who argues that too many Americans lack "moral hardiness" and believes that "cleverness should not be confused with character."[30] For Walt (and Mearsheimer), the United States must develop a more "disciplined attitude" to foreign policy if it wants to make its "privileged position acceptable to others and maintain geopolitical primacy for as long as it can."[31]

Of course, Walt does not go as far as another famous realist critic, Hans Morgenthau, once did when he reflected on the future of US politics in the aftermath of the Vietnam War.[32] There are certainly some realists today—perhaps best described as libertarian realists—who are concerned with the militarization of American life.[33] But what is clear in Walt's comments on the future of US foreign policy is that "serious" conservative IR thinkers recognize that a major change is required in the structuring of the American political system if the military excesses of the Bush years are to be avoided.[34] John Gray, the Professor of European Thought at the London School of Economics, concludes his eclectic (some would say fashionable, after his bestselling *Straw Dogs: Thoughts on Humans and Other Animals*) examination of apocalyptic religion and the "death of utopia" by arguing for a return to the "lost tradition of realism."[35] For Gray, there is no doubt why realism is "viewed with suspicion": it is "too austere for a culture that prizes psychological comfort above anything else." Like Walt, Gray acknowledges that realist thinking must begin to take "seriously" the threats posed by environmental crises and avoid "crackpot *realpolitik*."[36] Still, he argues that realism is a tradition that can overcome the secular myths that create the "debris of utopian projects" (which, for Gray, include the US neo-conservative project of the Bush years).[37]

In this new realist critique articulated by Walt, Gray, and others, there is a clear desire to bring an *ethos* of caution and an attitude of professionalism into a foreign policy that has been dominated by blind faith and moral certainty, and has been driven by a management of insecurities (political, economic, or social) that has resulted in a succession of disastrous situations outlined so forcefully by Joseph Stiglitz and Linda Bilmes in *The Three Trillion Dollar War*.[38] While contemporary realist arguments (including Walt's ideas and Gray's philosophical musings) may appear refreshing after the take-over of US foreign policy and national security debates by the neo-cons, it is also quite possible that this seemingly rekindled sense of realist caution may simply be about establishing a new "great power" geopolitical framework. This craving for a return to great power politics as an analytical approach that, among other things, may be able to restore order and stability (and certainty and security) in US politics (and in IR circles indirectly too) is perhaps best evidenced in reflections over the status of China. Walt observes that China and the United States "have continued to pursue mutually profitable economic ties and have avoided direct confrontation even when potential sources of tension were present."[39] Mearsheimer concludes his *Tragedy of Great Power Politics* by arguing that China is the primary threat for the United States. Indeed, Mearsheimer urgently affirms: "It is not too late for the United States to reverse course and do what it can to slow the rise of China."[40] In a way, it may be the case that American realists in academia and in policy circles have been patiently waiting their turn to redirect US foreign policy and national security. And now that the neo-cons have started to fade, US politics/culture may be ready for a replacement of the war on terror with what some (starting with Mearsheimer) may call an "offensive realism" (toward China in particular). As the influence of the neo-conservative American Enterprise Institute on foreign policy gives way to strategies prepared by the Cato Institute and its members,[41] current American insecurities and geopolitical anxieties may not so much be removed (by a new realist sense of order, priority, stability, or certainty) as they may be shifted towards new geopolitical objects and targets. The emerging realist recovery of the American (in)security field is thus no guarantee that the militarization of everyday life and the formation of societies of control will soon be past realities.

As some of the novel (sometimes popular) approaches to questions of insecurity and geopolitical anxiety—the ideas sketched by realists like Walt and Mearsheimer, Fukuyama's project of global awareness towards non-traditional security issues, or even the perspectives championed by proponents of the climate change debate—take hold in US politics and culture, a new all-encompassing expression or vision of US hype(r)-power is likely to appear in order to try to make sense of the disparate events, situations, and often crises that will populate the landscape of security studies and IR. A candidate for such an all-encompassing vision is Joseph Nye's concept of "smart power."

In December 2007, *The American Interest* published a dialogue between Nye and Richard Armitage (the former US Deputy Secretary of State), led by John Hamre, the CEO of the Center for Strategic and International Studies in Washington, DC. Nye and Armitage had been co-chairing the Center's Commission on Smart Power, a project "designed to provide recommendations to the next President of the United States on how to restore America's credibility and influence in the world."[42] Nye clarified his views on smart power in *The Powers to Lead*, a primer on leadership that, according to General Brent Scowcroft's recommendation on the back cover, would "benefit anyone from Washington to Wall Street."[43] The book sets out the case for a smart power based on "Contextual IQ" that, among other dynamics, focuses on understanding "evolving environments," develops the ability to "Capitalize on Trends" ("create luck"), and responds to crisis and "time urgency."[44] Building on the assumption that the tension between "idealism" and "realism" is a false dichotomy, Nye suggests that smart power is about tapping into "diverse sources of power, including our soft power, to attract others. It is about how we can get other countries to share our goals without resorting to coercion, which is limited and inevitably costly." Armitage adds that smart power is concerned with a strategy that returns foreign policy to more "traditional values of hope and optimism."[45] Simply put, smart power operates from the assumption that America has to have a purpose that is greater than a "single threat" focus. As Nye puts it, we (meaning Americans) "can do more damage to ourselves by overacting to terrorist threats than the terrorists could ever do."[46] Like Walt in *Taming American Power*, Nye and Armitage call for a liberal realism dedicated to providing "international public goods" to deal with problems such as climate change, poverty, or infectious diseases and to supporting a governmental structure and institutional architecture that will provide the "mental bandwith" necessary to multi-task the management of regional challenges and various geopolitical/geo-economic problems.[47]

The emergence of a smart power approach to foreign policy may be a welcome development for those concerned with America's future role in international affairs. Yet, as suggested above, there is no guarantee that smart power will be able to reduce the effects of militarization on everyday life or the dangers resulting from the proliferation of techniques of control. In fact, smart power may be a perfect *trompe l'oeil* mechanism for power politics, geopolitical mastery, and biopolitical management and surveillance. Veiled by smart power techniques and strategies, America's hype(r)-power may well be unable to respond to its *Unsicherheit* (that is to say, once again, its political, economic and cultural experience of uncertainty, insecurity and unsafety), both at home and abroad.

Geopolitics and American insecurity

The essays collected in this volume all seek to provide warnings about the future of US foreign policy. Often, they develop disturbing critiques of American political and security culture. There is in fact a recognition that the post-9/11 domain of geopolitics that includes issues such as global warming, bioterror, or the rise of allegedly new military powers like China (among other concerns) may produce forms of smart politics and smart governance that, far from opening up possibilities for life or living, will instead continue to narrow the mostly technocratic and technostrategic focus of contemporary politics. This is the point where, as Timothy W. Luke suggests (in his chapter in this volume), smart power actively enables the passage from hyper-power to hype-power.

Many of the essays in *The Geopolitics of American Insecurity* are haunted by the awareness that designing irresponsible wars or deploying novel forms of violence out of American society/culture through a belief in smart power and/or governance will take us further away from being able to grasp the significance of war and violence (and possibly challenge them both), a point made powerfully by Larry N. George's chapter. Amidst contemporary discussions on the taming of America's (hyper)power, on the assault on reason, on new approaches to risk and uncertainty, or on the emergence of smart power, Hannah Arendt's words of caution are a loud echo throughout this book. As Arendt so prophetically put it: "The greater the bureaucratization of public life, the greater will be the attraction of violence."[48]

But the essays in this book are also influenced by the critical concerns with state (bio)power recently articulated by intellectuals such as Giorgio Agamben (particularly, his writings on *homo sacer*, or bare life, and the state of exception). Faced with the realization of hyped-up attempts at smart power and governance, but also of their horrific failure at times (with the proliferation of governmental irresponsibilities, as was blatantly displayed in the aftermath of Katrina), the contributors to this volume recognize that it is not just in the "wild zones" of IR or in the "detention camps" of global anti-terror politics where sovereign power today decides who will live and who will die (as we saw all too tragically in Myanmar in May and June 2008, after yet another humanitarian disaster). Rather, it is also in the worlds that we inhabit, the safe zones in which we move, transit, or live on a daily basis, that new modalities of biopolitical and media-technological control or surveillance operate. It is in those mundane, familiar, and normalized spaces that terror is being fought and transnational crime is being tracked down. Throughout those common sites "in here" (and not just those exceptional locations "over there"), new forms of global insecurities are not at all ameliorated by smart power (in fact, they generally are exacerbated).

In many ways, our post-9/11 times are strange times for an analysis of IR. As we intimated above, we live in an era when many of the ideas, concepts, perspectives, or provocations explored by critical IR theorists, critical geopolitics scholars, or critical security studies thinkers (such as the use of fear in politics, the ideological biases found in traditional interpretations of security, the role of biopower in the daily organization of life, and so on) are simultaneously being addressed in writings, presentations, or images provided by mainstream or non-critical public intellectuals (sometimes pundits, or journalists, or politicians), such as Al Gore, Francis Fukuyama, or Robert D. Kaplan (to only name a few). We have come to a point where an education or some training in Michel Foucault's analytics of, for instance, biopower or governmentality (and a corollary capacity to learn to use critical theoretical concepts and introduce them back into the everyday practice of smart power) would become a perfect preparation for landing a job in government or with the security industries (or, perhaps, as part of the Military-Industrial-Media-Entertainment Network, or MIME-net, as Der Derian appropriately labels it[49]). As Eyal Weizman powerfully demonstrates in *Hollow Land: Israel's Architecture of Occupation*,[50] postmodern or critical social theory (Gilles Deleuze's work on territory and the "war machine," in particular) is already being exploited to such effects by the Israeli military. Interested in exploring the potential of "swarming" tactics (a concept derived from Deleuze and further explored by Hardt and Negri in *Multitude*) and in making "good" use of "network-centric war" in its endless campaign against terror, the Israeli military now is interested in developing proficiencies in the theoretical intricacies of postmodern thought.

Part of the mission of the following chapters is also to resist (to the extent that it can be done) some of the "smart" (mis)appropriations of the writings by critical theorists like Agamben, Deleuze, or Foucault (among others). Faced with this latest form of co-optation of critical or emancipatory thought, the chapters in this volume, all in their own ways, insist on the fact that critical and postmodern social analytical perspectives are crucial, not because they can teach soldiers, border patrol officers, risk analysts, social scientists involved in the "Human Terrain" programme, designers/architects, camp directors, or police men and women to become better biopolitical agents, but because they allow us to raise urgent (even if sometimes destabilizing) ethico-political questions about life under generalized conditions of hype(r)-power.

Outline of the book

The diagnoses of the contemporary American political condition provided by Timothy W. Luke and Larry N. George in the two chapters that begin this volume offer bleak warnings that US foreign policy will continue to engage in a dangerous form of geopolitics. In "Hyper-power or hype-power?", Luke mobilizes the idea of the United States as a "hyped" power in order to challenge America's post-9/11 claims of global control, hegemony, and potency (or hyper-power). Luke's chapter suggests that a great deal of American state power today is far more about hype (an exponential, media-based, visual, and virtual projection of military and commercial might and capacity to master world events) than it is about conventional or "hard" force. Yet, as endless cycles of visual/virtual media-hype proliferate America's post-9/11 claims to power or hegemony, geopolitical insecurities the world over and social, cultural, and economic anxieties at home are likely to abound for years to come. America's hype-machine is incapable of addressing a whole range of common, almost mundane, security threats or material concerns. An obscene projection of simulated potency, argues Luke, is privileged to the detriment of a quotidian apprehension of actual socio-economic crises and problems (as the handling of the Katrina disaster by US governmental agencies blatantly revealed).

George's chapter, "American insecurities and the ontopolitics of US pharmacotic wars," continues the rather grim overview of the present and future state of US foreign policy initiated by Luke by suggesting that what is mainly being hyped up by contemporary regimes and discourses of American power is war or, rather, the American nation's belief in the salutary and curative dimensions of battle and conflict. While anchoring his study of war and power in a broader historico-discursive context, George explores a key mechanism by which American elites (and the populations that follow their ideas or ideologies) deal with the fragility, instability, or even hollowness of US hype(r)-power (as suggested by Luke). This crucial mechanism is what George refers to as "ontopolitics," or the construction and maintenance of national political identity, and one of its main modalities of expression is what George calls "pharmacotic war." Pharmacotic war (from the Greek word *pharmakos*, which means drug or cure, but also poison) is the idea that the US nation's endless thirst for combat, antagonism, warfare, and destruction of enemies or "evil" ones is driven by a socio-historico-cultural certainty that war is a "performance-enhancing" drug, a medicine operating at the level of the social body that can exacerbate claims to hyper-power and accentuate (or hype) hyper-power's hoped-for results. But this belief in ritualized, sanctified, but also purgative and sacrificial, war (and actual battles)—or in the beneficial ontopolitical effects of America's gun-slinging cultural history—turns out to be a poison (once again, another meaning of *pharmakos*) for the domestic community, for US subjects/citizens and, of course, for many people across the world too. Indeed, as the US nation is redeemed and revealed through war, external foes and domestic scapegoats constantly have to be found and sometimes killed, thus inevitably keeping the allegedly protected community always on the edge, always in danger or at risk, and always insecure. George's identification of the pharmacotic element in US wars (returning in full force after 9/11 and in the war on terror) captures a basic cultural and ideological dimension in the relationship between war and national security that both realists and liberals in IR have ignored or been incapable of theorizing.

In "Power, violence, and torture," Alexander D. Barder develops some of the concerns introduced by Luke and George by using Arendt's distinction between violence and power. Barder turns to Arendt in order to examine situations of counterinsurgency and the phenomenon of wars of attrition. Arendt's nuanced analysis in "On Violence" warns against the conflation of power and violence in politics, suggesting that this common historical mixture (in the West, above all) contributes to the destruction of moral and political legitimacy. Barder illustrates the destructiveness of the violence deployed against a "moralized" enemy by the French in Algeria during the 1950s, and he explores its effects on the public sphere, both at home (France, in his case) and abroad. Arendt was deeply concerned about the future of war, bureaucratic politics, and the public sphere (arguing in one lecture that future politics would play itself out in a state of "constant emergency" where new experiments in population control would take place). But Barder suggests that the violence that was so nefarious to the legitimacy of the French political system in the 1950s and 1960s may not be so destructive for contemporary America. Turning to Sheldon S. Wolin's writings on the "imperial citizen"—a citizen pacified in the consumer culture of contemporary capitalism and sanitized by the media spectacles of the Military-Industrial-Media-Entertainment Network—Barder intimates that it is difficult to imagine a modality of power that could challenge a form of politics whereby violence and torture have become the pharmacotic (that is to say, the "performance-enhancing") drugs of the nation.

In the next chapter, "*Torturefest* and the passage of pedagogy of tortured pasts," Marie Thorsten writes about the way the US-led war on terror will be taught and represented in the future cultural politics of the American nation. For Thorsten, the ethico-political problem we are confronted with is that both "enhanced interrogation techniques" (a euphemism for torture) and a cleansed cultural landscape silence or normalize acts of torture and other brutal forms of violence, often perpetrated by US soldiers. Normalizing torture in US society and beyond takes place through a reduction of torture to the actions of a few "bad apples" in popular accounts. Thorsten develops further the theme of imperial citizenry encountered in Barder's chapter, and she explores the issue of the fragility of the public sphere and its ability to articulate alternative conceptions of the political. In an age when representations of war, terror, and torture are both sanitized and justified through popular TV shows like *24*, how can the actions of America and Americans in the war on terror be displayed in the everyday cultural spaces where we normally learn about history (in pedagogy, in the classroom, in textbooks), and how will this affect the moral imaginations of future generations? Will the United States (and its public sphere) be able to articulate critical pedagogical examinations of state power and violence, or will new generations be subjected to information-age strategies of "active forgetting"? Among other things, Thorsten suggests that some contemporary alternative visual and cultural representations of torture and the war on terror (a few documentary films, for example) may be crucial contemporary tools to use if one seeks to avoid this "active forgetting."

It is not only in the spaces created or imagined by pedagogy or popular culture where our moral and political imaginations are subject to strategies seeking to maintain official histories and produce uncontested values. Biopolitical strategies of governance are also creating new geographies of control, policing, and technological utility that seek to redesign the spaces we inhabit. In "Designing security," Mark J. Lacy looks at responses to anxiety and insecurity that attempt to create a tasteful and seductive militarization of everyday life. In response to geopolitical anxieties and the fear of crime, there has been a growing hype about new technologies of control and protection (biometrics, RFid, smart materials, biomimicry). Introducing Deleuze's concept of control society, Lacy examines how a design-security complex is creating forms of control that are perhaps different from the ones that Deleuze actually imagined (visions that have been prevalent in the popular cultural representations of future societies), with objects that are tactile, light, elegant, and designed to be seamlessly integrated into our everyday lives. Whether this emerging control society will offer the protection and security through design that many contemporary politicians promise remains to be seen. In fact, the focus on designing out insecurity may be the latest technique for trying to erase anxiety from the population, something that is without doubt a form of hype(r)-power.

In "Deserting sovereignty?," Mathew Coleman begins by providing a critical evaluation of Hardt and Negri's work. For many scholars, activists, and world observers angry at the hype(r)-power of the state fueled by neo-conservative ideology and desirous to find a challenge to the emerging smart powers of control society, Hardt and Negri (since the publication of their book *Empire* in 2000) have provided a powerful political alternative. Coleman suggests that the way Hardt and Negri deal with the global phenomenon of undocumented cross-border migration, however, is problematic because of their adherence to contract theory and their commitment to *autonomia* (the idea of the self-valorizing dimension of labor, something that can make labor totally independent from capitalism). What is missing in Hardt and Negri's theorization is a more careful, refined, and localized analysis of how much of the immigration debate, particularly in the United States, has been able to merge public policy issues with foreign policy and national security matters, thus creating a biopolitics of increased militarization of borderland life. While a rather conventional policing of workplaces and of "productive" but undocumented labor is still going on, newfangled regimes of biopolitical governance, control, and normalization operated through new strategies of population management are proliferating. Coleman concludes his chapter by suggesting that, while Hardt and Negri may criticize others for failing to think beyond sovereignty, critical (in)security analysis needs to delve further into the intensified militarization of life that is being deployed across territories and is generally obsessed with scapegoating strangers (or foreign/alien bodies), something that Michel Foucault described as the "biocriminal domain."

Some of Hardt and Negri's insights on empire, biopower, and world order continue to be discussed in "The biopolitics of American security policy in the twenty-first century," authored by Julian Reid. Intent on pushing some of Hardt and Negri's claims about empire toward a more detailed reflection on the relationship between biopower and sovereignty, Reid takes issue both with scholars who argue for a deepening of global civil society and with those who seek to analyze American foreign policy simply in terms of a "return to imperialism." For Reid, the current intellectual landscape of IR lacks the analytical tools that can make sense of the globalization of biopower. What Reid calls the "international constitution of power" in contemporary IR requires critical scholars to examine, interrogate, and further theorize the key role that biopolitical forces (often operating through so-called liberal instruments or agents of world politics, such as the United Nations or non-governmental organizations) play in the war on terror and in the construction of the global political order such a war supports. Thus, far from opposing empire to imperialism, global civil society to the war on terror, and biopolitics to sovereignty, what is needed is an analytical perspective that can allow IR theorists and security studies specialists to examine how biopower and state power are intricately woven and combined to produce a geopolitics that endlessly seeks to frustrate the possibility of a "politics of life."

In his chapter, "Human security, governmentality, and sovereignty," Kosuke Shimizu extends the discussion on global biopolitics/governmentality and their ramifications to contemporary geopolitical insecurities. Shimizu looks at contemporary discourses on human security, narrative productions (often relayed by liberal agencies or actors in IR) that seek to shift the debate on transnational security away from the nation-state and towards global civil society. Through Shimizu's close discursive analysis of texts, pamphlets, and official documents intent on propagating a specific view of what humanity is or should be (these narratives claim to detail, explain, or capture the many dimensions of human security), the universalizing impulse behind these discourses becomes obvious. Local particularities, contextual situations, individual preferences, and a plural or disseminated approach to life and the living are foreclosed by these narratives on global human security that seek to arrive at a perfect organization or governmentalization of a uniformly understood humanity. In contrast to this universalizing discourse on the governmentality and security of life/living, Shimizu reintroduces the warning calls of thinkers like Arendt and E. H. Carr (for IR) who, when confronted with either "human rights" discourses or liberal democratic ideologies that claimed to know what it means to be human, were eager to point to the dangers of these normalizing narratives.

The theme of governmentality/governance and global insecurity is pursued in Geoffrey Whitehall's chapter, "The aesthetic emergency of the avian flu affect." Whitehall outlines how "affective governance" operates in the production of an internationalizing state of exception organized in the wake of the bird flu pandemic scare. This transnational state of exception (perhaps the negative or flip side of the universalizing humanity sought after by the human security discourses discussed by Shimizu) points to the dynamics of an international civil war of which the war on terror is merely one component. Similar to the endless making and showing of disaster movies in today's society, the background hum in our everyday lives is the belief that we should always be prepared for the next catastrophe to happen. Through the case of the avian flu anxiety, Whitehall demonstrates how affective governance (the governing of human bodies through the manufacture of strong emotions) is contributing to an internationalizing biopolitics of control that supplements the biopower of the contemporary sovereign state (or Empire) with organizations such as the World Health Organization. Here again, reminiscent of Reid's argument, the division between state power and global biopolitical forces is shown to be artificial. Whitehall's chapter reveals how this international state of exception (organized around the avian flu panic) is leading to new architectures of control that will decide who lives and who dies in future bioterror emergencies. State and transnational bureaucracies that devise strategies to survive these future (supposedly inevitable) threats need to be understood not as instruments of state power (as much as the police or the military are), but a (state) power over life and death. Unfortunately, the apparent depoliticization of issues related to bio-emergency or the preservation of everyday life—the drive for ever more technical and productive solutions, and the complex grid of public or private bureaucracies and agencies that will implement strategies of protection—makes it increasingly difficult to escape these ecologies of panic, thus limiting people's capacity to design alternate social environments or invent different networks of production (of food, for example) and mobility (for example, public transportation or communication) that may be more protective of individual life than systems of control and surveillance (that typically are driven by a public mobilization of (geo)political fear).

One of the key modalities of contemporary anxiety revolves around consumption and ecological danger. Cars have always had a tendency to reflect America's hyperpower (economic, commercial, cultural, and political too). Over the past decade or so, the Sports-Utility Vehicle (SUV) has emerged as a powerful symbol of or metaphor for America's hype(r)-power. The political and cultural economy of automobility (and of the SUV, in particular) is the theme developed in Simon Dalby and Matthew Paterson's chapter, "Over a barrel." Dalby and Paterson intimate that much of the discourse on the SUV and oil imperialism today (at a time when oil and gas prices become symptoms of deep economic insecurity in many Western countries) fails to grasp the structural problems of a society designed for automobility and around carboniferous capitalism. Rather than obsessing over the possibility advanced by Nye of creating a nation driven by a quest for "soft power," the authors of this chapter suggest that what is needed instead is a different geopolitics, one that would be geared towards the notion of "soft energy." Smart and soft power could be the answers to many of America's contemporary geopolitical insecurities. But what Dalby and Paterson also begin to argue is that this smart power and carbon capitalism agenda may simply be the latest form of an efficient and productive biopolitical management of populations and ecologies (or what Luke has described elsewhere as "green governmentality"[51]), a new regime of biopower that shuts down deeper political questions about how we want to live with others and with nature. Still, soft energy could lead to a redesigning of everyday life, not in the often paranoid fashion of the *SAFE* exhibition discussed by Lacy, nor as the outcome of an affective governance through catastrophic panic or pandemic anxiety (as Whitehall suggests), but through the design of infrastructures for people and not for cars.

As hinted at above, an important theme runs through many of the chapters in this book: the idea of the depoliticization of the public sphere in an age of hype(r)- power, and the corollary militarization of everyday life in societies of control. Once again, the chapters in this volume are cautious about making claims in favor of smart power or for the "taming" of American power. Instead, all of them seek to pose questions about America's (and, sometimes, the rest of the world's) addiction to pharmacotic war and hype(r)-power. In fact, the volume in its entirety illustrates how many of the anxieties, insecurities, and injustices produced by hype(r)-power are unlikely to be smartly eliminated from future American politics by either intelligent design or through "tamed" power. As Thorsten's chapter shows, the regimes of public pedagogy and everyday visualization in which we live continue to simplify and distort histories of war, violence, and insecurity. Attempts are made to confront the pain and suffering caused by war's terror, but societies of control insist on installing mechanisms of effective and affective governance that often keep people away from images that may disturb or unsettle. Death was kept hidden (and to some extent still is) in the onslaught of optimistic life stories that filled both the battlespaces and the mediascapes of Iraq and Afghanistan. And there still does not seem to be much of a desire to confront the brutality of war in a manner that could escape the hysterics of tabloid geopolitics. However, what is silenced in the official narratives of corporate entertainment and political culture finds an expression in low budget movies where parts of the political and cultural unconscious of American life are sometimes revealed. One of Joe Dante's recent zombie films, *Homecoming*, and the independent Canadian movie *Fido* have been able to gain some viewership in the United States (and beyond) because of their biting satire of the absurdity of our distaste at confronting images and stories of those who have died in the war on terror (on both "sides"), often in our names or for our own alleged "protection" from death. The final chapter in the volume, Patricia Molloy's "Zombie democracy," analyzes those two films and addresses the representation of the zombie in contemporary cinema. A crucial point she makes is that sanitization (of meaning, images, stories, and indeed death) can only produce more violence, destruction, and, eventually, more death. By contrast, a "zombie democracy" would not turn away from the haunting of the political that official or popular narratives often try to repress in order to perpetuate the cycle of addiction to pharmacotic war in the nation. Thus, it may be that, by walking with zombies, the temptations of hype(r)-power and violence begin to be challenged.

Notes

1 The films *28 Weeks Later* or *I am Legend*, for example, show the police and the military turning on citizens in a "state of emergency" environment.
2 The notion of hyper-power (as attached to the United States, after 9/11, above all) was developed by former French Foreign Minister Hubert Védrine. For Védrine, hyper-power (or *hyper-puissance* in French) was supposed to convey not only the hegemonic aspirations of the United States as a nation both before and after 9/11, but also (and more crucially) its unilateralist and interventionist military ambitions (something that the United States quickly put into motion in the months that followed the 9/11 attacks). On Védrine's notion of hyper-power, see Thomas Weiss, "The Illusion of UN Security Council Reform," *The Washington Quarterly*, Vol. 26, No. 4 (2003), pp. 147–61. In this Introduction, we mobilize the term hyper-power too, but modify its grammatical structure (and refer to it as "hype(r)-power") in order to indicate that hype or exaggeration is always already part of this American *ethos* of geopolitical power, force, and violence (an understanding we derive from Timothy W. Luke's chapter in this volume). The meaning of hype(r)-power will become clearer to the reader as the volume progresses.
3 Barry Bergdoll, "Preface," in ed. Paola Antonelli, *Design and the Elastic Mind* (New York: MoMA Press, 2008), p. 10.
4 See Zygmunt Bauman, *In Search of Politics* (Cambridge: Polity Press, 1999), p. 5.
5 Ibid., p. 50.
6 Al Gore, *The Assault on Reason: How the Politics of Fear, Secrecy and Blind Faith Subvert Wise Decision-Making, Degrade Democracy and Imperil America and the World* (London: Bloomsbury, 2007), p. 34.
7 Ibid., p. 36.
8 Ibid., p. 37.
9 Ibid., p. 35.
10 Ibid., p. 44.
11 More will be said about these scholars below.
12 See Michael Hardt and Antonio Negri, *Multitude: War and Democracy in the Age of Empire* (New York: Penguin Press, 2004), p. 3.
13 Hardt and Negri, *Multitude*, back cover.
14 On tabloid geopolitics, see François Debrix, *Tabloid Terror: War, Culture, and Geopolitics* (New York: Routledge, 2007).
15 Thomas Barnett, *Blueprint for Action: A Future Worth Creating* (New York: Putnam's Sons, 2005); Tony Blankley, *The West's Last Chance: Will We Win the Clash of Civilizations?*

(Washington, DC: Regnery, 2006); Ted Galen Carpenter, *America's Coming War with China: A Collision Course over Taiwan* (New York: Palgrave, 2006); Tom Tancredo, *In Mortal Danger: The Battle for America's Border and Security* (Nashville: Cumberland House, 2006); Jed Babbin and Edward Timperlake, *Showdown: Why China Wants War with the United States* (Washington, DC: Regnery, 2006); Patrick Buchanan, *State of Emergency: the Third World Invasion of the United States* (New York: Thomas Dunne Books, 2006); Kenneth Timmerman, *Countdown to Crisis: The Coming Nuclear Showdown with Iran* (New York: Three Rivers Press, 2006).

16 See Francis Fukuyama, "The Challenges of Uncertainty: An Introduction," in ed. Francis Fukuyama, *Blindside: How To Anticipate Forcing Events and Wild Cards in Global Politics* (Baltimore: Brookings Institution, 2007), p. 1. For an alternative approach to risk and security, see the Special Issue on "Security, Technologies of Risk, and the Political," *Security Dialogue*, Vol. 39, No. 2/3 (2008).

17 Stanley Hoffmann, "An American Social Science: International Relations," in ed. James Der Derian, *International Theory: Critical Investigations* (New York: New York University Press, 1995), p. 237.

18 Fukuyama, "The Challenges of Uncertainty," p. 2.

19 Richard Falk, *This Endangered Planet: Prospects and Proposals for Human Survival* (New York: Random House, 1971).

20 Among these critical geopolitical approaches, see Derek Gregory, *Geographical Imaginations* (Oxford: Blackwell, 1993); John Agnew and Stuart Corbridge, *Mastering Space: Hegemony, Territory, and International Political Economy* (New York: Routledge, 1995); Gearóid Ó Tuathail, *Critical Geopolitics: The Politics of Writing Global Space* (Minneapolis: University of Minnesota Press, 1996); Michael Shapiro, *Violent Geographies: Mapping Cultures of War* (Minneapolis: University of Minnesota Press, 1997); Gearóid Ó Tuathail and Simon Dalby (eds.), *Rethinking Geopolitics* (New York: Routledge, 1998); David Campbell, *Writing Security: United States Foreign Policy and the Politics of Identity*, second edition (Minneapolis: University of Minnesota Press, 1999); and Matthew Sparke, *In the Space of Theory: Postfoundational Geographies of the Nation-State* (Minneapolis: University of Minnesota Press, 2005).

21 Among recent analyses of biopower and biopolitics, see Naoki Sakai and Jon Solomon (eds.), *Translation, Biopolitics, and Colonial Difference* (Hong Kong: Hong Kong University Press, 2006); Elizabeth Dauphinee and Cristina Masters (eds.), *The Logics of Biopower and the War on Terror* (London: Palgrave, 2006); Michael Dillon, "Governing Terror: The State of Emergency of Biopolitical Emergence," *International Political Sociology*, Vol. 1, No. 1 (2007), pp. 7–28; Julian Reid, *The Biopolitics of the War on Terror: Life Struggles, Liberal Modernity, and the Defense of Logistical Societies* (Manchester: Manchester University Press, 2007); and Roberto Esposito, *Bios: Biopolitics and Philosophy* (Minneapolis: University of Minnesota Press, 2008).

22 Fukuyama, "The Challenges of Uncertainty," p. 3.

23 Ibid., p. 5.

24 See "American Scenarios: A Discussion with Walter Russell Mead, Eliot Cohen, Ruth Wedgewood, Anne Applebaum, Bernard-Henri Lévy, Josef Joffe, Peter Schwartz, and Francis Fukuyama," in Fukuyama, *Blindside*, p. 107.

25 See Simon Dalby, *Creating the Second Cold War: The Discourse of Politics* (New York: Guilford Press, 1990); Timothy W. Luke, "The Discipline of Security Studies and the Codes of Containment: Learning from Kuwait," *Alternatives*, Vol. 16, No. 3 (1991), pp. 315–44; James Der Derian, *Antidiplomacy: Spies, Terror, Speed, and War* (Oxford: Blackwell, 1992); and David Campbell, *Writing Security: United States Foreign Policy and the Politics of Identity*, first edition (Manchester: Manchester University Press, 1992).

26 Nassim Nicholas Taleb, *The Black Swan: The Impact of the Highly Improbable* (New York: Random House, 2007).

27 See John Mearsheimer and Stephen Walt, *The Israel Lobby and US Foreign Policy* (New York: Farrar, Straus and Giroux, 2007).

28 Stephen Walt, *Taming American Power: The Global Response to US Primacy* (New York: Norton, 2006), p. 18.

29 Ibid., p. 18.
30 See Robert D. Kaplan, "On Forgetting the Obvious," *The American Interest*, Vol. 2, No. 6 (2007), p. 8.
31 Walt, *Taming American Power*, p. 245.
32 Morgenthau was concerned with the fact that the "great issues of our day—the militarization of American life, the Vietnam war, race conflicts, poverty, the decay of the cities, the destruction of the natural environment—are not susceptible to rational solutions within the existing system of power relations." See Hans Morgenthau, *Truth and Power: Essays of A Decade, 1960–70* (New York: Praeger, 1970), p. 6.
33 See, for example, Christopher Layne, *The Peace of Illusions: American Grand Strategy from 1940 to the Present* (Ithaca: Cornell University Press, 2007); and Christopher Layne and Bradley A. Thayer, *American Empire: A Debate* (New York: Routledge, 2007), p. 127.
34 We can see these new realist ideas entering the mainstream of American political debate. US Presidential candidate Barack Obama has his own take on realism. In a University of Chicago Press advertisement for the recent reissue of Reinhold Niebuhr's *The Irony of American History*, Obama writes: "[Niebuhr] is one of my favorite philosophers. I take away [from his work] the compelling idea that there's serious evil in the world, and hardship and pain. And we should be humble and modest in our belief we can eliminate those things. But we shouldn't use that as an excuse for cynicism and inaction." See www.press.uchicago.edu/cgi-bin/hfs.cgi/00/285412.ctl.
35 John Gray, *Black Mass: Apocalyptic Religion and the Death of Utopia* (London: Allen Lane, 2007), p. 192.
36 Ibid., p. 200. Realism's reluctance to take seriously threats such as human-generated climate change is examined in Mark J. Lacy, *Security and Climate Change: International Relations and the Limits of Realism* (London: Routledge, 2005).
37 Gray, *Black Mass*, p. 1.
38 See Joseph Stiglitz and Linda Bilmes, *The Three Trillion Dollar War: The True Cost of the Iraq Conflict* (New York: Norton, 2008).
39 Walt, *Taming American Power*, p. 181.
40 John Mearsheimer, *The Tragedy of Great Power Politics* (New York: Norton, 2001), p. 402.
41 Such as Ted Galen Carpenter, the author of *America's Coming War with China*.
42 Richard Armitage, John Hamre, and Joseph Nye, "Smart Power: An Interview," *The American Interest*, Vol. 3, No. 2 (2007), p. 34.
43 Joseph Nye, *The Powers to Lead* (Oxford, Oxford University Press, 2008).
44 Ibid., p. 83.
45 Armitage, Hamre, and Nye, "Smart Power," p. 34.
46 Ibid., p. 35.
47 Ibid., p. 37. The desire for a smart power approach appears to be driven also by a growing recognition (and anxiety) that China's own "smart power" may be trumping American diplomacy and power politics through the "powerful combination of enhanced geopolitical acumen and better professional diplomacy." In "Smart Power, Chinese Style," Kishore Mahbubani observes that the "typical time horizon in Washington hovers somewhere between the daily spin for the evening talk shows and the next election cycle." Past geopolitical humiliations, Mahbubani notes (in a move that may be geopolitical "hype"), have led to the creation of a China that is focused on where it wants to be fifty years in the future. See Kishore Mahbubani, "Smart Power, Chinese Style," *The American Interest*, Vol. 3. No. 4 (2008), p. 71.
48 See Hannah Arendt, "On Violence," in H. Arendt, *Crises of the Republic* (London: Penguin Books, 1972), p. 141.
49 See James Der Derian, *Virtuous War: The Military-Industrial-Media-Entertainment Network* (New York: Basic Books, 2001).
50 See Eyal Weizman, *Hollow Land: Israel's Architecture of Occupation* (London: Verso, 2007).
51 See Timothy W. Luke, *Ecocritique: Contesting the Politics of Nature, Economy, and Culture* (Minneapolis: University of Minnesota Press, 1997).

1 Hyper-power or hype-power?
The USA after Kandahar, Karbala, and Katrina

Timothy W. Luke

This brief critique explores the hollowness of today's pre-eminent sovereign power, or even hyper-power—the United States of America. With its various associated coalitions of the willing from other nation-states, the USA allegedly still stands tall during an era in which sovereignty is less certain, territoriality is contested, power is unclear, and pre-eminence is resisted by misunderstood and ill-named jihadists of multiple stripes. The misadventures of Kandahar, Karbala, and Katrina, however, are exposing some all too common mistakes: the vehicles of international affairs are driven across the landscape of world events at high rates of speed, their drivers glancing occasionally out of the windshield as they stare into the rearview mirror at images and ideas long since past, believing somehow that they will guide them through what lies ahead. Not knowing where they are, not certain where they are going, they believe that they remember where they, or at least their precursors, have been. Memories and myths of the Cold War, World War II or Victorian imperialism pop up in the rearview mirrors or on the passing terrain, but the troubled travel across it should never be guided by the cloudy reflections in the mirror or on the windows. Disaster ensues.

This chapter asks all on board the vehicles of state to stop staring at what has passed, and immediately glance out of the windshield and side windows anew. Their field of vision, across the troubled terrain of contemporary world affairs, must shift. This study of power, then, probes the merits of Paul Virilio's assertion about analytical vision, namely that "to see is to be lying in wait for what must spring up from the ground, nameless; for what presents no interest what so ever, what is silent will speak, what is closed is going to open, it is always the trivial that is productive, and so that constant interest in the incidental, in the margins of what ever sort, that is, in the void and absence."[1] These features are not to be found easily in the rearview mirror, but they sit silent and nameless at the margins, closed out by inattention, full of significance in the voids, absences, and incidences as change lies in wait across the ground and all around. Kandahar, Karbala, and Katrina are but a handful of them.

"Shock and awe," as "hype-power" uses it, very plainly rests upon "the *sudden militarization of mass information*" by interventionist powers as well as local resistances that recognize and reconfigure this reality as they "*democratize ubiquity, instantaneity, omniscience, and omnipresence*" with their own insurgent weapons of mass communication.[2] A new balance of terror, or a ballet of violence, begins as the warhead videos of precision-guided munitions (cruise missiles, laser-guided artillery shells, smart bombs, etc.) are counter-poised against improvised explosive device (IED) explosions on the six o'clock news, jihadist snuff films of foreign hostages or video of victims hit by suicide bombers detonating their shrapnel vests in the noontime market place. Hype plays a major role in all these maneuvers.

Indeed, as of this moment on September 2, 2008, the duration of this war already exceeds America's involvement in World War II against Japan by many days (1,993 in 2008 vs. 1,365 in 1945 on V-J Day, September 2, 1945) and against Germany by almost as many days (1,943 in 2008 vs. 1,248 in 1945 on V-E Day, May 8, 1945). Rumsfeld, as we know now, and as many feared before it all began, was dead wrong. Six days has become nearly 2,000, six weeks has piled up to 285 weeks, and six months is now pushing 65 months—and the clock is still ticking. The "short war in Iraq" sought by the world's sole hyper-power has morphed into what is now being advertised by its architects as a stupendous and colossal "Long War for the World." Whether it is or is not remains "to be determined." Yet, today's peculiar hyper-power wars would have been impossible to launch, wage, or continue without the "hype-power" that sustains them.

Hyper-power and hype-power

At the end of the Cold War, French Foreign Minister Hubert Védrine argued that the victory of the USA over the USSR elevated it above the status of "mere superpower" to an unprecedented condition of "hyper-power." In making this claim, Védrine archly wished to exceed the superlativity of superpower by attributing far greater, or actually even more excessive, reserves of power to the USA as it prepared to preside over a world remade by the collapse of its worn-down ideological enemy—the Soviet Union and the bloc of satellite states in the Warsaw Pact. Many have accepted this characterization of the United States as a hyper-power, the world's sole remaining superpower or, as Niall Ferguson more apprehensively characterizes it, a true geopolitical and geo-economic "colossus" close to attaining "full spectrum dominance" over the world economy, global culture, international politics, and planetary environments.[3]

"Hyper" is, of course, a common prefix that denotes a condition or status that is "above," "beyond," or "over" that of the ordinary. It can mean "excessive" as well as imply an existential situation of being in a state with more than three dimensions, as with "hyperspace," or unfolding with non-sequential linkages, as in "hypertext." Védrine's ironic characterization of "hyper-power" (*hyper-puissance* in the original French) clearly includes bits of all these qualities.

Where did hyper-power arise, and what does it rest upon? As Paul Kennedy's conditional retraction of his imperial overstretch thesis from the 1980s put it, the Reagan era's "revolution in military affairs" underpinned this hyper-powered dominion in the 1990s. Even though the United States basically quadrupled its national debt from 1981 to 1991 in a reckless military build-up, this feckless fiscal policy essentially

> had paid an unforeseen dividend. Not only did the Soviet Union collapse as it strained to match the Reagan-Weinberger arms extravaganza, but the United States also went on to collect a triple peace dividend in the 1990s: falling defense spending as a share of GDP, accelerating economic growth and a quantum leap in military capability that left other powers far behind.[4]

The shock of 9/11 still lingers over many in the United States and around the world. Nonetheless, this terrorist incident also transpired within an economy that accounted for over a third of the world's global product in 2002, as opposed to just 10 percent in 1980. The American economy now underpinning this war on terror is

> two and half times larger than the Japanese economy, eight and half times larger than the Chinese economy, and thirty times larger than the Russian. U. S. military expenditures exceed the combined defense budgets of the EU, China, and Russia. Yet the cost of the U.S. military has declined steeply in relative terms, from an average of 10 percent of GDP in the 1950s to just 4 percent in the 1990s and a forecast 3.5 percent in the first half of the present decade.[5]

Hyper-power is celebrated for its neoliberal efficiency, although its real material effectiveness is much more open to question.

Strangely enough, as the hyper-power supposedly rises, there are many examples of "declinism" or "endism" for American hegemony, superpower, empire, or leadership in the world system going back to the crisis-ridden years of the 1960s and 1970s. For nearly two generations over the past four decades, one can look at critics and complainants setting their briefs out for why arrogance, poverty, racism, laziness, corruption, inequality, ignorance, or greed would very soon collapse the American state and society. Of course, year after year, it did not. This outcome could still occur, but it has not yet happened. Instead, today the United States seems to be continuously growing in power and privilege—even as arrogance, poverty, racism, laziness, corruption, inequality, ignorance, or greed can be seen as deepening and spreading at the same time. And, even more brazenly, the United States continues to cast itself as Ronald Reagan's "shining 'city upon a hill'," despite all of the assertions of the declinist school of anti-American hegemony. From Paul Kennedy to Gabriel Kolko to Samuel Huntington to Noam Chomsky, critics jointly have judged the USA to have the world's greatest power, while at the same time seeing it as ready to suffer the world's quickest collapse. Whether it is the "distemper of democracy," "imperial overstretch," "the limits of power," "military humanism," or "blowback," the end is, and has been, near for American hegemony for decades.[6] And yet an unusual new order persists.

Joseph Nye's soft power thesis is one explanation for why American power continues, but it has been attacked as incomplete. Here, Ferguson is basically correct when he questions how much American soft power really matters:

> If the term is to denote anything more than cultural background music to more traditional forms of dominance, it surely needs to be demonstrated that the United States can secure what it wants from other countries without coercing or suborning them, but because its cultural exports are seductive.[7]

Ferguson's questioning raises major doubts about soft power: is American culture alone so seductive, or must its soft power also be made much more seductive? Seduction itself can be real, but does it need to be made ever more extravagant, excessive, and exaggerated to gain greater effect?

Nye trips over the branches of hype-power with his notion of soft power.[8] His pious characterization of such power softening its subjects rests upon obtaining compliance without "force or inducement," because "it is the ability to entice and attract soft power that arises in large part from our values."[9] How this occurs is essentially cast as a quasi-charismatic event in which, Nye asserts, "a country may obtain the outcomes it wants in world politics because other countries want to follow it, admiring its values, emulating its example, aspiring to its level of prosperity and openness."[10] Taken uncritically on its own terms, and particularly in the context of the 1990s, when Nye fabricated this notion, soft power might seem quite convincing. Yet, are these values as such actually all that attractive?

Force or inducement might not be operational routines in soft power, but hyper-power on its own also appears quite ominous, unattractive, or even repulsive. Something major is missing here in the foamy boundaries between the hard power and soft power of hyper-power, and the absent element seems to be hype-power. How does a country get what it wants without force or inducement? Nothing necessarily attracts on its own without intense promotion, publicity, or proclamation of some sort. How do others know about those examples to emulate, levels to aspire toward, openness to be had, prosperity to be made widespread, values to admire or leaders to follow without 24/7 hype-power? To see hype-power at work, one must recognize how mighty marketing can be, or how might itself markets its own merits. Hyper-power could predispose others to be more pliable, or even foreshadow the ill effects of noncompliance. Still, compliance itself seems to arise as much from endless excess, exaggeration, or extravagance, as it does out of excellence. Consequently, one must explore the reach and the grasp of hype to consider the degree to which soft power presumes its preparatory actions when speaking of others' admiration, emulation, aspiration, or compliance. The ability to entice and attract is not necessarily symptomatic of anything charismatic; it might be the expression of something far more problematic.

All of the inventories of hyper-power capability in the United States are important, but one must ask if they actually energize the conduits of hype behind many American decisions and dictates. Hype essentially colloquializes the classical trope in rhetoric used to define the purposeful exaggeration, excessive emphasis, and extravagance of overstatement, or "hyperbole," which literally means "overshooting" in Greek. Hype is a strategy of media management, spin control or mass marketing to boost public attention and engagement with exaggerated claims. Excessive coverage, extravagant marketing, or extended publicity are the tactics of hype. Arguably, even the contemporary literature of imperialism itself cannot be disconnected from this PR machine. When used by poets as a rhetorical device, hyperbole can stir powerful emotions or lasting impressions. When mobilized in politics, it aims to elicit comparable effects.

Hype relies upon "weapons of mass communication," and thereby creates a strategic impasse at the local, molecular, or neighborhood level, as military interdictions in a policing register, a civic action mode, or a hearts-and-minds motif all underscore how a "deterrence of the strong by the weak" is unfolding.[11] The weapons of mass destruction that define hyper-power do not disappear as much as have their significance degraded as digital video downloads from the internet, home video, and cell phone cameras all are integrated into the weapon arrays of mass communication that permit brutality to be documented and inertia to be universalized through instantaneous, ubiquitous, and atrocious "information bombing" by the Pentagon and terrorist networks alike. Thus, one sees hype-power underpinning a "state of siege," which invests space "no longer on the level of the city-state, of the threatened region or nation state but, this time, on the level of the entire world."[12]

Caught up in a world shaped by the population crisis, the environmental crisis, the nuclear crisis, the fiscal crisis, or the energy crisis, hype comes into its own. Whereas hyper-power might be expected to react decisively and then act coercively in crises to contain their alleged disruptions, hype-power simply anticipates and adapts to draw renewed capacity out of instability. Hype-power presides over the populations of crisis, occupies the environments of crisis, constitutes the nucleus of crisis, and attracts the money of crisis because it sustains its order out of the energies of crisis. Whereas hyper-power maps into the post-1991 era the apparatus tied to "*the equilibrium of terror*" that rested within a "*triumph of the strategy of deterrence*" relying upon "*intercontinental ballistics*," hype-power exceeds the order of "*geostrategic proximity*," as the New World Order battles against "*the decline of territorial politics*" in which "*the permanent disequilibrium of a strategy of tension*" favors gaining command, control, and communication of "*global logistics*."[13] Hyper-power perhaps aimed to invent conditions of "a *relative peace*," but hype-power acknowledges the transpolitical inversions of speed and space leading to the permanence of "a *relative war*."[14]

Hyper-power is hard heavy coercion. Where it exists it can do whatever it wishes. Hype-power, however, imagines its goodness and greatness at such exaggerated levels of apparent stolid sincerity that it floats on implication, impulse, or intrigue. Talk about it is central to it even existing for deployment. Hence, one hears Democrats asserting that "we are the first global power in history that is not an imperial power,"[15] while Republicans claim that "America has never been an empire ... [and that] [w]e may be the only great power in history that is not an imperial power."[16] Even as it sits atop territorial remnants of its nineteenth-century imperialism, and twentieth-century anti-totalitarianism, the United States extravagantly denies its unfree side in celebrating its founding in/of/for freedom. A vast majority of Americans believe it is very good that American ideas and customs circle the world with their influence. But they see this result as merely attractive order and not as a system of extractive exploitation. Former secretary of State Colin Powell formulated hype-powered globalism very well when he stated: "The United States does not seek a territorial empire. We have never been imperialists. We seek a world in which liberty, prosperity, and peace can become the heritage of all peoples, and not just the exclusive privilege of a few."[17] Exaggeration perhaps knows no greater excess than political pieties like these.

Hype-power, then, is clearly a more distributed and efficient gridwork of governmentalizing influence amid

> the special problems that beset the production of locality in a world that has become deterritorialized, diasporic, and transnational. This is a world where electronic media are transforming the relationships between information and mediation, and where nation-states are struggling to retain control over their populations in the face of a host of subnational and transnational movements and organizations.[18]

To succeed on these terrains, extravagance and excess plainly are effective techniques on the street and at home.

Hyper-power essentially presumes territorial order, if not continuous command, control, and communication in, and over, territorially bounded communities. The United States pretends to have this power, but it is obvious that its main strength lies in sweeping swiftly into localities with "shock and awe," or sitting endlessly inside neighborhoods with glimmer and glitz, exaggerating its authority with cruise-missile strikes, or better yet, cruise-missile nose-cam videos of prior successful through-the-side-window PGM (precision-guided munition) strikes. For hype-power, CBS and CNN, Bank of America and Citibank, Microsoft and Minnesota Mining and Manufacturing, or Nike and the NBA, are the best assets to use continuously. They are Washington's hype stockpile.

Some fear American hyper-power, but most cannot resist US hype-power. Indeed, as Arjun Appadurai argues,

> the fact is that the United States, from a cultural point of view, is already a cast free-trade zone, full of ideas, technologies, styles, and idioms (from McDonald's and the Harvard Business School to the Dream Team and reverse mortgages) that the rest of the world finds fascinating. This free-trade zone rests on a volatile economy; the major cities of the American borderland (Los Angeles, Miami, New York, Detroit) are now heavily militarized. But these facts are of little relevance to those who come, either briefly or for more extended stays, to this free-trade zone. Some, fleeing vastly greater urban violence, state persecution, and economic hardship, come as permanent migrants, legal or illegal. Others are short-term shoppers for clothes, entertainment, loans, armaments, or quick lessons in free-market economics or civil-society politics. The very unruliness, the rank unpredictability, the quirky inventiveness, the sheer cultural vitality of this free-trade zone are what attract all sorts of diasporas to the United States.[19]

The attractors of hype here pull populations into the polysemic pluralism of the USA, which becomes a pastiche of transnationalizing localities. The Democratic Popular Republic of Korea might be building nuclear weapons for deterrence against Washington, DC, but Kim Jong Il imagines himself as Elvis, John Ford, and Luke Skywalker—all at once—striking out against Empire. Indeed, as Appadurai contends, "for every nation-state that has exported significant numbers of its populations to the United States as refugees, tourists, or students, there is now a delocalized transnation, which retains a special ideological link to a putative place of origin but is otherwise a thoroughly diasporic collectivity."[20]

These hype-powered ethnoscapes, in turn, are dense networks of localities in which multiculturalism, tribalism, ethnonationalism, and sectarianism persist in relative stability. Refugees from superpower struggles since the 1940s have been drawn to the United States despite multicultural anxieties about the United States' own diversity. When put in this perspective,

> applied to New York, Miami, and Los Angeles (as opposed to Sarajevo, Soweto, or Colombo), the trope of tribalism both conceals and indulges a diffuse racism

about those Others (for example, Hispanics, Iranians, and African-Americans) who have insinuated themselves into the American body politic. It allows us to maintain the idea of an Americanness that precedes (and subsists in spite of) the hyphens that contribute to it and to maintain distinction between tribal Americans (the black, the brown, and the yellow) and other Americans. This trope facilitates the fantasy that civil society in the United States has a special destiny in regard to peaceful multiculturalism—intelligent multiculturalism for us, bloody ethnicity or mindless tribalism for them.[21]

Such polyglot pluralism can precipitate a cultural crisis, but hype-power just spins up its own dynamic cultures of crisis and further feeds its own excess.

Hype-power actually appears to be remarkably cost-effective in comparison to the weighty tallies counted up for the imperial armadas and armies of superpower by other thinkers like Chomsky, Johnson, or Kolko. As Robert D. Kaplan notes, today's empirean administration has discovered since 1991 that "the entire planet was a battle space for the American military," but the Pentagon also is learning "that the fewer troops that policed it the better."[22] As a result, hype-power's intense exaggeration of America's military prowess has led to an extraordinary outcome, since

> the turn of the twenty-first century found the United States with bases and base rights in fifty-nine countries and overseas territories, with troops on deployments from Greenland to Nigeria, and from Norway to Singapore, all this while defense appropriations amounted to only 3.3 percent of America's gross domestic product—compared to 9.4 percent during the Vietnam War and 14.1 percent during the Korean War.[23]

Empire as biopolitics: an empirean order?

Any celebrations or denunciations of American hyper-power as a new imperialist hegemon become affirmations of its new empire-building project by exaggerating hype-power to extravagant excess. In many ways, the root cause of these transformations, and the force that must respond to their effects, undoubtedly is the global political economy of "Empire." Consequently, what is now in question with US hype-power are the structures and agents of globalizing biopolitical power as well as the worldwide regimen of global governance responsible for organizing its globality, systematization, and biopolitics as Empire. During the 1990s, Michael Hardt and Antonio Negri claimed something was "materializing before our very eyes," namely, "Empire," or some new cluster of "an irresistible and irreversible globalization of economic and cultural exchanges," out of which emerged "a global order, a new logic and structure of rule—in short, a new form of sovereignty," and that it now is "the political subject that effectively regulates these global exchanges, the sovereign power that governs the world."[24] Yet, Empire actually does not seem all that "imperial." Instead it seems to be a new "empirean" order—one that is regarded as acceptable by many, all-important by a few, but not all that overwhelming by most. This empirean order is not empyrean, but it persists in the biopolitical organization of the planet and its multitudes. How and why this system causes transformations are vital questions that preoccupy Hardt and Negri in two quite remarkable works—*Empire* (2000), and then *Multitude* (2004), but it is explored here as a new empirean regime.

Francis Fukuyama's celebration of "accumulation without end" roughly captures the central characteristics of empirean exercises in the ongoing "omnipolitanization" of the planet through continuous economic and social development.[25] Hype-power's excesses depend upon these cycles of material growth, and the dense, intense, and vast communities that occupy "the omnipolis" are most easily controlled through extravagant spin. Such patterns of omnipolitanization arise, as Virilio asserts, from highly clustered concentrations of urbanized values and technified practices accumulating all at once. These urbanized spaces increasingly should be regarded as a

> *world-city*, the city to end all cities [and] in these basically eccentric or, if you like, *omnipolitan* conditions, the various social and cultural realities that still constitute a nation's wealth will soon give way to a sort of 'political' *stereo-reality* in which the interaction of exchanges will no longer look any different from the – automatic – interconnection of financial markets today."[26]

Once everyday life attains this condition of continuous remediation, weapons of mass communication easily displace weapons of mass destruction.

To sustain omnipolitanizing processes, an empire-centered order is vital. There are many unanticipated changes coming from the global movement of people and goods in today's interdependent economy. Over 5 billion tons of goods were shipped worldwide in 1998, which is up from less than 850,000 million tons in 1955.[27] Two million people cross international borders everyday, and over 2.6 trillion air kilometers were flown in 1998 continuing the nine percent annual growth rate since 1950.[28] Once again, these almost invisible and innocuous quantitative increases in human traffic all contribute to shaping the battlespace of empirean conflicts. They shape the qualitative transformations in popular struggles over each contested neighborhood of the omnipolis, which are themselves essentially producible only in these complex empire-driven conditions that generate these flows of ideas, money, people, and things.

With this sea change in everyday life, or "the postmodernization of the world economy," Hardt and Negri maintain, "the creation of wealth tends evermore toward what we will call biopolitical production, the production of social life itself, in which the economic, the political, and the cultural increasingly overlap and invest one another."[29] While they put many of their conceptual chips on performativity in cyberspace, the attributes of this empire-driven regime also bear marks of constant communicative capacity in the televisual discourses, Kanban capitalism, bioengineered products, and informatic collectives becoming more common amid postmodern globalization's "immaterial paradigm of production."[30]

Who, where, when, why, and how such mechanisms of governmentality are enacted, implemented, or maintained are important questions to the multitude of Empire, which is not "a political body with one that commands and others that obey, the multitude is *living flesh* that rules itself."[31] As power has evolved from less coercive into more productive forms, powerful agencies that survey the multitude's various populations, inventory their energies, enhance their capabilities, and enforce their norm have become critically significant in the "Global War on Terror" (GWOT), because the surveys, inventories and enforcements are failing. Whether the source is the Ba'athists in Baghdad, Al Qaeda anywhere, the Taliban in Afghanistan, or a hurricane in the Gulf, the biopolitical well-being of the multitude is more endangered, and empire only tries to defend society. Yet, the conflict is illusive, molecular, continuous, brutal, and not well-suited to Empire's capabilities for response. With globalization, "the right of the social body to ensure, maintain or develop its life" becomes a key site of contestation and control.[32] Now, however, these biopolitical agendas unfold locally and globally. This point is critical inasmuch as when "the multitude is imprisoned and transformed into the body of global capital, it finds itself both within and against the processes of capitalist globalization."[33] But what is the social body of the multitude, how is it imagined, who exercises its rights, and where does its life arise and go? The possibilities are endless: for some it is at the mall; others, it is the intifada. For some others, it is the diaspora. And for yet some others, it is in a FEMA (Federal Emergency Management Agency) trailer on a backwoods bayou.

Given these realities for the multitude, does empire, or do some other empirean governance structures closer to the populace, work "to incite, reinforce, control, monitor, optimize, and organize forces under it: A power bent on generating forces, making them grow, and ordering them, rather than one dedicated to impeding them, making them submit, or destroying them"?[34] Empire in some concrete sense does represent a new planetary "field of intervention" (as Foucault puts it[35]) for collectives of sovereignty, territoriality, and demography to unfold these regimens of governmentality on a worldwide scale, albeit in a still very discontinuous and highly unequal manner.[36] Through CNN, the United Nations, McDonald's, The World Bank, Wall Street, the WHO/FAO/UNCTAD regime, and, more recently, the World Wide Web, many new subpolitical institutions appear to order, organize, and operate an empirean authority rather than a more traditionally imagined imperial order amidst multitude's social body, since the culture and constitution of this social body is deeply contested.[37]

The world's multitudes, as a result, remake the world through, around, and beyond empire, because "the multitude can move through empire and come out the other side, to express itself autonomously and rule itself."[38] In the meantime, like much of cyberspace, for large swaths of Earth's biophysical ecology, and for most global markets, "Empire's rule has no limits," and it is "characterized fundamentally by a lack of boundaries."[39] Consequently, empirean order is unusual in that

> autonomous movement is what defines the place proper to the multitude ... A new geography is established by the multitude as the productive flows of bodies define new rivers and ports. The cities of the earth will become at once great deposits of cooperating humanity and locomotives for circulation, temporary residencies and networks of the mass distribution of living humanity.[40]

Recognizing this, powerful countries like the USA, Australia, China, Japan, France, or Great Britain all push their own visions of "homeland security" with their state apparatuses over empirean civil society. Yet, the multitude's and empire's movements often cause these national/statal efforts to produce outcomes that are too little, too late, and too light.[41] In turn, the global omnipolis of warring neighborhoods surfaces amid, around, and above the national-statal system. Outside of Kabul, beyond the Green Zone, and away from the French Quarter, is the multitude only left with hyper-power occasionally, hype-power more often, and anarchy otherwise?

Hardt and Negri's analysis of an empire made of rule is simultaneously innovative, critical, and problematic. Nevertheless, one must ask, does it capture the causes behind the conflicts of the New World Order after 1991?[42] Hardt and Negri believe that the national and supranational institutions of Empire's powers are, in fact, flowing through the multitude, but these apparatuses also seem to promote and exacerbate continuous conflict (for example, in the GWOT) to attain relative peace. More concretely, they claim:

> The concept of Empire posits a regime that effectively encompasses the spatial totality, or reality that rules over the entire "civilized" world. No territorial boundaries limit its reign. Second, the concept of Empire presents itself not as a historical regime originating in conquest, but rather as an order that effectively suspends history and thereby fixes the existing state of affairs for eternity. From the perspective of Empire, this is the way things will always be and the way they were always meant to be. In other words, Empire presents its rule not as a transitory moment in the movement of history, but as a regime with no temporal boundaries and in this sense outside of history or at the end of history. Third, the rule of Empire operates on all registers of the social order extending down to the depths of the social world. Empire not only manages a territory and a population but also creates the very world it inhabits. It not only regulates human interactions but also seeks directly to rule over human nature. The object of its rule is social life in its entirety, and thus Empire presents the paradigmatic form of biopower. Finally, although the practice of Empire is continually bathed in blood, the concept of Empire is always dedicated to peace—a perpetual and universal peace outside of history.[43]

Most importantly, then, this empirean order seems to cycle and recycle, like the loops of commodity chains or the connectivities of cybernetic networks, in a fashion that suspends time, works outside of history, pushes beyond embedded practices, or breaks temporal boundaries.[44] Yet, it also essentially fails inasmuch as relative peace is actually relative war. The "new cartography" for an alternative global society could be "written today through the resistances, struggles, and desires of the multitude,"[45] but much of it appears to rest within the shifting sign wars of hype-power rather than the traditional strategic games of hyper-power. Empire's biopolitics cannot be ignored, but empirean order is something different. And one must look past both the apologies for and the attacks upon the US presence in the world to interpret the workings of empirean control.

Fukuyama's vision of empirean policing as "benevolent hegemony" is absurd on its own merits, as he admits, when describing how it has no interest in providing certain public goods, like policing Africa, fighting climate change, ending world hunger, or reconciling with Iran. To say that a nation founded from 1492, 1607, or 1776 has forged a people that one might characterize by "the fact that Americans are not, at heart, an imperial people," and that they lack "a staying power that does not come easily to people who are reasonably content with their own lives and society,"[46] is essentially laughable. A century later, the United States still sits in Hawaii, Guam, Cuba, and Panama; and, half a century later, the United States still garrisons bases across Europe, Japan, and Korea. Americans might not be an imperial people, but the United States has an empirean system. It may involve an "incoherent empire," "a new American militarism," or an "empire of bases."[47] But its empireanizing is also something more. And this ineffable element is hype.

Conclusions

Ferguson suggests that "the United States has acquired an empire, but Americans themselves lack the imperial cast of mind. They would rather consume than conquer. They would rather build shopping malls than nations ... The problem is that despite occasional flashes of self-knowledge, they have remained absent-minded—or rather, in denial—about their imperial power all along."[48] Without the *mens rea* of imperialists, it is near impossible to regard the New World Order of American hegemony since 1991 as imperialism. There is no imperial idea, ideal, or ideology above and beyond some minimal order in the world made anew by the end of the Cold War. Yet, there are conditions in the New World Order that parallel imperial controls with empirean design.

Rather than imperialism, then, this empire-like condition simply could be interpreted in these almost *sui generis* terms as an empireanizing development. In Ferguson's analysis, US hype-power is rooted

> in the business of providing a limited number of public goods: peace, by intervening against some bellicose regimes and in some civil wars; freedom of the seas and skies for trade; and a distinctive form of "conversion" usually called Americanization, which is carried out less by old-style Christian missionaries than by the exporters of American consumer goods and entertainment. Its methods of formal rule are primarily military in character; its methods of informal rule rely heavily on nongovernmental organizations and corporations and, in some cases, local elites ... It prefers the idea that foreigners will Americanize themselves without the need for formal rule.[49]

Oddly enough, Ferguson falls into the epicycles of exaggeration of hype-power, even as he touts its practices.

Fearing further public backlashes against its authority, like those after the fumbling, fatuous responses to Hurricanes Katrina and Rita or the rebuilding of Afghanistan and Iraq, the US government staged a major media event at the National Institute of Health to announce a new website (www.pandemicflu.gov), new antiviral drug purchases, new vaccine production funds, new legal relief from product litigation for vaccine procedures, and new local government "first responders" support funds. It too was mere hype-power in action. To stage the event, the White House had to admit the H5N1 avian flu had been a public health menace since 1997, and a killer of humans since 2003. Yet, only in 2005 did President Bush cast this virulent flu strain as another "danger to our homeland" to justify his new "comprehensive national strategy" of increasing global surveillance, stockpiling medicines, and integrating plans for public responses from a transnational alliance of 88 foreign countries through the US national bureaucracy down to all of its state, county and municipal governments.[50] With this event on November 1, 2005, President Bush basically bridged the war on terror over to the struggle with nature by mobilizing the health care sector to work hand in hand with the security industry. As part of a global response, the President asserted: "By making critical investments today, we'll strengthen our ability to safeguard the American people in the awful event of a devastating global pandemic, and at the same time we'll bring our nation's public health and medical infrastructure more squarely in the 21st century."[51]

Nonetheless, like the rebuilding of Baghdad, the United States is unprepared to act effectively against most natural disasters, no matter whether they are diseases or storms. In the face of the avian flu, as one medical associate of the New England Center for Emergency Preparedness notes, "with few exceptions, the United States lacks the ability to develop, manufacture and administer vaccines in response to specific threats as they arise."[52] Like Katrina, the H5N1 virus is one of those exceptions where there is no ready counter-response for use against it. The hurricane response system in the Gulf states was unable to process images coming to it from network news programs, CNN, the Weather Channel, and major newspapers. Believing every American must have a car, the Department of Homeland Security (DHS) basically ignored the carless, the homeless, and the jobless, leaving the city to concentrate them and their misery at the New Orleans Superdome.

It was a response, but it only made American hyper-power appear that much worse. The dogged desperation of those thousands trapped inside the Superdome moved many to lob their own information bombs through CNN and the Weather Channel as collaborating hype-power subversives. Indeed, they demonstrated the reach and depth of hype-power at one of its most central sites: an iconic NFL stadium. Even so, the responses of DHS were still sadly inadequate. The Bush administration, lacking true hyper-power, dumped the responsibility for disaster relief that it had through Homeland Security to states, counties, and cities, which all had insufficient capacity to respond. Hence, the United States was left relying mostly on medieval, pre-industrial technologies, like the fortified redoubts of the Superdome to withstand a Category 4 hurricane that the structure barely survived. Given this veritable Baghdad-like response to a public safety crisis that was days in the making in the summer seas of the Gulf, one must continue to explore how and why this system of hype-power production is maintained globally in the current neo-liberal world order. Like Katrina in 2005, the USA in 2008 really is unprepared to respond to many new security threats. To strike against Syria, North Korea, or Iran with anything more than hype-power is almost unimaginable. It also remains to be seen if the empirean order and its hype-powered regimes would survive the shock of such a strategic move, or would they be left, like Katrina's survivors, wandering or floating about in the wreckage left behind.

Today, the enticement of excess becomes an excess of enticement whose continuous conversions come via consumption, entertainment, and spin. The empireanized sign up with the empirean order to emulate, enjoy, and enlarge the extravagance of empireanizing agents and structures. A financial crisis might cause collapse, but fiscal integrity itself is suspended to survive the crises of disorder that the empirean order brings forth as its public goods and private satisfactions. Fortunately for the United States and its hype-power, Ferguson's scathingly accurate survey of the high price to Washington of sustaining its hyper-power simply underscores Oscar Wilde's arch observations about why one should doubt those who know the price of everything but the value of nothing. What Ferguson questions as unsustainable hyper-power only adds to the maintenance of hype-power. Any attention its extravagant excesses garner again underscores the power of exaggerated capabilities that causes others to accede to such excessive extravagance.

Hype-power also follows from the limited utility of weapons of mass destruction sought by would-be hyper-powers as "the war of images and sounds tends to supplement the war of projectiles of the military arsenal."[53] As secure spaces under the dominion of states—whether they are micro-powers or hyper-powers—are infected, divested, or repositioned with contested places where weapons of mass communication mediate struggles between empirean hype-power and resistant networks, relative war prevails all the time across every neighborhood in the omnipolis of the planet's empireanized order. It is not pretty, but the scores of beheaded bodies along roadsides, mini-genocides in the hills or deserts, collateral damage in urban slums, home-made missile barrages, stealth drone strikes, and professional soldiers dying one, two, or three at a time in defense of empirean stability are the toll of relative war.

These excesses are an extravagant waste, but their significance remains open to greater exaggeration and faster spin. They are not megadeaths from megatons, but they are marks in a new equilibrium of terror as neighborhoods battle neighborhoods, localities terrorize localities, and armies of one clash with the uprisings of other ones. The "*inertia of a relative war*" perhaps is typified by intifadas from the 1980s to the present from Palestine to the Philippines all across the omnipolitan mediascapes as "transpolitical anarchy" back home and in diasporic wanderings.[54] Whether it is Bosnia, Baghdad, Beslan or Chad, Colombia, Chechnya, hype-power fuels its reign from the ravages of relative war at molecular levels of rage.

Indeed, the spin needed to produce minimal levels of compliance tumbles out of exaggerated, excessive, and endless enmities captured in networks of biopolitics. As Virilio puts it:

> The hate and extreme horror of what is close, familiar, are merely the indirect and political unperceived consequences of the logistical capacities that reach the extremities of the world without delay. *No more delay, no more relief*, the neighborhood becomes insipid, leading to the introversion of communities, the inertial confinement of *societies infinitely too small to make civil peace*.[55]

The hyper-power's spectacle of its long-range coercive reach from Kuwait to Afghanistan to Iraq in so many Desert Storm-type operations truly is a "desert screen" (as Virilio would have it), and this weaponized mass-communication regime now screens the deserts of hype-power's slipping dominion over so many unruly localities of inequality and injustice. The revolt on the street builds its IEDs to serve as information bombs as they are recorded, replayed, and reassessed in 24/7 endless loops of informationally exaggerated discourse all across the empirean domains. Whether for "freedom everywhere" or "world jihad," it is armies of one caught in relative war in neighborhood-level urban warfare that crystallize the excess of empirean oversight. Short wars once might have concluded in relative peace; the long war is simply another name for the extravagant excesses of unending relative war.

At the 2002 West Point graduation commencement, President Bush likened the GWOT to the Cold War: "Our struggle is similar to the Cold War."[56] By 2004, the state of relative war in Iraq was being presented by US Army General John Abizaid as a long struggle against totalitarianism, not unlike the 1930s or 1950s, which would become "a long war." And, in his 2006 State of the Union address, the President reiterated in quite hyped-up terms how "the short war in Iraq" was just the beginning of an existential choice for today's post-9/11 order. As Bush then saw it, it was going to be a long war:

> We must be clear in our principles and willing to act. The only alternative to American leadership is a dramatically more dangerous and anxious world. Yet, we must also choose to lead because it is a privilege to serve the values that gave us birth. American leaders—from Roosevelt to Truman to Kennedy to Reagan—rejected isolation and retreat, because they knew that America is always more secure when freedom is on the march. Our own generation is in a long war against a determined enemy ... Together let us protect our country, support the men and women who defend us, and lead this world toward freedom.[57]

Here is hype-power *in nuce*: freedom on the march, warrior presidents of the past, the privilege of leading the world to freedom all bobbing along the televisual flotsam of old war movie re-runs, CNN news flashes 24/7, and cynical citation of past grandeurs.

Iraq is not a mission once accomplished, now botched by neoliberal, maladministrative, and strategic incompetence. As the latest fire-fights suggest, it is the current "successful surge" of a battle that is part of a "Long War," like that of "man against the elements" in New Orleans. Hyper-power is useless there, so hype-power is always on the move to manage the empirean system's conflicts. Whether it is another Cold War, World War III, World War IV, or anti-totalitarianism, the conditions of relative war using such weapons of mass communication guarantee that it will be a very long war over the world.

Notes

1 Paul Virilio, *Negative Horizon* (New York: Continuum, 2005), p. 29.
2 Paul Virilio, *Desert Screen: War at the Speed of Light* (New York: Continuum, 2005), p. 8; italics in original.
3 Niall Ferguson, *Colossus: The Price of America's Empire* (New York: Penguin, 2004), pp. 1–29.
4 Ibid., p. 262.
5 Ibid., p. 263.
6 See Joyce Kolko and Gabriel Kolko, *The Limits of Power: The World and the United States, 1945–1954* (New York: Harper and Row, 1972); Samuel Huntington, "The Democratic Distemper," *Public Interest*, Vol. 41 (Fall 1975), pp. 9–38; Paul Kennedy, *The Rise and Fall of the Great Powers* (New York: Vintage, 1989); Noam Chomsky, *Hegemony or Survival: America's Quest for Global Dominance* (New York: Holt, 2004); and Chalmers Johnson, *Blowback: The Costs and Consequences of American Empire* (New York: Holt, 2004).
7 Ferguson, *Colossus*, p. 21.

8 See Joseph Nye, *Soft Power: The Means to Success in World Politics* (New York: Public Affairs, 2004).
9 Ibid., p. 8.
10 Ibid.
11 Virilio, *Desert Screen*, p. 8.
12 Ibid., p. 9.
13 Virilio, *Negative Horizon*, p. 189, italics as in original.
14 Ibid., p. 188.
15 See *Washington Post*, August 21, 2001, p. A1.
16 See Andrew Bacevitch, *The New American Militarism: How Americans Are Seduced by War* (New York: Oxford University Press, 2005), p. 201.
17 Secretary of State Colin Powell, "Remarks at the Elliott School of International Affairs, George Washington University," available at www.state.gov/secretary/rm/2003/23836.htm.
18 Arjun Appadurai, *Modernity at Large: Cultural Dimensions of Globalization* (Minneapolis: University of Minnesota Press, 1996), pp. 188–9.
19 Ibid., p. 175.
20 Ibid., p. 172.
21 Ibid., p. 171.
22 Robert D. Kaplan, *Imperial Grunts: The American Military on the Ground* (New York: Random House, 2005), p. 6.
23 Ibid., p. 7.
24 Michael Hardt and Antonio Negri, *Empire* (Cambridge, MA: Harvard University Press, 2000), p. xi.
25 Francis Fukuyama, *The End of History and the Last Man* (New York: Free Press, 1992), pp. 89–97.
26 Paul Virilio, *Open Sky* (London: Verso, 1997), p. 75.
27 See Hilary French, *Vanishing Borders: Protecting the Planet in the Age of Globalization* (New York: Norton, 2000), p. 34.
28 Ibid., p. 34.
29 Hardt and Negri, *Empire*, p. xiii.
30 Michael Hardt and Antonio Negri, *Multitude: War and Democracy in the Age of Empire* (New York: Cambridge, MA: Harvard University Press, 2004), p. 142.
31 Ibid., p. 100.
32 Michel Foucault, *The History of Sexuality, Vol. I: An Introduction* (New York: Vintage, 1980), p. 136.
33 Hardt and Negri, *Multitude*, p. 101.
34 Foucault, *The History of Sexuality, Vol. I*, p. 136.
35 Michel Foucault, *The Foucault Effect: Studies in Governmentality*, eds. Graham Burchell, Colin Gordon, and Peter Miller (Chicago: University of Chicago Press, 1991), pp. 92–3.
36 See Robert D. Kaplan, *The Ends of the Earth: A Journey at the Dawn of the 21st Century* (New York: Random House, 1996); or Thomas Friedman, *The World Is Flat: A Brief History of the Twenty-First Century* (New York: Farrar, Strauss and Giroux, 2005).
37 Fredric Jameson, *Postmodernism, or the Cultural Logic of Late Capitalism* (Durham: Duke University Press, 1992).
38 Hardt and Negri, *Multitude*, p. 101.
39 Hardt and Negri, *Empire*, p. xiv.
40 Ibid., p. 397.
41 See Thomas Friedman, *The Lexus and the Olive Tree* (New York: Knopf, 1999); French, *Vanishing Borders*; or Stephen Krasner, *Problematic Sovereignty: Contested Rules and Political Possibilities* (New York: Columbia University Press, 2001).
42 For more on this question, see Fukuyama, *The End of History and the Last Man*; William Greider, *One World, Ready or Not: The Manic Logic of Global Capitalism* (New York: Simon & Schuster, 1996); Timothy W. Luke, "Discourses of Disintegration/Texts or Transformation: Re-Reading Realism in the New World Order," *Alternatives*, Vol. 18, No.

2 (1993), pp. 229–58; Pierre Bourdieu, *Acts of Resistance: Against the Tyranny of the Market* (New York: The New Press, 1998); and Timothy W. Luke, "Real Interdependence: Discursivity and Concursivity in Global Politics," in ed. François Debrix, *Language, Agency, and Politics in a Constructed World* (Armonk, NY: M.E. Sharpe, 2003), pp. 101–20.
43 Hardt and Negri, *Empire*, pp. xiv–xv.
44 See Timothy W. Luke, "Placing Powers, Siting Spaces: The Politics of Global and Local in the New World Order," *Environment and Planning A: Society and Space*, Vol. 12 (1994), pp. 613–28.
45 Hardt and Negri, *Empire*, p. xvi.
46 Francis Fukuyama, *America at the Crossroads: Democracy, Power, and the Neoconservative Legacy* (New Haven: Yale University Press, 2006), p. 113.
47 See Michael Mann, *Incoherent Empire* (London: Verso, 2003); Chalmers Johnson, *The Sorrows of Empire: Militarism, Secrecy, and the End of the Republic* (New York: Metropolitan Books, 2004); or Bacevich, *The New American Militarism*.
48 Ferguson, *Colossus*, p. 29.
49 Ibid., p. 13.
50 See www.whitehouse.gov/news/releases/2005/11/20051101-1.html.
51 Ibid.
52 See Kendall Hoyt, "Bird Flu Won't Wait," *New York Times*, March 3, 2006, p. B10.
53 Virilio, *Desert Screen*, p. 88.
54 Virilio, *Negative Horizon*, p. 190; italics in original.
55 Ibid., p. 190.
56 See www.whitehouse.gov/news/releases/2002/06/20020601-3.html.
57 See www.whitehouse.gov/news/releases/2006/01/2-6-131-10.html.

2 American insecurities and the ontopolitics of US pharmacotic wars

Larry N. George

Introduction

International insecurity today stems from many sources. Some of these, such as global climate change or the unanticipated effects of genetically modified organisms (GMOs), are novel and unprecedented, while others (global pandemics or impending fossil fuel shortages, for instance) are familiar in kind if not in scale. One source of growing insecurity around the world, however, is both familiar and unprecedented: the already overwhelming and still-increasing military preponderance of the United States.[1] With some four percent of the world's population, the United States currently spends approximately as much on preparing for and fighting wars as the rest of the world combined. Its conventional armed forces are already an order of magnitude more powerful than those of any currently imaginable foe, and its nuclear arsenal is so superior to those of any possible combination of adversaries that, for the first time in at least four decades, one country is now arguably on the brink of attaining a usable nuclear first-strike capability.[2] This combination of essentially limitless destructive capability and strategic invulnerability will render the American armed forces capable of unilaterally annihilating any or all significant counterforce and countervalue targets—indeed, human life itself—anywhere on the planet without fear of remotely commensurate military retaliation. American presidents, who exercise unique command authority over this arsenal, will thus soon wield the power to summon the angel of death itself, the undiscriminating Destroyer Angel of the Bible (*lammal'ak hammashit* in Hebrew or *olothreuon* in Greek) who, once unleashed, cannot be called back, not even by God.[3]

The remarkable expansion of post-Cold War American conventional and nuclear warfighting and force projection capabilities can only partially be explained by traditional power politics, or by rationally calculated, national interest-driven responses to the evolving geopolitical and geoeconomic challenges and opportunities. This raises the question of the roles that domestic political considerations, driven by Americans' own material, ideological, and ontopolitical insecurities, may be playing in this unprecedented military buildup. This chapter will suggest that these insecurities are to a significant extent the legacies of recurring cycles of *pharmacotic wars*. The term "pharmacotic war" refers to the simultaneously beneficial and harmful effects of war on political communities, and to the ways wars are structured like, and resemble, mass collective human sacrifices. It derives from the semantically ambiguous and

Janus-faced Classical Greek word *pharmakon* (which meant both medicine and poison, performance-enhancing drug and addictive toxin) and from the etymologically related Ionian Greek word for the human sacrifice or "scapegoat" ritual, *pharmakos*. Pharmacotic violence and pharmacotic war simultaneously strengthen and endanger the state by temporarily transforming political division or derangement into divinely ordained political order and unanimity, through the mystical power of collective projection and targeted hatred, victimage, and enmity directed against designated internal scapegoats and demonized external foes.[4]

Pharmacotic violence is purgative and cathartic. It ritually cleanses the community of evil, impurity, and guilt; carries away the accumulated burdens of past violence and iniquity; and restores the community's sense of righteousness, its avenues of communication with its gods, and its sacred ties to the divine. Pharmacotic war re-sacralizes and re-sanctifies the polity. Pharmacotic violence and pharmacotic war are also ontopolitically unifying. They temporarily restore political harmony and integrity by repressing difference and plurality through the common targeting of a single designated object of community demonization and hatred (a domestic scapegoat or a foreign enemy). Pharmacotic wars also violently reinscribe on the world fundamental moral and political metaphysical distinctions between inside and outside, friend and foe, good and bad (or evil), and security and insecurity. By tapping into the same ancestral cultural reservoirs of embodied archetypes and collectively experienced meanings that fed ancient rituals of collective victimization, demonization, and ultimately human sacrifice itself, pharmacotic wars create political power from that aspect of the collective unconscious that is structured not, as in Lacan's formulation, like a language, but, in the words of Phillipe Sollers, like a lynching.[5]

While specific, limited acts of pharmacotic violence (the scapegoating rituals of the ancient Near East, for example, or capital punishment today) may partially and temporarily reunify a community, only pharmacotic war can fundamentally reunite and reground a polity in a way that enables the comprehensive reordering and reconstruction of that body politic. "War," as Jean Bethke Elshtain has observed,

> retains the power to incite parts of the self that peace cannot seem to reach ... Our deeply rooted conviction, sustained by veterans of battle fronts and home fronts and transmitted to others is that wars—good wars that unite us—offer a communal endeavor, the sharing of sacrifice and danger. Modern society appears to have found no other way to initiate and sustain action in common with others on this scale.[6]

Traditionally, such sacralizing wars have been capable of restoring order in deranged polities, or of transforming decentralized *Gesellschaft* civic associations or rhizomic societies into hallowed nations occupying a sacred and secured homeland. This is accomplished by reconsecrating the sacred bond that unifies and articulates the four elements of the traditional mythical national body politic: the gods of the community, the king (or, in earlier polities, the king-priest), the nation's sacrificial heroes and martyrs, and the citizenry or "people." At any given moment, each of these four constituent elements of the nation's sacred identity is represented in the nation's imaginary by a specific metonymic figure. Because nations are both imagined and historically evolving communities, the figures who occupy those metonymic positions may change over time, particularly in the wake of pharmacotic wars. The political etiologies of specific wars may, conversely, be significantly affected by the identity and character of the individuals or groups playing these metonymic roles in a given historical moment.

These roles also confer substantial political power. Occupying the king-priest site within the sacred national political imaginary during wartime, for example, can be an incomparable source of fungible symbolic political capital and power, even conferring quasi-royal status on the president or prime minister of a modern, ostensibly secularized, polity.[7] The same is true of culturally hegemonic ethnic groups who metonymically come to stand for or represent the "people" through their conspicuous participation in wars and other patriotic blood sacrifices. This is why, during wartime, the ontopolitical stakes involved in what would ordinarily be "merely" symbolic, ideological, or partisan struggles among groups often escalate so dramatically. But pharmacotic wars can also addict a community to the treacherous political panaceas of militarization, regimentation, predation, collective demonization, projection, and scapegoating. Such wars thus exhibit characteristics of both *pharmakos* and *pharmakon*—hence, the term "pharmacotic".

In referring to US wars as pharmacotic, I mean specifically that they enable political leaders periodically to exploit blood sacrifice to reconstitute, strengthen, and stabilize the American political order. But they do so in ways that ultimately prove simultaneously medicinal, poisonous, and addictive to the US body politic. The use of American military power can be highly fungible for both foreign policy and domestic political purposes, but like an addictive drug the exploitation of war only increases the need for future doses. And because American political institutions, practices, and norms—indeed, the country's very political identity—are so deeply informed by the narratives of past American wars, each successive war politically strengthens and emboldens those forces that earn political capital from the prosecution of those wars, enabling them to shape the country's future in their own image and according to their own nationalistic ideals and militaristic values. But it also aggravates the inherited problems (the mortmain) created by the cumulative pharmacotic effects of these wars.

That wars shape and inform political institutions and political cultures, and can at least temporarily enable governments to displace or defer internal societal, economic, or political problems, is hardly a revelation.[8] What is less well understood is how war can shape a nation's political *identity*, that is to say, the collective self-image with which the people of a nation identify, the position, status, and role of each subject within that imagined community, and the sense of commonality engendered by the various practices through which that collective self-conception is reproduced.[9] The arena of national identity politics—the ways that efforts to define, impose, and enforce a particular ideological conception of the nation's identity affect the ongoing struggles for equality or dominance among politically mobilized groups within the nation—has in recent years frequently emerged as the most prominent site where even traditional political controversies over policy alternatives, ideology, material interests, or governmental power and resources are fought out. Understanding the roles played by pharmacotic wars in these ontopolitical struggles, and the ways that such ontopolitical conflicts can shape the content and course of the nation's wars, are thus crucial to uncovering the underlying dynamics of the insecurities driving American foreign policy and international relations today.

Many of the most troubling insecurities driving recent American foreign policy derive from the delinking of foreign policy from American political identity struggles following the end of the Cold War. This has resulted in recurring efforts to restore centralized executive authority and overcome the increasing instability of American political identity by (re)constructing an imagined national identity sufficiently robust, integral, and secure to sustain the ambitious foreign policy agendas of the post-Cold War US national security state. Many of the resulting ontopolitical conflicts are familiar: struggles among ideologically constituted identity groups for political influence and power, especially in the electoral arena, for example, or efforts by political parties and other organized political interests to construct new political identities or reshape existing ones according to ontopolitically coded, ideologically determined positions on particular issues.

This chapter focuses on how, during such times of political disunity, pharmacotic wars increase the relative power, and legitimate the claims to ontopolitical primacy of certain groups, through the violent reassembly and reconstruction of national identity. Pharmacotic wars transubstantiate the blood shed by martyrs and heroes into new ontopolitical bonds of national identity and solidarity. By actively participating in these wars, certain subnational groups can, over time, accumulate substantial ontopolitical power, influence, and authority. This enhanced ontopolitical status may in turn confer a privileged relationship with the sovereign or centralized executive authority, a special bond with and even a sense of ownership over the nation's patriotic symbols, and an enhanced right to redefine the nation's core values, ideals, and commitments, and even to determine the future shape of its institutions, laws, policies, and political practices.

Ontopolitics, pharmacotic war, and the security dilemma

Ontopolitical pharmacotic violence—the construction and sustaining of national political identity and the consecration of sacralized political authority through armed conflict and sacrificial bloodletting—has always been a part of American wars and foreign military interventions. War's ontopolitically regenerative function is, of course, coeval with the nation-state system itself. Nation-states have always constituted themselves through attempts to overcome both external estrangements and insecurities associated with the ever-present threat of war, and internal derangements and insecurities—economic, social, cultural, and psychological—resulting from the outcomes of past wars and the need to prepare for future wars.[10]

From the beginning, national identity always had more to do with bellicose bloodletting than with genealogical blood ties. The symbolic and ideological elements of most ethnic and national identities are essentially politically orchestrated echoes of pseudo-fraternal bonds forged in ancient wars and periodically renewed through subsequent collective blood sacrifices.[11] What genuinely ancient consanguinities may be associated with such identities are to a disturbing degree the genetic legacies of the historically misogynistic brutality of war (for example, rape, capture, relocation, enslavement, forced concubinage, marriage, and childbearing, along with other forms of sexual violence, bondage, and domination of women by military conquerors).[12] The ethnic groups from which the national identities of Western European nation-states supposedly stem, for instance, were never actually organic, "vertical," or even autonymic, but rather were violently assembled through successive military conquests by war-leaders whose "martial charisma" and ferocity both attracted vassal warriors and forcibly incorporated other followers drawn from among the remnant populations of conquered or defeated communities and "peoples."[13] In a context of virtually continual intercommual armed violence, these early "ethnic" war-leaders established their power and legitimacy by redistributing war booty (including captured and enslaved women) among the warriors whose kin would come to comprise these ethnic groups, and then consolidated and institutionalized their own pseudo-patriarchal authority by retroactively conjuring mythical proto-ethnic identities, and then "projecting their charisma back in time" through fictional narratives recounting their own imagined, divinely ordained, royal lineages:

> Casting themselves as members of long-lived dynasties, they lay claim to authority not only on the contingency of present, potentially transitory, military success; but also on their lineage, portrayed as uniquely and divinely favored. These dynastic claims bolster their reputations as leaders, but more importantly serve to merge the multiple identities of their current polyethnic following into the "ethnicity" (or *gens*) of the noble leadership ... "[E]thnicity" is essentially an exclusive attribute of the social elite, conferred for their advantage onto the mass of their satellites.[14]

In their original form, these early European ethnic foundation myths and narratives included concepts of divine kingship similar to ancient Mesopotamian and Greek understandings of "sacral kingship"[15] that were in turn directly linked to Bronze and Iron Age pharmacotic scapegoating rituals, myths and legends of pharmacotic human sacrifices, and pharmacotic wars.[16] In the earliest forms, then, of the proto-ethnicities that mythically antecede modern European nationalisms can already be seen the ontopolitically generative articulation of sacrificial political authority, collective political identity, and originary political insecurity that continues to both feed and feed on the security dilemma inherent in the anarchic modern state system today.

Since the sixteenth century, the security dilemma has compelled modern states to formulate and implement domestic and foreign policies that intensify the nationalistic solidarity and patriotic loyalty of their subjects. Internally, states have developed a battery of political strategies and administrative practices (ranging from the promulgation of nationally unifying rituals, symbols, and myths to novel forms of surveillance, policing, and biopolitics) intended to strengthen centralized state authority by "grounding" it in an ostensibly integral and homogeneous national identity. External wars have continued to be fought over disputed territories, dynastic successions, economically valuable resources, religious affiliations, imperial expansion, and other conventional geostrategic and geopolitical matters. But these disputes more and more have come to be understood and defined in ontopolitical terms. Increasingly, both the insecurities provoked by the armaments of neighboring states and those arising from domestic challenges to state legitimacy have been addressed by vigorously reasserting and reinforcing the mystical bonds of national kinship through the cultivation of sacred symbols, rituals, and myths of patriotic militarism. In these, the blood sacrifices of the nation's martyrs and heroes are transubstantiated into mystical blood ties that bind and unify the subjects of the state into an imagined and idealized sacred national family.

Such efforts to construct and reinforce centralized national identities, however, always have been complicated and confounded by the persistence of counter-hegemonic ethnic, religious, and other subnational or transnational political identities. In recent decades, the proliferation of increasingly pluralizing, complex, self-constructed, heterogeneous, contested, fragmentary, contradictory, and rhizomic political identities has further exacerbated the ontopolitical difficulties facing contemporary nation-states like the Unites States that continue actively to employ war and militarism as instruments of statecraft. Such "national security states" require the periodic mobilization—or, at minimum, the passive consent—of a unified, disciplined, and conformist citizenry comprised of subjects who embrace their *national* political identity as primary, determinate, and definitive, and who also subordinate other aspects of their identities to it.

Such a mobilization has become more difficult in recent decades though. With the dramatic reduction of traditional security threats since the middle of the last century, many of the unique roles and traditional functions of the state have diminished in importance, or are increasingly performed by private organizations, intergovernmental institutions, and transnational corporate and financial businesses and other nongovernmental organizations. In reaction, many states have begun to develop a biopolitical and ontopolitical interest in *securitization*, that is to say, in redefining, re-identifying, and broadening the category "security threats" to now include problems such as drug trafficking, loss of control over fossil fuel supplies, immigration, political violence committed by nongovernmental organizations ("terrorism"), and other global challenges. Pharmacotic war has played a crucial role in this securitization process. By taking advantage of the pharmacotic effects of war, states can sacralize the otherwise often questionable—and frequently counterproductive or even disastrous—deployment of national military forces to cope with these sorts of challenges while temporarily quelling internal sources of insecurity. The sacrificial aura surrounding pharmacotic war can even overcome the reluctance of contemporary citizenries to tolerate significant military casualties, in favor of demanding that the deaths of martyrs and heroes be avenged and their blood sacrifices redeemed.

But these benefits for states can only be won, however, within the harsh terms of the *pharmakon* (the simultaneously salutary and poisonous political effects) of war. The deranging effects of such wars will typically include the political elevation and empowerment of those partisan factions and ethnic or other ontopolitically constituted groups who most enthusiastically embrace patriotic militarism and contribute the greater portion of the blood sacrifice. Such groups will tend to embrace cultural norms and value systems that celebrate the heroic martial virtues of honor, glory, sacrifice, and unconditional love of country, and favor decisive and violent action over political negotiation, diplomacy, or reconciliation. Members of these groups will typically be more accepting of the use of coercive violence by public officials and of interpersonal violence in their own private lives. As such, they will tend to be overrepresented in the armed forces, as well as on both sides of domestic criminal law enforcement. They will be more likely to identify more intimately with, and uncritically support, their country's war leaders, and they will develop parochial material interests in the further arming, militarization, and securitization of the state.

Over time, such groups will often develop nationalistic obsessions and insecurities that resemble collective manifestations of the classic defense mechanisms of the ego, including denial, displacement, projection, aggression, and scapegoating. Because they view both their own political system and the world at large in starkly binary terms of friend and foe, they are more susceptible to pro-war propaganda and to dualistic, Manichean political ideologies that identify them and their nation with Good and their enemies of the moment with Evil. They may become obsessed with seeking out domestic traitors to punish, and foreign enemies against whom to prosecute patriotic wars. The pious among them will come to believe that they and their country are doing God's work on Earth, and that the violence they engage in is not only just, but divinely ordained and blessed. By temporarily breaching the barriers that separate the sacred from the profane, sacrificial pharmacotic wars can enable such groups to reshape their own—and, through their example and influence, the rest of the nation's—religious beliefs, rituals, and practices into conformity with militant and crusading (and often millennarian or even apocalyptic) theologies of righteous vengeance and salvation through sacralizing blood sacrifice.

Modern states, then, can exploit the pharmacotic effects of war to overcome the ontopolitically centrifugal, pluralizing, and decentralizing tendencies of contemporary societies. But they do so only at significant peril. This understanding suggests another interpretation of both Clausewitz's dictum regarding war as the continuation of politics (in this case, *ontopolitics*) by other means and Foucault's inversion of it (politics continues war internally and ontopolitically by other means). For those states still addicted to the ancient drug (*pharmakon*) of war, sacrificial violence may remain the underlying condition of, and the most effective remedy for, the internally diremptive effects of ontopolitical pluralization and the proliferating insecurities arising from it (insecurities that animate so much of contemporary international relations).

The genealogy of pharmacotic war

The Ionian Greek *pharmakos* ritual has been associated by some scholars with the more familiar and overtly political *ostracism* ritual.[17] There and throughout the ancient Near East, human sacrificial or scapegoat expulsion rituals were carried out both during regular calendrical festivals and in response to existential wars or political crises. These ceremonies served a number of crucial ontopolitical functions: to purge the community of social or political toxins that might debilitate the body politic; to restore and reconsecrate the integrity, collective identity, and sacred unity of the political community (along with its traditional values, fundamental metaphysical categories, and the moral and social norms that were derived from these); to reassert, re-establish, and re-sacralize the territorial boundaries of the state; and to reaffirm the sacred ties among the polity's leaders, the government, the body politic, and the gods. This link between the ontopolitically re-sacralizing and regenerative functions of internally directed pharmacotic scapegoating and externally oriented pharmacotic war was institutionalized in the Ionian Greek *pharmakos* ceremony that was conducted annually during the Thargelia festival and also sporadically during times of looming disaster or political derangement, such as droughts, famines, plagues, or imminent military defeats. As Jan Bremmer puts it:

> The scapegoats [*pharmakoi*] were expelled on the sixth of the month Thargelion, the first day of the two-day festival of the Thargelia. It is rather surprising to note that on the same day that the scapegoats were expelled the Greeks also celebrated the fall of Troy, the victories at Marathon and Plataea, and even the victory of Alexander the Great over Darius (Ael. VH. 2.25). Evidently the expulsion of evil was felt so intensely that this seemed to be the appropriate day to celebrate these victories.[18]

For these Greeks, the salutary political effects of pharmacotic sacrifice were clearly related to similar effects arising from the then-emerging forms of what the conservative historian Victor Davis Hanson calls the "Western way of war,"[19] which entailed the formalization of the norms of warfighting designed to confine war's ill effects to the combatants in the field.[20]

These pharmacotic rituals recall the commonplace motif found in Greek (and Hebrew) literature and mythology of human (and especially female child) sacrifice to save the city from disaster or ensure military victory.[21] In expressing gratitude to the gods for the temporary security provided by divinely sanctioned military victory (while enacting appeals for exemption from divine vengeance and punishment for the violence, hubris, and impiety that inevitably accompany war), these myths and ceremonies of collective and public ritual scapegoating or atonement also provide clues to the originary grounding of the metaphysical principles that underpin Western and Helleno-Abrahamic concepts of public morality, social order, and political authority and power.[22] The *pharmakos* and ostracism ceremonies together could ritually overcome the chronic fear of the dissolution of the political, metaphysical, and moral unity and order that was maintained through the centralized religious, military, and political authority of kings.

In these ceremonies, the mystical foundations of political power could be restored and re-sanctified through a ritualized act of sacrificial expulsion or killing that, by violently transgressing the fundamental metaphysical distinctions between high and low, inside and outside, good and bad (or evil), and the living and the dead, could momentarily breach the liminal boundaries that separate the human from the divine. This violence was cathartic and apotropaic. By inflicting on the designated scapegoats the originary territorializing violence of inclusion and exclusion, it was intended to ward off or even cure the polity of the divinely inflicted evils (drought, plague, famine, or military defeat). Because everyone in the community was required to take part in this expulsion or even killing of the victims, it also served as a rite of aggregation and reunification of the polity in the face of chronic physical, metaphysical, and ontopolitical insecurity. From the community's point of view, this process was largely mystical: if the underlying logic of pharmacotic violence were publicly acknowledged or openly thematized, its effects would be diminished or canceled out. In this sense, pharmacotic violence functions like magic or sorcery. Indeed, one Greek term for magician or sorcerer was *pharmakeus* (and sometimes *pharmakos*).

Such a sacrificial pharmacotic violence could provisionally resolve political crises. However, the logic of the *pharmakon* meant that, over time, its cumulative effects would become malignant. Such violence could enable the temporary reinvestment of traditional moral and political norms, meanings, and identities, and it could also provisionally restabilize conventional metaphysical principles of hierarchy and order. But political identities and "fundamental" values sustained through pharmacotic violence were always volatile and turbulent. Resecuring these across time required further sacrificial violence at home and abroad, thus fueling tragic cycles of pharmacotic violence and war to which numerous ancient polities became habituated and that gradually restructured those communities' political cultures, institutions, and values, shaped their internal ontopolitical struggles, and (in many cases) determined the historical roles they would eventually come to play.

Modern pharmacotic war

Modern societies have, for the most part, abandoned this overt public performance of pharmacotic human sacrifice. To be sure, many "atavistic" pharmacotic sacrificial practices—from monarchical spectacles of retributive public punishment to pogroms, lynching, institutionalized capital punishment, routinized administrative torture, ethnic cleansing, wartime slaughter of civilians, or genocidal massacres (all of which, in many ways, function politically like ancient sacrificial rituals) continue even in the "developed" Helleno-Abrahamic world. Such practices are, however, today widely regarded as institutionally incompatible with the emerging biopolitical organization of society.[23] Nevertheless, several key features of modern societies continue to generate pressures to turn towards pharmacotic violence and war, in part by tapping into deeply inscribed psychological and neuropolitical predispositions,[24] but also by drawing upon vestigial remnants of earlier cultural practices, social formations, and political institutions.[25]

A modern pharmacotic war is triggered by a violation that produces victims who can be inscribed as heroes or martyrs. The violation typically consists of an attack against a military or quasi-military political target, but carried out in such a way that the target can be construed as an "innocent" victim. Politically driven narrative construction and mythopoeisis ensues whereby the attack and the responses to it are thematically interpreted and inscribed within familiar plot lines involving victimhood, martyrdom, righteous vengeance, and the restoration of security and sacred justice and order. These are often recentered around a metonymic patriotic axis linking together the martyred victims, the nation's "core" ethnic population, and the president, prime minister, or other head of state. The process of reincorporating this idealized body politic confers on the sovereign the sacred authority to designate the "evil" (or "evil" ones) responsible for the violation, to identify those within the country who might in some way be associated or affiliated with that evil, and to wage war against the external manifestations of evil until sacred political order is restored.

The "rallying" effect of such a pharmacotic violation of the body politic is analogous to that of a performance-enhancing drug (*pharmakon*). That political effect, of course, eventually wears off, thus requiring ever increasing "dosages" (further pharmacotic sacrifices and wars), but also producing dangerous side effects and derangements in the body politic. Over the short-term, however, the pharmacotic war typically provokes a general increase in patriotic zeal and enthusiasm, generating windfall surplus political capital for incumbent leaders, and granting them substantial political leeway and autonomy (even in areas of policy not directly related to the unfolding, sacrificially structured violence). The resulting recentralization of power is compounded by the ensuing dampening of political criticism and dissent as political discourse is constricted (becoming much more uniform, intolerant, rigid, conformist, and supportive not only of the incumbent leadership's response to the violation but typically also of its larger political goals and agendas). As the pharmacotic war unfolds, this produces a political "supplement" that flows outward from the reconsecrated patriotic "core" axis, thus augmenting the personal political capital of the executive officials of the government (while increasing the political influence of their party, political allies, and affiliated constituencies).

The symbolic condensation of the nation's sovereignty, its sacralized martyrs and heroes, its ontopolitically "core" ethnic population, and its executive leadership into a newly revitalized and reconsecrated body politic leaves the incumbent government's political adversaries, opponents, and critics vulnerable to castigation, demonization, and even scapegoating as unwitting agents, vacillating enablers, or even tacit supporters of the nation's newly designated existential foes. The press is typically cowed, and opposition parties, social movements, and individual dissenters readily intimidated into silence and inaction. Subaltern voices are either silenced or heard almost exclusively in the roles of either victims of or collaborators with the nation's newly designated enemies, or as patriotic supporters of and cheerleaders for the government's response to the attack.[26] As constitutional, institutional, and other traditional checks on centralized executive power are weakened by the sanctification of the now-sovereign executive authority, extraordinary and even otherwise illegal political practices are lent credibility and legitimacy, generally leading to intensified public surveillance, increased governmental secrecy, and expanded covert operations both inside and outside the country, compromising or undermining civil rights and liberties, and threatening democratic institutions.

With the weakening of institutional checks and balances and public accountability generally, new avenues for patronage, cronyism, collusion, and other forms of favoritism and corruption appear under the sacred cover of reconsecrated domestic authority and foreign military operations now construed as acts of righteous vengeance. Religious denominations, sects, movements, organizations, priestly castes, or sometimes entire faiths (that enjoy confessional affinities or political associations with either the sacralized victims or the newly re-empowered incumbent national leaders, have a substantial following within the nation's core metonymic identity group, and are able to associate their own parochial dogmas, doctrines and beliefs with the unfolding pharmacotic events) may begin to gain competitive sectarian advantages and enhanced theological credibility.

Pharmacotic war and political culture

The *pharmakon*, or drug of war, can become politically addictive, particularly for certain kinds of communities. A society that continually prepares for and periodically engages in pharmacotic warfare will generate public institutions, private interest groups, and networks of powerful individuals that are dependent on continued and expanding militarism. Its political culture will come to revolve around militaristic themes, symbols, and images—flags, battle anniversaries, war memorials, anthems, and the like—and its official historical narrative will fill with heroic sacrificial myths and legends of martyrdom, just revenge, and divinely ordained victory. War will increasingly define patriotism, and dissent against the nation's growing addiction to war will be regarded as treason. Governments of such states and social orders will be drawn towards new wars as readily available means for enhancing their own legitimacy and for temporarily displacing domestic political problems.

Eventually, however, the double-edged logic of the *pharmakon* as both medicine and poison to the body politic will begin to reverse the initially salutary effects of the political exploitation of this pharmacotic supplement. The sacrificial nature of scapegoating and demonization will come back to haunt the community and its leaders. Pharmacotic violence and war necessarily entail the repression, purgation, forced conversion, exclusion, expulsion, eradication, elimination, or extermination of designated sacrificial victims and dehumanized foes. But these targeted enemies upon whose negation the formerly troubled polity has reconstructed its political identity always also represent repressed elements of the community itself (as well as "othered" groups within or outside the community). Their scapegoating inevitably produces a *haunting* of the polity by *revenants*—remnants, remainders, reminders, afterimages, or ghosts—of the expurgated ontopolitical elements (for an additional reading of the return of the sacrificed ones, see Patricia Molloy's chapter in this volume). The resulting disturbances or threats to the newly reconstituted national identity must eventually either be reincorporated into or expelled from the *polis* through further iterations of pharmacotic violence. Through the very processes by which pharmacotic violence and war seek to reintegrate, reunify, and reconsecrate the community, they simultaneously sow the seeds of further ontopolitical instability.

Whether a particular pharmacotic war will successfully restore the nation's political identity and its institutions is often determined by how well or poorly the incumbent government manages the contradictory or double-edged logic of the *pharmakon* that structures these wars. Factors such as the character of the nation-state's designated enemy, the plausibility and resonance of the mythopoeitic narrative framing the conflict, the war's costs in lives and treasure, or its political impact can make a significant difference here. If the demonized foe is a peer state, its military defeat and conquest can significantly enhance the legitimacy and political capital of the victorious government's leaders (as occurred in the United States and the Soviet Union following the Allied defeat of Nazi Germany). If that defeat is incomplete or excessively costly, the pharmacotic rivalry between the two states can be indefinitely protracted, thus aggravating other controversies (as with Germany after World War I, Russia after the Cold War, or both Iran and Iraq today) and often contributing to future pharmacotic wars. If the demonized enemy is a militarily weak state (for the United States, Spain in 1898, Grenada in 1983, Panama in 1989, or Taliban Afghanistan more recently) or a non-state actor (the Medellin Cartel or even Al-Qaeda before 9/11), the pharmacotic "boost" from the resulting asymmetric war will usually be ephemeral at best. And if a pharmacotic war against such an adversary goes wrong (as in Korea, Vietnam, or Iraq today), the government may find itself facing severe and accumulating domestic ontopolitical problems. Not only will the human and material costs of the war increasingly be counted against the administration/political leadership, thus resulting in the diminishment of its legitimacy and in a loss of fungible political capital, but the fortunes of those on both sides of the decision to initiate pharmacotic violence will increasingly be reversed. The incumbent government may then suffer political repudiation or defeat, and the president, prime minister, or autocrat responsible for the ill-fated pharmacotic war may be humiliated or punished. Parties, factions, ideological tendencies, and interest groups affiliated with the beleaguered administration will increasingly fall into disfavor, lose political power and advantage, and may even be targeted for political retaliation (often taking the form of counter-scapegoating).

Ontopolitics and American pharmacotic wars

As a *Herrenvolk* polity evolving towards plutocracy (while aspiring to become a "civilizational" empire), the United States has long had a predilection for pharmacotic war.[27] Since its "Founding," the country's constitutional framework, imperial insignia, and public buildings and monuments have been modeled on those of ancient Rome, and its liberal Lockean civil society has been gloved in the iron gauntlet of a Hobbesian liberal state. During the Cold War, US internationalist elites imagined their Soviet adversary as a Spartan garrison state, and their own suddenly hegemonic country as a contemporary Athens (a maritime commercial democracy blessed with a war-swollen treasury and a long-range force-projection capability reluctantly drawn into the role of hegemonic alliance leader and enforcer). But the flaws in this analogy were always glaring. Haunting the popular American image of Soviet tyranny was the always barely repressed self-image of an *American* Sparta: an insecure republic at the heart of which resided a heavily armed "core" white *ethnos* physically and psychologically encircled by, economically dependent upon, and obsessed with maintaining its ontopolitical identity and hegemony over a variegated population of subaltern metics and foreigners.

The United States has always relied on the ontopolitically restorative effects of both pharmacotic violence and pharmacotic wars to sustain its patriotic myths.[28] As a multicultural and polyethnic settler state, its national identity has traditionally not been defined in ethnic terms, but rather in terms of territorial, civic-republican, legalistic, and religious elements bound together, expanded, and sustained through violence.[29] Yet, as Anthony Smith, the British scholar of nationalism, notes, polyethnic nation-states are often "dominated by a single stategic *ethnie* which seeks, to a greater or lesser extent, to incorporate, or influence, the surrounding smaller or weaker *ethnie*."[30] In such states, one ethnic community, having "antedated, and so influenced by its normative patterns and economic location succeeding ethnic waves of immigrants" will often try to "forge a wider 'political culture' by extending, and perhaps attenuating, its own traditions, or by universalizing them to include the new ethnic migrants or the new incorporated *ethnie*."[31] This cultural hegemony may, according to Smith, be achieved through a combination of economic sanctions and institutional constraints, ultimately backed up by the threat of coercive violence.[32] It may also be established and maintained through pharmacotic war.

In the prevailing American political imaginary, ethnic groups and racialized populations are placed in two distinct social, economic, and political hierarchies, organized roughly by (1) the order in which "voluntary" immigrant groups arrived and were assimilated into the national community and (2) the conditions under which conquered, colonized, or enslaved populations were forcibly incorporated into the country's social and economic order. At the top of both these hierarchies, of course, sit white Americans of European, and particularly Anglo-Saxon Protestant, descent. The two hierarchies do not, however, precisely intersect, and thus there has always existed a permanently vacant site in this imagined social order, a politically generative "spark gap" with a tremendous potential to multiply the political power of whatever group occupies it (and where, as a result, various groups have historically struggled for dominance over the *point d'appui* or "quilting point" of that order).

Historically, the ethnic groups that have frequently come closest to forging a hegemonic American political culture in its own image have been white Anglo-Saxon Protestant northerners and Southern Anglo-Saxon and Scotch-Irish Protestants (hereafter simply called "southern whites").[33] It is almost exclusively among this latter group that one still encounters ethnically (and even racially) couched interpretations of the terrritorial, civic-republican, constitutional-legal, and religious elements of American national identity, interpretations often sanctified by reverence for the patriotic blood sacrifices that sustain the holy covenant binding the citizens of this "New Israel" to the nation's consecrated territory, its hallowed constitution, and God. The dominance of this white southern *ethnie* over the early political life of the United States, interrupted for a century by the interregnum that followed its defeat in the Civil War, in recent decades has been restored with a vengeance, so much so that, today, in the words of one of the (now repentant) architects of this remarkable political restoration, "[f]rom the Pentagon to Congress and the White House, the South, more that the North, speaks with the voice and carries the insignia of national command."[34]

Today, with approximately a quarter of the nation's population, the eleven states of the former Confederacy can effectively block federal legislation, decide the outcome of the electoral college's presidential vote, and (in alliance with the broader diaspora of descendants of southern whites who politically dominate nearly all of the non-coastal Western states), continue to shape the content of American domestic politics and foreign policy. All three branches of the federal government have been dominated for decades by southern whites or their appointees. Every elected American President since John F. Kennedy has either hailed from the south or won that office by actively mobilizing white southern voters. All but one sitting Supreme Court justice was appointed by these presidents, and, until the 2006 US midterm elections, nearly all of the most powerful positions in both the House and Senate had been occupied by Southerners. Indeed, for a period in the mid-1990s, the entire top of the federal government's chain of succession, from the President to the Vice-President, Speaker of the House, and President pro tempore of the Senate, were not only southern white men, but also had been baptized into the same southern Christian denomination.

This disproportionate political influence has meant that, in recent decades, issues of special concern to white Southerners—race, religion, hostility to the federal government, patriotic militarism, "traditional family values"—have become the most prominent and persistent topics in American political discourse and, not infrequently, the decisive issues in American elections.[35] Ethnically conscious white Southerners historically have regarded the country's most salient political issues—slavery, federalism, incorporation, segregation, foreign policy—less as tractable controversies amenable to political negotiation and compromise than as fundamental existential threats to their survival as a distinctive people and culture (or as matters of ontopolitical security and insecurity). One effect of southern white political hegemony, not surprisingly, has been the disturbing trend toward recoding conventional political controversies, both at home and abroad, as matters of national security, often requiring the use of armed force. This is one of the major reasons why recent American foreign policy solipsistically has continued to regard the various global problems that have emerged since the end of the Cold War (such as climate change, ecological deterioration, fossil fuel supply shortages, inter-ethnic violence and genocide, drug trafficking, economic globalization, epidemic diseases, population growth and migration) not as transnational challenges requiring multilaterally coordinated solutions arrived at through international diplomacy, but instead as threats to American national security to be dealt with through intensified domestic policing, the forcible imposition of American-style market rules and norms, and, wherever possible, the violent elimination of the foreign sources (real or imagined) of these dangers.

The pharmacotic narrative history of US wars

The wars of the United States have always been used to unite the citizenry, shore up the country's national mythos, and restore the sacred axis linking martyrs, heroes, and war presidents to the ontopolitically "core" American white (southern) ethnos, thereby reincorporating and reconsecrating the imagined and idealized American body politic. The Revolutionary War and the Civil War are the most obvious examples of this phenomenon,[36] but the country's many foreign wars and military interventions also provide revealing illustrations. Conventional narratives of these wars, from the Spanish-American War, World Wars I and II, the Vietnam War, and the Grenada and Panama invasions to the Persian Gulf War and now the "War on Terror" and the Iraq War, all follow a remarkably predictable plot line that conforms to the deep structure of ritual pharmacotic sacrifice.

At the outbreak of each of these wars, the country is politically divided, either by a close and hotly contested (and perhaps even questionably or dubiously decided) presidential election (McKinley, Wilson, George W. Bush), or polarized by an incumbent administration's pursuit of significant institutional reorganizations or policy innovations that benefit their own electoral base but threaten substantially to reshape the political status quo (McKinley, Franklin Roosevelt, Johnson, George W. Bush). An "unprovoked" attack is carried out (or is manufactured, or fabricated) against a symbolically resonant military or quasi-military target (the *Maine*, the *Lusitania*, the US Pacific Fleet at Pearl Harbor, the *Maddox* and *Turner Joy* in the Gulf of Tonkin, the Panama Canal, the Kuwaiti oil fields, or the Pentagon on 9/11). Innocents are killed, often in a manner that symbolically connotes sexual violation or child abuse. These victims may be civilians (the crowd outside the Boston Customs House, American women abused by Spanish officials in Cuba, the passengers of the *Lusitania*, child hostages and fictitious premature Kuwaiti babies in incubators, office workers in the Twin Towers, the passengers and crew of Flight 93) or unwary ordinary military personnel engaged in routine peacetime activities (night-duty sailors on the *Maine*, Pearl Harbor soldiers preparing for breakfast or church, the crews of the *Maddox* and *Turner Joy* on routine patrol in international waters in the Gulf of Tonkin, a US Army lieutenant kicked "in the groin over and over again" as his wife is "sexually threatened"[37] immediately before the US invasion of Panama, Pentagon office staff at their desks on the morning of 9/11).

The attack bonds the nation in solemn, unanimous outrage. Flags, posters, patriotic bumper stickers, and other patriotic symbols appear everywhere. Church attendance swells, patriotic sermons are delivered, and pious nationalistic rituals (such as the singing of the martial *Star Spangled Banner* or the reciting of the Pledge of Allegiance at public events) are performed with renewed spiritual meaning, ardor, and earnestness. The citizenry rallies behind the president, who paraliptically calls for restraint, while vowing retribution against the perpetrators. Conservative Christian preachers clamor for divinely sanctioned vengeance (often exhibiting impressive theological adroitness in delicately calibrating a rhetoric of righteous vengeance in the face of the inconvenient Sermon on the Mount). In the inevitably contradictory and paradoxical rhetorical interweaving of the mutually incongruous Christian doctrines of human forgiveness and divine vengeance (typically managed through the elision of the teachings of the pacifist Christ of the Gospels with tales of the warlord Jesus taken from the pulp fictional book of *Revelation*) and the sacrificially structured violence that follows, American political culture's underlying pharmacotic narrative structure can clearly be seen.[38]

A sacrificial theo-political narrative begins to take shape, scripted around the archetypal categories of victim, perpetrator, and rescuer. White, heterosexual, Christian, middle-class, rural, suburban or small town victims of the attack are singled out and held up as sacrificial martyrs to the nation. Those held responsible (correctly or falsely) for the attack are demonized and designated as the country's new mortal foes or existential enemies. An ideologically defined struggle ensues in which various groups seek to associate their political opponents' beliefs, policies, or identities with those of the perpetrators. Members of domestic groups with real or imagined ethnic, religious, ideological, or other links with the perpetrators of the attack (German-Americans in World War I; American Nisei in World War II; Black nationalists and antiwar student activists during the Vietnam War; Muslim Americans, feminists, and liberals generally since 9/11) are denounced, pilloried in the press, castigated by jingoistic politicians and other public figures, surveilled and monitored, and, in some cases, threatened, assaulted, imprisoned, confined to concentration camps, disappeared, tortured (or, in recent years, deported for torture), or killed. Accusers wrangle over how broadly to cast the net of responsibility for the attacks. Some, wary of the dangers in unleashed pharmacotic scapegoating, try to limit responsibility as narrowly as possible. Others, sensing an opportunity to capitalize politically on the popular clamor for sacrificial vengeance, seek to incriminate as broad a range of potentially guilty individuals as possible.

Emergency security measures are imposed, accompanied by moral panics, witch hunts, abuses of police powers, and other violations of civil rights and liberties (the prosecution of anti-draft speakers during World War I, the roundup and incarceration of Japanese-Americans and criminal justice system abuses directed against African-Americans and Mexican-Americans during World War II, Cointelpro and other abuses of police powers during the Vietnam War, imprisonment without due process, extraordinary renditions, and disappearances of Arabs and Muslims following 9/11, along with legally dubious surveillance of antiwar groups and other abuses of civil liberties associated with the Patriot Act). Dissenters (anti-imperialists in 1898, socialists in World War I, antiwar Vietnam veterans, anti-corporate globalization activists after 9/11) and opposition party leaders (Republican isolationists during World War II, liberal Democrats during the Vietnam War, and Iraq War opponents before 2005) are intimidated or silenced.[39] Both public agencies and private organizations typically contribute to this hunt for collaborationists, traitors, and other scapegoats.

As noted earlier, whether this projection, demonization, scapegoating, and the rallying effect and temporary national unity that result actually generate fungible political capital for the incumbent government depends on how well or poorly the president manages the pharmacotic dimensions of the ensuing war. In some cases (the Spanish-American War, World War II), the political consequences are momentous: a national partisan realignment, or the generational prolongation of single-party political dominance. In other cases (Korea, Vietnam, Iraq?), poorly handled pharmacotic wars destroy presidencies, cost the presidents' parties the White House, and undermine support for the incumbent administration's party, ideology, and policies.

Conclusion

The basic structure of pharmacotic sacrifice has shaped the politics of war since the Bronze Age. But it has taken different forms in successive historical periods. Since World War II, and particularly since the Cold War, traditional great-power wars have given way to internal wars, asymmetrical interstate wars, and novel types of conflict between state versus non-state actors. Today, the United States is largely secure from direct military threats from other states. But it cannot be confident of victory in asymmetric wars. And it remains vulnerable to non-conventional attacks by non-state actors and transnational groups.

The political exploitation of the pharmacotic dimensions of such wars is always tempting, but remains extremely risky. Unless the United States radically reconfigures its broad geoeconomic and geostrategic commitments and involvements, the sorts of insecurities that have prompted American leaders over the years to conduct one ill-fated and counterproductive pharmacotic foreign war after another will likely continue to fuel future American sacrificial violence, both at home and abroad.

Notes

1 See Rey Chow, *The Age of the World Target* (Durham: Duke University Press, 2006). In a different register, see Stephen Walt, *Taming American Power: The Global Response to U.S. Primacy* (New York: Norton, 2005).
2 See George W. Bush, "The National Security Strategy of the United States," (Washington, DC: White House, 2002); Charles Glaser and Steve Fetter, "Counterforce Revisited: Assessing the Nuclear Posture Review's New Missions," *International Security* Vol. 30, No. 2 (2005), pp. 84–126; James J. Wirtz and Jeffrey Larsen (eds.), *Nuclear Transformation:*

The New U.S. Nuclear Doctrine (New York: Palgrave, 2005); Keir A. Lieber and Daryl Press, "The End of MAD? The Nuclear Dimension of U.S. Primacy," *International Security* Vol. 30, No. 4 (2006), pp. 7–44; and Jeffrey Lantis *et al.*, "Correspondence: The Short Shadow of U.S. Primacy," *International Security* Vol. 31, No. 3 (2007), pp. 174–93.

3 See Exodus 12: 23; I Corinthians 10:10.

4 A superficial sampling of works that address the sacrificial dimensions of politics would include: Giorgio Agamben, *Homo Sacer: Sovereign Power and Bare Life* (Stanford: Stanford University Press, 1998) and *Remnants of Auschwitz: The Witness and the Archive* (New York: Zone, 2005); Georges Bataille, *Visions of Excess: Selected Writings, 1927–39* (Minneapolis: University of Minnesota Press, 1985) and *The Accursed Share, Vol. III* (New York: Zone, 1991); René Caillois, *Man and the Sacred* (Urbana: University of Illinois Press, 2001); William Connolly, *The Ethos of Pluralization* (Minneapolis: University of Minnesota Press, 1995); Jacques Derrida, *Dissemination* (Chicago: University of Chicago Press, 1981); Paul Dumouchel (ed.), *Violence and Truth: On the Work of René Girard* (Stanford: Stanford University Press, 1988); Barbara Ehrenreich, *Blood Rites: Origins and History of the Passions of War* (New York: Holt, 1997); Bracha L. Ettinger, *The Matrixial Borderspace* (Minneapolis: University of Minnesota Press, 2006); René Girard, *Violence and the Sacred* (Baltimore: Johns Hopkins University Press, 1977), *The Scapegoat* (Baltimore: Johns Hopkins University Press, 1986) and *Things Hidden Since the Foundation of the World* (Stanford: Stanford University Press, 1987); Chris Hedges, *War is a Force that Gives Us Meaning* (New York: Anchor Books, 2003); Julia Kristeva, *Powers of Horror: An Essay on Abjection* (New York: Columbia University Press, 1982); Philippe Lacoue-Labarthe, *Typography* (Stanford: Stanford University Press, 1998); Bruce Lincoln, *Death, War, and Sacrifice: Studies in Ideology and Practice* (Chicago: University of Chicago Press, 1991); Bruce Lincoln, *Holy Terrors: Thinking about Religion after September 11* (Chicago: University of Chicago Press, 2003); Jean-Luc Nancy, *The Inoperative Community* (Minneapolis: University of Minnesota Press, 1991); Andrew Norris (ed), *Politics, Metaphysics and Death* (Durham: Duke University Press, 2005); and Ivan Strenski, *Contesting Sacrifice: Religion, Nationalism, and Social Thought in France* (Chicago: University of Chicago Press, 2002).

5 See Terence McKenna, *Violence and Difference: Girard, Derrida, and Deconstruction* (Urbana: University of Chicago Press, 1992), p. 5.

6 Jean Bethke Elshtain, *Women and War* (New York: Basic Books, 1987), p. 10.

7 As in Winston Churchill's famous appearance on the balcony of Buckingham Palace with the British royal family on VE Day in 1945.

8 See Peter Gourevitch, "The Second Image Reversed," *International Organization*, Vol. 32, No. 4. (1978), pp. 881–912.

9 See the excellent collection of essays by Hent de Vries and Samuel Weber, *Violence, Identity and Self-Determination* (Stanford, CA: Stanford University Press, 1997).

10 The pivotal treatment of this theme is G. W. F. Hegel's *Philosophy of Right* (Amherst: Prometheus Books, 1991), (§321–40).

For a superb commentary on these passages, see Michael Shapiro, *Violent Cartographies: Mapping Cultures of War* (Minneapolis: University of Minnesota Press, 1997), Chapter 2. On this topic, see also R. B. J. Walker, *Inside/Outside: International Relations as Political Theory* (Cambridge: Cambridge University Press, 1990); James Der Derian, *On Diplomacy: A Genealogy of Western Estrangement* (London: Blackwell, 1991); David Campbell, *Writing Security: United States Foreign Policy and the Politics of Identity* (Minneapolis: University of Minnesota Press, 1993), especially Chapter 3; David Campbell and Michael Dillon, *The Political Subject of Violence* (New York: St. Martin's Press, 1993). For an illuminating exchange, compare Azar Gat, *War in Human Civilization* (Oxford: Oxford University Press, 2006) and Gopal Balakrishnan, "The Role of Force in History," *New Left Review* (Sept.–Oct. 2007), pp. 23–56.

11 See Jacques Derrida, *Politics of Friendship* (London: Verso, 2005); and R. Brian Ferguson, *The State, Identity, and Violence* (London: Routledge, 2002).

12 See Wendy Brown's brilliant genealogy of the resulting paradox of the prerogative of masculinist states in *Manhood and Politics* (Boston: Rowman and Littlefield, 1988), Chapter 7. See also Wendy Brown, *States of Injury* (Princeton: Princeton University Press,

1995), pp. 186–96; and Cynthia Enloe, *Globalization and Militarism: Feminists Make the Link* (Lanham: Rowman and Littlefield, 2007).
13 See Patrick J. Geary, *The Myth of Nations: The Medieval Origins of Europe* (Princeton: Princeton University Press, 2002); and Michael Kulikowski, *Rome's Gothic Wars* (Cambridge: Cambridge University Press, 2007).
14 Andrew Gilett, "Ethnogenesis: A Contested Model of Early Modern Europe" *History Compass* Vol. 4, No. 2 (2006), p. 245.
15 Jan Bremmer, "The Scapegoat between Northern Syria, Hittites, Greeks, Israelites and Christians" (Unpublished manuscript, 2007). See also Gunnar Heinsohn, "The Rise of Blood Sacrifice and Priest-Kingship in Mesopotamia," *Religion* Vol. 22 (1992), pp. 109–34.
16 See Gilett, "Ethnogenesis," p. 246; Jan Bremmer, "Scapegoat Rituals in Ancient Greece," in ed. Richard Buxton, *Oxford Readings in Greek Religion* (Oxford: Oxford University Press, 2000), pp. 271–93; Walter Burkert, *Structure and History in Greek Mythology and Ritual* (Berkeley: University of California, 1979), pp. 59–77; Robert G. Hamerton-Kelly, *Violent Origins: Ritual Killing and Cultural Formation* (Stanford: Stanford University Press, 1987); Georges Dumézil, *Mitra-Varuna: An Essay on Two Indo-European Representations* (New York: Zone, 1988); Lincoln, *Death, War, and Sacrifice*; Pierre Bonnechère, *Le sacrifice humain en Grèce ancienne* (Athens: Kernos, 1994); James M. Deem, *Bodies from the Bog* (Boston: Houghton Mifflin, 1998); and Eammon P. Kelly, *Kingship and Sacrifice: Iron Age Bog Bodies and Boundaries* (Bray, Ireland: Archeology Ireland, 2006).
17 See Jean-Pierre Vernant and Pierre Vidal-Naquet, *Myth and Tragedy in Ancient Greece* (New York: Zone, 1988); Sara Forsdyke, *Exile, Ostracism, and Democracy: The Politics of Expulsion in Ancient Greece* (Princeton: Princeton University Press, 2005); Robert Parker, *Miasma* (Oxford: Oxford University Press, 2008), pp. 257–80.
18 See Bremmer, "The Scapegoat between," p. 21.
19 Victor Davis Hanson, *The Western Way of War: Infantry Battle in Classical Greece* (New York: Knopf, 1989). See also Hanson, *Carnage and Culture: Landmark Battles in the Rise of Western Power* (New York: Doubleday, 2001). For critical perspectives on Hanson's thesis, see John Lynn, *Battle: A History of Combat and Culture* (New York: Basic Books, 2004); and Hans van Wees, *Greek Warfare: Myths and Realities* (London: Duckworth, 2004).
20 Here, too, we can see early precursors of later Western notions of civilian or noncombatant immunity, just war, and *ius in bello*. These paradoxical, double-edged pharmacotic effects of such notions were again illustrated recently in the post-9/11 pro-war rhetoric of groups ranging from advocates of Samuel Huntington's theo-civilizational warfare to proponents of a secular or holy war against "Islamofascism" to "Christian Realists" and "liberal hawks."
21 See, for example, the biblical story of Jephthah; the child sacrifices at Crete in the myth of Theseus; the sacrifices of the Theban girls and the daughters of Orion during the Orchomenos war; the sacrifice of the daughters of Erechtheus in response to the threat of Eumolpos to Athens; and the self-sacrifice of other martyred Athenians, including Agraulos, the daughters of Leos, the king Kodros, and Menoecus listed by Bremmer in "The Scapegoat between," p. 6. This theme clearly preoccupied Euripides, who linked it allegorically to the terrifying implications of Athens' looming defeat in the Peloponnesian War.
22 The following discussion draws on Bremmer, "Scapegoat rituals"; Bonnechère, *Le sacrifice humain en Grèce ancienne*. Other structurally isomorphic and politically analogous practices occurring in ancient South Asia, China, Mexico, and the Andes provide substantiating and confirming examples of the phenomenon's ubiquity, but lie beyond the scope of this chapter. These and related issues will be taken up in Larry N. George, *Pharmacotic War: Sacrificial Violence and the Future of American Power* (in progress).
23 See Michel Foucault, *Discipline & Punish: The Birth of the Prison* (New York: Vintage, 1979); *The History of Sexuality, Volume I: An Introduction* (New York: Vintage, 1980); and *"Society Must Be Defended"* (New York: Picador, 2003). The concept of pharmacotic war also addresses the important theoretical tension between Foucault and Gilles Deleuze and Felix Guattari over the relation between war and politics. On this topic, see Julian

Reid, "Deleuze's War Machine: Nomadism Against the State," *Millennium* Vol. 32, No. 1 (2003), pp. 57–85.
24 See William Connolly, *Neuropolitics: Thinking, Culture, Speed* (Minneapolis: University of Minnesota Press, 2002); Andrew Schmookler, *Out of Weakness: Healing the Wounds that Drive us to War* (New York: Bantam, 1988); Lawrence LeShan, *The Psychology of War* (New York: Helios, 2002); and Jerry S. Piven *et al.*, *Terror and Apocalypse: Psychological Undercurrents of History, Volume II* (Lincoln: Writer's Showcase, 2002).
25 See Ehrenreich, *Blood Rites*; Hent de Vries, *Religion and Violence: Philosophical Perspectives from Kant to Derrida* (Baltimore: Johns Hopkins University Press, 2002); Mark Pizzato, *Theatres of Human Sacrifice: From Ancient Ritual to Screen Violence* (Albany: SUNY Press, 2005); Michael Welch, *Scapegoats of September 11th* (New Brunswick: Rutgers University Press, 2006); and Bruce Lincoln, *Religion, Empire & Torture: The Case of Achaemenian Persia, with a Postscript on Abu Ghraib* (Chicago: University of Chicago Press, 2007).
26 See Susan Faludi's scathing account of the comprehensive silencing after 9/11 of the voices of women who failed to conform to the sudden need for a renewed American *mythos* of heroic male rescuers and helpless women victims in her *The Terror Dream: Fear and Fantasy in Post-9/11 America* (New York: Holt, 2007).
27 On this topic, see Barbara Jeanne Fields, "Slavery, Race, and Ideology in the United States of America," *New Left Review* No. 181 (1990), pp. 95–118; W. E. B. Du Bois, *Dusk of Dawn: An Essay toward an Autobiography of a Race Concept* (New Brunswick: Transaction, 1995); Anatol Lieven, *America Right or Wrong: An Anatomy of American Nationalism* (Oxford: Oxford University Press, 2004); Joel Olson, *The Abolition of White Democracy* (Minneapolis: University of Minnesota Press, 2004); Chris Hedges, *American Fascists: The Christian Right and the War on America* (New York: Free Press, 2006); Kevin Phillips, *American Theocracy: The Peril and Politics of Radical Religion, Oil, and Borrowed Money in the 21st Century* (New York: Viking, 2006); and Thomas Schaller, *Whistling Past Dixie: How Democrats Can Win without the South* (New York: Simon and Schuster, 2006).
28 Patriotic American historians often have been quite unapologetic about this history. See, for example, Richard Maxwell Brown, *No Duty to Retreat: Violence and Values in American History and Society* (Oxford: Oxford University Press, 1991); Victor Davis Hanson, *Carnage and Culture* and *Ripples of Battle: How Wars of the Past Still Determine How We Fight, How We Live, and How We Think* (New York: Doubleday, 2003); James Webb, *Born Fighting: How the Scots-Irish Shaped America* (New York: Broadway, 2005); and Robert Kagan, *Dangerous Nation: American Foreign Policy from Its Earliest Days to the Dawn of the Twentieth Century* (New York: Vintage, 2006).
29 The most impressive history of this mythopoeisis is still Richard Slotkin's trilogy: *Regeneration through Violence: The Mythology of the American Frontier, 1600–1860* (Middletown: Wesleyan University Press, 1973); *The Fatal Environment: The Myth of the Frontier in the Age of Industrialization, 1800–1890* (New York: Harper Collins, 1985); and *Gunfighter Nation: The Myth of the Frontier in Twentieth-Century America* (New York: Harper, 1993). See also Campbell, *Writing Security*; Michael Bellesiles, *Lethal Imagination: Violence and Brutality in American History* (New York: NYU Press, 1999); and Christopher Waldrep and Michael Bellesiles, *Documenting American Violence: A Sourcebook* (Oxford: Oxford University Press, 2006).
30 Anthony David Smith, *The Ethnic Origins of Nations* (Oxford: Blackwell, 1986), p. 150.
31 Ibid., p. 150.
32 Ibid.
33 On southern white ontopolitical culture and the violence associated with it, see Fox Butterfield, *All God's Children: The Bosket Family and the American Tradition of Violence* (New York: Harper, 2002); Elliot Jaspin, *Buried in the Bitter Waters: The Hidden History of Racial Cleansing in America* (New York: Basic Books, 2006); Jonathan Markovitz, *Legacies of Lynching: Racial Violence and Memory* (Minneapolis: University of Minnesota Press, 2006); John Moore, *Carnival of Blood: Dueling, Lynching, and Murder in South Carolina, 1880–1920* (Colombia: University of South Carolina Press, 2006); and Webb, *Born Fighting*.
34 Phillips, *American Theocracy*, p. 133.

35 See Thomas Frank, *What's the Matter with Kansas? How Conservatives Won the Heart of America* (New York: Owl Books, 2005).
36 A burgeoning literature interprets the Civil War as an ontopolitically sacralizing and sacrificial conflict (I am grateful to the historian Kerry Candaele for introducing me to this literature). See, in particular, Mark E. Neely, *The Civil War and the Limits of Destruction* (Cambridge: Harvard University Press, 2007); Drew Faust, *This Republic of Suffering: Death and the American Civil War* (New York: Knopf, 2008); Adam Gopnik, "In the Mourning Store: Burying the Civil War Dead," *The New Yorker*, January 21, 2008, pp. 77–81; and Mark Schantz, *Awaiting the Heavenly Country: The Civil War and America's Culture of Death* (Ithaca: Cornell University Press, 2008).
37 As President George H. W. Bush himself put it. See "Fighting in Panama: The President; Excerpts from Bush's News Conference on Central America," *New York Times*, December 22, 1989, p. A16.
38 A good illustration of this is Jerry Falwell's pro-Iraq War sermon of January 31, 2004, which, predictably, nowhere quotes Jesus himself. Instead, it references "the full revelation concerning Jesus pictured in the book of Revelation 19, where He is depicted bearing a 'sharp sword' and smiting nations, ruling them with 'a rod of iron'." See Jerry Falwell, "God is Pro-War," available at www.worldnetdaily.com/news/article.asp?Article_ID=36859.
39 An illustration of how thin the blue line between mainstream American conservatism and open fascism is today can be gathered from the widespread citing (including on the floor of Congress) of a pseudo-quote, concocted by conservative writer J. Michael Waller, and falsely attributed to Lincoln, calling for the punishment as traitors of anti-war elected representatives. The fabricated quote is: "Congressmen who willfully take action during wartime that damage [sic] morale and undermine the military are saboteurs, and should be arrested, exiled or hanged." See Mary Ann Ankers, "Honest, It Wasn't Abe's Comment," *The Washington Post*, February 16, 2007, p. A21.

3 Power, violence, and torture
Making sense of insurgency and legitimacy crises in past and present wars of attrition

Alexander D. Barder

> All right, [General Jacques] Massu won the battle of Algiers; but that meant losing the war.
>
> Paul-Henri Teitgen[1]

> The terrorists are as brutal an enemy as we've ever faced. They're unconstrained by any notion of our common humanity, or by the rules of warfare.
>
> George W. Bush[2]

Introduction

In the aftermath of the 9/11 attacks, there emerged two distinct responses that would shape American geopolitical actions throughout the world. The first was essentially to declare the United States at war. The full power of the American state was geared towards a "Global War on Terror" (GWOT) against states, organizations or individuals that were deemed a threat to American security. This was conceived as no ordinary war: traditional threat perceptions had metamorphosed (from an emphasis on other concrete geopolitical centers of power) and multiplied to an extent that even internal political and societal characteristics had to fall under the American purview. The day after the attacks, President George W. Bush declared that "[t]his will be a monumental struggle of good versus evil" against an enemy that "hides in shadows, and has no regard for human life." Consequently, the "United States of America will use all [its] resources to conquer this enemy."[3] Bush later added that this coming war "will not be short" for the reason that it "is a conflict without battlefields or beachheads, a conflict with opponents who believe they are invisible."[4] This unconventional war prized the ability to gather "actionable" intelligence to preempt terrorists from carrying out their attacks. Especially in the months following 9/11 when there continued to be a widespread perception that another attack was imminent, the need for intelligence became paramount. In this context, the traditional procedures and rules governing the acquisition of such information were redefined by the Bush administration to include the possibility of "coercive" interrogations or even techniques amounting to torture against individuals in American custody. The Geneva Conventions governing the laws of warfare were said to be "quaint" in this new setting.[5] The infamous, and later retracted, Bybee ("torture") memo of August 1, 2002 attempted to characterize torture as only occurring in extreme cases that "would ordinarily be associated with a sufficiently serious physical condition or injury such as death, organ failure, or serious impairment of bodily functions."[6] Over the last few years, the press has become more vigilant in documenting what "coercion" means for those detainees in US custody and how instrumental the Bush administration has been in attempting to legitimize and institutionalize these forms of interrogations.[7] From the establishment of "black" CIA sites and so-called "extraordinary renditions" to the use of interrogation techniques such as waterboarding or total sensory deprivation over long periods of time, the Bush administration has essentially accepted that these techniques must become part of the overall war on terror.[8]

The second important change in American geopolitical thinking that took place in the aftermath of 9/11 was the emphasis on democracy promotion as a means of attaining global stability and peace. This idea became much more pronounced after the campaign in Afghanistan and the lead-up to the war in Iraq in March 2003. By the second inaugural presidential address, in early 2005, it had become a matter of policy "to seek and support the growth of democratic movements and institutions in every nation and culture, with the ultimate goal of ending tyranny in our world."[9] American military power, it was argued by many within the Washington beltway, should be put to use in certain cases by removing tyrannical regimes such as Iraq, Syria, and Iran. In November 2003, Bush himself argued that "[t]he establishment of a free Iraq at the heart of the Middle East will be a watershed event in the global democratic *revolution*."[10] Indeed, this "revolutionary" idea of transforming the Middle East, beginning with the ouster of Saddam Hussein, was a long held desire on the part of the neo-conservative clique present throughout the Bush administration and among those in the public sphere. In the same speech at the National Endowment for Democracy, Bush added: "[t]he United States has adopted a new policy, a forward strategy of freedom in the Middle East. In every region of the world, the advance of freedom leads to peace."[11] This articulation of a global policy for the advancement of freedom was meant to be a way for the United States ultimately to legitimize its actions in the global war on terror. It was designed to show that, while some of the means employed in this war might be considered unpleasant, there is still a silver lining to it all, one that would reveal itself in the end. This was essentially a policy of hope. "Freedom is the permanent hope of mankind," Bush declared.[12] And the war to topple the Ba'athist regime in Iraq would be the example *par excellence* of the transformative power of freedom.

Yet, in the five years since the American invasion and occupation of Iraq, this project of ushering a democratic revolution in the heart of the Middle East has been met with a growing anti-American insurgency, Sunni/Shia sectarianism or civil war, and widespread anger throughout the region towards American intentions. The inability to provide basic security, economic reconstruction and civil society revitalization along with a political process that major participants would consider legitimate has contributed to a growing sense that American options for success in Iraq are running out. The latest gamble of "surging" the number of US troops in Baghdad and the Anbar province, while yielding some tangible results in the fight against Al-Qaeda in Iraq, has highlighted the general political impotence of the Iraqi government encamped in the "Green Zone" and demonstrated the remarkable lack of political authority and legitimacy of the American mission among Iraqis. Rather than helping towards a resolution to the persistent violence between sectarian groups, the latest attempt at a military buildup appears to be a way of forcing a necessary political solution (i.e., reconciliation between sectarian groups) through military means. Nonetheless, with American public support of the war reaching record lows, and with an ever louder accompanying call for withdrawing American soldiers, the White House has found itself in a predicament that has afflicted many states in similar situations before: the diminishing returns of military violence and *zugzwang* decision-making. While the apparent ease of the initial invasion of March and April 2003 seemed to have shown the world the immensity and irresistible nature of American hard or hyper "power," the inability to secure the subsequent peace highlights the limitations of what this military prowess can effectively accomplish once on the ground.

The contemporary situation in Iraq has become a glaring example of a major military power that finds itself in a quandary of diminishing military returns. Historically, the fight against an insurgent enemy that has the backing of a large section of the population has often been considered one of the most difficult types of military operations. From the Spanish rebellion against Napoleon in the early nineteenth century through the armed struggles for independence by colonial subjects that later applied the lessons of Lenin and, especially, Mao, great powers have had enormous difficulties in combating, let alone winning, conflicts against the irregular/partisan combatant who hides among the local population. When it comes to struggles for self-determination, the use of raw military power becomes, as time goes forward, ever more contradictory, particularly when deployed by a liberal-democratic state whose *raison d'être* remains the maintenance of order based on the rule of law. The case of the Algerian war for independence against France from 1954 to 1962, which has received a great deal of attention recently for its perceived parallels with the current conflict in Iraq, is revealing precisely on this point. At the acme of French military supremacy against the insurgent forces coming after the victories in the battle of Algiers and the major countrywide offensive under General Maurice Challe in 1959, a stark realization emerged within the French political establishment in Paris (later reflected in the return of de Gaulle to power) that *une Algérie Française* could no longer be maintained without destroying the republic. Such military victories could not compensate for the lack of legitimacy in the eyes of the local population, and subsequently among the French public, a problem that had plagued the entire endeavor from the start. Even with the various plans put forward for political, legal and civil rights, the French were never able to reassert an ideal of legitimate rule for a majority of the Muslim population.[13] At the same time, the progressive institutionalization of torture within the French military ultimately destroyed the credibility of the armed forces and that of the state for the French public. When it became apparent that the same reviled Nazi interrogation techniques were being used by the French military (tortures that many French men and women still alive at the time suffered during World War II), the nascent anti-war movement gained more credibility and started to demonstrate against the war. At the same time, the adoption of torture started to destroy the discipline of the army and its historically problematic relationship to the state. How these realizations came about in the case of the Algerian war will be explored in the first part of this chapter.

Returning to the present situation, if the defining military and political struggles of the twenty-first century lie in an asymmetric global war on terror against shadowy terrorists on the one hand, and localized insurgents in such places as Iraq and Afghanistan on the other, then we start to get a sense of the immense problems involved in trying to win such a war strictly through military means. But the very language of total war often used today in describing this conceived conflict with a violent *activity*, as opposed to one with ideology, continues to misrepresent the nature of the war. There appears to be no end to this war, or at least, no well-conceived way to measure the progress of it (or lack thereof) and determine what subsequent changes of policy should occur. Furthermore, the creation of the total or absolute enemy—one who lacks not only the legality, but even the legitimacy, to take up arms, the so-called "unlawful combatant" who stands beyond the law and whose emergence is, in reality, a matter of *decisionistic* will by the President of the United States (the criminal bandit that must be expunged in the Schmittian sense)—takes over and warps the normative fabric that underlies the conventional laws of war and, as we will see, the normative project of democracy promotion itself. The current controversies that surround the allegations of torture displace the grounding of legitimacy by subverting it. This is one of the key lessons that Alistair Horne's work on the Algerian war (discussed below) elucidates.

Previous cases of post-colonial conflicts resulting in long-standing military occupations demonstrated the intrinsic limits of a narrow operative concept of power—often understood in terms of the applicability of violence in order to function as coercion—in securing legitimacy, authority, and rule. Hannah Arendt's writing on the notions of power and violence captures this fundamental dichotomy and its implications for the concept of legitimacy. While violence remains wedded to a means/ends rationality, power, according to Arendt, is an intrinsically intersubjective ability to act in common within the public realm, one that gives rise to legitimacy and political authority. Arendt's political theory, and her distinctive approach to the question of power and violence, will be tackled in the second part of this chapter in order to understand the dilemmas that occupying powers face in situations of counter-insurgency turning into wars of attrition. Still, Arendt's overall theoretical objective remains tied to a particular conceptualization of the public sphere and to the idea of a politically engaged citizenry that can act and freely participate in civic matters. To push forward Arendt's analysis, this chapter questions whether her definitions and analysis, while largely correct in the case of Algeria, can remain applicable today. By bringing in Sheldon S. Wolin's recent work on the emergence and meaning of "post-modern democracy," the intent is to show how the traditionally conceived symbiosis between the concept of legitimacy and the idea of power developed by Arendt has become decoupled. In other words, the continuous expansion of "lighter" de-centralized bureaucratic and administrative controls over the population, the connections between state and corporate interests to the detriment of the public good, and the transformation of the role of the citizen into a marginalized voter, or what Wolin calls an "imperial citizen," become salient features of a new political totality that, with Wolin, we can label "Superpower." This totality essentially creates widening gaps between the public sphere, the citizen, and political-economic power, gaps that enable the perpetuation of endless, and in a sense completely internalized, wars.

Lessons from the Algerian war: torture and the collapse of the French political legitimacy

With the Iraq war not going according to plan, comparisons with previous conflicts involving a local insurgency have been developed in order to determine the particular parameters for successful counter-insurgency strategies. Because of this, the Algerian war for independence in the late 1950s has received a great deal of attention among members of the press, pundits, and think-tank analysts. A study of the Algerian war of independence has also become a matter of great importance to American military officers keen on understanding the contexts and pitfalls of French counter-insurgency operations in urban settings. Scott McConnell in *The American Conservative* writes that even "some Pentagon special operations officers attended a screening of Gillo Pontecorvo's classic 1966 docudrama, 'The Battle of Algiers'."[14] The classical historical narrative (in English) of the French war in Algeria remains Horne's *A Savage War of Peace*, which was recently reissued by *The New York Review of Books*. It has even been said that Horne's chronicle found its way to President Bush's reading list thanks to none other than Henry Kissinger who recommended the book to the President.[15]

In the preface to this recently reissued work, Horne identifies three major lessons that policy-makers should learn from the Algerian episode: the way in which Algerian insurgents, knowing that they could not defeat the French military head-on, concentrated on sowing destruction upon the weaker police units, thus greatly damaging morale and forcing the French army to defend these units; the use by insurgents of neighboring Morocco and Tunisia as sanctuaries where they could regroup, arm and train for the interior struggle (sanctuaries that the French were unable to effectively attack because of international political implications, a situation that today may be repeating itself in the case of Iraq with Syria and Iran); and, most importantly, the use of torture as an interrogative method that the French had condemned in the first place because they themselves had been the victims of such vile acts in their own resistant struggle against the German occupation during World War II. To this day, there are many works published in France that deal with specific aspects of the role of the French military at the time of the Algerian insurrection and with its ethical/political implications.

The particular political context the French found themselves in at the start of the Algerian rebellion remains pertinent to a discussion of the eventual change in tactics employed by the French military. With the humiliating defeat of the French army at Dien Bien Phu in 1954 fresh in the minds of officers serving in Algeria, the Algerian rebellion was very much a challenge to the honor of, not so much France herself, but the very institution of the army as a fighting force. The subsequent debacle of the Suez operation in 1956 also weighed heavily on the minds of the officer corps and contributed even more to the officers' image of the French political class as fundamentally pusillanimous in the face of a direct challenge. Nonetheless, the lessons of Indochina were not lost on these officers. Mao became a necessary reading for the officers' class, and the lessons of partisan warfare were eventually to be applied in earnest in Algeria. The French officers' use of partisan tactics, Horne argues, required not only winning skirmishes, but also, and more importantly, the need to "crush and eradicate the whole of the clandestine political organization behind them."[16] This led, according to Horne, to turning the officers into "highly political animals," something that would have grave repercussions as the war progressed. The brutality of the initial engagements, the attacks by the FLN (Algerian National Liberation Front, or *Front de Libération Nationale*) on civilian targets, and the inability directly to confront the enemy in battle (because of the insurrectionary nature of the conflict), forced a crueler manner of fighting on the part of the French military and police. Summary executions, torture, mass detentions, collective forms of punishments were all used to try to pacify the countryside with initially mixed results. Essentially, French officers were not only attempting to maintain order in Algeria, but also felt that they had to prop up a domestic political will in the context of the degenerating French Fourth Republic, a political system that often led to decisional paralysis. This highly charged political environment, involving a national insurgent force fighting against a nation-state's military, is cogently captured by Colonel Thomas X. Hammes' recent study of what he terms "fourth-generation warfare." For Hammes, the insurgent "[does] not attempt to win by defeating the enemy's military forces. Instead, ... it directly attacks the minds of enemy decision makers to destroy the enemy's political will."[17]

It is the battle of Algiers, which began on September 30, 1956, that fundamentally marked a change in fortunes for both sides in the war. Immortalized in the classic film *La Battaglia di Algeri* (The Battle of Algiers) by Gillo Pontecorvo, the battle of Algiers brought to the fore the reality of urban terrorism and its violent responses. The FLN's militant network in Algiers, residing primarily in the dense Arab populated Casbah, orchestrated a series of attacks on European cafés, which included the assassination of the mayor of Algiers. Using elegant women as bombers, the FLN network, under Yacef and his henchman Ali la Pointe, was able to extract a harsh overreaction on the part of the French authorities. At the same time, the FLN called for a general strike to call international attention to the plight of the Algerian population, particularly at the United Nations. The French commander in charge of Algiers, General Jacques Massu, was under considerable pressure from Paris and the civilian authorities to launch an almost limitless attack on the terrorist network in an effort to restore order. The widespread use of torture—electric shocks known as *la gégène*, beatings, having one's stomach filled with water, the use of simulated drowning (what today might be called waterboarding), along with a full range of other psychological and degrading treatments—were institutionalized in the French military at the time of the battle of Algiers. Torture, however, produced results. Slowly, the French paratroopers uncovered Yacef's network, until the final confrontation in the Casbah in which Ali la Pointe was killed and Yacef captured. All of this decimated the FLN as a fighting force in the city of Algiers, at least for a few years.

The recently published memoir by General Paul Aussaresses, who participated in the battle of Algiers as an intelligence officer, openly recognizes the use of torture by the French troops: "The methods I used were always the same: beatings, electric shocks, and, in particular, water torture, which was the most dangerous technique for the prisoner."[18] Aussaresses describes in detail the "understanding" that emerged within the French military (from the top officers) for the need to employ counter-insurgency strategies that allowed brutal and degrading physical/psychological treatment and even summary executions. Aussaresses writes that "[r]egarding the use of torture, it was tolerated if not actually recommended. François Mitterrand, as minister of justice, had a de facto representative with General Massu in Judge Jean Bréard, who covered our actions during the night."[19] More importantly, what Aussaresses also argues is that the sheer volume of individuals caught up in the dragnet of counter-insurgent operations precluded the normal functioning of the judicial system based on the rule of law, the very foundation of any liberal-democratic order. As Aussaresses puts it:

> Only rarely were the prisoners we had questioned during the night still alive the next morning. Whether they had talked or not they generally had been neutralized. It was impossible to send them back to the court system, there were too many of them and the machine of justice would have become clogged with cases and stopped working altogether.[20]

This idea of a "clogged" judicial system likewise remains a problem today for the American forces in Iraq where the number of detainees in US custody continues to rise, especially now that a military "surge" has been ordered.[21] The question of how individuals in Iraq are, or should be, treated within the current detainee system and its corresponding effects on the American efforts to stabilize the country have been considerably overlooked in the overall debate on an Iraq strategy. While the US military has sought to find ways to transfer a majority of these detainees into Iraqi custody, a continuing fear among American officers is that the dysfunctional Iraqi judicial system across sectarian lines would either result in situations of torture or of "neutralization" of individuals similar to what happened in Algeria, or in the release of individuals who could continue to pose a "terrorist" threat. Aussaresses declares that this was a major concern among the French forces, and it led them not to follow proper judicial procedures. Again, Aussaresses recalls:

> Many terrorists would have been freed and given the oppurtunity of launching other attacks. Even if the law had been enforced in all its harshness, few persons would have been executed. The judicial system was not suited for such drastic conditions ... *Summary executions were therefore an inseperable part of the tasks associated with keeping law and order.*[22]

While Aussaresses' memoir makes it clear that torture and summary executions played a crucial role as a means of imposing law and order, the prevalent use of torture greatly troubled the conscience of many civil servants in the French political and civil establishment. Horne recounts one of the most noteworthy objections to the use of torture by the Secretary-General of the *Préfecture* (the capital city of the region), Paul-Henri Teitgen. Asked to put a prisoner to torture because of information that he might possess about bomb locations, Teitgen refused. Himself a victim of torture at the hands of the Nazis when he was deported to Dachau during World War II, Teitgen memorably wrote:

> But I refused to have him tortured. I trembled the whole afternoon. Finally the bomb did not go off. Thank God I was right. Because if you once get into the torture business, you're lost ... Understand this, fear was the basis of it all. All our so-called civilization is covered with a varnish. Scratch it, and underneath it you find *fear*. The French, even the Germans, are not torturers by nature. But

when you see the throats of your *copains* [buddies] slit, then the varnish disappears.[23]

As Horne argues, Teitgen recognized the inherent corruptibility that torture brought to any operation and operator. Even those who have themselves administered torture have come away from it with different forms of psychological damage. Aussaresses admits that "[w]e did everything we possibly could to avoid having the youngest soldiers bloody their hands and many would have been unable to see it through anyway."[24] Horne revealingly recounts the results of a poll among French soldiers who were asked what their worst experience in Algeria was: 132 of them said that it was either participating in or witnessing acts of torture, whereas 126 referred to the hardship of the campaign, and only 6 mentioned the wounds they had suffered as a result of the war.[25]

It is, however, in the long-term effects on the political and social domains that the pathologies of the use of torture were most clearly evident. Torture, in this case at least, when used to extract information, represents a type of violence that is fundamentally rooted in expediency and asserts its justification precisely as a forceful method that lies beyond the existing legal framework (at least, in liberal-democratic systems). Torture has to be beyond the law because its institutionalization is understood to inherently corrupt and distort the essence of the normative democratic framework, particularly through the applicability of due process. It then comes as somewhat of a surprise to read that a distinguished civil-libertarian professor of law like Alan Dershowitz would advocate the institutionalization of torture within American jurisprudence today. For Dershowitz, the inevitability of torturing individuals for information during a "ticking time-bomb" situation necessitates torture's codification and inclusion into the law:

> I have no doubt that if an actual ticking bomb situation were to arise, our law enforcement authorities would torture. The real debate is whether such torture should take place outside of our legal system or within it. The answer to this seems clear: If we are to have torture, it should be authorized by the law.[26]

However, Dershowitz, in this same piece, readily admits that excess is bound to occur: "We know from experience that law enforcement personnel who are given limited authority to torture will expand its use."[27] And yet he argues that vesting the judiciary with "torture warrants" would allow for the "accountability and transparency" that "requires compliance with the rule of law."[28] Dershowitz's argument and that of those who propose the institutionalization of torture, even in extreme or rare situations, operates on the fictional basis that, as David Luban notes, the torturer as a "conscientious interrogator overlooks a division of moral labor in which the person with the fastidious conscience and the person doing the interrogation are not the same."[29] The emergence of what Luban calls a "torture culture" through a series of ambiguous perceptions concerning the legal status of detainees is a slippery slope. As a result, torture's violence begins to dominate the entire spectrum of a political bureaucracy. For Luban, the abuses at Abu Ghraib could not be limited to "a few bad apples." Rather, Abu Ghraib is the direct manifestation of a "torture culture" that places the domination of one individual over another as essential to the production of information in the political system in general. The relationship between torturer and tortured is in "a microcosm, raised to the highest level of intensity, of the tyrannical political relationships that liberalism hates the most."[30] Inimical to the fundamental tenets of political liberalism, torture corrupts the totality of the juridical process.

This is exactly what contributed to a growing lawlessness throughout the ranks of the army and the civilian government that quickly began to characterize the Algerian conflict. Horne continues his analysis by quoting Teitgen's description of the implication of allowing torture to become institutionalized:

> Even a legitimate action ... can nevertheless lead to improvisations and excesses. Very rapidly, if this is not remedied, efficacy becomes the sole justification. In default of a legal basis, it seeks to justify itself at any price, and, with a certain bad conscience, it demands the privilege of exceptional legitimacy. In the name of efficacy, illegality has become justified.[31]

While there emerged on the part of the French public a general awareness and condemnation of this resort to torture in the mid to late 1950s, and such a public outcry eventually was felt in the dwindling popular support for the war effort in the final years of the Fourth Republic, it was the glaring crisis between the idea of republican legality and the perception of legitimacy that marked the loss of the war for France. The mass anti-war rallies led by notable intellectuals such as Jean-Paul Sartre and Simone de Beauvoir gave momentum to the idea of questioning the basis of the republic. By early 1958, the Fourth Republic was in its death throes. The complete inability of the French political class to establish a consensus among various parties or factions and to form a stable government revolved around the Algerian question. At one point, France did not have a government in power for 37 days, from April 15, 1958 until the arrival of Charles de Gaulle at the behest of the military. This would open the door for the military to play a greater role in France's internal political affairs. The military, under General Raoul Salan, the French military commander in Algeria until he was replaced by de Gaulle in late 1959, categorically refused any attempt at finding a political solution to the conflict (i.e., a form of autonomy or self-determination for the Muslim population). Even the return of de Gaulle through a quasi-military coup in mid-1959 did not quell the growing political unrest that was plaguing the military. By 1960, the situation began to unravel with de Gaulle's realization that self-determination for the Muslim population of Algeria was a de facto necessity for the long-term well-being of France. However, a cadre of military officers led by four Generals revolted in 1961 in what became know as the Generals' putsch. Though easily put down, this attempted rebellion marked a growing internecine fighting inside France. The violence wrought by the emergence of the infamous OAS (*Organisation Armée Secrète*), headed by Salan, a radical terrorist organization that targeted Muslims and Frenchmen alike (particularly policemen and minor political officials; most notably they killed the mayor of Evian where negotiations were being held between the French government and the FLN), culminated in a wave of utterly senseless attacks that hastened the inevitable acceptance of a fully independent Algeria. This descent into a total violence against both the republican state and the external Algerian foe was championed by Salan, at the moment of his trial, who claimed that it was derived from a higher concept of legitimacy, one that, however, was not rooted in the laws of the republic. By what authority, he asked, did the French president de Gaulle possess the right to cede French territory? This, the German jurist and political theorist Carl Schmitt astutely notes, was his only retort against being forced into the position of absolute criminality within the framework of the laws of the republic.[32]

The Algerian conflict dramatically highlights two fundamental facets of politics that become clearer within the context of asymmetrical or post-colonial conflicts. On the one hand, the dominant power, France in this case, was able to prevail militarily throughout the conflict. It did so especially in the countryside by increasingly resembling the insurgent and adopting its tactics. In the case of the battle of Algiers, the legal order morphed into a series of institutionally justified criminal acts, tortures, summary executions, deportations, and so on (although it should be said that the French government's official position was that the Geneva Conventions did not apply to the Algerian conflict given that Algeria was considered a French territory and that the insurgents were said to be criminals rather than a recognized lawful party to the conflict and, as such, could only be subjected to French criminal law).[33] In essence the democratic rule of law was subverted for the sake of a political necessity that looked ever more dubious and unachievable in the eyes of the local population and the French public alike. This subversion of the law greatly affected the support and legitimacy of the French government at home, and it resulted in the eventual fall of the Fourth Republic. What, in effect, transpired over these years in France was a demonstration of the inherent inability of violence *tout court* to establish a principle of legitimacy for ruling, not only Algeria, but metropolitan France as well. The episode of the French military in Algeria (so well documented by Horne) illustrates the divergence between violence and power, which cannot simply be understood in terms of a command-obedience relationship, that is to say, a relationship that is rooted in a constant threat of violence. The prevalent use of torture, amplifying this direct relationship of violence between individuals, and an essential antithesis to liberalism, destroyed the moral and political legitimacy of the French state at home and abroad. This is why, at about the same time these violent events took place, and throughout the 1960s, the philosopher Hannah Arendt sought to draw our attention to the necessity of maintaining the distinction between violence and power, particularly if we cared to understand how political legitimacy was actualized and operated. For her, a conflation of the two notions (power and violence) was the mistake of political theorists whose thoughts had been marked by unremitting violence. For Arendt, the post-colonial conflicts of the 1950s and 1960s perfectly illuminated the inherent opposition between violence and power. They demonstrated why the privileging of violence in politics ultimately destroys the public domain that is the only place where politics as freedom can be made possible.

Making sense of power, violence and legitimacy, yesterday and today

In her essay *On Violence*, Arendt established a series of conceptual distinctions (between power, violence, strength, force, and authority) in order to avoid a confusion that, she believed, was common in political theory.[34] Power, for her, had to be considered as "the human ability not just to act but to act in concert. Power is never the property of an individual; it belongs to a group and remains in existence only so long as the group keeps together."[35] For her strength referred to a "singular" individual property that could be witnessed in relation to others, as in physical strength. Force, Arendt argued, could be understood as the "indirect energy released by physical or social movements."[36] More importantly, authority could be vested in the individual for the purpose of eliciting obedience without resort to persuasion or command. And authority was contingent upon respect. Violence, on the other hand, was a type of fabrication or poiesis, a way of "multiplying individual strength," and it was necessarily instrumental in nature.

What, then, is the relationship between violence and power that seems to be at the heart of past and contemporary debates about war, torture, and legitimacy? Does violence aid in the creation of power? Or does it destroy it? More importantly, what is the relationship between violence and the establishment of legitimacy? Arendt can help us to answer these questions. She writes:

> Power and violence are opposites; where the one rules absolutely, the other is absent. Violence appears where power is in jeopardy, but left to its own course its end is the disappearance of power. This implies that it is not correct to say that the opposite of violence is nonviolence: to speak of nonviolent power is actually redundant. Violence can destroy power; it is utterly incapable of creating it.[37]

For Arendt, colonial powers could never properly secure what they thought was their legitimate rule with more and more violent and repressive means. While violence can win battles and destroy the ability of any group to act in concert (as was the case in the battle of Algiers), the inability to firmly establish rule and order through the emergence of genuine authority is grounded in the steady deterioration of power— a power rooted in plurality, opinion and consent—that violence brings. Thus, the legitimacy required for the proper establishment of governance founders because violence, relying on "implements" rather than on common action, is fundamentally in need of justifications towards reaching a particular end (in the case of the Algerian conflict, security and hegemony for the French colonial authority). The further the end, however, the further removed the justification for violence (and its link to the political).[38] At the same time though, Arendt also understood the concept of legitimacy to be "based on an appeal to the past,"[39] a past that necessarily had to be revered as the foundation of the republic and its constitution.[40] In the case of colonial appropriation, there could be no past to appeal to because the historical legacy of colonialism was rooted in an original act of violent pilfering and occupation.

Arendt recognized the boomerang effect that violence creates with regards to power. The collapse of the French government in the mid-1950s and the ensuing military rebellions were directly related to an over-expansive use of violence. The legitimacy that a liberal-democratic political order requires through an appeal to the consent of the governed inevitably begins to be called into question when the liberal-democratic institutions have recourse to unrestrained forms of violence. The turn to violence, then, essentially closes off the public sphere as a place of debate and political engagement. This is why Arendt suggested that colonial powers were ultimately faced with the choice of either "decolonization or massacre."[41] The persistence of conflict often characteristic of asymmetrical wars, or the downward spiral of violence against not only the insurgents, but also internal enemies who are seen to compromise the war effort (as was claimed by Salan and the OAS in the Algerian case, or against the anti-war demonstrations in the United States after the war in Iraq began), results in a form of terror that ends up "destroying all power" and ultimately provokes the "paralysis of the whole country."[42]

Arendt's determination of the conceptual nuances between power, violence, and legitimacy was intimately tied to an idea of the public realm as that domain in charge of actualizing the possibility of genuine political action. Power and the public sphere were mutually co-constitutive; one could not survive without the other. But Arendt's own pessimism is evident in that the longevity of the public realm was in danger because of a modern process that she characterized as "world alienation" and that impacted liberal-democratic societies.[43] She could not believe that a global public place could emerge that would actualize new forms of power capable of restraining the instrumentalization of politics.

These concerns about the place of modern politics, the fate of the public realm, and the possibilities of an active citizenship are also present in Sheldon S. Wolin's reissued classic *Politics and Vision*. Wolin tackles what he terms a "formless form" as a new political structure that cannot be subsumed under any traditional categorization of government (i.e., democracy, tyranny, monarchy, and so on).[44] Economic rationality as efficiency is conceived to be vital, and far more crucial, than civic virtue, and it becomes a main asset for governance. Wolin uses the term "Superpower" to denote this emergence of a distinct political-economic identity that, historically, started to become internalized through the great struggles of World War II and the subsequent Cold War. But Superpower culminates in the aftermath of the 9/11 attacks, a time when, as Wolin writes, American and European political leaders "seemed to revert to the anti-communist categories of the past. The Cold War reflexes that shaped the American Superpower's transition from anti-communism to anti-terrorism helped blur the unique features of its new foe."[45] For Wolin, however, the emergence of Superpower is not to be ascribed only to a distinct and overawing modality of military rule or violence. Rather, Superpower represents the nexus between corporatist interests and the state. It refers to the "technologization" of politics and society, and to the transformation of popular culture into a referent for Superpower. Superpower is characterized by a rolling back of social welfare programs, especially for the very poor, and it is marked by a political and religious "fundamentalism" that seeks to create rigid boundaries around legitimate discourse inside the public sphere.[46] In the context of Superpower and of this central place given to a "political economic" conception of society, the role of democratic governance as the direct manifestation of a politicized citizenry gets to be progressively removed. Wolin argues:

> Superpower has no need for a conception of the citizen as he who takes part in politics ... *Superpower needs an imperial citizen*, one who accepts the necessarily remote relations between the concerns of the citizen and those of the power-holders, who welcome being relieved of participatory obligations, and who is fervently patriotic. Superpower's ideal citizen is apolitical but not alienated.[47]

Indeed, as Wolin remarks, it is noteworthy that Bush enjoined the American people to "unite, spend, and fly" right after he declared the beginning of an endless war against terror, but did not ask for the US citizenry to involve itself in the war effort in some precise political capacity.[48]

Wolin believes that the misconception among the anti-war constituency in the United States today is that the pathologies of American governance are rooted in a continued mode of deception by the power elites who desperately seek to justify war or wish to promote social inequalities. Rather, the "utter helplessness" of the imperial citizen, and its inability "to constitute itself as an effective public actor capable of countering the situation that unequal economic power has corrupted,"[49] is built into the fabric of Superpower, a modality of power/governance that further cements the position of the imperial citizen as an essentially atomized subject. The ongoing irony, as Wolin understands it, is that, while democracy is being acclaimed as the only remaining legitimate form of government, its operative capacity to generate a well-educated, well-informed, and active citizen has been persistently undermined because of the growing concern with the fact that "mass democracy" itself may become utterly ungovernable. The totalizing impulse of Superpower towards a perpetual economico-political expansion by way of co-optation, assimilation, and depoliticization of external or internal opponents is thus characterized as a form of "inverted totalitarianism." But Wolin's use of the term totalitarianism here is not meant to constitute a direct homology with past totalitarian systems, although they may share a few similar features. The key difference, for Wolin, is that Superpower does not (need to) possess the kind of "instruments of terror" relied upon by the Nazi or Stalinist systems.[50] Instead, Superpower's main feature consists in giving free rein to the forces of global capitalism at the same time that a type of cultural and social rule over a complicit but patriotic citizenry is established. Thus, the crucial feature of the body politic as a whole, and of the citizen in particular, inside Superpower is passivity. The occasional bouts of internal militancy, for civil rights or anti-war rallies, for example, are easily "appeased by minor concessions," which in fact result in the maintenance of the status quo.[51] Wolin concludes on an important point: "Political action, when it does not fail altogether, seems capable only of achieving expedients that fall woefully short of dealing with deeply embedded injustices."[52]

Wolin's analysis of Superpower and of today's imperial citizen is essentially a manifestation of Arendt's worst fear, namely, that modern liberal-democracy, along with the "rise of the social" (or the supremacy of private interests whereby power, as Arendt understands it, is made irrelevant), effectively abolish the public realm as a space for political action. Wolin shows us to what extent the contemporary public realm and its citizenry, as the traditional underpinnings of liberal-democracy, have been transformed and made to function for a totalizing type of governance based on fear, conformity, passivity, and, eventually, economic rationality. In this fashion, and in the context of the GWOT (starting with the war in Iraq), Superpower has been able to maintain a paradoxical situation: justifying and perpetuating an endless series of wars across the globe while, at the same time, sheltering a majority of the members of the imperial citizenry from the costs and images of those wars. What we are witnessing, then, is the emergence of a series of internal structural responses to a new form of global imperial rule that would appear to be inconsistent with the traditional notions of liberal-democratic governance, but that nonetheless has successfully adapted itself to this role. While Michael Hardt and Antonio Negri see the transformation of the concept of legitimacy into such an imperial set up as being rooted in a form of efficacy against "the threat of disorder" perpetuated by the "enemy,"[53] what is important to note is that this process of legitimation could never have become internalized and rendered operative without the transformation of the democratic citizen into an imperial citizen.

What this transformation has accomplished in the case of torture discussed above is not so much its use and acceptance (the acceptance in the popular imagination of absolute physical violence by one or many individuals against another individual being) as a necessary instrument of imperial rule, but, rather, a passive tolerance by the public (or what is left of it) of a series of more subtle practices of extraction of information deemed simply to be "coercive." What this argument suggests is the passage to a normalization of torture and thus to the ability of the state to safeguard a concept of legitimacy (torture and legitimacy are no longer antagonistic under Superpower). This process is further facilitated by the growing devolution of the war machine (in the employment of private contractors in many different capacities, the use of extraordinary renditions of individuals to third party countries such as Syria and Egypt, and so on) whereby practices of war and violence are distanced from the state and responsibilities become much more diffuse and murky.

Conclusion

What the French state and its military experienced in Algeria was a collective revolt against the idea that the way the war was being fought was legitimate. The past experience of France's occupation by Nazi Germany acted as a constant reminder of the kind of intolerable acts the military should not commit. The rebellion of the military was precisely rooted in this crisis of political legitimacy brought on by the widespread use of torture in Algeria. Arendt was correct in seeing the process of colonial independence as a case of fundamental tension between violence and power, a situation where, at its most extreme, the result is the total paralysis of the state (in the case of France, the fall of the Fourth Republic and the quasi-civil war that the Algerian conflict provoked). Today, the problem is different since the possibilities for spontaneous public action have become much more limited. The public sphere has become compromised by the triumph of the privatization/commercialization of the self in the form of an imperial citizen. Today's disengaged citizenry, the product of a governmentality defined by the necessities of political-economic rationalities, reflects a passive conformity that has morphed the concept of legitimacy into an acquiescence of imperial rule. The GWOT and the so-called democratic revolution post-9/11 are therefore both rooted in the same logic that manifests itself in a new perpetual war, a war in the shadows, and according to which (as Bush originally argued) there are no "beachheads" and opponents believe they are "invisible." The idea of Superpower shows us how the United States has been able to usurp the principle of democratic governance and has used it to mask its more nefarious practices without running the risk of delegitimizing itself in the eyes of its imperial citizens (who are far too preoccupied with their own private lives, apathetic, and passively accepting any new security requirement and freedom limitation in the name of the war on terror).

Superpower's force is its remarkable resilience and its ingenuity to adapt to all sorts of situations by always being able to tap into the comforting yet explosive potentials of economic profit. Of course, occasional disturbances do occur and try to call into question the direction of a policy or a war strategy, and they sometimes seek to shed light on vile practices such as "coercive" interrogations. But after some time, the status quo reasserts itself, and past abuses are quickly forgotten once the latest Homeland Security warning has been broadcast.

All of this does not mean, however, that the idea of American "legitimacy" in the eyes of the world has not suffered because of allegations of abuse at Guantanamo, the images from Abu Ghraib, or a general perception that the war in Iraq is immoral or unjust. But the crucial linkage between this sort of global discernment towards US actions in the war on terror (and the general cynicism towards the US idea of "democracy promotion") and an actual fundamental change in the way the United States acts in the world is not and will not be forthcoming because of the absence of a public realm capable of intervening and supporting a new crisis of legitimacy. This is also not a matter of changing political leadership. The internal constitution of Superpower is made up of a series of processes (economic, political, social, cultural, and so forth) that are beyond any one political leader's control. If anything, the current political inertia with regards to the future of America's role in Iraq reveals precisely the consequences of the passivity of not only the imperial citizen, but also the political elites. As Thomas Powers has recently put it, "[n]one of the presidential candidates seems to know why we are failing, or to understand what is imperial about the way we deal with Iraq, *or to sense that a bigger war is just another mistake away.*"[54]

Notes

An earlier version of this chapter was presented at the 2007 International Studies Association conference in Chicago, IL. I would like to thanks François Debrix, Mark J. Lacy, Scott Nelson, and Geoffrey Hill for their valuable comments.

1 Paul-Henri Teitgen, quoted in Alistair Horne, *A Savage War of Peace: Algeria 1954–1962* (New York: New York Review of Books, 2006 [1977]), p. 207.
2 George W. Bush, *President Discusses War on Terror at National Endowment for Democracy* (2005 [cited August 29, 2007]); available at www.whitehouse.gov/news/releases/2005/10/20051006-3.html.
3 George W. Bush, *Remarks by the President in Photo Opportunity with the National Security Team* (2001[cited August 28, 2007]); available at www.whitehouse.gov/news/releases/2001/09/20010912-4.html.
4 George W. Bush, *Radio Address of the President to the Nation* (2001 [cited August 27, 2007]); available at www.whitehouse.gov/news/releases/2001/09/20010915.html.
5 Alberto Gonzalez, *Decision Re Application of the Geneva Convention on Prisoners of War to the Conflict with Al Qaeda and the Taliban* (2002); available at www.msnbc.msn.com/id/4999148/site/newsweek/.
6 Jay Bybee, *Standards of Conduct for Interrogations under 18 Usc 2340–2340a* (Office of Legal Council, 2002 [cited August 28, 2007]); available at www.humanrightsfirst.org/us_law/etn/gonzales/memos_dir/memo_20020801_JD_%20Gonz_.pdf#search=%22bybee%20memo%20pdf%22.
7 See, in particular, Barton Gellman and Jo Becker, "Pushing the Envelope on Presidential Power," *The Washington Post*, June 25, 2007, p. A01.
8 See, for example, Jane Mayer, "Outsourcing Torture," *The New Yorker*, February 14, 2005,

available at www.newyorker.com/archive/2005/02/14/050214fa_fact6?currentPage=1; Jane Mayer, "The Black Sites," *The New Yorker*, August 13, 2007, available at www.newyorker.com/reporting/2007/08/13/070813fa_fact_mayr; Katherine Eban, "Rorschach and Awe," *Vanity Fair*, July 17, 2007, available at www.vanityfair.com/politics/features/2007/07/torture200707.
9 George W. Bush, *Second Term Inaugural Address* (2005 [cited September 3, 2007]); available at www.whitehouse.gov/news/releases/2005/01/20050120-1.html.
10 Bush, *President Discusses War on Terror*, no page given.
11 George W. Bush, *Global Message* (2003); available at www.whitehouse.gov/news/releases/2003/11/20031107.html.
12 Bush, *Second Term Inaugural Address*.
13 There were, however, quite a few Algerians who served as auxiliaries in the French army. Referred to as *harkis*, they were systematically butchered at the end of the war when it is estimated that between 30,000 and 150,000 of them perished. See Horne, *A Savage War of Peace*, p. 538.
14 Scott McConnell, "Algeria, the Model," *The American Conservative*, April 23, 2007, available at www.amconmag.com/2007/2007_04_23/article.html.
15 Gary Kamiya, "Bush's Favorite Historian," *Salon*, May 8, 2007, available at www.salon.com/opinion/kamiya/2007/05/08/alistair_horne/index_np.html.
16 Horne, *A Savage War of Peace*, p. 167.
17 Thomas X. Hammes, *The Sling and the Stone: On War in the 21st Century* (St. Paul: Zenith Press, 2004), p. 2.
18 Paul Aussaresses, *The Battle of the Casbah: Terrorism and Counter-Terrorism in Algeria, 1955–1957*, trans. Robert L. Miller (New York: Enigma Books, 2002), p. 128.
19 Ibid., p. 128.
20 Ibid., p. 126.
21 Alex Barker and Demetri Sevastopulo, "Hands Tied the Us Struggles to Get out of the 'Detention Business' in Iraq," *The Financial Times*, July 16, 2007, p. 9.
22 Aussaresses, *The Battle of the Casbah*, p. 127; my emphasis.
23 Horne, *A Savage War of Peace*, p. 204. Aussaresses writes that the prisoner in question, a communist party member, caught while placing a bomb at a gas plant, was tortured against Teitgen's explicit instructions: "[Honoré] Gévaudan later told me that they had to use torture to force [Fernand] Yveton to talk, in spite of the fact that Paul Teitgen had expressly forbidden it" (*The Battle of the Casbah*, p. 107).
24 Aussaresses, *The Battle of the Casbah*, p. 128.
25 Horne, *A Savage War of Peace*, p. 233.
26 Alan Dershowitz, "Is There a Torturous Road to Justice?," *The Los Angeles Times*, November 8, 2001, page B19, available at ontology.buffalo.edu/smith/courses01/rrtw/Dershowitz.htm; see also his *Why Terrorism Works: Understanding the Threat, Responding to the Challenge* (New Haven: Yale University Press, 2002).
27 Dershowitz, "Is There a Torturous Road to Justice?" page B19.
28 Ibid., page B19.
29 David Luban, "Liberalism, Torture, and the Ticking Bomb," *Virginia Law Review*, Vol. 91, No. 6 (2005), p. 1449.
30 Ibid., p. 1430.
31 Horne, *A Savage War of Peace*, p. 207.
32 Carl Schmitt, "Theory of the Partisan: A Commentary/Remark on the Concept of the Political," *New Centennial Review*, Vol. 4, No. 3 (2004 [1963]) , pp. 45–6.
33 The International Committee of the Red Cross was involved in attempting to convince the French that the Geneva Conventions covered insurgent combatants. However, as reported in a press article in 2005 originally published in the Swiss daily *Le Temps*, "France actually refused to see itself as being at war with the Algerian nationalists. Consequently, if there were no war, the detainees could not claim prisoner of war status. They were referred to as 'PAM,' the French acronym for 'taken captive while in possession of weapons.' Their fate was in the hands of the French magistrates and they were to be brought systematically before the courts. The ICRC was therefore obliged

to obtain special authorization from those magistrates – a long, complex process since the judges were going to do everything in their power to stop the delegates from getting through." See Luis Lema, "Torture in Algeria. The Report That Was to Change Everything," *Le Temps*, August 19, 2005, available at www.icrc.org/Web/Eng/siteeng0.nsf/html/algeria-history-190805.

34 Hannah Arendt, *On Violence* (New York: Harcourt, 1970).
35 Ibid., p. 44.
36 Ibid., p. 45.
37 Ibid., p. 56.
38 Ibid., p. 52.
39 Ibid.
40 Hannah Arendt, *On Revolution* (Westport: Greenwood Press, 1982).
41 Arendt, *On Violence*, p. 53.
42 Ibid., pp. 55–6.
43 Hannah Arendt, *The Human Condition* (Chicago: University of Chicago Press, 1998), p. 257.
44 Sheldon S. Wolin, *Politics and Vision: Continuity and Innovation in Western Political Thought* (Princeton: Princeton University Press, 2004), pp. 557–9.
45 Ibid., p. 560.
46 Ibid., pp. 560–1.
47 Ibid., p. 556; my emphasis.
48 Ibid., p. 590.
49 Ibid., p. 589.
50 Ibid., p. 591.
51 Ibid., p. 592.
52 Ibid.
53 Michael Hardt and Antonio Negri, *Multitude: War and Democracy in the Age of Empire* (New York: Penguin, 2004), p. 30.
54 Thomas Powers, "The Reason Why," *The New York Review of Books*, September 15, 2007, available at www.nybooks.com/articles/20597; my emphasis.

4 *Torturefest* and the passage to pedagogy of tortured pasts

Marie Thorsten

> If there were no photographs, there would be no Abu Ghraib ... It would have been, "OK, whatever, everybody go home."
>
> Sergeant Javal Davis[1]

Introduction

Questions about how wars are fought soon turn into questions about how wars will be taught. But "teaching" a war also occurs in everyday media, before wars come to an end. Critic A. O. Scott recently commented that a spate of new films dealing with the Iraqi conflict embrace "confusion, complexity and ambiguity" but lack the "sweet relief," "bitter catharsis," or "moral certainty" we have come to expect from films that followed other wars.[2] They also fail to give us a sense of collective grief, as did the Vietnam War films. It may be too early for Iraq War films, since, as Scott asks, "how can you bring an individual story to a satisfying conclusion when nobody has any idea what the end of the larger story will look like?"[3] As another critic added, the war is just "so close and so raw" that people lack "perspective" to make assessments about collective ideas regarding who we were "then."[4]

The critics' reservations assume that image-making follows, rather than is integral to, war-making, and that citizens pursue a linear path when they experience the fact of their nation at war and, later, when they study and memorialize that war once it is over. Still, the optical lens is a component rather than an afterthought of war. "Visual intelligence" continuously influences the way people perceive and respond to conflict.[5] And war typically motivates people through images of sacrifice, heroism, and national unity, thus clearly drawing a line between allies and enemies. The recent outpouring of films and other artistic/educational representations of the global war on terrorism is sandwiched between such a "bring it on" sense of moral certainty that Bush used to launch the wars in Afghanistan and Iraq and another imagined assurance that takes the form of a collectively agreed upon national memory. Another phrasing of Scott's question might be: "How can individual media pieces, including films, help Americans to think through less comfortable aspects of the war on terrorism as well as its eventual textbook conclusion to ensure that the larger story will not be forgotten despite all its complexity?"

Such an inquiry can be taken up in a submotif of the current surge of "terror-tainment," one that addresses one of the most obtrusive lies of the Bush administration:

the claim that "this government does not torture people." A veritable festival of popular cultural (mostly visual) items has recently emerged to respond to this claim and thus contribute to discussions of torture in the public sphere. It would be naïve to hope that such works of visual culture could "solve" the question of torture, but their very act of dissension raises another question: how can a record of public non-consent survive against the many circumstances of public life that favor forgetting that any debate ever existed at all?

Eventually, watchdogs of posterity will decide how to write about Bush's denial—"this government does not torture people"—for future generations. But, as a reiteration of officialdom, the denial might actually *become* the textbook. Traditionally, this has been the purpose of most school textbooks: to legitimate state narratives and to draw meaning from the visual images that sustain them. Children's textbooks are relevant beyond the classroom. Indeed, by being understood as the imprimatur of a society or nation,[6] and by presenting comforting conclusions with a safe emotional distance, sanctified textbook narratives rub closely against other homogenizing nationalistic tendencies, including the prospect of permanently legitimizing state torture through legal mechanisms. The ethical debate over torture may end up being chiseled into aseptic conclusions with or without preemption from popular culture. But currently this very debate is conditioned by the contorting of "torture" itself to satisfy demands for enhanced sovereignty, solidarity, nationalism, and acquiescence to power. After all, the word "torture" is derived from the Latin word *tortura*, which means "to twist".

This chapter conducts a preliminary consideration of the capacity to put this contortion of torture on public display through an examination of recent works of popular culture that are noteworthy for their educational resourcefulness. The concern is whether such media can provoke some intervention against the normalization of torture in American public life, and also whether their contentiousness itself can survive the passage from the chaos of current media to the illusory comfort of future national narratives. This is particularly important amid the critical impasse between the "shock and awe" beginning of Bush's war on terrorism and the many attempts to filter the now discredited war into an unproblematic national memory of the not so distant future.

The critics' assumption that there is a comforting linear progression or passage from war to pedagogy (via film, in particular) is increasingly elusive in the era of prolific media. Moreover, when disparaged wars come to be remembered, whether through films, memorials, or textbooks, the certainties that marked these wars' beginnings are put into doubt by increasingly global constituencies (witness the continuous criticism of Japan's displays of war memory by Koreans, Chinese and other victims of Japan's imperial aggression).[7] Educators need not be just the purveyors of unitary national creeds, but can also be guides who integrate rather than avoid challenges from singular visual spectacles, or from ambiguous themes developed in films and other media.[8] Such time-consuming endeavors, however, may be a luxury available to only a few.

Visual wars: from spectacles to texts

The war on terrorism is the most globally visual war ever. Its development and progression have pivoted around distinct photographic representations: the collapse of the World Trade Center towers on September 11, 2001; the fall of Saddam Hussein's statue on April 9, 2003 (paired with the US "Mission Accomplished" slogan); and, finally, the visual disclosures of the Abu Ghraib prison abuses made available to the public in April 2004. This visual/iconic triptych depicts, first, America as victimized, second, America as victorious, and, finally, with the incongruous photographic evidence of gross human rights violations, America as duplicitous (or, as US Senator Lindsey Graham has put it, the image of the United States "becoming the enemy in the name of trying to defeat your enemy")."[9]

The Abu Ghraib photos, unchecked by US government interpretation, and produced by low-ranking soldiers for their own amusement, offered a different visual reality than the one previously proclaimed through the "Mission Accomplished" moment. As one of the convicted interrogators succinctly argued (reproduced in the quotation at the opening of this chapter), the photos *became* the scandal. Visual evidence of naked and hooded prisoners, placed in bizarre, stressful, painful, scatological, and sexually humiliating positions, generated protest and censure throughout the world. These images led to a criminal investigation and to the conviction of low-ranking soldiers too. Above all, the exposure signaled the precipitous decline of American moral authority.

The Abu Ghraib photos may well sustain their intervening function of discrediting the narrative of American triumph, as suggested above. But they may also prove just as forgettable as the "Mission Accomplished" slogan since the "politics of spectacle" are "highly unstable, subject to multiple interpretations, and often generate unanticipated side effects," as Douglas Kellner reminds us.[10] The 279 photos and 19 videos, handed to the Army's Criminal Investigation Command on January 13, 2004 by Spc. Joseph Darby,[11] first seemed to destabilize the "shock and awe" image of a triumphant America defeating terrorism. The eerie sight of the electrically rigged prisoner in Abu Ghraib, hooded with a prayer rug, once threatened to become *the* flashbulb memory of the Iraq War for generations to come. Yet, the very sensational nature of these photos—after all, the interrogators at Abu Ghraib were encouraged to be "creative"—has also allowed the images to be trivialized as the "Animal House on the night shift."[12] Visual spectacles are bolstered by their spins into what François Debrix has called "tabloid geopolitics," or the centering of American identity, security, and discourses of morality on sensationalist, simplistic punditry in talk shows and other media venues (often performed by populist hosts, pseudo-intellectuals, and conformist policy professionals alike).[13]

The visual spectacle of the war on terror, Judith Butler writes, "numbs the senses and, like the sublime itself, puts out of play the very capacity to think."[14] To restore the human sensitivity lost through such numbness, some critics have been waxing nostalgic about the 1960s protest culture, and particularly about the films that followed the Vietnam War. But those films had their problems too (they were about America rather than Vietnam), and they still beg the question of whether they even mattered in terms of influencing American posterity and pedagogy. Indeed, when James W. Loewen conducted a study of how the war in Vietnam was being taught in American high schools in the 1990s, he found that teachers were afraid of controversy and reluctant to encourage students to become critical of American institutions. Or they just did not have the time to teach about the failed war amid other curricular/

educational demands. Almost all of the twelve typical texts Loewen surveyed failed to adequately explain the moral legitimacy of the US involvement in Vietnam or the extent of the anti-war demonstrations on the home front. The key visual images that adults old enough to remember that war typically recalled—the "napalm girl," the My Lai massacre, the self-immolation of a Buddhist monk—were all avoided in order not to challenge US war efforts, whether past, present, or future. Citing a number of other studies of American high school classes, Loewen confirmed estimates that the average time teachers spent on the Vietnam War amounted to less than five minutes in the entire school year.[15]

It is difficult to imagine the war on terror, and its continuous, round-the-clock Iraq news coverage, reduced to five minutes of uncontroversial tedium in future school classes or textbooks. National narratives are never fully compressed between two book covers. Despite texts and curricula, they might still be contested for decades and centuries to come. Nevertheless, these national accounts are remarkably resilient when they are memorialized in textbooks, museums, and monuments. And controversies over the production of unitary narratives or memories can leave wounds unhealed for generations to come, something that is well known to victims of Japan's aggression in World War II. At the start of the American-led invasion of Iraq, officials often cited postwar Japan as a model of successful US occupation, one that had made allies out of former enemies. Instead, given the travesty that the Iraq intervention has become, Japan may in fact offer a different sort of historical precedent, namely, what to tell future generations about the most disparaged chapters of a nation's history.

In Japan, and in the United States as well, "official" representations of World War II (approved by the state, legitimated by the public) generally existed prior to the outpouring of dissertations, documentaries, mini-series, and blockbuster films that now have revisited and potentially "revised" these more unitary and unproblematic inscriptions of history. Few people had televisions then. Print reporting was considerably minimal compared to today's standards. And in Japan during the US occupation, censorship (often self-imposed) served to preserve the sanctioned ways of representing the war.

The Iraq conflict begun in 2003 has already lasted longer than the American experience in World War II. Like past wars, it has been sanctioned in single-purpose visuals and discourses. But, if one wishes to find them, a range of non-state crafted (and, as such, globally diverse) opinions have been "out there" in public culture too. Thus, the crucial question today is how to make information matter and last.

Popular culture can help to archive the social impact of the war on terror. Between the years 2004 and 2007, 10 important popular cultural sites, linked with relevant educational resources, sought to directly address, implicate by analogy, or provoke a public discussion over the so-called truth about the American use of torture. These popular cultural and educational works came in various forms:

Website/television programs (the non-governmental organization, Human Rights First, analyzed torture themes on contemporary TV programs on its homepage, with a special section dedicated to the "Primetime Torture" project[16]).

Plays (Victoria Brittain and Gillian Slovo's *Guantanamo: Honor Bound to Defend Freedom*, 2004[17]).

Documentary films (*Ghosts of Abu Ghraib*, directed by Rory Kennedy, 2007;[18] *Promise to the Dead: The Exile Journey of Ariel Dorfman*, directed by Peter Raymont, 2007;[19] *The Torture Question*, directed by Michael Kirk, 2005;[20] *Taxi to the Dark Side*, directed by Alex Gibney, 2007[21]).

Feature films (the re-released *The Battle of Algiers*, directed by Gillo Pontecorvo, 2004, originally made in 1966;[22] *Rendition*, directed by Gavin Hood, 2007;[23] *Road to Guantanamo*, directed by Michael Winterbottom and Mat Whitecross, 2006[24]).

Art Exhibits (Fernando Botero's "Abu Ghraib" collection, 2007[25]).

World War II demonstrated art's capacity to influence political culture by elevating the cultural Self and bestializing the Other.[26] But the 10 educational/visual/artistic efforts listed above differ from World War II films or cartoons, for example, because they do not represent one punctual statement. Instead, they present themselves to the public as one particular link in a network of complex information, and not as the bearers of one totalizing, regime-maintaining, message. Thus, these materials are not just "think pieces" in and of themselves. Their authors, directors, producers, or contributors lead viewers towards many public symposia and/or educational sources provided by human rights organizations, news articles, clips of political statements, various policy papers, personal testimonies, interviews, legal documents, and additional films/visual media. Some of these supplementary materials are intended for the general public while others are explicitly marked "for teachers" and adapted to the needs of high schools and universities. With such resources, what can be called a "torturefest" reveals civil society's response to educate people on the political and historical conditions that brought about the abuses evidenced in Afghanistan, Iraq, Guantanamo, or the various locations of "extraordinary rendition."

The chronopolitics of torture

The war on terror's "smoke them out of their holes"[27] machospeak disgorges a similar dehumanization as that employed by propaganda makers of World War II. But even such an odious thing as racial dehumanization is subject to refashioning.

Butler feels that public endorsement of the idea of the inhuman is more likely inculcated through the Other's absence, that is to say, through the media denial of visualization of the Other, especially of his/her suffering. To recover a sense of humanity and the ability to grieve for the loss of life is not only about reiterating the universality of the human, but also about understanding human precariousness. What counts as human is already mediated by "schemes of intelligibility" that tell us "what will and will not be human, what will be a livable life, what will be a grievable death."[28] Schemes of intelligibility about human precariousness are often provided through images whose purposes are precisely to delay the moment of re-humanization, of the rediscovery of the image of the precarious Self or Other.

One such popular cultural product is the Fox TV series *24*, an innovative, extraordinarily popular program based on a tense twenty-four hours of barely futuristic counter-terrorism operations. The viewer of *24* does not have time to ask many questions about the postulated bestiality of the enemy/Other or to ponder over the issue of humanity in general. The narrative is tailored to the twenty-first-century high-tech politics of time, or what Paul Virilio has referred to as the "chronopolitical."[29] In *24*, this means not only trading space for time (which Virilio calls "deterritorialization"), but also demoralization as "chronopolitics." The war on terrorism requires forgetting about ethical rules whenever time-ticking situations (determining life or death for millions) are concerned. *24* began airing immediately after 9/11; the first season was written before the 9/11 attacks. Subsequent episodes conveniently forget the "real life" abuses in Afghanistan, Guantanamo, or Abu Ghraib. Always living on the apocalyptic edge, *24*'s family-values patriot-protagonist, Jack Bauer, performs "sublime" acts by dispelling any misgivings about ethics: what moral rules matter when the lives of millions are at stake? Likewise, in *24*, each season's enemy has to be tortured, not because of his inherent bestiality, but because there is no time to think when the national security hangs in the balance.

Torture in popular culture is usually performed by medieval or menacing people, pathologically or politically strange "others." But as Jack Bauer went from episode to episode vindicated and unscathed, people (in the United States in particular) began to recognize *24* as a wishful representation of Bush's America: the righteous, although unappreciated, global policeman who knows just when to break the rules but always has good intentions, and always saves the world.

Those who do support Bush's counterterrorism tactics have rallied around this refreshing gift from American primetime television. The conservative think-tank, the Heritage Foundation, hosted a symposium titled "*24* and America's Image in Fighting Terrorism: Fact, Fiction, or Does it Matter?" During this symposium, the head of Homeland Security, Michael Chertoff, defended the show for representing "real life" situations. The co-creator and executive producer of *24*, Joel Surnow, a self-described "right wing nut job," boasted that the military and the administration love the program.[30] The show's "political message," writes Jane Mayer, is to depict contemporary trade-offs between liberty and security in the war on terror, and the program shows "the fight against Islamist extremism much as the Bush Administration has defined it: as an all-consuming struggle for America's survival that demands the toughest of tactics."[31] Surnow candidly added that *24* "is ripped out of the Zeitgeist of what people's fears are" and that "America wants the war on terror fought by Jack Bauer."[32]

The enemies of *24* are not the just the terrorists but also the humanitarian liberals who want to protect international agreements and civil liberties. Following such a reasoning, the actual left would probably put a real-life Jack Bauer into Leavenworth Penitentiary for life, according to conservative commentator Patrick Buchanan. Jack Bauer is a "take-no-prisoners patriot who puts love of country and loyalty to friends first, and fights by his own rules," the sort of American vigilante who knows that "the only good terrorist is a dead terrorist."[33] Bauer knows that, "without victory in the war on terror, freedom may not survive." The fact that *24*'s audience is "so loyal and large" tells us something about Americans, argues Buchanan. While they defend their liberties, most Americans (at least, those who watch *24*) also agree with Bush that "the enemies of 9/11 are so evil, so depraved, they forfeit the right to be treated honorably."[34]

The show thus crossed the line of verisimilitude, creating social acquiescence to reinforce the very reality that inspires it. Doing "anything it takes" is one of the recurring lines of the series (thus inferring the meaning/authorization of torture), and it was also a line reiterated by Bush in his September 15, 2001 "smoke them out" speech. Tony Lagouranis, a former Army interrogator who served for a year in Iraq, has revealed that, when he and fellow soldiers were told to scrap the Geneva Conventions and be "creative," it was hard for them to come up with ideas since their only training had been Geneva-consistent. But it was not uncommon for soldiers to learn methods of enhanced interrogation from TV shows. Lagouranis admits that he has sensed the effects of *24* more distinctly since coming back to America where he has been actively speaking out against military torture and giving his frank assessment on why torture does not work (the information is not reliable, or it is limited, or false). In such speaking engagements, he is surprised that the members of the public often bring up the "case" of *24* to defend torture, and he believes that the messages from the media, more than those from the government, are inculcating the idea that torture is necessary to defend the United States from terrorism.[35] David Danzig, Director of the "Primetime Torture" project for Human Rights First,[36] claims that, according to his own conversations with instructors in military techniques, *24* is one of the biggest obstacles to teaching since, as one instructor put it, "everybody wants to be like Jack Bauer. They all think that it may be possible or there are times when you should have to cross the line."[37]

The main issue, philosopher Slavoj Zizek suggests, is that *24* and its spin-offs are helping to normalize the acceptance of torture, returning humans to the conditions of the Middle Ages. When a hero such as Jack Bauer can "retain human dignity in accomplishing acts of terror" and, on top of this, acquire an "additional tragic-ethic grandeur," then such atavistic human adaptation to an illogical war becomes "the ultimate confirmation" of "moral catastrophe."[38]

Responding to *24*

To challenge the democratically unhealthy mutual reinforcement between national ethos and primetime entertainment, other popular culture pieces have attempted to slow down the fast and convenient American rationales produced in tabloids and television shows such as *24*. They have hoped to restore some time for reflection, the very thing that has been bulldozed by chronopolitics, and to allow more nuanced inquiries into the precariousness of human life and human suffering. They assume that citizens, even at a high school age, are capable of processing complex knowledge. For educators in democracies, the meaning of citizenship is not just about the feeling of belonging to a particular nation-state or about the duty to offer unquestioned national sacrifice when called upon. Education also involves instilling in young minds the responsibility to question the premises of a nation's wars, to discuss controversial public issues, and to continuously check the moral authority of the leaders.[39] Critical pedagogy draws on the assumption that education occurs throughout everyday life and by way of dialogue in the public sphere, not just within the brick and mortar confines of formal schooling. The media, in particular, do not need to be seen only as forms of entertainment or as reinforcements of authority. Rather, the media can facilitate sharing, discussion, and negotiation of the knowledge that takes place across various (real or virtual) social formations. In these social settings, citizens can influence one another without pressure from formal government figures or institutions, and they can find the courage to decenter and interrogate the cultural Self whenever necessary. These are the very points made by Henry Giroux who, after the Abu Ghraib photos disclosure, was motivated to tap into the pedagogical thread of Theodor Adorno's 1967 essay, "Education after Auschwitz," an essay written with the hope that future German generations would not repeat the atrocities of their elders. To resist totalitarianism, especially the "Auschwitz principle," requires true "human autonomy," Adorno insisted, or a "force of reflection and of self-determination, the will to refuse participation."[40]

In the interest of summoning a critical pedagogy that could reverse the capacity of a show like *24* to teach how to torture, the "Primetime Torture" project has developed training manuals for junior officers so that they cannot be so easily influenced by fictional media portrayals of torture. The project's authors have been meeting with TV producers and writers to help them understand the negative ramifications of popular programs that endorse torture. In particular, they have insisted on the fact that such programs are widely viewed overseas and thus contribute to the tarnishing of America's image in the world.[41] Toward these goals, Brigadier General and West Point Dean, Patrick Finnegan, along with Danzig, Lagouranis, and two other former interrogators, met with *24* producers in the fall of 2006 to try to dissuade them from continuously depicting torture as an effective method of interrogation. They were probably not successful in getting *24* to include the more proven "realistically" problematic aspects of torture. Lagouranis, for example, recounted that *24*'s producers were "receptive" but "resistant to change." Overall, "Primetime Torture" makes the point that torture scenes on American TV dramatically increased after 9/11 (from fewer than four acts every week before 9/11 to more than one hundred per week in recent years), but also that the characters who perform torture have changed. Now, so-called good guys as well as bad guys use torture, and when the good guys torture, it is necessary, effective and even patriotic.

Other narrative works also dilute the national discourse that boasts the effectiveness of "enhanced interrogations." As Alexander D. Barder shows (see his chapter in this volume), the grittily realistic *Battle of Algiers* movie (originally made in 1966) provided a case study for planners of the US-led war against terrorism, revealing to them that torture does "work," but only temporarily, up to the point where it produces worse results than what the war planners were facing in the first place. In Algeria, the French (who also fudged with the semantic use of "torture") won the "battle." But they ended up losing the "war" because they failed to assess how strong the Algerian resistance was throughout the nation. Torture only fanned the flames of the much wider Algerian peoples' movement that emerges through the smoke in the final scenes of the film.

Another historical case study is offered in the documentary that follows scholar and writer Ariel Dorfman, who was moved by the events of 9/11 to retrace his experience in "the other September 11," that of 1973, when the CIA offered tactical and financial support to overthrow the Chilean President Salvador Allende. For representing a political paradox—a democratically elected socialist—Allende was forced to commit suicide (it is usually believed), and was later replaced by one of the most brutal military dictators, Augusto Pinochet. With a family background of several experiences of exile,

Dorfman's hope (through this documentary on his role in the Allende government before he was forced to flee to the United States) is to encourage viewers of the film to feel "more human than less human," that is to say, more inclined to seek justice and compassion rather than revenge.[42]

After 9/11, to ponder the question "what kind of world shaped the minds of the people who plotted and carried out the unforgivable acts of September 11?" would seem to amount to a denial of the pure evil that was inflicted that day or would appear to create an attempt to excuse or even sympathize with such acts.[43] Film director Rory Kennedy, when making *Ghosts of Abu Ghraib*, nonetheless ended up asking a similar kind of question, but not about foreign terrorists this time, but about Americans themselves. Kennedy had originally aspired to make a film about genocide, asking why apparently decent people are drawn to commit atrocities, and gathering some insight from the research conducted by Stanley Milgram, the psychologist who led the famous "obedience study" in 1961.[44] Kennedy reveals that, contrary to her expectations, the prison guards/soldiers at Abu Ghraib were surprisingly "just like you and me." But they were "thrown into circumstances that are unimaginable" in their tour of duty there. They lacked any kind of guard training, endured daily mortar attacks, and were subjected to confusing orders. These things are not excuses, she acknowledges, but they helped make the guards into people they themselves did not believe they were.[45]

The film *Road to Guantanamo* and the play *Guantanamo: Honor Bound to Defend Freedom* are additional popular cultural sites that place Guantanamo's detainees at the heart of *torturefest*. These two works draw our attention to the precariousness of life by raising the question of what happens when the detainees deemed to be outside the realm of the Geneva Conventions and other international agreements as "unlawful combatants" (even though they are only suspects) happen to be British citizens. The feature film *Rendition* brings the story of illegal prison treatment home to Americans by showing what an average young wife goes through when her Egyptian-born husband is transferred to an undisclosed country under suspicion of terrorist activity. The film's homepage identifies all of the main characters with the identity qualifier "American" in order to underscore that this could be any US spectator's experience too. For this reason, it was controversial for viewers who hoped the film would better reflect its "true story" based on Khalid El-Masri's ordeal, a German citizen raised in Lebanon and married to a wife from Lebanon. Both the DVD and homepage also offer additional resources to examine the problem of "extraordinary renditions," or the "outsourcing" of terror suspects to other countries where they can be tortured and often hidden as "ghost detainees" in "black sites." Given the "this could be you" promotion, however, it is not clear whether many who watched the film only, and not the educational links, really understood that extraordinary renditions were indeed already real.

Another important documentary is *Taxi to the Dark Side*, which takes its name from Dick Cheney's own euphemism for sending somebody to be tortured ("dark side" is also a phrase used by some of *24*'s producers). This documentary is connected with the "Democracy Now!" project and recounts the last few weeks of an unassuming Afghan taxi driver who died after sustaining injuries inflicted by American soldiers at Bagram (a US military base in Afghanistan).

Art has often represented the voices of the oppressed. For Colombian artist Fernando Botero, "art is a permanent accusation."[46] Botero's own artistic response to

Abu Ghraib was to offer an "anti-visual" visual accusation of American power as a so-called model of compassion. Without viewing the famous photographs, the Colombian artist nonetheless drew dozens of sketches of the experiences of the Iraqi prisoners based only on what he refers to as "fidelity" with his own readings. As a result, the fifty oil paintings that became a traveling exhibit in 2005 are arguably even more explicit than the infamous, more choreographed, original photos.[47] Botero's signature fleshy and blithe bodies have become muscular and solemn, reasserting masculinity against humiliation. The prisoners' blindfolds compel the viewer to see the horrors at Abu Ghraib. Botero was especially concerned with the fact that Americans would not be able to see his paintings since US art institutes and galleries initially refused to showcase the exhibit. In 2004, the Capobianco Gallery in San Francisco was forced to close after its owner was physically assaulted, and the gallery was repeatedly vandalized for showing another painting depicting the Abu Ghraib scandal. In 2007, however, the University of California at Berkeley and American University both decided to display Botero's paintings to mostly impressed and supportive reviews.

To remember or forget things not yet past

If the scandalous photos of Abu Ghraib work as Proust's *madeleine*, then one "bite" could activate reflection about the role of America in the war on terror, furthering education on the intersection between universal human rights and the journey to the infamous "dark side." Whether the photos survive as such a flashbulb memory, however, remains to be seen. Some American high schools have begun teaching about post-9/11 America and the war on terror, often using extensive and thoughtfully written curricular guides designed to facilitate a range of thinking.[48] But to the extent that teaching is being conducted on the Iraq War and other matters of the war on terror, it is "incredibly delicate," as one teacher put it, since teachers fear reactions from parents, administrators, or some students.[49] This reaction is understandable given the climate of ideological intimidation that pervaded American education immediately after 9/11 and still lingers to some degree today.

Susan Graseck, the Director of the Choices Education Program (under the heading of the Watson Institute for International Studies at Brown University), is an established leader in curricular guides for high school students in the area of international studies. She states that she hopes students will study issues surrounding the global war on terror for the main reason that "it matters to them."[50] The Choices Program's guide for teaching about Iraq includes not only lessons about the requisite historical and geographical facts, matters of national interest, and simulation activities, but also lesson plans that challenge students to evaluate media images and political rhetoric.[51] At the high school level, many teachers make considerable efforts to withhold their own judgment and allow students to role-play many positions, even some they do not necessarily agree with, all in the name of allowing students to make up their own minds on the topic. In some US high schools, students have even become activists, writing or speaking to their representatives in Congress, holding demonstrations, or, in a recent case of high school presidential scholars visiting the White House, directly petitioning the President to end torture (Bush's response to them was, typically, that "the United States does not torture").[52]

But forgetting often trumps remembering. When the Tipton Three were about to be released from Guantanamo in response to considerable international pressure affirming their innocence, they were not given any sort of apology or compensation. Instead, they were taken to a special place nicknamed the "Love Shack" where they were unshackled and allowed to munch on Pizza Hut pizzas, McDonald's burgers, and Pringles chips while watching DVDs. "This was because they knew they had messed us about and tortured us for two and a half years, and they hoped we would forget it," speculated Asif Iqbal.[53]

There are indications that such a Guantanamo-Pringles effect may be at work in American daily life too. Journalist Thomas L. Friedman charges that Americans are forgetting about Iraq because of fatigue over the failure of the so-called "surge" (the extra 20,000 troops Bush ordered to Iraq in 2007) and because of the inability of the Democrats to bring about any troop withdrawal.[54] Many have bemoaned America's lack of an anti-war movement, and to the extent that there has been one, its key figure, Cindy Sheehan, resigned from it in exhaustion.[55] "Iraq fatigue" became a commonplace expression by 2008.

But the recent debate over torture also forgets that the American use of it did not begin in late 2001 or in 2002, in Afghanistan or at Guantanamo. Democracies, including the United States, have used torture at least since the nineteenth century, even though torture (that is to say, the "intimidation, abuse of public trust, extraction of false confessions [and] the blind eye of officials") is clearly antithetical to the idea of democracy. What gradually has changed though, according to Darius Rejali, is the introduction of a "clean torture" that leaves few marks on the body and happens behind closed doors. This is the very kind of torture that is conveniently and easily forgotten.[56] Methods of "clean torture" have long been exported to other regimes, and taught to Latin American leaders who graduated from the notorious CIA-funded School of the Americas (now located at Fort Benning, Georgia). Naomi Klein argues that it is strange that Americans say "Never before!" when it comes to US torture when, really, they should be protesting "Never again!" What is really different today is not the use of torture but, as Zizek suggests, its emergence from the shadows and its public legitimization.[57]

Jack Bauer's real-time torture frenzy to "save lives," even if it means hurting others, also forgets the real-life detonation of the bombs that already were said to have "saved lives" on August 6 and 9, 1945. Historian Herbert P. Bix reveals that the Truman administration's decision to drop the nuclear bombs over Hiroshima and Nagasaki in 1945, presented for decades as necessary to save lives, won public support through careful cultivation of the myth of "good intentions." American nuclear bombs, together with other conventional bombs dropped over Japan, killed between 600,000 and 900,000 Japanese noncombatants. These overwhelming civilian casualties could be made conscionable to do-good Americans only through the careful use of governmental rhetoric highlighting the special conditions of battle, the righteousness of the mission, and the good intentions of the leaders and soldiers. "What counted was the motive," explains Bix, "not the consequences of the act or the nature of the weapons used."[58] "Collateral damage" became a euphemism to hide the killing of civilians in the nuclear age and to exempt the United States from any moral or legal accountability for those acts. As Bix puts it, "it is the military's way of saying: judge the commander, the pilot, the combat soldier, even the US mercenary and torturer not by what he did but by his subjective state of mind when he did it."[59]

The sudden public/popular cultural interest in twenty-first-century American torture cannot only be explained as a hangover from the 1945 nuclear bombs, French colonialism in Algeria, or mindless television, although all these things do matter. The fact that people comply easily with authority—a compliance that might devolve into accepting the abuse, torture, and murder of civilians—is conditioned by what Michel Foucault identified as the "trace of torture" found in the practices of everyday life. What Foucault had in mind was life as managed by the "great enclosed, complex and hierarchized structure," or "the body of the state."[60] According to Foucault, feudal societies once used the spectacle of torture to repress criminals. But by the nineteenth century, the punishments became more private than public, more hidden than carnivalesque, more about the suspension of rights than about leaving marks on the body, and more about tedious investigations and classifications than about open confrontations between torturers and criminals. Modern societies that organize, regulate, classify, and impose norms and rules that turn entire populations (and not just prisoners from afar) into passive objects of authority, carry over this trace of torture into the daily lives of those they administer, in schools, clinics, and other agencies/institutions of everyday social welfare.[61]

This docility alone is "useful," and it becomes more easily obtained as the education policies threaten to turn schools into endless examination-cramming and data-displaying centers. One might wonder, then, if this conversion of complex social history into data crunching and immutable discourse is not enough in itself to satisfy educational goals for authoritarian leaders. But there are still other educational "benefits" that can be obtained from the re-normalizing of torture in public policy and life. Foucault's social histories show that the crowds that gathered around the scaffolds gave their hearty enthusiasm to the veritable political ritual, joining in the triumph of the executioner's liturgical punishment. Since a docile population is not a lively population, then, with the return of torture from the shadows into TV's primetime comes the possibility of a bolder and more enthusiastic endorsement of the sovereign. One can refer, once again, to the certainty of pro-Jack Bauer conservative pundits like Buchanan (and many others) who happily endorse a strong leader who will do "whatever it takes" to get the job done. But Rejali warns that "it would be ignoring history to assume that what happens in an American-run prison in Iraq will stay in Iraq." Rejali adds: "Soldiers who learn torture techniques abroad get jobs as police officers when they return, and the new developments in torture you read about today could yet be employed in a neighborhood near you."[62] Educational messages in schools or in TV programs that instill the resurrected enthusiasm of scaffold spectators will create a nation of better Jack Bauers. But, as Rejali intimates, there is always a glitch. As Foucault's feudal lords discovered, enthusiastic crowds can end up turning against their sovereign leader, sympathizing with prisoners, and arguing for more rights.

Against such a possibility, strategies of language contort the meaning of torture in order to redesign allegiance to the owner of the scaffold and perform the illusion of international compliance. High profile American legal scholar Alan Dershowitz proclaims: "I am against torture. But if we do it, we must do it democratically." Newly appointed Attorney General Michael B. Mukasey chimes in: "Torture is 'repugnant,' but I am not sure if it is illegal." And Bush confirms: "Torture means organ failure. Therefore, the United States does not torture." Such utterances are not conducive to producing the kind of constructive ambiguity that could build bridges and enable more fluidity across borders. Rather, these statements are classic instances of Orwellian doublespeak—hiding one meaning while proclaiming another—securing the totality of American imperialism.

Conclusion

Such an American geopolitical and imperialistic totality was initiated in the "with us or with the terrorists" rhetorical launch of the war on terror. It has also been bolstered by the unitary effects of mind-numbing visual spectacles, tabloid geopolitics, and pop cultural verisimilitudes. In the not-so-distant past, it could be reasonably assumed that nations were interested in protecting the unitary purposes of war in national memories. This is especially the case for the victorious. With the American loss in Vietnam, other narratives of affirmation—the American victory in the Cold War, the show of democracy in the concurrent civil rights movement, the collective admission of shame in the film oeuvres—could partly contain the shame of defeat.

In the synchronic rather than diachronic space between the global war on terror and an imagined final-answer textbook, concerned citizens have pushed for more informed debate on torture in America. The 10 visual popular culture works described in this chapter hope to intervene on behalf of the public sphere, in the interest of an open national narrative, before such a narrative becomes too linear and reaches a predictable conclusion. These alternative sites present viewers with complex and moving stories and perspectives connected to a range of useful information sources. Even those works that are marked "for teachers" do not underestimate the capacity of citizens (or students) to process raw or complex issues (that have to do with a conflict that has not yet ended) so that the power of visual intelligence can be reclaimed and a culture that tries to normalize torture can be refused.

Without interference from a demanding and critical public, the Abu Ghraib photos, for example, are in danger of being reduced to the dim memory of some "bad apples" doing disturbing things on a night shift. And a textbook paragraph on this event may end up sounding very much like the spin that Cheney gave to it in 2007, already seeking to create the impression of a faraway past. Indeed, Cheney declared: "Some years ago, when abuses were committed at Abu Ghraib prison—again, a facility that had nothing to do with the detainee program run by the CIA—the abuses that came to light rightfully outraged many people ... The wrongdoers were arrested and prosecuted, and justice was demanded."[63]

As I reached the final draft of this essay, it became apparent that almost none of the Iraq War films, including the *torturefest* films I have referred to here, have done well at the box office (although *Taxi To the Dark Side* got an Oscar for Best Documentary). Of the Iraq War films that did receive attention, critics especially praised *No End in Sight* (also nominated for Best Documentary) for being "unbiased" in its analysis of the aftermath of the 2003 Iraq invasion and of the blunders of the United States that helped turn that conflict into a seemingly endless war. Director Charles Ferguson edited the film from several hundred hours of interviews with key Washington officials, focusing on three principal errors: the failure to use the infrastructure and personnel already in place under Saddam's regime, the failure to use enough US coalition troops to maintain order, and the disbanding of the Iraqi army. While such errors of policy are detailed with surprising candor in the documentary, there is nothing mentioned of the American treatment of prisoners and suspected terrorists in Abu Ghraib (even though Ferguson did include a few references to torture in his book that followed up the film).

This omission of the moral failure of the war helps unite people around the acceptance of a US *strategic* failure, a theme also repeated when the *New York Times* asked nine military and foreign policy specialists to comment on "what most surprised them" or what "they wished they had considered in the prewar debate."[64] Often echoing *No End in Sight*, the experts alluded to inability to control the looting of cultural heritage, the lack of security for the population, the arrogance and rashness of the Bush administration, the absence of proper equipment, a failure of intelligence, and so on. But not a single mention of torture or mistreatment of prisoners was made. These admissions of failure are certainly needed today. But will they be able to lead to further examinations of pre-existing cultural attitudes that allowed the enemy to be so thoroughly dehumanized?

The media facilitate the education process long before citizens come to an agreement on how to teach and memorialize the past for posterity. Just as Butler has argued that the grief necessary to contemplate the precariousness of lost lives requires a slowing down process, so too will the reflections on the entire meaning of the ill-conceived war (and its violence and tortures) demand time and thoughtfulness on the part of educators and students. For the critical pedagogy of *torturefest* to be effective, it needs to harness the confidence of citizens to seize their own self-definitions without the lure of mind-numbing assumptions about national ethos and victimization, and without the intimidation of fearing to be either "with us or with the terrorists." More cross-cultural narratives of humanity and suffering are entering the American airwaves, and it will become more difficult to forge distinct lines between us and them, Self and Other, in forthcoming reckonings of the war on terrorism. But one of critical pedagogy's greatest challenges will remain the time-ticking chronopolitics of everyday life, the demand to move faster and faster and to constrict grieving and learning with a view toward enabling a way of life comforted by the presence of a knowledge that is leaner, more manageable, and less subject to time-consuming ethical contemplations.

Notes

1 Sergeant Javal Davis, 372nd Military Police, interviewed in *Ghosts of Abu Ghraib*, dir. Rory Kennedy (HBO, 2007).
2 See A. O. Scott, "A War on Every Screen," *New York Times*, October 28, 2007, available at www.nyt.com/2007/10/28/movies/28scot.html.
3 Ibid., no page given.
4 Peter Travers, quoted in Dan Harris, "The Movies Go to War," *ABC News*, October 28, 2007, available at www.abcnews.go.com.
5 For a critical theoretical perspective, see Paul Virilio, *War and Cinema: The Logics of Perception* (London: Verso, 1989). For works on the use of cinema in the Pacific War, see eds. Abe Mark Nornes and Fukushima Yukio, *The Japan/American Film Wars: World*

War II Propaganda and Its Cultural Contexts (Chur, Switzerland: Harwood Academic Publishers, 1994).
6 Laura Hein and Mark Selden, "The Lessons of War, Global Power and Social Change," in eds. Laura Hein and Mark Selden, *Censoring History: Citizenship and Memory in Japan, Germany, and the United States* (Armonk: M.E. Sharpe, 2000), p. 4.
7 Ibid., p. 4.
8 Julieta Savova, quoted in Falk Pingel, *UNESCO Guidebook on Textbook Research and Textbook Revision* (Paris: UNESCO, 1999), p. 33.
9 I am paraphrasing Senator Graham's testimony to the Armed Services Committee. See Lindsey Graham, quoted in PBS Frontline, *The Torture Question*, dir. Michael Kirk (PBS, 2005), available online at www.pbs.org/wgbh/pages/frontline/torture/view/.
10 Douglas Kellner, *Media Spectacle and the Crisis of Democracy* (Boulder: Paradigm Publishers, 2005), p. 78.
11 Joan Walsh, "The Abu Ghraib Files," *Salon.com*, March 14, 2006, available at www.salon.com/news/abu_ghraib/2006/03/14/introduction/.
12 See Javal Davis, interviewed in *Ghosts of Abu Ghraib*, no page given.
13 See François Debrix, *Tabloid Terror: War, Culture, and Geopolitics* (New York: Routledge, 2008).
14 Judith Butler, *Precarious Life* (London: Verso, 2004), p. 148.
15 James W. Loewen, "The Vietnam War in High School American History," in eds. Hein and Selden, *Censoring History*, pp. 150–72.
16 See "Primetime Torture," available at www.humanrightsfirst.org/us_law/etn/primetime/index.asp. The website also provides extensive resources, including "Tools for Teachers."
17 See also Victoria Brittain and Gillian Slovo, *Guantanamo: Honor Bound to Defend Freedom*. (London: Oberon Books, 2004). Supplementary materials, including a "Study Guide," can be found on the Chicago Timeline Theater's webpage for the play's performance at www.timelinetheatre.com/guantanamo/.
18 See *Ghosts of Abu Ghraib*, dir. Rory Kennedy (HBO Documentary Films, 2007). Supplementary materials can be found at www.hbo.com/docs/programs/ghostsofabughraib/resources.html. They include numerous curriculum guides, voter registration and links to Amnesty International's own site for the film.
19 See *Promise to the Dead: The Exile Journey of Ariel Dorfman*, dir. Peter Raymont (White Pine Pictures, 2007). Educational links here can be found at www.whitepinepictures.com/promise/index.htm.
20 See *The Torture Question*, dir. Michael Kirk (PBS, 2005), available at www.pbs.org/wgbh/pages/frontline/torture/view/. Supplementary materials can be found on this website, including materials expressly marked "For Teachers."
21 See *Taxi to the Dark Side*, dir. Alex Gibney (ThinkFilm, 2007). It is accompanied by a detailed press kit available at www.taxitothedarkside.com. Even more extensive educational resources can be found on the "Why Democracy?" Project website at www.whydemocracy.net/film/4?PHPSESSID=14ce838237bb0287504a84e1b9ed86b0.
22 See *The Battle of Algiers*, dir. Gillo Pontecorvo, DVD (Criterion Collection, 2004 [1966]). Supplementary materials are on the DVD set, including interviews with US government officials, educators, and filmmakers in the light of post-9/11 counterterrorism efforts.
23 See *Rendition*, dir. Gavin Hood (New Line Cinema, 2007). Supplementary materials can be found on the film's webpage under "Worldview," available at www.renditionmovie.com/.
24 See *Road to Guantanamo*, dir. Michael Winterbottom and Mat Whitecross, DVD (Sony Pictures, 2006). Supplementary materials can be found at "Production Notes for Revolution Films, *Road to Guantanamo*," available at thecia.com.au/reviews/r/images/road-to-guantanamo-production-notes.rtf. Amnesty International USA also provides a number of resources for viewing this film.
25 See "Fernando Botero: Abu Ghraib," Center for Latin American Studies, University of California at Berkeley, January 30–March 23, 2007, available at www.socrates.

berkeley.edu:7001/Events/spring2007/01-29-07-boteroopening/index.html. See also Botero's "A Permanent Accusation," January 27, 2007, available at www.youtube.com/watch?v=VoleMx-sxqQ.
26 See John Dower, *War without Mercy: Race and Power in the Pacific War* (New York: Pantheon, 1987); and eds. Nornes and Yukio, *The Japan/American Film Wars*.
27 George W. Bush, "America's New War: Resolve and Remembrance," transcript of the President's speech, September 15, 2001, available at *CNN.com* transcripts, no page given.
28 Butler, *Precarious Life*, p. 146.
29 Paul Virilio, *Speed and Politics: An Essay on Dromology* (London: Verso, 1986).
30 Marc Lee, "*24*—Isn't It Just Torture?" *The Telegraph*, October 1, 2007, available at www.telegraph.co.uk.
31 Mayer, "Whatever It Takes," p. 2.
32 Ibid., p. 2.
33 Patrick J. Buchanan, "What Would Jack Bauer Do?" *WorldNet Daily Commentary*, January 23, 2006, available at www.worldnetdaily.com/news/article.asp?ARTICLE_ID=48457, no page given.
34 Ibid., no page given.
35 Quoted in transcript to "Is Torture on Hit Fox TV Show '24' Encouraging US Soldiers to Abuse Detainees?," *Democracy Now* (Independent Media), February 22, 2007, available at www.democracynow.org.
36 See Human Rights First, "Primetime Torture," no page given.
37 See "Is Torture on Hit Fox TV Show '24'?," no page given.
38 Slavoj Zizek , "Jack Bauer and the Ethics of Urgency," *In These Times*, January 27, 2006, available at www.inthesetimes.com/article/2481/.
39 Hein and Selden, "The Lessons of War," p. 5.
40 See Adorno, quoted in Henry Giroux, *Against the New Authoritarianism: Politics after Abu Ghraib* (Winnipeg: Arbeiter Ring, 2005), p. 141. Along with Giroux, I maintain that the abuses at Abu Ghraib cannot be compared to the singular horrors of Auschwitz. But the tendency of people to willingly go along with the politics and demands of unscrupulous leaders is something that must be addressed through greater awareness of the influence of the media and of the capacity of education to enforce discipline or inspire Adorno's hoped for lessons about reflection. See Giroux, *Against the New Authoritarianism*, p. 136.
41 Human Rights First, "What Can Be Done: Human Rights First's Primetime Torture Project," available at www.humanrightsfirst.org/us_law/etn/primetimc/project.asp.
42 Ariel Dorfman, quoted on the homepage of *Promise to the Dead*, available at www.whitepinepictures.com/promise/Ariel%20Dorfmanctvcacomp.pdf.
43 See Butler, *Precarious Life*, p. 40.
44 Milgram recruited participants and tested their willingness to inflict pain on others when ordered to do so.
45 See Kennedy, Director's Commentary, *Ghosts of Abu Ghraib*.
46 See Botero, "A Permanent Accusation," no page given.
47 Ibid., no page given.
48 See "9/11 Teaching Resources," sidebar to Kathleen Kennedy Manzo, "Teachers Tiptoe into Delicate Topics of 9/11 and Iraq," *Education Week*, September 6, 2006, pp. 1 and 22–4.
49 Ibid., pp. 22–4.
50 Ibid.
51 See Choices Program, *Conflict in Iraq: Searching for Solutions* (Providence: Watson Institute, 2007).
52 See Transcripts to "American Morning," *CNN.com*, June 26, 2007, pp. 5–6, available online.
53 See "Composite Statement of Tipton Three," available at www.ccr-ny.org/v2/legal/september_11th/docs/Guantanamo_composite_statement_FINAL.pdf.
54 Thomas L. Friedman, "Remember Iraq," *New York Times*, October 24, 2007, available at www.nyt.com.

55 See "Anti-War Mom Cindy Sheehan Gives up Her Protest," *CNN.com*, May 29, 2007, available online.
56 Darius Rejali, "Torture: American Style," *The Boston Globe*, December 16, 2007, available at www.boston.com.
57 Naomi Klein, "'Never Before!' Our Amnesiac Torture Debate," December 9, 2005, *The Nation*, available from the CommonDreams.org News Center at www.commondreams.org/views05/1209-22.htm.
58 See Herbert P. Bix, "The Immunity of Non-Combatants and the Myth of Good Intentions: Sixty-One Years after Hiroshima and Nagasaki," *Japan Focus*, August 20, 2006, available at www.japanfocus.org.
59 Ibid., no page given.
60 Michel Foucault, *Discipline and Punish: The Birth of the Prison* (New York: Vintage, 1979), p. 16.
61 Ibid., pp. 115–16.
62 Rejali, "Torture: American Style," no page given.
63 Quoted in Mark Silva, "Cheney: 'We Do Not Torture,' even 'Tougher Customers'," *Baltimoresun.com*, November 2, 2007, available online.
64 L. Paul Bremer III *et al.*, "Reflections on the Invasion of Iraq" (opinion), *New York Times*, March 16, 2008, available online.

5 Designing security

Control society and MoMA's *SAFE: Design Takes on Risk*

Mark J. Lacy

The philosopher Gilles Deleuze describes the emergence of societies of control in a brief essay first published in 1990. The objective of control societies, he argues, is to use new technologies and biopolitical policy instruments to "modulate" bodies, behaviors, markets, territories, buildings, ecologies, battlespaces, networks, and bio-criminals. But it is also to break down the distinction between interior and exterior "sites of confinement." The dream of modular life in control society is to adapt fast to all problems and opportunities that emerge—terrorism, human-generated climate change, new economic practices, global diseases, financial crises, new forms of networked social interactions—in order to, in the words of Michel Foucault, optimize a state of life.[1] Control society combines geopolitical hype(r)-power (as Timothy W. Luke describes it in his chapter in this volume) with increased privatization of safety to form a "biopolitics 2.0." With this combination, new technologies make possible the proliferation of mini-panopticons, individuals become active components in the fabric of control, and "border checks" are found everywhere.[2] As a character in Philip K. Dick's novel *A Scanner Darkly* (an exploration of a future war on drugs) observes:

> Ahead, one of those giant shopping malls surrounded by a wall that you bounced off like a rubber ball—unless you had a credit card on you and passed in through the electronic hoop. Owning no credit card for any of the malls, he could depend only on verbal reports as to what the shops were like inside.[3]

Biopolitical control's desire is to be able to adapt to future problems that emerge from the complexity of control society, and to enhance the ability of communities and individuals to thrive and profit in these risky environments. The management and production of "safe" modular life are the political challenges of control societies.[4]

Obsessed with keeping the future in check, control societies seek techniques to "geo-engineer" a safe future or to devise financial means of profiting from "catastrophic risk."[5] For example, there are projects that are hoping to find ways to adapt to the risk of climate change. Unable to design adequate economic solutions in the present, the focus is no longer simply on resilience (the ability to bring a society/organization quickly back to its previous, pre-accident/catastrophe state).[6] Rather, the concern is now with adaptation,[7] or to modify a state of life. At the level of catastrophic risk, the precautionary principle is supplemented with the adaptation principle.[8] In a scenario that could emerge out of a Michel Houellebecq novel, the most extreme plans suggest that responses to global warming/climate change will involve "bioengineering ourselves and our environment to survive and thrive on an increasingly hot and potentially less hospitable planet."[9] The less "extreme" solutions involve measures such as orbiting mirrors to reduce sunlight reaching the earth, a policy identified by the Intergovernmental Panel on Climate Change.[10] Faced with the possibility of uncontrollable—and unimaginable—futures, contemporary politics is obsessed with the intensification of control society, as if anxiety about the uncertainty of the future could be controlled through an obsessive pursuit of perfect security and control in the present.[11] As William Gibson mentioned in a discussion of his novel *Spook Country*, uncertainty about the future influences his writing. As he put it: "When I wrote my fourth novel, *Virtual Light* [published in 1994], I set it in a very near future—probably about now—to punk things up a bit, not honour the sci-fi rules and write a book that would date terribly. But for my last two books, I have become convinced that it is silly to try to imagine futures these days."[12] Indeed, in *Children of Men*, Alfonso Cuarón decided that the most realistic and convincing way to depict England in the year 2027 was to visualize the future in terms of a society that had stopped developing around the time the film was released (in 2006).[13] The desire for safe life—often taking on exaggerated and obsessive forms—in control society may be a response to this predicament (or uncertainty) about the future. Or, as Zygmunt Bauman comments:

> Governments cannot honestly promise their citizens a secure existence and a certain future; but they may for the time being upload at least part of the accumulated anxiety (and even profit from it electorally) by demonstrating their energy and determination in the war against foreign job-seekers and other alien gate-crashers, intruders into once clean and quiet, orderly and familiar, native backyards.[14]

This chapter is a response to the exhibition *SAFE: Design Takes on Risk* that was featured in 2005 at New York's Museum of Modern Art (MoMA). Museums and art exhibitions are often spaces of cultural and political anxiety over historical memory, contemporary insecurities, and future dangers.[15] On one level, the various projects/products displayed in *SAFE* reflect a concern with obsessive attempts at controlling risk and with anxieties about "designing-out" threats from everyday existence.[16] Many of the pieces or interventions in the exhibition provide examples of what Anthony Dunne and Fiona Raby have described as "design noir."[17] If contemporary design has become analogous to Hollywood blockbusters, then design noir is about challenging "safe" products to bring out other possibilities, thus subverting material objects in order to illuminate alternative choices for living.[18] Design noir aesthetically challenges and disturbs the consumer. The challenge "is to blur the boundaries between the real and the fictional, so that the conceptual becomes more real and the real is seen as just one limited possibility among many."[19] But *SAFE* also illustrates Beatriz Colomina's argument that

> modern architecture is inseparable from war. It recycles the techniques and materials developed for the military. The postwar form of domesticity turns out to

be a powerful weapon. Expertly designed images of domestic bliss are launched throughout the entire world as part of a carefully orchestrated campaign.[20]

Colomina goes on to suggest that, during the Cold War, New York's MoMA played an important role in this campaign. While expressing anxiety over the "militarization" of our domesticity (more than simply showcasing diverse responses to the issue of protection and risk), *SAFE* also illustrates a potential "synergy" between designers and the policy architects of control society. As William Burroughs observed in "The Limits of Control," "[w]hen there is no more opposition, control becomes a meaningless proposition. It is highly questionable whether a human organism could survive complete control."[21] In this sense, control society "modulates" itself too in order to become more acceptable, humane, and seductive. Yet, it is also the case that the imaginary of designer security and the consumption of protection—or the promise of a designer solution to anxiety—may become increasingly important in the re-imagining of security, protection, and progress for an age haunted by images of future insecurity.

Societies of control

In an article initially published in the French daily *Le Monde* in 1978, Deleuze commented on the bombing of South Lebanon since 1969 with the "almost unanimous complicity of other states (with various nuances and restrictions)."[22] He observed that the problem was not simply that Israel thinks "it will defeat the militants by creating more refugees, thereby creating more militants."[23] Rather, the Israeli-Palestinian conflict was becoming a "model that will determine how terrorism will be dealt with elsewhere, even in Europe. The worldwide cooperation of states, and the worldwide organization of police and criminal proceedings, will necessarily lead to a classification extending to more and more people who will be considered virtual 'terrorists'."[24] Deleuze also suggested that the situation was analogous to the Spanish Civil War when Spain served as "an experimental laboratory for a far more terrible future."[25] In another piece titled "Postscript on Control Societies," a brief essay first published in *L'Autre Journal* in 1990,[26] Deleuze begins to outline the logic of the "experimental laboratory" of control.[27] From Deleuze's perspective, societies are moving away from disciplinary society, a formation of power that Foucault associated with European societies from the seventeenth to nineteenth centuries, and that reached its apogee at the beginning of the twentieth century. The disciplinary societies described in Foucault's writings operated through the organization of major sites of confinement. In those, "individuals are always going from one closed society to another, each with its own laws: first of all the family, then school ('you're not at home, you know'), then the barracks ('you're not at home, you know'), then the factory, hospital from time to time, maybe prison, the model of the site of confinement."[28] Commenting that some observers have given the impression that Foucault's analyses of disciplinary society were his "final word" on power and discipline, Deleuze suggests that Foucault was aware that the disciplinary society was not eternal, and he attempted to outline the logic behind a spatial transformation in the organization of control.[29] Deleuze's contention is that, while we may live with the remnants of disciplinary society for years to come, we need to recognize that we are now moving toward "control societies," a term he draws from Burroughs' work (incidentally, Deleuze notes Foucault's "deep admiration" for Burroughs' writings).[30]

To be clear, by writing that we are moving towards control societies, Deleuze is not suggesting that disciplinary societies were not concerned with "controlling" individuals and populations. But what is significant in control societies is that the "interior is breaking down."[31] Control societies have the potential to unfold in a manner that those "who are concerned with our welfare no longer need, or will need, places of confinement."[32] Deleuze observes that the future prisons, schools, and hospitals are already places of "permanent discussion" (he notes, in particular, the expansion of home visits by doctors, new technologies of incarceration, or working from home). For workers in control society, "instant communication" means that the sites of confinement are breaking down so that workers are potentially always available to work. More broadly, capitalism is moving towards a system of "metaproduction" where businesses market finished products from dispersed systems of producers (often in the Third World) that exist in constant competition with one another. One of Deleuze's primary ethico-political concerns is that the transformation of the "old factory system" into metaproduction—and into a dispersed system of "sites of confinement" that depend on technologies of control/instant communication for their efficient operation—could limit resistance to economic practices.[33] Marketing and branding—the design of the corporate image—take the seduction of consumerism to new levels. As Deleuze puts it: "We're told businesses have souls, which is surely the most terrifying news in the world."[34] Equally disturbing for Deleuze is the fact that these developments are presented in terms of "new freedoms" that are actually contributing to "mechanisms of control as rigorous as the harshest confinements."[35] He reflects that we might come to see the "harshest confinement as part of a wonderful happy past" (I will return to this line of inquiry in the conclusion to this chapter).[36] From Deleuze's perspective, disciplinary societies began to break down after World War II, with developments in the "third generation of machines" (computers, information technologies) and with the emergence of "amazing pharmaceutical products, nuclear technologies, and genetic engineering."[37] Control of the genetic code and the "potential of silicon in third generation machines" now create the possibility of a "practically unlimited diversity of combinations."[38]

The emergence of control society did precede 9/11. But the Global War on Terror, along with the fear of crime or of the "dangerous classes," are currently two of the key driving forces that are breaking down the divide between interior and exterior spaces of control and confinement in the name of new freedoms and new securities. To give an example of one of the many ways the interior is breaking down, since 9/11, there has been an emphasis on airports deploying new biometric technologies (such as Privium) to make moving through airports safer and faster.[39] These technologies are presented as major leaps forward in the way we will be able to move through airports, and as new freedoms: no more waiting in long lines; more time to hook up your wireless devices or computers to networks and check your emails. The space of the airport becomes less exceptional, designed to be more like the home or work, and conceived more like a hotel or a shopping mall, with all sorts of services for business or relaxation. At the same time, the airport also becomes less exceptional because all spaces—including security systems inside homes or office buildings—have the potential to become more like airports.[40] Indeed, discussion in the media of plans to make traveling on trains subject to the same types of technologies used in air travel was noticeable after the events of 7/7 in London. It is in this sense that Deleuze suggests that control society will depend less on sites of confinement because everywhere will become part of systems of control, driven by the desire to fight all types of risks and insecurities. To be sure, there are—and most likely will continue to be—sites of confinement for those who are detected as "untrustworthy" travelers. But their significance could decrease as new technologies control and police movements. In fact, moving will be harder without access to the correct codes.

A crude vision of what "disciplinary society" looked like has been depicted in many cinematic visions about the future. For example, in George Lucas's 1970 film *THX 1138*, humans are depicted to live in a carefully controlled and policed underground city/prison where every move is subject to surveillance and visceral reminders of authority, from one site of confinement to the next, abound. At home, individuals are sedated with drugs and televised spectacles of punishment or sex. *THX 1138* shows how an individual undertakes to escape from this "society of surveillance" to reach the outside world, a space that—for reasons that are not explained—remains beyond the control of the police state. Indeed, in many sci-fi films, the key issue is how to escape disciplinary societies and their surveillance. In Steven Spielberg's *Minority Report*, Tom Cruise's character has to remove his eyes in order to avoid biometric control. In all those films, there is an interior that can (has to) be escaped *from*. Indeed, these futuristic visions are almost nostalgic in their depictions of a disciplinary society that nonetheless keeps an exterior as a possibility of freedom. Many futuristic films intensify aspects of the present and place them in the future (for example, the Abu Ghraib-like prisons on the United Kingdom borders in *Children of Men*). At the same time, cinematic imaginings of the future contribute to the shape of the present and illustrate potentials that remain unexplored. *Blade Runner* (1982), for example, influenced many aspects of contemporary popular culture.[41] But cinematic depictions of the future also play a role in creating anxiety about and dialogue on what we do not want the future to be like. Thus, cinema becomes an "experimental laboratory" that forms ideas about what types of technologies and architectures are undesirable.

Deleuze observes that we do not "have to stray into science fiction to find control mechanisms that can fix the position of any element at any given moment—an animal in a game reserve, a man in a business (electronic tagging)."[42] Indeed, rather than science fiction movies like *THX 1138*, it is perhaps contemporary television police dramas that best capture the desires of control society (and may constitute a form of policing through televisual-deterrence and through an exaggeration of the current capabilities of many technologies, or what we may call the "CSI effect") to develop "ceaseless control in open sites."[43] The television series *CSI: Crime Scene Investigation*, for example, constantly demonstrates the potential of new technologies of policing and control. All movements leave traces (DNA, credit card transactions, and images on CCTV cameras), *CSI* intimates, and so there is literally nowhere to escape to and no way to commit the perfect crime.

What I want to focus on in the rest of this chapter is the issue of the design of control society (something that popular TV shows today highlight but do not question). Once again, Deleuze writes about control society in terms of the "harshest confinement." But, in Deleuze's work, we do not get a sense of what life in control society could feel or look like, of how technologies of control could blend into our habitats, or of how control itself could enfold our bodies, thus endo-colonizing our lives.[44] Deleuze does explain that the logic that results in the interior and exterior distinction is breaking down. We fill in the blanks with the austere and brutal images of policing and control depicted in the works of Burroughs (with his sinister "control men") or Dick, or in films such as *Minority Report, Blade Runner, THX 1138*, or *Children of Men*. Or, maybe, we imagine the future in terms of the almost silent and invisible Privium-like technologies of airport control. This is undoubtedly the dream of those designing the future of societies of control.[45] But what if the aesthetics of control that is breaking down the distinction between interior and exterior spaces is unfolding in a fashion that is different from the dystopic visions we are so familiar with? Steven Shaviro provides an interesting commentary on control society in his book *Connected*. In a move that makes some problematic assumptions about the relationship between the visual and the tactile, Shaviro nonetheless notes that, today, "control is less visual than tactile. It invites our hands-on participation."[46]

Designing security: *SAFE: Design Takes on Risk*

The plans for *SAFE: Design Takes on Risk* began in March 2001 under the title *Emergency*. The exhibition was intended to focus on "emergency-response equipment and tools."[47] A decision was made after 9/11 to shelve the exhibition, but those who knew about the plans expressed a desire to keep it moving by focusing instead on the themes of safety and design.[48] The resulting exhibition at MoMA in 2005 was concerned with showing how different designers around the planet responded to the desire to make life less risky or less anxious, thus protecting our bodies and emotions as well as enabling us to live with what curator Paola Antonelli describes (in her essay in the MoMA volume that accompanies the *SAFE* exhibit) as "grace under pressure." In an interview included in the *SAFE* volume, Cameron Sinclair, the founder of *Architects for Humanity*, discusses research on internally displaced people in Kosovo. Various designers worked on five-to-ten-year transitional shelters that could be placed in lands where people lived before being displaced. People could live in the shelters while their communities were being rebuilt, thus giving the opportunity for people to restart everything by using "their own vernacular."[49] Sinclair commented:

> It was very important that we had an equal number of relief experts and designers, in order to achieve a balance between ethics and aesthetics. By the end of the jury session, those who had come in from the relief world began embracing the aesthetics of the projects, and the architects started talking about the critical needs of the people and not as much about aesthetics, realizing the issues were equally important.[50]

SAFE includes many design solutions needed to manage or aid the "bare life" (as Giorgio Agamben puts it) that exists in zones of emergency, and to facilitate adaptation to disaster and poverty.[51] As Deleuze notes, capitalism still keeps two-thirds of all the people in the world in extreme poverty, people who are "too numerous to have debts and too numerous to be confined."[52] Control will have to deal not only with "vanishing frontiers," but also with "mushrooming shantytowns and ghettos."[53] Among *SAFE*'s innovative design solutions are the "Global Village Shelter," the "Shapla Arsenic Removal Filter," the "Safe Sari," the Freeplay Foundation and Freeplay Energy plc. "Lifeline Radio," and the "Spider Boot Antipersonnel Mine Foot Protection System." Of course, from the perspective of Agamben's "bare life," these are the kind of projects that can illustrate the separation between humanitarianism and politics, and can maintain "a secret solidarity with the very powers they ought to fight."[54] But difficult ethico-political questions about the "humanitarian paradox" in *SAFE* are not asked. *SAFE* leaves many of these questions outside the domain of critical interrogation of design taking on risk. To the extent that ethico-political questions emerge in *SAFE*, they appear only in the examination of design in the "tame zones" of modern life, a move that reinforces the depoliticization of the "natural" disaster areas of global life.

The projects mentioned above, however, are juxtaposed to other critical aesthetic and design interventions on the issue of obsession with safety and risk in control society. This is well exemplified through the project, "How to Disappear Kit and Vending Machine," created by an interdisciplinary design team based in Denmark. This intervention seeks to comment on the problem of living in an information/surveillance society. The kit can be purchased from vending machines, and it instructs consumers on ways to dodge surveillance (offering them a selection of "disappearance gadgets"). Perhaps concerned that the kit will be viewed as subversive or even dangerous, we are told by *SAFE*'s curators that, "[a]t once humorous and critical, the kit urges the user not to disappear but rather to take an active role in social debate."[55] *SAFE* also showcases the "Securitree" by Torolab from Mexico. This piece is a metal tree of surveillance cameras that was designed as part of a project intended to provoke people to think about questions of policing, wealth, and inequality. In *SAFE*, we also find the "paraSITE" homeless shelter that exploits the energy of a "host" building and is thought of as a form of social protest by way of placing objects in locations where people would rather not see them.

As important as these critical design interventions are for issues of control and surveillance, what *SAFE* begins to outline through these pieces is the potential for a design-control complex to evolve or mutate with the innovative and more critical concerns of contemporary designers. Just as societies of control attempt to capture bodies, diseases, machines, or information that produce risks for safe life, so the logic of control seeks to capture developments seemingly on the "exterior" in order to better "modulate," refine, or control. Even supposedly "critical" or "counter-cultural" design responses to contemporary life can become part of control society. Everything can be (re)captured. Indeed, in the introductory essay to the *SAFE* exhibit volume, Antonelli places the philosophy of Heidegger (who raised disturbing questions about technology) next to the Kabbalah (popularized through celebrities such as Madonna), thus suggesting that design plays a role in the normalization of "disruptive change." As she puts it:

> The idea that displacement, sometimes even destruction, is necessary for progress

can be found in many schools of thought across the centuries, from Heraclitus and the Kabbalah, all the way to Martin Heidegger. Designers are trained to balance risk-taking with protection, and to mediate between disruptive change and normalcy. They make revolutions viable, understandable, and accessible for other human beings.[56]

Body-armor

SAFE is organized around six main themes: shelter; armor; property; everyday; emergency; and awareness. Each theme seeks to break down the distinction between interior and exterior and illustrates the "composite possibilities" of technologies and materials. Again, one of the key points made by Deleuze is that control is "a *modulation*, like a self-transmuting molding continually changing from one moment to the next, or like a sieve whose mesh varies from one point to the next."[57] An everyday illustration of this would be the modulation of movement made possible by automated bollards that control flows of traffic. For example, the UK's City of Manchester government announced that "in Manchester City Centre, a number of streets have automated bollards to control access. Access is restricted to authorised users only, for security purposes. There are strict criteria to be met when applying for a key card."[58] Armed with the correct codes and key cards, anyone can move quickly through city center streets whose points of entry are not fixed but, rather, parts of a "universal modulation." The design of control society is making possible the creation of products that enable fast transformation in our body-armor so that we can cope with all types of risks and insecurities. As Antonelli asserts: "Today, the simple need for protection has mutated into the complex universe we call fashion."[59] It is not simply a case of adapting our behavior in "risk society." But we can now adapt our own "armor" for the purpose of safe living:

> Advances in technology have opened up many composite possibilities, especially with the introduction of insulating gels, fiber composites, and new fibers such as Kevlar or Gore-tex. This progress has made armor lighter and more flexible, hence allowing for more freedom of movement and agility, an important feature when a rapid escape becomes necessary in case of an emergency. Moreover, the possibility of infusing chemical properties in the materials themselves has brought about antibacterial and SPF fabrics, to name just a few of the many areas of innovation.[60]

SAFE includes the work of the fashion designers who have created the "Killing Zone Shirts," shirts that incorporate a variety of materials such as metal foil and swan feathers to add ballistic protection to everyday clothing.[61] There is also the "Bazooka Joe" sweater, a pullover from the Bezalel Academy of Art and Design in Jerusalem that integrates filters and values for transformation into "emergency mode." We can also find in SAFE the "Subtle Safety Defensive Ring." This ring is both a fashion accessory and a weapon. As Antonelli explains, "the ring is an alternative solution to the recommended practice of a woman placing her keys between her fingers in case of an attack."[62] Antonelli further notes that "security is a complex system that

96 M. J. Lacy

needs to be addressed dynamically, by building it into several 'security valves,' and especially by allowing for human discretion and intervention."[63] Thus, security is individualized, made flexible, light, and, of course, modular. In his essay on "Design for Destruction," Phil Patton mentions that, during the 1950s, when American cars were designed for the "most aggressive forms of external protection," European automobile manufacturers began to explore the "crumple zone," resulting from the evidence that "the stronger the body, the more the energy of a collision was transmitted to people inside."[64] The security of heavy modernity—defensive shields against Cold War threats, bunkers to survive a nuclear war, or prisons to confine the dangerous classes—has now mutated into the technologies of what Bauman refers to as "liquid modernity."[65] Indeed, as Antonelli informs us, "the recent argument against SUVs interestingly points to the existence of passive and active safety, and shows how misguided we can be in our attempt to find safety in size and mass rather than the ability to escape a crash by rapidly swerving a smaller, lighter car out of the way."[66] Once again, good design today is about "grace under pressure," not about the hard and industrial aesthetics of policing and discipline. It is what we can call a "zen" security. "Disciplinary man," Deleuze observes, "produced energy in discrete amounts, while control man undulates, moving among a continuous range of different orbits. *Surfing* has taken over from the old *sports*."[67]

Our modular bodies and accessories should be able to adapt to risks with increasing speed. At home, the "interior" can be designed with products that are "beautiful and meaningful" but that can also provide safety and emotional or psychological security.[68] Again, the composite possibilities of new technologies create a variety of design objects for safe living. For example, the section of *SAFE* on "Shelter" includes Futurefarmer's "Homeland Security Blanket," an experiment in *communectivity*. This product operates as follows: "As a means to 'disseminate information,' these blankets disseminate temperature change and an indicating light ... alerts the user of current threat and comforts them accordingly."[69] The idea is that one can be curled up under a blanket and one will be able to feel changes in the government's level of alert. One can literally wrap one's body into "safety." One website showcasing these blankets declares: "Think of this as an electric blanket on night patrol. The next feature we'd like to see is a support to turn this into a portable fallout shelter."[70] The "Homeland Security Blanket" may be an ironic comment on the breaking down of the interior and the exterior. But it gives us a sense of how fashion and *communectivity* can co-evolve and permeate our most intimate environments.

Interior design

The section of *SAFE* on "Property" includes a number of works by Matthias Megyeri, a designer known for his "Sweet Dreams Security" project. Megyeri's products in the MoMA exhibit include the "Mr. Smish and Madame Buttly Razor Wire," the piece that serves as the main logo for the entire *SAFE* show (it is also displayed on the cover of the accompanying catalog). This particular product is a barbed wire made up of small but blunt looking metal butterflies. *SAFE* also showcases Megyeri's "Landscape Glass Objects," a series of sharp recycled glass pieces designed to adorn garden walls. The "Sweet Dreams Security" project has been described as a "comment on the growing demand for security in our modern culture, mixed with the saturation of exaggerated niceness in everything that surrounds us: iron railings with bunny rabbits for posts; barbed wire with angular butterflies and fish; personalized, sharp glass shards to top a brick wall; heart-shaped ring chains with teddy bear padlocks; catlike CCTV cameras with bat wings; and burglar-alarm boxes crowned with daisies."[71] But the irony of the project is left rather ambiguous by Antonelli. She writes: "The resulting products merged the need for protection with the desire for beauty, redefining padlocks, fences and razor wire as lovable objects."[72]

Another important project in the exhibit, Olivier Peyricot's "Vigilhome," begins with a declaration from the designer that, "because of our fears, modern comfort will be combative, in kit form, claustrophobic."[73] Peyricot's contribution to *SAFE* is a shelter fully equipped for a "paranoid survivalist." The shelter contains absurdly large boxes of cereals and pills to fight hunger and stress, along with bright red gun-shaped toolboxes that look like children's plastic toys but contain everyday utensils. The accompanying commentary suggests that the "Vigilhome" "is an exaggerated solution for comfort, safety, and well-being, and a support to help one overcome paranoid perceptions of reality. Peyricot understands the contemporary dangers in progressive isolation, and translates the threat into a real battle against one's self and the outside world."[74] The irony here is obvious. Indeed, "the Vigilhome was designed with a large audience and all kinds of demands in mind."[75] Peyricot's work is a comment on the infantilization of control society, that is to say, on the potential for control to infantilize us with products that provide illusions of control and security, and perhaps are designed with a childlike and "fun" aesthetic (absurd examples of this are the "Power Pizza," a laptop protective case disguised as an Italian style pizza box, or the "Hello Kitty SARS masks," protective masks with cartoon characters on them).

In another essay found in the *SAFE* exhibition volume, Susan Yelavich makes it clear that private spaces—the "realm of the interior"—were accorded a special status in the MoMA show. Yelavich writes that, "[n]o matter how transparent the walls, they still retain the powerful memory of defense against threat."[76] For Yelavich, there is a growing convergence in design cultures between the "fringe" and the "mainstream," one that is moving "even faster now that the primal fascination with the arc of the dome thrives in tandem with the new capabilities of the computer to morph the box into a vortex of curves."[77] Framing her position in such terms as "primal fascination" or "organic morphologies," Yelavich proceeds to show how the womb ("our first piece of real estate") is driving design culture, as exemplified in works that focus on "nature and the spaces of nurture." Among these projects are Javier Senosian Aguilar's "Shark-shaped House" (a piece that highlights the "umbilical relationships of the house to the land,"[78] with furniture integrated into the architecture so one can "recline like an animal in a cave"), Frank Gehry's attempt at developing a "biomorphic architecture" with modern materials, and other works that use software designed for animation in order to transpose the language of the "curve" from nature into urban apartments. Thus, Yelavich writes about surveillance in the home in terms of "intrusions" that are "simply a kinder, gentler iteration of Jeremy Bentham's Panopticon—a prison design with a central tower to give wardens a 360 degree view of their prisoners while remaining invisible to them."[79] Yelavich further argues that we may become "schizophrenic" in such a design setting (that induces a "kind of design hypochondria"). While we want protective devices "benignly woven into the fabric of our daily lives," we also seek protection from "acts of God and war" not covered by the "average insurance policy."[80] The composite possibilities of design make possible our immersion in ecologies of control.[81]

Exterior design

There is also a sense of anxiety in *SAFE* about designs for safe living in the "exterior" domain. Our home, according to Yelavich, should be our secure "womb." And the visual impact of architectures of protection in public spaces should be minimized. Yelavich points to the Archer Courts' housing project in Chicago that had the "luxury of moving the stigma of chain link" (something that, she notes, was also used by Gehry as a "metaphorical conceit" in his own house). Fencing was stripped away from this housing project because it made the buildings' corridors look like prison cellblocks. Yelavich comments that this removal of fencing replaced an atmosphere of danger with an "aura of safety and the pleasure and dignity that comes from recognizing that the space is designed, not just maintained."[82] It is important to note, however, that these changes were made in tandem with the implementation of new systems of protection such as buzzers, security locks, and surveillance cameras. But, for Yelavich, the removal of fencing demonstrates the "ability of design language to express that safeness without the infantilizing systems that society so often reverts to in moments of panic."[83] People should not be made to feel as if they inhabit a prison-like environment of control and surveillance. Yelavich concludes:

> Whether womb or tower, bunker or spire, the job of design is to create nests people can leave as well as return to. Otherwise, we will make no culture to defend, and we will deprive ourselves of the culture we thrive on – the culture of design. If we are not to be infantilized by fearmongers, design must be understood as both shelter from danger and amulet against its inevitability. Uncertainty has many virtues: it breeds iconoclasm, opening up space for the personal, the crafted, and most thankfully, in our paved-over world, the unpredictable.[84]

Thus, our modular bodies can be secured with the composite possibilities of new technologies. Our homes can be "endo-colonized" (to use Paul Virilio's term) through increasingly powerful technologies of surveillance and protection. At the same time, the aesthetic of control is about reducing the visual impact of policing in the environments we move through. It is in this sense that the distinction between the exterior and the interior breaks down, with technologies of control benignly woven into our lives. For example, the "Help Point for the New York Subway" project is designed to enable 24/7 contact with security personnel, and its compact design makes it less prone to vandalism. It has incorporated "a blue LED into its intercom in an attempt to provide a sense of safety and security in a manner that is not obtrusive during everyday activities, but is recognizable during an emergency."[85] Urban environments become modular in the same way bodies are. They too become ready for fast transformation into protective mode. There is a number of such urban environments' "modular" objects in *SAFE*: for example, Philippe Million's "Barrier Bench" (a bench that can be turned quickly into a defensive barrier).[86] One can also find the "Mojo Barrier" designed for music concerts. It remains upright because of the weight of the crowd, but can collapse in the event of a stampede. Other projects of this kind include the "Obelisk Security Bollards" and the "NoGo Barrier" (prepared for the New York Financial District Streetscape and Security Design project), two sculptures that are specifically designed to merge into the streetscape.

Even the most vulnerable elements of society can be benignly integrated through design into the urban environment in a manner that makes an aesthetic contribution to the landscape of the city. Alongside work on design solutions for emergencies around the planet, *SAFE* also incorporates works on homelessness, such as Lucy Orta's "Refugee Wear Intervention" piece, featuring protective clothing for homeless people. We find a rather similar product in Cameron McNall and Damon Seeley's prototype for "Urban Nomad Shelter Inflatable Homeless Shelter." This design project is presented in a photo of a city parking lot filled with those shelters, all in bright different colors. What is interesting here is that, at the same time that the shelters are made to look like a comfortable environment for the homeless (or "urban nomads"), the tactile qualities of the PVC materials with nylon-reinforced bases, along with the various colors, create a unique viewing experience. This combination makes the city scene look more intriguing and vibrant (the point where situationism and homelessness meet, in a way). Indeed, this piece makes being an "urban nomad" fun, as childhood desires or memories of camping and exploring are now transposed to the city. Of course, this product is unlikely to offer a global solution to homelessness. But the logic behind the product reveals a potentially powerful logic in the design of control society: making urban environments seductive and safe by removing industrial harshness or visual pollution from them through an almost childlike focus on colors, fun and interesting materials, and shapes. Here, the increased complexity of "silent" technologies of surveillance and control is mirrored by an increased emphasis on an infantilization of design that is actively embraced and openly celebrated.

SAFE also displays design products that respond to the issues of protest and policing. Here, designers are clearly concerned with resisting military/policing technologies, and with intensifying the spectacle as a component of contemporary resistance. For example, Ralph Borland's "Suited for Subversion" project is a "civil disobedience suit" supposed to be worn by protestors in order to avoid being hit by police batons. This insect-like bright red "bubble" is intended as a conceptual statement on the risks faced by protestors, and the idea of it is drawn from the "white overall" tactics and theatrics of Ya Basta or Tute Bianche (that Michael Hardt and Antonio Negri talk about).[87] "Suited for Subversion" also has a camera that is mounted over the head to record police actions. The system transmits a signal directly to an external source, thus avoiding the problem of confiscation of film or information by the police. Moreover, the suit contains a speaker that can amplify the sound of the wearer's heartbeat. This creates the impression of a swarm of bright red insect people. In a group situation, when many people are wearing this suit, "one would hear heartbeats increasing as tension and excitement mount, like a natural soundtrack arousing the crowd."[88] But Antonelli adds that, "at the same time, the heartbeat exposes the vulnerability of the individual. The fragility of the human body is exploited as a tool, a shield, almost as a weapon, against police munitions."[89] Although it is a comment on state and corporate power, this product also points to the potential of design in control society. Tactile, colorful, and childlike materials in design are combined with the latest network information technologies. But it also illustrates an important point about the logic of surveillance in control society: surveillance will not simply be centralized anymore; rather, it will become *molecular*. In this fashion, we can all be components in the fabric of control. And everything should be visible, like the transparent plastic bags hung from steel rings in Paris and designed as a response to bomb scares.[90]

Concluding remarks

There is often a misunderstanding about Deleuze's comments on control society. To talk about living in control society, some argue, is to declare that we are experiencing an Orwellian nightmare where resistance is futile. Control society becomes the equivalent of the "iron cage" of heavy modernity. To be sure, Deleuze was concerned with the "ceaseless control" found in open sites and with the constant communication potentials some of us have to live with. But the desire for control actually creates new problems. As Deleuze puts it:

> It's true that, even before control societies are fully in place, forms of delinquency or resistance (two different things) are also appearing. Computer piracy and viruses, for example, will replace strikes and what the nineteenth century called "sabotage" ("clogging" the machinery) ... The key thing may be to create vacuoles of noncommunication, circuit breakers, so we can elude control.[91]

Control societies are obsessed with the constant search for control and security by way of design. The complexity of control creates unintended consequences, with new forms of vulnerability and insecurity. Yet, it is precisely this promise of design security and control that has become such a powerful political fantasy, particularly after 9/11. Carolyn Nordstrom writes that, if "you want to believe in security, don't visit ports. A journey to these borderlands shows that security is an illusion." She adds: "[t]he notion of security is the magician's trick: smoke and mirrors, with a good dose of misdirection."[92] Nordstrom indicates that the "formal voice" of security becomes a mantra made up of reassuring words that are meant to silence anxieties about the ports so that goods can continue to enter the United States. Faced with so many official declarations about security, she notes how she had to remind herself about all the evidence she had accumulated that actually exposed the gap between reality and rhetoric.[93] Thus, control today is no longer the "iron cage" depicted in *THX 1138*, for example. It is rather the more messy world of the type of surveillance depicted in the HBO police drama series *The Wire*,[94] with police forces faced with financial constraints, corruption, bureaucratic inertia, and networks of organized crime that constantly adapt to new forms of control. Societies of control are faced with constant reminders about the fragility of their intended control and about the limits of their ability to capture the future. In these societies, we know that, while we can have more long-term and more complex biopolitical projections of our security and safety, we also live with a political economy of protection that remains geared towards the short-term, based on dreams of hype-power (as Luke puts it in his chapter in this volume), and reliant on the mantras of security and pharmacotic war (as described in Larry N. George's chapter). Deleuze, once again, declares that:

> Control is short-term and rapidly shifting, but at the same time continuous and unbounded, whereas discipline was long-term, infinite, and discontinuous ... One thing, it's true hasn't changed—capitalism still keeps three quarters of humanity in extreme poverty, too poor to have debts and too numerous to be confined: control will have to deal not with vanishing frontiers, but with mushrooming shantytowns.[95]

At the same time, there are and will continue to be resistances to technologies of control. In 2003, Benetton announced that it would weave radio frequency identity (RFid) chips from Royal Philips electronics into its clothes in order to track the worldwide movement of its products. These chips were intended to enable faster and more efficient scanning of deliveries, more personalized customer service, and better protection from theft or bootlegging.[96] The "Boycott Benetton" campaign responded to this RFid chips project with satires of Benetton's infamous advertising campaigns that would use slogans like "I'd rather go naked." The satirical ads would state that, "[i]n the future, it may be impossible to go anywhere without a complete history of your travels being recorded by RFid tag readers."[97] The media attention created by that resistant strategy resulted in Benetton abandoning the chips scheme (although the company suggested that it may still use the RFid chips in the future).[98]

The breakdown of the interior-exterior divide increasingly may be orchestrated by individuals or families who can create ecologies of control that are not centralized. For example, there are now products designed to secure animals and children. A company like PetsMobility produces the "PetsCell," a "revolutionary waterproof A-GPS CDMA cell phone for your Pet" (as the company puts it). PetsMobility declares that

> there's no hiding with the PetsCell™. You can locate a pet in places where traditional GPS does not work, like in homes, garages or under foliage where scared or curious animals will likely venture. Establish a remote programmable geofence around a yard or campus, and use handy notification features that alert your cell phone when a breach occurs.[99]

But one can also find a number of product solutions that enable control and surveillance of children. Another company, Alltrack USA, has developed cellular wireless networks that allow you to track the location of your vehicle at all times and in "real time." Alltrack's selling point is that these devices are particularly useful for parents who want to check their kids' whereabouts. As Alltrack states: "This means you can see your teen's car from anywhere in the world, including while at home, at work, on a business trip or on vacation."[100] "Real time" tracking like this can alert you when "up to 10 predefined boundaries have been crossed," but it can also inform you of the vehicle's speed.[101]

Governments around the world increasingly base their authority on the promise of delivering efficient societies of control that can design safe life. In the United Kingdom, a government report titled *Building on Progress: Security, Crime and Justice* set out to use new technologies to manage crime and terror (in particular, to create a more complex and thorough biometric identity management system). One such suggested technology involves awareness campaigns and aims at developing partnerships with business communities in order to "crime-proof their products, services and processes to the highest standards. One example could be introducing fingerprint activation of MP3 players."[102] In November 2007, Prime Minister Gordon Brown pursued this theme in a speech to the House of Commons in which he described the steps taken to make all institutions more vigilant and resilient. Brown insisted on the idea of the modulation of activity through targets. Or, as he put it, "[f]rom now on, local authorities will be required as part of their performance framework to assess the measures they have taken to protect against terrorism."[103] Further, 160 British counter-terrorism advisers will train civilians to use CCTV footage more effectively and to identify suspicious activity. "We will now work with architects and planners to encourage them to 'design-in' protective security measures into new buildings, including safe areas, traffic control measures and the use of blast resistant materials," announced Brown.[104] The promise of "designing-in" protective measures will most likely continue to be an important part of the language of security in countries concerned with terror and crime.

This rhetoric about "designing-in" protection is a response to the management of the war on terror and to the sense that the official language of security needs to be reworked. In a recent issue of *The American Interest*, Joseph Nye and Richard Armitage introduce the term "smart power."[105] This is a new vision of security that the citizenry supposedly desires: no unnecessary wars but, instead, a security system that draws on the smartest innovations in the informational economies of network society, benefits from the smart use of new technologies to control terrorism and design-in protection, and facilitates the circulation of goods and people through new forms of control. In the United States, Al Gore had already deployed a notion of "smart growth" in his 2000 presidential campaign in the context of urban sprawl and climate change. Post-9/11, "smart power" has been retrofitted to describe both a foreign and a domestic policy that desires control through the designing-in of protection and the redesigning of the security brand of the United States.

In the future politics will increasingly be concerned with balancing the desire for control and designing-out insecurity against future anxieties. In the United States, visions of safe life in control society will be constantly haunted by images of future destruction that propagate throughout popular TV shows such as *Heroes*, *Southland Tales*, or *24*. With the help of such representations, the official language of security is and will be about keeping all those fears under control through the corollary promise of more "control society," a society designed for "grace under pressure," once again. As Jacques Derrida observed, fears of nanotechnology are based on their invisibility and their potentially uncontrollable nature. He wrote that "[t]hey are the micrological rivals of microbes and bacteria. Yet our unconscious is already aware of this; it already knows it, and that's what's scary."[106] The other side of this equation may be, however, that the promise of control society does provide hope against all sorts of anxieties. At some level, we want to believe in control society, in the promises embodied in biometric iPods or in the Homeland Security blanket. We want to feel that a society of or with control is possible, so that it can erase the fear of apocalyptic terror attacks. Jürgen Habermas commented that, after 9/11, we began to "recognize the central importance the towers held in the popular imagination, and the irreplaceable imprint on the Manhattan skyline and their powerful embodiment of economic strength and projection toward the future."[107] If the images of future destruction that haunt US culture (mostly) become a reality again, that destruction will be perceived as an attack on the desires and promises of control society that have surfaced after 9/11 (and are now articulated in the official language of security and often illustrated through art or design exhibitions like *SAFE*). The promise of control and of designing security renews our "projection toward the future." Thus, such a promise plays a larger role in the contemporary imaginary of security politics than we realize. And it is unclear what type of politics could emerge from an attack on a society that has "designed-in" its protection, and what measures would be required to recreate additional projections toward the future.

Notes

I would like to thank the following for their comments on this chapter: Paolo Palladino, Cindy Weber, Debbie Lisle, Bulent Diken, Nayanika Mookherjee, François Debrix, Mick Dillon, and Peter Wilkin.

1 Michel Foucault, *"Society Must Be Defended"* (London: Penguin, 2004).
2 On the dissemination of border controls, see Mathew Coleman's chapter in this volume. On the proliferation of multiple mini-surveillance regimes, see Geoffrey Whitehall's chapter also in this volume.
3 See Phillip K. Dick, *A Scanner Darkly* (London: Gollanz, 2006), p. 6.
4 On the topic of "modularity," see Zygmunt Bauman, *In Search of Politics* (Cambridge: Polity, 1999), pp. 157–61. Ethico-political questions with regards to this new biopolitics of control have been raised by many academics concerned with international relations/security studies. See, in particular, Louise Amoore, "Biometric Borders: Governing Mobilities in the War on Terror," *Political Geography*, Vol. 25, No. 3 (2006), pp. 336–51; Louise Amoore, "Vigilant Visualities: The Watchful Politics of the War on Terror," *Security Dialogue*, Vol. 38, No. 2 (2007), pp. 215–32; William Bogard, *The Simulation of Surveillance: Hypercontrol in Telematic Societies* (Cambridge: Cambridge University Press, 1996); Didier Bigo, "Security and Immigration: Toward a Critique of the Governmentality of Unease," *Alternatives*, Vol. 27, No. 1 (2002), pp. 63–92; Phillipe Bonditti, "From Territorial Space to Networks: A Foucauldian Approach to the Implementation of Biometry," *Alternatives*, Vol. 29, No. 4 (2004), pp. 465–82; Elizabeth Dauphinee and Cristina Masters, *The Logics of Biopower and the War on Terror* (London: Palgrave, 2007); Bulent Diken and Carsten Lausten, *Culture of Exception: Sociology Faces the Camp* (London: Routledge, 2005); Michael Dillon, "Virtual Security: A Life Science of (Dis)Order," *Millennium*, Vol. 32, No. 3 (2003), pp. 531–58; Jef Huysmans, Andrew Dobson, and Raia Prokhovnik, *The Politics of Protection: Sites of Insecurity and Political Agency* (London: Routledge, 2006); Julian Reid, *The Biopolitics of the War on Terror: Life Struggles, Liberal Modernity and the Defence of Logistical Life* (Manchester: Manchester University Press, 2006); and Cynthia Weber, "Designing Safe Citizens," *Citizenship Studies*, Vol. 12, No. 2 (2008), pp. 125–42.
5 See Philip Bougen, "Catastrophe Risk," *Economy and Society*, Vol. 32, No. 2 (2003), pp. 253–74.
6 See Yossi Sheffi, *The Resilient Enterprise: Overcoming Vulnerability for Competitive Advantage* (Cambridge, MA: MIT Press, 2007).

7 See Mark Lacy, *Security and Climate Change: International Relations and the Limits of Realism* (London: Routledge, 2005).
8 François Ewald, "Two Infinities of Risk," in ed. Brian Massumi, *The Politics of Everyday Fear* (Minneapolis: University of Minnesota Press, 1993), pp. 221–8.
9 Cited in Bill McKibben, "Can Anyone Stop it?," *The New York Review of Books*, October 11, 2007, p. 40.
10 Robin McKie and Juliette Jowitt, "Can Science Really Save the World?" *The Observer*, October 7, 2007; available at observer.guardian.co.uk/focus/story/0,,2185343,00.html.
11 See ed. Brian Massumi, *The Politics of Everyday Fear* (Minneapolis: University of Minnesota Press, 1993).
12 William Gibson, quoted in Tim Adams, "Space to Think," *The Observer*, August 12, 2007, available at www.books.guardian.co.uk/departments/sciencefiction/story/0,,2146989,00.html.
13 See Alfonso Cuarón, DVD commentary on *Children of Men* (Universal Studios, 2007).
14 Bauman, *In Search of Politics*, p. 51.
15 See Timothy W. Luke, *Museum Politics: Power Plays at the Exhibition* (Minneapolis: University of Minnesota Press, 2002).
16 "'Designing-out insecurity' was first used in a report by the British Cabinet Office. See British Cabinet Office, *Building on Progress: Security, Crime and Justice*, March 2007, available at www.homeoffice.gov.uk/documents/security-crime-justice-policy.
17 Anthony Dunne and Fiona Raby, *Design Noir: The Secret Life of Electronic Objects* (London: Birkhauser, 2001).
18 Ibid., p. 46.
19 Ibid., p. 64.
20 Beatriz Colomina, *Domesticity at War* (Cambridge, MA: MIT Press, 2007), p. 12.
21 William Burroughs, "The Limits of Control," in eds. James Grauerholz and Ira Silverberg, *Word Virus: The William Burroughs Reader* (London: Flamingo, 2000), p. 339.
22 Gilles Deleuze, "Spoilers of Peace," in G. Deleuze, *Two Regimes of Madness: Texts and Interviews 1975–1995* (New York: Semiotext(e), 2006), p. 161.
23 Ibid., p. 162.
24 Ibid.
25 Ibid.
26 Gilles Deleuze, "Postscript on Control Societies," in Deleuze, *Negotiations, 1972–1990* (New York: Columbia University Press, 1995), pp. 177–82.
27 See William Bogard, "The Coils of a Serpent: Haptic Spaces and Control Societies," *Ctheory.net*, posted on September 11, 2007, available at www.ctheory.net/articles.aspx?id=581; see also Michael Hardt and Antonio Negri, *Empire* (Harvard: Harvard University Press, 2001).
28 See Deleuze, "Postscript on Control Societies," p. 177.
29 Gilles Deleuze, "What Is the Creative Act?," in Deleuze, *Two Regimes of Madness*, p. 321.
30 Ibid., p. 321.
31 Deleuze, "Postscript on Control Societies," p. 178.
32 Deleuze, "What Is the Creative Act?," p. 321.
33 See also Hardt and Negri, *Empire*.
34 Deleuze, "Postscript on Control Societies," p. 181.
35 Ibid., p. 178.
36 Ibid., p. 175.
37 Ibid., p. 178.
38 Gilles Deleuze, *Foucault* (London: Continuum, 1999), p. 131. Unlike his comments on control society, Deleuze does not appear disturbed by the possibility of a new type of human being. "It is the advent of a new form that is neither God nor man and which, it is hoped, will not prove worse than its previous two forms," he writes. See ibid., p. 132.

39 Peter Adey, "Secured and Sorted Mobilities: Examples from the Airport," *Surveillance and Society*, Vol. 1, No. 4 (2004), pp. 500–19.
40 On this topic, see Diken and Lausten, *Culture of Exception*; and Debbie Lisle, "Site Specific: Medi(t)ations at the Airport," in eds. François Debrix and Cynthia Weber, *Rituals of Mediation: International Politics and Social Meaning* (Minneapolis: University of Minnesota Press, 2003), pp. 3–29.
41 See Matthew Honan, "The *Blade Runner* Nexus," *Wired*, September 26, 2007, available at www.wired.com/entertainment/hollywood/magazine/15-10/fl_bladerunner.
42 Deleuze, "Postscript on Control Societies," p. 181.
43 Ibid., p. 175.
44 Paul Virilio and Sylvère Lotringer, *Pure War* (New York: Semiotext(e), 1997). For useful explorations of design, architecture, and war, see ed. Igmade, *5 CODES: Architecture, Paranoia and Risk in Times of Terror* (Berlin: Birkhäuser, 2006); Stephan Trüby, *Exit-Architecture: Design Between War and Peace* (New York: SpringerWien, 2008); ed. Michael Sorkin, *Indefensible Space: The Architecture of the National Security State* (London: Routledge, 2008); Richard Ross, *Architecture of Authority* (New York: Aperture, 2007); eds. Shumon Basar, Antonia Carver, and Markus Miesen, *With/Without: Spatial Products, Practices and Politics in the Middle East* (Dubai: Bidoun and Moutamarat, 2007).
45 See Lucas D. Introna and David Wood, "Picturing Algorithmic Surveillance: The Politics of Facial Recognition Systems," *Surveillance and Society*, Vol. 2, No. 2/3 (2004), pp. 177–98.
46 Steven Shaviro, *Connected, or What It Means to Live in the Network Society* (Minneapolis: University of Minnesota Press, 2003), p. 32.
47 Paola Antonelli, *SAFE: Design Takes on Risk* (New York: The Museum of Modern Art, 2005), p. 13. Many of the themes of *SAFE* are developed further in Paola Antonelli, *Design and the Elastic Mind* (New York: The Museum of Modern Art, 2008). For a useful reflection on the future of design and technology, see John Thackara, *In the Bubble: Designing In A Complex World* (Cambridge: MIT Press, 2005).
48 See Aaron Dalton, "Designer Gear for the Apocalypse," *Wired*, October 17, 2005, available at www.wired.com/culture/lifestyle/news/2005/10/69208.
49 Antonelli, *SAFE: Design Takes on Risk*, p. 52.
50 Ibid., p. 53.
51 See Giorgio Agamben, *Homo Sacer: Sovereign Power and Bare Life* (Stanford: Stanford University Press, 1998).
52 Deleuze, "Postscript on Control Societies," p. 181.
53 Ibid., p. 181.
54 Agamben, *Homo Sacer*, p. 133.
55 Antonelli, *SAFE: Design Takes on Risk*, p. 78.
56 Ibid., p. 15.
57 Deleuze, "Postscript on Control Societies," p. 179; author's emphasis.
58 See www.manchester.gov.uk.
59 Antonelli, *SAFE: Design Takes on Risk*, p. 80.
60 Ibid., p. 80.
61 Ibid., p. 87.
62 Ibid., p. 112.
63 Ibid., p. 15.
64 Phil Patton, "Design for Destruction," in Antonelli, *SAFE: Design Takes on Risk*, p. 29.
65 See Zygmunt Bauman, *Liquid Modernity* (Cambridge: Polity, 2000).
66 Antonelli, *SAFE: Design Takes on Risk*, p. 12. For a useful discussion of the paradoxes of safety, see Donald A. Norman, *The Design of Future Things* (New York: Basic Books, 2007).
67 Deleuze, "Postscript on Control Societies," p. 180; author's emphases.
68 Antonelli, *SAFE: Design Takes on Risk*, p. 10.
69 "Homeland Security Blanket, 2002," FutureFarmers Project Site, available at www.futurefarmers.com/survey/homeland.php.
70 See "Blanket Security," Gizmodo, available at gizmodo.com/gadgets/homeland-security/blanket-security-122472.php.

106 M. J. Lacy

71 Antonelli, *SAFE: Design Takes on Risk*, p. 101.
72 Ibid., p. 100.
73 Quoted in Antonelli, *SAFE: Design Takes on Risk*, p. 65.
74 Ibid., p. 65.
75 Ibid.
76 Susan Yelavich, "Safety Nests," in Antonelli, *SAFE: Design Takes on Risk*, p. 17.
77 Ibid., p. 18.
78 Ibid., p. 19.
79 Raul Barreneche, "In the Belly of the Beast," *Interior Design* (June 2003), pp. 169–74; cited in Yelavich, "Safety Nests," p. 19.
80 Yelavich, "Safety Nests," p. 24.
81 Not all the products meant to secure the "interior" involve *communectivity*. For example, the "Safe Bedside Table" product is a table that turns into a club that could be used to ward off intruders. Part of the "Hidden Wealth" project, the "Incognito dinnerware," has deliberately hidden classic Rococo hand-painted details that are visible only when the cups and saucers are turned upside down.
82 Yelavich, "Safety Nests," p. 25.
83 Ibid., p. 25.
84 Ibid.
85 Antonelli, *SAFE: Design Takes on Risk*, p. 187.
86 Ibid., p. 98.
87 See Michael Hardt and Antonio Negri, *Multitude: War and Democracy in the Age of Empire* (London: Penguin, 2004).
88 Antonelli, *SAFE: Design Takes on Risk*, p. 84.
89 Ibid., p. 84.
90 Ibid., p. 12.
91 Deleuze, "Control and Becoming," in Deleuze, *Negotiations*, p. 175.
92 Carolyn Nordstrom, *Global Outlaws: Crime, Money, and Power in the Contemporary World* (Berkeley: University of California Press, 2007), p. 191.
93 Ibid., p. 194.
94 An important theme of *The Wire* concerns the bureaucratic constraints, corruption, political rivalries, and socio-economic problems that frustrate police attempts to combat the drugs trade in Baltimore.
95 Deleuze, "Postscript on Control Societies," p. 181.
96 See Elisa Batista, "What Your Clothes Say about You," *Wired*, March 12, 2003, available at www.wired.com/gadgets/wireless/news/2003/03/58006; see also Bruce Sterling, *Shaping Things* (Cambridge, MA: MIT Press, 2005).
97 See www.boycottbenneton.com.
98 There is currently a "Boycott Gillette" campaign aimed at opposing a similar strategy by Gillette to devise tracking systems in the sale of razors.
99 See www.petsmobility.com.
100 See www.alltrackus.com.
101 Ibid., no page given.
102 See HM Government, *Building on Progress: Security, Crime and Justice*, March 2007, p. 35.
103 See Gordon Brown, "In Full: Brown Anti-Terror Speech," November 14, 2007, available at news.bbc.co.uk/1/hi/uk_politics/7094620.stm.
104 Ibid., no page given.
105 See "'Smart Power': Joseph Hamre Talks with Joseph Nye and Richard Armitage," *The American Interest*, Vol. 3, No. 3 (2007), available at www.the-american-interest.com/ai2/article.cfm?MId=16&id=346.
106 Jacques Derrida, "Autoimmunity: Real and Symbolic Suicides," in ed. Giovanna Borradori, *Philosophy in a Time of Terror: Dialogues with Jürgen Habermas and Jacques Derrida* (Chicago: University of Chicago Press, 2003), p. 102.
107 Jürgen Habermas, "Fundamentalism and Terror," in ed. Borradori, *Philosophy in a Time of Terror*, p. 28.

6 Deserting sovereignty?
The securitization of undocumented migration in the United States

Mathew Coleman

There has been an explosion of critical research on American security (and insecurity), prompted in large part by the US-led war on terror and its contingencies (for example, extraordinary renditions, racial profiling, military tribunals, or preemptive warfare). One important result has been a multi-disciplinary popularization of a central theme in the critical geopolitics/critical international relations literature of the 1990s: that accounts of identity and its differences constitute the (geo)political. For example, it is now held as commonsensical that security, rather than a no-nonsense expression of national interest or strategy in a conflict-prone world economy, is a boundary-drawing knowledge of performative temperament whose power lies in its ability to geographically "enframe and incite certain conceptual, moral and/or aesthetic understandings of self and other, security and danger, proximity and distance, indifference and responsibility."[1] The message, then, is that spatialized discourses about identity and difference continue to inhere in statecraft, and that complex global political economic realities are still frequently reduced by practitioners of state (particularly in US foreign policy practice) to simplistic territorial mappings of "identity here" and "difference there."

At the same time, one cannot help but notice that perhaps the two most cited early twenty-first-century books dealing with the shape and substance of global politics—Michael Hardt and Antonio Negri's *Empire* and *Multitude*—do not dwell on such matters. If anything, their argument cuts across the grain of much contemporary research in the social sciences and humanities on the politics of security. On the one hand, Hardt and Negri's work downplays the importance of US security politics and practice. As Hardt writes, although still an important ingredient in global conflict, US power is dysfunctional and ham-fisted; it is an "old monster" soon to be dead and buried.[2] On the other hand, Hardt and Negri are skeptical about the present-day utility of identity/difference accounts of the political. As they put it, the new post-Bretton Woods and post-Cold War organization of power means the *replacement* of the "contradictory couple identity-difference" with the "complementary couple commonality-singularity."[3] Indeed, if many are re-evaluating post-Cold War life in terms of the ongoing relevance of enmity and violence to world politics, Hardt and Negri have turned the other way to ask about the newly collective and democratic properties of an increasingly common social life.

Central to Hardt and Negri's argument about the increasingly anachronistic properties of identity/difference-structured accounts of world politics (yet not frequently taken up) is the revolutionary challenge that they claim migration poses to the state and to possibilities for effective state governance. In this chapter, I offer a recapitulation and a critical assessment of this aspect of their argument. As will become clear, I find that their position brings a breath of fresh air to contemporary analyses, particularly as Hardt and Negri refuse to see migration through the lens of security and its violences. At the same time, I find their analysis difficult because of the way they neglect the securitization of migration, something which, I argue, is a product of their pseudo-contract theory account of state power and of their commitment to what I will call "autonomy-in-migration."

I start the chapter off with a brief review of Negri's earlier experiments in autonomist Marxism. My claim is that the language and tension in this earlier work helps us to better appreciate Hardt and Negri's subsequent books and, specifically, their tendency to treat migration as relatively autonomous from the state. A second section dwells on the analysis of migration and the state, predominantly in *Multitude,* but also in *Empire.* I suggest that Negri's earlier "refusal of work" argument is exaggerated in Hardt and Negri's recent collaboration in the form of a "refusal of the state" argument that downplays the ways in which migrant life is hemmed in by states. In order to ground this discussion, a third section looks briefly at major trends in US immigration enforcement, and in particular at the expansion of interior enforcement as an important supplement to border enforcement. My hope is that this section will stand somewhat by itself as relevant to security debates regardless of what one thinks of Hardt and Negri's argument. This said, a fourth and final section presents three criticisms of Hardt and Negri's treatment of migration in explicit relation to the material discussed in the third section.

The refusal of work

Critics and admirers alike are quick to draw out the implications of Hardt and Negri's unconventional deployment of (in no particular order) Foucault, Deleuze, Spinoza, and Marx. In contrast, arguably little attention has been given to how both *Empire* and *Multitude* follow from Negri's own contributions to the post-World War II variants of Italian Marxism referred to as *operaismo* and *autonomia.*[4] An appraisal of Hardt and Negri on what we might call the migration-state nexus—or on the challenge posed to the state by migration—should not avoid Negri's earlier theoretical experiments. For example, his contributions to *autonomia* are the grounds for Hardt and Negri's discussion of migrants' refusal of sovereign authority as outlined in *Empire* and *Multitude.*

It is difficult to speak of either *operaismo* ("workerism") or *autonomia* ("autonomy") in general terms.[5] As Steve Wright notes (about *autonomia* in particular), the concept is "ideologically heterogeneous, territorially dispersed, organizationally fluid, politically marginalized: [the] ... analogy of an archipelago is an apt one."[6] At the same time, we can distill some broad features of both notions. *Operaismo,* for instance, emerged in the 1960s as a critique of the Italian post-war economic miracle, and in particular of the automation of production in Italy's northern factories. Its key theoretical innovation was to de-emphasize the all-powerfulness of capital in relation to labor. The main thrust of this argument was that capitalists' adoption of new technologies and management schemes was a response to workers' refusal to submit to capitalist authority. From this perspective, workers' repeated disruption of capital's mechanisms of control (called "recomposition") sets the stage for capital's "decomposition" of the proletariat into a more acquiescent class form.[7]

Despite this inventive inversion of the capital/labor relationship, *operaismo* was criticized on the left as overly "factoryist," or too narrowly about production and Fordist wage struggle.[8] It was deemed insufficiently attentive to emerging countercultural, feminist, and immigrant movements, to the restructuring of capitalist power in terms of state austerity measures, and to the explosion in part-time and non-guaranteed work.[9] Those gathered under the umbrella of *autonomia*—including most notably Negri—took these criticisms as a starting point for a new look at capitalist rule.

Autonomia can be roughly described to encompass a trio of theoretical innovations. First, *autonomia* theorists took *operaismo*'s claim about the subsumption of labor under capital to refer to the reality of a "social factory," or the total immanence of capital to the social world.[10] As Negri argued in his take on Marx's "Fragment on Machines," the "[r]eal subsumption of labor can't but be (in the same moment) [the] real subsumption of society."[11] That no sphere was autonomous from capital signaled for *autonomia* the misplaced intention on the left (in Euro-communism, above all) for economic change via the state. Negri put it bleakly: parliamentary representation, and more generally any attempt to capture state office for revolutionary ends, was but "the conscious extension of the capitalist mode of production to the whole of society and its ('socialist') state management."[12] The immanence of capital also meant doing away with the shop floor as the basic site of political strategy and theory building. This brought theoretical as well as practical attention to a range of subject positions traditionally ignored by the left.[13]

Second, notwithstanding this focus on the all-pervasiveness of capitalism, *autonomia* theorists, and in particular Negri, explored labor's "self-valorizing" power. The concept of self-valorization was intended not just as a corrective to the Marxist concept of valorization (that is to say, capital's lopsided ability to put human productive activity to work), but also as a critique of theories of disvalorization (capital's absorption and destruction of human skills) as well as a Situationist praxis about "the diversion of elements of domination into vehicles of liberation."[14] This followed from *operaismo*'s critique of capital's univocity, but at the same time went beyond it. For example, by drawing attention to capital's inability to put labor to work in a full sense as well as to capital's incomplete colonization of human skill, self-valorization gutted capital of anything but a parasitical, second order enslavement to labor. As Negri explained: "The whole of capitalist development, ever since the working class established itself … has been nothing other than the obverse of, a reaction to, a pursuit of proletarian self-valorization—an operation of self-protection, of recuperation, of adjustment in relation to the effects of self-valorization."[15] Negri went on to add that, although labor and capital are "hostile to the point of destroying each other reciprocally," the destruction of the enemy was only possible for workers since the capitalist class requires its enemy in order to survive.[16]

Third, and closely related to the concept of self-valorization, was the so-called "refusal of work" idea, in many ways a concept (and strategy) at the heart of *autonomia*. As Negri described it, the refusal of work concerns the material destructuration and/

or political destabilization of capitalism and the state through absenteeism, slack time on the job, sabotage, protest, wage pressure, wild cat strikes, and so on.[17] At the same time, the refusal of work was not intended to be merely destructive. As Harry Cleaver summarizes it: "The refusal of work with its associated *seizure of space* (eg., land, buildings) or *time* (eg., weekends, paid vacations, non-work time on the job) or *energy* (eg., an entropy raising diversion from work) creates the very possibility of self-valorization."[18] Indeed, for Negri, refusal led to the "total utilization of wealth in the service of collective freedom," in place of the "void" of capitalist development.[19]

These three points are not a comprehensive account of *autonomia*. But they are useful as they hint at two important deployments of "autonomy" in Negri's work. On the one hand, and in keeping with the social factory thesis, Negri's post-war scholarship ridiculed *political* autonomy.[20] In no uncertain terms, he lampooned parliamentary reformism, for instance, as a cooptation of labor in the "state-form of capitalism."[21] At the same time, Negri drew attention to the autonomy of *labor*, or what he called a "working class outside capital."[22] The refusal of work strategy was an explicit recognition of this. At first glance, the concept seems to speak to the "cramped" position that labor finds itself in with respect to capital, that is to say, its inability to decisively abandon capital, or its limited room for movement.[23] However, if paired with the concept of self-valorization, as was mentioned above, refusal of work is the sharp end of a much bigger wedge. Indeed, as Negri put it, if moments of sabotage ("recomposition") invite capitalist disciplinarity ("decomposition"), then, beyond that reinforcement of capitalist violence, the refusal of work frees a "last front that is the antagonistic and general persistence of living social labor" in a system otherwise fully colonized by exchange value.[24] In so doing, it inaugurates "a process of separation" or "rupture" from capital.[25] It was in this sense that Negri spoke of the refusal of work as "liberated labor" building "liberated spaces."[26]

In a provocative essay and book, Nicholas Thoburn points out that these two renderings of autonomy (that boil down to the social factory thesis, and the self-governing aspect of labor power) are in tension.[27] As Thoburn explains, despite his insistence on the immanence of capital, Negri minimizes capital's colonization of social life and, in its place, he emphasizes the conditions under which labor might break from capitalist rule.[28] Thoburn refers to this as Negri's embrace of an "autonomy-in-production" argument that Thoburn goes on to criticize as a "mirror-image of neo-Gramscian thought by replacing the relative autonomy of the social with that of production."[29] My concern here is not whether neo-Gramscian thought can be characterized in this way. Rather, I am interested in how Negri's work, as a result of this prioritization of autonomy-in-production, treats labor as "a figure of plenitude" rather than as a proliferation of "impossible, minority positions where social forces constrain movement."[30] Moreover, I am interested in how this lack of constraint comes to the fore in Negri's more recent work with Hardt. As I argue in the next section, Hardt and Negri's take on migration in particular can be read as an exaggeration of Negri's autonomy-in-production position in so far as they de-emphasize the "cramped" position migrants find themselves in with respect to the state.

The refusal of the state

There are many ways one can think about *Empire* and *Multitude* in relation to Negri's experiments in autonomist theory. As with the latter's turn away from the "mass worker" and toward a broader range of "socialized workers," Hardt and Negri too put "marginality at the center" of their analysis and de-prioritize the workplace as the locus of revolutionary power.[31] Hardt and Negri also emphasize the real subsumption of society to capital. A good chunk of *Empire*, for example, is dedicated to exploring how contemporary capitalism is a "society of control" in which power "reaches down to the ganglia of the social structure" and literally produces life itself.[32] At the same time, the real subsumption of society to capital is not total for Hardt and Negri. In *Empire*, for instance, the state and capital always play second fiddle to labor's ability to produce both "outside measure" and "beyond measure."[33] So, in at least three ways (the importance of marginal work, the immanence of capital, and self-valorization), Hardt and Negri's analysis follows from Negri's earlier work. This said, there is a much more pronounced emphasis in Hardt and Negri's studies on the dissolution of constituted forms of power and on revolutionary politics as an open horizon of possibilities. This is nowhere more apparent than in their analysis of contemporary migration.

For Hardt and Negri, migration (a catch-all term that includes documented and undocumented laborers moving to the global north, hobos, seasonal laborers, and the global poor moving between cities and states all over the planet) sheds light on the constitution of contemporary globality. As they explain, migrants of all sorts "teach us about the geographical divisions and hierarchies of the global system of command. Migrants understand and illuminate the gradients of danger and security, poverty and wealth, the markets of higher and lower wages, and the situations of more and less free forms of life."[34] But, in fact, Hardt and Negri contend, migrants do much more than signpost an uneven global political economy. Indeed, they also call that very economy into question.[35] This is so in two ways. On the one hand, migrants' mass mobility poses a challenge to the statist inside/outside territorialities through which, in part, global capitalist accumulation proceeds. As Hardt and Negri remark, the migrating global multitude "recognize the geographical hierarchies of the system and yet treat the globe as one common space."[36] On the other hand, the knowledges, skills, habits, desires, and practices migrants bring with them and develop on their border-crossing journeys come together to produce social relations unmoored from the often territorialized logic of identity/difference. The result is an "open source society, that is, a society whose source code is revealed so that we all can work collaboratively to solve its bugs and create new, better social programs."[37] In sum, migration is for Hardt and Negri a limit concept concerning effective state territoriality as well as an emerging form of placeless social self-organization.

Hardt and Negri's provocation on migration is a refreshing alternative to both polemical treatises about the demographic and other (security) threats posed by migrants[38] and more measured or mainstream research about how to best cope with the pressures of migration.[39] In both these literature strands, although with clearly different outcomes, migration is taken more or less at face value, that is to say, as a disruption warranting state intervention in the form of a policy fix. It is not so with Hardt and Negri. Rather than a disturbance to be better managed, Hardt and Negri understand migration as an insurgency or flight that opens up new political, economic and social horizons. In other words, if in varying degrees much of the ink spilled about migration these days treats it somehow through the lens of security (here interpreted as a set of discourses, knowledges, and technologies that produces troublesome, or nomadic, constituencies as "referent objects" of statecraft to be disciplined and/or made to live differently[40]), Hardt and Negri's own emphasis is rather on the state itself as a source of insecurity and on migration as a progressive challenge to the state's forms of violence.

This is perhaps one of the more obvious ways that Hardt and Negri's research links up profitably with critical geopolitics' and critical international relations' problematization of the state and statecraft. At the same time, unlike the aforementioned schools, Hardt and Negri arguably make short shrift of the state and of processes of securitization. Although they outline how, for example, undocumented migrations from the global south to the global north are criminalized and policed, their interest is ultimately to examine how the "mobile multitude" of "illegal labor" turns national spaces into a "new geography" of "subterranean and uncontainable rhizomes."[41] Indeed, in keeping with *autonomia*'s emphasis on the dependence of capital on labor, their basic point is that "the multitude have to be allowed to extend always wider across the world scene" because this is what drives the productivity on which capital is reliant.[42] Thus, although the state securitizes itinerant populations, in effect it has no choice but to let them move freely across its borders.[43]

But there is more to this "global citizenship" reading of migration than the state speaking out of both sides of its mouth, as it were. Key here is Hardt and Negri's discussion of migration as an exodus from sovereign authority. As they explain it, exodus is a revolutionary "act of refusing the relationship with the sovereign,"[44] a decision by the ruled to "to take leave of domination, to take leave of the Power of the State" (as Negri paraphrases).[45] At one level, the concept of exodus can be considered a repackaging of *autonomia*'s refusal of work argument. For instance, in much the same way Negri spoke of labor collapsing capital's structure of command via sabotage and of the creation of liberated spaces of self-valorization, the exodus argument suggests that the state is exhausted if its structures of authority are both subverted and refused by those subjected to them. However, if both arguments share a logic of subtraction (i.e., the collapse of power through withdrawal), there is nonetheless a very important difference of emphasis between the two. In particular, the refusal of work argument echoed a still meaningful state-capital nexus, one to be reckoned with. This is well exemplified in Negri's controversial essay "Domination and Sabotage" in which labor's attempt to destructure the state and capital invites the former's monstrous, violent and crisis-ridden return.[46] In contrast, what Hardt and Negri give us under the moniker of exodus is a politics of liberation based essentially on contract theory.[47] Although Hardt and Negri, for instance, warn about the rearguard wars that will need to be fought by those abandoning sovereignty against the forces of the state, in hot pursuit,[48] this comes off as a side story in a larger script about how the ruled can provoke the withering away of the state by simply refusing their relationship of protection/obedience and right/obligation with the sovereign. From this perspective, simply reneging on the sovereign contract begets an opening.

In sum, what we have in Hardt and Negri's migration-as-exodus argument is an imagining of the migrant as a "figure of plenitude" with respect to the state, that is to say, a subject only fractionally caught up in the state's legal, disciplinary and other arts of government. In other words, to riff off Thoburn's analysis, Hardt and Negri extend Negri's earlier "autonomy-in-production" perspective into a yet stronger "autonomy-in-migration" argument, or a decidedly "uncramped" account of migrant life with respect to the state.

US immigration enforcement: a geopolitical-biopolitical hybrid

I now want to shift the focus a bit and move from Hardt and Negri's abstracted discussion of migration and the state to a brief overview of contemporary US immigration enforcement. My hope is that this will help us to think about the limitations of Hardt and Negri's account of migration as a revolutionary problematic, something I will return to in the subsequent, and final, section of this chapter.

Immigration law reform, or the process of immigration lawmaking by elected representatives in conversation with the executive branch, is a key part of how immigration policy is made in the United States. Notwithstanding widespread insistence across the political spectrum that this process is, at root, open and inclusive, a certain "anti-immigrantism" can be said to constitute US immigration law reform politics.[49] That is, despite the 1965 Immigration and Nationality Act's elimination of national origin and race as the basis for US immigration policy, immigration lawmaking adheres to a "restrictive ideal of national community" that treats immigrants as "objects of our vigilance, suspicion, and perhaps even our hostility."[50] So, for example, although most, if not all, legislative debates about immigration proceed via the proviso that it is an important source of cultural, economic and political renewal for the polity, fears about balkanization, and about how local scale immigrant incorporation might shift the balance of political-economic power away from non-whites, mean that immigration is routinely articulated by national and local lawmakers in terms of ethnic, demographic and racial survival.[51] This is particularly the case when immigration is perceived through a foreign policy lens. As one critic has recently put it, the "merger of immigration and terrorism policy promotes the notion that immigrants are suspects first and welcome newcomers second, if at all."[52]

The identity/difference correlates of immigration law reform politics are perhaps most pronounced when it comes to the question of the undocumented migrant, a figure that has been more or less constantly in lawmakers' crosshairs over the past three decades.[53] What exactly is it about undocumented migration that makes it such a steadfast object of scrutiny for lawmakers? A first cut at this question suggests that what is at stake (in many ways echoing Hardt and Negri) is the undocumented migrant's refusal to submit to sovereign authority at the borders of the state. For example, much legislative and executive energy has been spent characterizing the migrant as a subject whose refusal of sovereign authority (in the form of unauthorized entry) inaugurates a sort of generalized lawlessness throughout the polity.[54] The logic at work here is that the undocumented migrant is dangerous by virtue of the "geographical 'crime' of undocumented entry" and the risk this poses to a larger culture of respect for the law.[55]

However, if the raw fact of unauthorized territorial incursion—and the contagion of illegality (withdrawal of obedience) it apparently foreshadows—has featured prominently in lawmakers' claims about the undocumented migrant's dangerousness, a case nonetheless can be made that lawmakers' securitization of undocumented migrants depends on much more than their crossing of some legal-geographic line in the sand. For example, much of the past three decades of immigration law reform debate in the United States can be summed up as an investigation of the multiple ways in which the undocumented migrant merges public policy issues (food stamp abuse, unemployment, health, sexuality, cultural assimilation, urban safety issues, welfare abuse, and so on) with foreign policy issues (underdevelopment, population pressure abroad, narcotics trafficking, terrorism, and so forth), and of how the result of this merger is an unwieldy policy landscape whose contingencies are difficult to manage by virtue of their spatial extensivity.[56] In other words, the undocumented migrant has been held as the bellwether of what we might call a "recombinant" topography of threat that throws into question the "domestic" as an identity, a logic, and a form of life (with certain guarantees) apart from the "international."[57]

One of the better examples of this phenomenon is the 1996 Illegal Immigration Reform and Immigrant Responsibility Act (IIRIRA). On the one hand, on the tenth anniversary of the 1986 legalization program and debate about its fiscal impact, IIRIRA responded to concerns that undocumented migrants' use of social services, public schooling, healthcare, welfare, and other public benefits was financially unsustainable. To this was added the possibility that accessibility to welfare was a pull factor that encouraged undocumented migration to the United States. In response, IIRIRA legislated new workplace enforcement practices as well as a long list of restrictions on federal benefits and allowances. On the other hand, in the wake of the 1993 World Trade Center bombing and with growing concerns about international terrorism, debate leading up to IIRIRA's passage focused on how best to stop terrorist groups from infiltrating the United States. Agreeing for the most part that the solution was more vigorously to police undocumented migration to the United States, lawmakers authorized more money for border enforcement, new terrorist and criminal grounds for immigration inadmissibility, and a wide array of vastly expanded deportation and exclusion procedures for a broad group of unlawfully resident aliens including terrorists, drug traffickers, incarcerated aliens, and undocumented laborers. The lawmakers' message was loud and clear: undocumented migration constitutes a newly deterritorialized field of threats and uncertainties, stretching from the local scale up, and incorporating all manner of increasingly indistinguishable policy issues and arenas, mundane or otherwise.[58]

At stake, then, in this articulation of the undocumented migrant-as-threat is arguably more than the classically geopolitical problem of legal trespass, or the problem of securing territory against unwanted incursions. Rather, the economy of danger that has gravitated (and continues to gravitate) around the figure of the undocumented migrant is about its embodied dissolution of public policy issues and spaces into foreign policy issues and spaces, and about how, as a result, a formerly predictable mode of life on the "inside" is put at risk in relation to a slew of "external" dangers, now not so distant. In other words, the undocumented migrant (as a deterritorializing agent of uncertainty) is as much a biopolitical as a geopolitical problematic, if by the former is meant in particular a broad spectrum of activities (and anxieties) concerning the (dis)orderliness and (un)regulability of everyday life in the context of pervasive non-local or extra-local forces.[59]

Of course, this biopolitical take on undocumented migration has not precluded a more narrow geopolitical response. The Mexico-US border, in particular, has become a site of intense investment where, for example, a masculine sense of national identity is put into question,[60] and where political elites play up a "loss-of-control" narrative for political advantage.[61] Indeed, in response to the extraordinary dangers said to be posed by undocumented migrants, federal monies allocated for border enforcement grew steadily throughout the 1980s and 1990s, and are now bigger than ever.[62] The result has been an unprecedented militarization of borderland life.[63] Moreover, deaths at the border—exhaustion and dehydration are the primary causes—have been on the increase over the past decade, and they are now at an all-time high, due in large measure to the now formidable barriers that force migrants to cross into the United States through some of the most inhospitable desert terrain on the continent.[64]

At the same time, the US response to undocumented migration has not been limited to bigger, longer, or more lethal fences. Taking cues from scholarship on the reconfiguration of immigration policing in the European Union context, what we see in the US case is the increasing importance of techniques of "population management" as a supplement to the inside/outside logic of "territorial management" at the border.[65]

For the sake of brevity, we can describe this as an emerging interior enforcement regime defined by three basic tactics. First, immigration law reform over the past 10 years has systematically closed the gap between immigration and crime enforcement. The result has been a "deep convergence" between criminal and immigration law, to the point that a criminal conviction is likely to trigger detention, deportation, and/or exclusion from the United States for a broad group of non-citizens.[66] Key to this criminalization of immigration enforcement has been an expansion of the immigration-only aggravated felony charge that is used to authorize removal from the United States' territory. Outlined initially in the 1988 Anti-Drug Abuse Act as a murder, drugs trafficking, and arms trafficking charge warranting deportation, has been expanded to include just about any criminal offense with an imposed sentence of one year or more.[67] Second, lawmakers have sought increasingly to isolate immigration enforcement from court oversight. Although this is merely the extension of a longer term deference of the courts to the legislature to make immigration law with little regard for its constitutionality, since the mid-1990s, we have seen a heightened attempt to strip the courts of many powers of review in aggravated felony (and other immigration) cases, as well as the introduction of new expedited, extra-judicial removal procedures applying broadly to undocumented aliens and carried out by front line immigration officers. In other words, while the plenary power doctrine has long granted immigration law and enforcement a certain extra-constitutional leeway, the more recent trend has been to try and excerpt a wider realm of immigration enforcement practices from the courts at the same time as immigrants are being brought into ever more intimate contact with criminal law for the purpose of removal. Third, and more recently, immigration enforcement has been devolved to include local-scale proxies—for the most part state troopers and local police officers, but also, theoretically, a range of municipal-scale employees such as social workers, rescue workers, healthcare workers, and so on—who previously enjoyed at best an arms-length relationship with federal immigration authorities.[70] Perhaps most noteworthy here is

116 M. Coleman

the recent enrollment of police forces and other proxy officers under former Attorney General Alberto Gonzales' "inherent authority" ruling that holds that local peace officers have the power to police both civil and criminal provisions of the Immigration and Nationality Act.[71] Among other things, this measure has brought attention to the contested constitutionality of emerging local landscapes of immigration policy as well as to the myriad, possibly conflicting, scales of immigration enforcement in the United States.[72]

The combined result of this criminalization, de-juridicalization, and devolution of immigration enforcement has been an "enforced reconnection" of immigrant life at the local scale with federal immigration law and authorities.[73] Indeed, this three-part reconfiguration of immigration enforcement has had a substantial impact on interior apprehensions by federal immigration authorities.[74] As summarized in Figure 6.1, interior apprehensions more than doubled between 1992 and 2003, and, since then, have remained above 100,000 cases annually. Moreover, as is also summarized in Figure 6.1, interior apprehensions steadily increased throughout the 1990s in relation to Border Patrol apprehensions, from a low of 4.9 percent in 1992 to a high of 12.3 percent in 2003.[75] Interior apprehensions are shown in more detail in Figure 6.2, and according to the 24 municipal-scale investigations districts where apprehensions are processed. Many of the cities on the map, with the exception of Los Angeles and San Diego, saw a sizeable increase in apprehensions in the mid-1990s, particularly after the implementation of IIRIRA in 1997. Perhaps more important though is the ratio of interior apprehensions to apprehensions by the Border Patrol in the US southwest, typically the most important site for US immigration policing. This is indicated through the shaded bars that measure the difference between annual

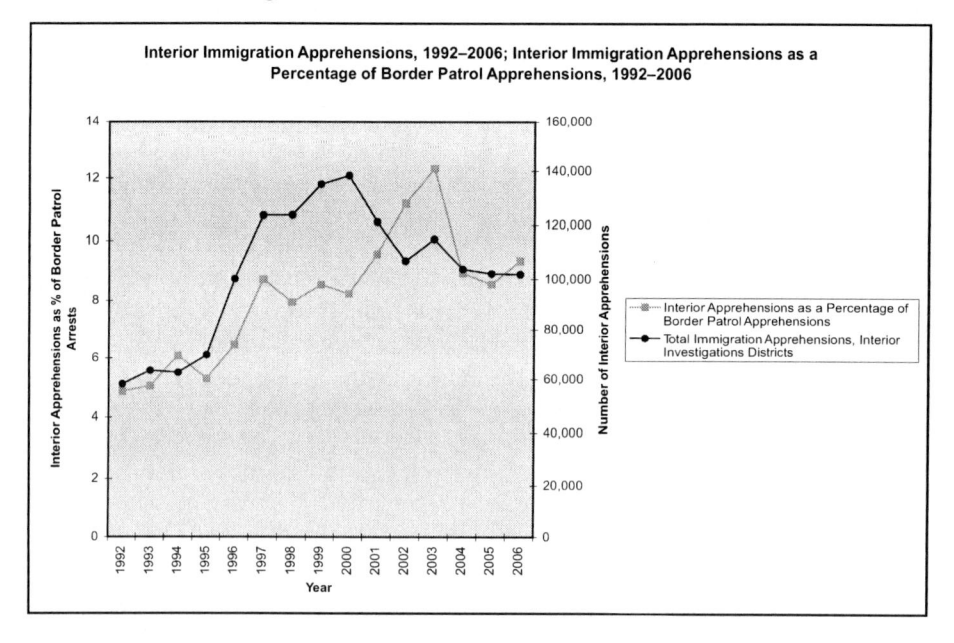

Figure 6.1 Interior immigration apprehensions vs. interior apprehensions as a percentage of border patrol apprehensions, 1992–2006.[68]

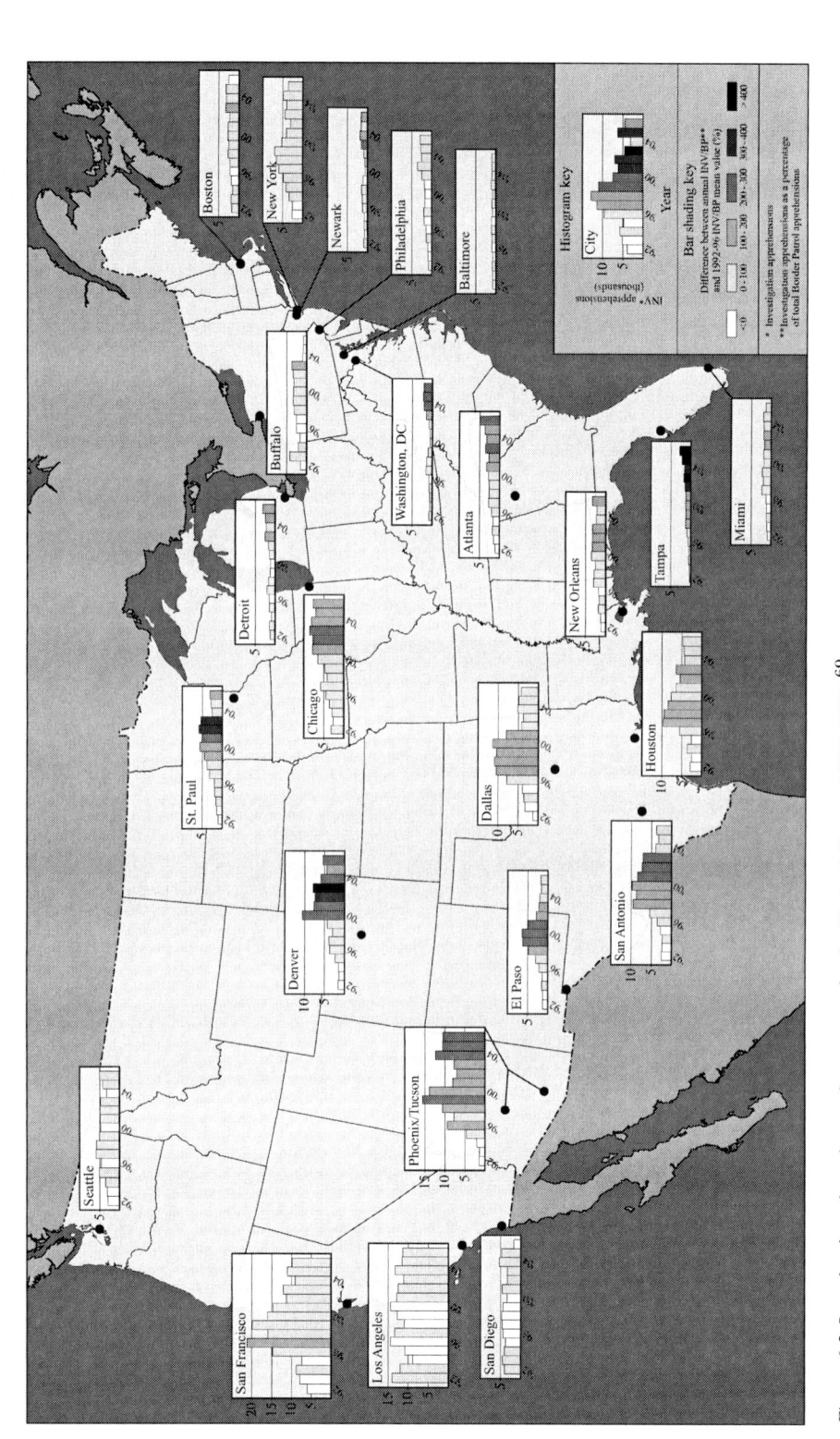

Figure 6.2 Interior immigration enforcement in the United States, 1992–2003.[69]

interior apprehensions as a percentage of Border Patrol apprehensions and the mean value of interior apprehensions as a percentage of Border Patrol apprehensions over the 1992–96 period (prior to the passage of IIRIRA). Figure 6.2 illustrates that interior apprehensions in cities typically accounted for a larger percentage of Border Patrol apprehensions at the end of the decade than at the beginning.

Although much is made publicly of worksite enforcement by federal immigration authorities, the above expansion of interior enforcement has entailed a drastic *decrease* in workplace arrests. For example, whereas in 1998 some 14,000 undocumented laborers were arrested at their places of employment for having overstayed visas or having entered the country without inspection, by 2003, this number had dropped to 445 arrests. Similarly, "intent to fine" notices issued to employers for employing undocumented workers dropped over the same time period from over 1,000 to approximately 160.[76] These numbers show quite clearly that interior enforcement, in the main, is not concerned with policing workplaces, a move clearly unpopular with agribusiness, the service industry, and other beneficiaries of inexpensive and hard-working undocumented labor.[77] Indeed, by far the most interior enforcement arrests concern operations where immigration enforcement itself is not, ironically, a primary goal. As Daniel Kanstroom puts it, what we see emerging is a "social control" model of immigration enforcement.[78] For example, a major part of interior enforcement concerns entitlements and services fraud investigations, as well as federal efforts to scour court dockets for aliens who might be deportable under the aggravated felony charge. Another major component involves criminal investigations. The ongoing Operation Community Shield run by the Department of Homeland Security in conjunction with multiple local law enforcement agencies across the country, for instance, is aimed specifically at street and prison gang members and has resulted in the arrest and deportation of thousands of individuals since its inception in 2005.[79] Similarly, Operation Predator, headed up by the Department of Homeland Security and local law enforcement agencies (and televised on *America's Most Wanted*), has resulted in the detention of some 8,500 alien sex offenders, the bulk of which have been deported.[80] In all these cases, what we see is the use of immigration law to facilitate the detention and deportation of undesirable and/or unproductive alien populations, singled out as spectacular objects of immigration law enforcement.

A rejoinder to Hardt and Negri

In the context of the above review of contemporary US immigration enforcement politics, Hardt and Negri's concept of exodus at best seems to be an incomplete framing of the relationship between migrants and the state. The first, and perhaps most straightforward, point to make is that migrants' desertion of sovereignty does not mean that sovereign power, in turn, deserts the migrant, or that the state acquiesces to the migrant's refusal of consent. Rather, the opposite can be said to be true: the migrant's itinerant refusal of sovereign authority at the territorial margins of the state is exactly what leads to its abiding designation as a threat by officials and practitioners of statecraft, on multiple public and foreign policy grounds. In fact, we can go one step further and suggest that the state itself is paradoxically more and more dependent on migrants' self-valorizing refusal of the state. For example, following Hardt and

Negri, if migrants' self-organization beyond the state means a costly and increasingly ineffective regime of territorial control, it is nonetheless the case that legislative (and other) elites use the threat of nomadism and the failure of border enforcement more generally to shore up authority for newly securitized states. In this sense, the spectacle of uncontrolled unauthorized migration does important work for the state even as it apparently erodes its legitimacy. As Didier Bigo explains, rather than being made secret, the tendency in the global north is for the disorderliness and unmanageability of migration (from the south) to be rendered hyper-visible as a contemporary political issue in order to "recapitalize trust in the state, not by reassuring but by worrying individuals about what is happening."[81] In other words, the "inferno of poverty and the odyssey of migration," as Hardt and Negri describe it, is as much a challenge to territorialized forms of authority as it is a "recomposition" of power by migrants, something which itself is the condition of possibility of an anxiety-ridden politics of "decomposition" by state elites.[82]

How do we explain Hardt and Negri's neglect of this politics of decomposition? The answer, I think, lies in their disembodied or abstract portrayal of sovereign power as an empty place or a sort of uninhabited political vacuum. In other words, sovereignty appears in both *Empire* and *Multitude* as an ungrounded conception of power rather than as a lived site of investment and/or affiliation. Indeed, the fact that a people—that is, in Hardt and Negri's terms, a section of the multitude co-opted by nationalist, racist, colonialist, or other violent modes of identification—does inhabit sovereign power as a space is never systematically broached in either book. As a result, Hardt and Negri sidestep the issue that the challenge posed by migrants (or, for that matter, by any deterritorializing force) is not simply about the transgression of territorial integrity in the abstract, but also about a constitutive challenge to a specifically territorialized (and subsequently securitized) form of life. Another way of representing the problem is to suggest that, if the multitude has a progressive subjectivity for Hardt and Negri, the people are still puzzlingly absent as a counter-revolutionary subjectivity obsessed with, and constituted through, the politics of (in)security.

A second point concerns Hardt and Negri's contract account of state authority, and how this contractual view tends to abridge the "where" of immigration-relevant statecraft to the rather narrow geopolitical problematic of border regions. Hardt and Negri ground the sovereign contract in the fiction of a perimetrical state territoriality (a signifying and intact international boundary). Having interpreted unauthorized migration as an erosion of that space, they then assert the impending collapse of the state. As with more traditional literatures in political geography and international relations, it is as if a whole and contiguous state territoriality is the *sine qua non* condition of effective sovereign power and authority.[83] In contrast, the case of US immigration enforcement suggests that, to gauge state power in this way (by the soundness—or questionability—of the sovereign contract at the territorial margins of the state), is to forget how the migrant-statecraft nexus might also be constituted elsewhere, for example along what Foucault has called a "battlefront that runs throughout society," or a whole range of "private warfares" that form the legal peace of the interior.[84] This is not to say that border enforcement is unimportant. Rather, the point is that migrants' transgression of borders in a narrow legal-territorial sense cannot culminate in the undoing of the state and statecraft because the sovereign power to police migration occurs through myriad *other spaces* as well. For example, while we should be extremely wary of the ways in which the undocumented migrant has been securitized as a threat by lawmakers, we can nonetheless agree that the result, particularly over the past decade in the United States, has been an enlarged immigration enforcement field (stretching from the local scale up, and in many cases in spaces far removed from the border) that gives tangible expression to undocumented migrants' otherwise questionable fusion of public and foreign policy issues and spaces. Indeed, if anything, the migrants' refusal to consent to sovereign authority at the territorial margins of the state, rather than bringing about the collapse of the sovereign state's power, has ushered in a comprehensive spatial reconfiguration of the way sovereignty controls immigration through all sorts of formally non-border spaces that now have become integral to immigration enforcement. Through a sort of mimicry of undocumented migrants' flight from sovereign authority, immigration enforcement has itself moved beyond the border. In a sense, immigration enforcers have become as nomadic as the migrants they pursue.

This last reflection brings us to a third point regarding what this relocated immigration-related statecraft actually entails, and moreover what immigration enforcement can tell us about the practice of state security in late modernity. Hardt and Negri's "autonomy-in-migration" argument tends to limit sovereign power in the realm of immigration enforcement to a spatial architecture of walls and fences, or, in other words, to the hierarchical practice of enclosing bodies into discrete nationalized spaces. But, as we saw in the US case, the sovereign power to police immigration is about much more than this basic gatekeeping function. On the one hand, what counts as immigration enforcement now implicates a sprawling economy of "domestic" policing, including entitlements investigations, identity fraud investigations, local routine policing (such as traffic stops), special task force operations (particularly in the realm of gang policing, narcotics enforcement, and sex crimes), restrictions on welfare and other public goods, street-level sweeps, and occasional worksite raids. On the other hand, this regime is administered not by border patrol agents per se, but via a complex proliferation of local scale "petty" sovereigns and "administrative" centers (some with possibly unconstitutional, or at least newfound, powers) whose goal is increasingly less the elimination of unauthorized migrant life on the "inside" than its regulation toward more productive ends.[85]

This newly unfolding landscape of immigration enforcement has significant implications for how we think about the provision of state security, something that is typically imagined as relevant only to the abstract spaces between states and, even there, only in terms of a relatively narrow range of classical foreign policy perspectives. Indeed, bringing together points two and three (mentioned above) concerning, respectively, the rapidly morphing ambit of what counts as immigration enforcement and where we might find it suggests that security in the field of immigration enforcement is an all-pervasive biopolitical reality that abides by no particular borders and no particular practices. The way Foucault sketches out the changing properties of security in *Security, Territory, Population* seems to be a particularly apt description of the situation.[86] If, for Hardt and Negri, state security becomes basically unthinkable in the wake of the multitude's abandonment or refusal of the state, for Foucault, the improbability of sovereign authority as singular, external, transcendent, and discontinuous with other (lower, presumably less important) forms of power signals not so much the end of security as, actually, its existing conditions of possibility. As Foucault puts it, security is in this context not about the defense of the sovereign or the defense of territory, but about the way "ever wider circuits" of increasingly varied content are folded into one another to comprise a densely articulated and always expanding field of tactics involving the economy, health, reproduction, criminality, and so on.

This critique, in fact, goes to the core of Foucault's warning call to get away from the lure of an "exchange of contracts" model of power whereby power is a commodity possessed and, therefore, transferable as well as revocable.[87] As he explains in *"Society Must Be Defended,"* schemas of power that work within the limitations of contract theory end up being overly centered on power as the kingly "right of the sword," and as such miss a multiplicity of subjugations, dominations, and securitizations that stem from well below and beyond the sovereign's office per se. Indeed, for Foucault, the contract model works explicitly to mask the multiple relations of power that permeate the social realm because, as an operation of power/knowledge, it limits where we go looking for politics to individualized and bureaucratized channels of consent, legitimacy, or obligation.

Hardt and Negri, of course, in reversing the terms of sovereign rule in accordance with *autonomia*'s inversion of power, do not fetishize the king in exactly this way. As we saw, they invert the typical contract model of power by virtue of what they say about the sovereign's parasitical dependence on the ruled. However, their primary focus on the migrant multitude's ability to withdraw their consent to be ruled brings attention to, in much the same way as Foucault warned against it, constituted power as a source of authority or force first and foremost bound up in the sovereign figure of Leviathan. Thus, although *Empire* and *Multitude* are generally celebrated as radical new theorizations about constituent power, it is certainly the case that, in focusing their attention on the self-valorizing powers of the multitude, Hardt and Negri do very little to unsettle state territorial sovereignty as the locus of constituted power, and they fail to query what actually comprises this power. While they criticize others for their inability to think beyond sovereignty in their various conceptualizations of contemporary global politics, they too fall into the same trap insofar as it is exactly against an unproblematized notion of kingly power that their account of constituent migrant power is developed.[88] Hardt and Negri might stand the sovereign upside down in relation to the migrating multitudes but they do not heed Foucault's injunction to lop off the king's head.

Notes

Thanks to François Debrix, Kevin Grove, and Mark J. Lacy for comments on an initial version of this chapter, and to Jim DeGrand for his mapmaking skills.

1 Gearóid Ó Tuathail and Simon Dalby, *Rethinking Geopolitics* (London: Routledge, 1998), p. 4.
2 Michael Hardt, "From Imperialism to Empire," *The Nation,* July 31–August 7, 2001, pp. 26–9. See also Nicholas Brown, Imre Szeman, Antonio Negri, and Michael Hardt, "Subterranean Passages of Thought: *Empire*'s Inserts," *Cultural Studies* Vol. 16 (2002), pp. 193–212.

3 Michael Hardt and Antonio Negri, *Multitude* (New York: Penguin, 2004), pp. 217–8.
4 There are, of course, important exceptions. See the essays by Callinicos, Bull, and Brennan in ed. Gopal Balakrishnan, *Debating Empire* (London: Verso, 2003).
5 Sylvère Lotringer and Christian Marazzi, "The Politics of Return," in eds. Sylvère Lotringer and Christian Marazzi, *Italy Autonomia: Post-Political Writings* (New York: Semiotext(e), 1980), pp. 8–23.
6 Steve Wright, *Storming Heaven: Class Composition and Struggle in Italian Autonomist Marxism* (London: Pluto Press, 2002), p. 152.
7 Mario Tronti, "The Strategy of Refusal," in eds. Lotringer and Marazzi, *Italy Autonomia*, p. 31. On *operaismo*'s inversion of power, see Harry Cleaver, "The Inversion of Class Perspective in Marxian Theory: From Valorization to Self-Valorization," in eds. Werner Bonefeld, Richard Gunn, and Kosmas Psychopedis, *Open Marxism* (Boulder: Pluto Press, 1992), pp. 106–44.
8 Wright, *Storming Heaven*, p. 81.
9 Nicholas Thoburn, *Deleuze, Marx and Politics* (London: Routledge, 2003), pp. 69–138; and Nicholas Thoburn, "Autonomous Production? On Negri's New Synthesis," *Theory, Culture and Society* Vol. 18 (2001), pp. 75–96.
10 On "society as capital," see Tronti, "The Strategy of Refusal," p. 28.
11 Antonio Negri, *Marx Beyond Marx* (Brooklyn: Autonomedia, 1991), p. 142.
12 Antonio Negri, "Domination and Sabotage: On the Marxist Method of Social Transformation (1977)," in *Books for Burning* (London: Verso, 2005), p. 254.
13 Wright, *Storming Heaven*, pp. 89–106.
14 Cleaver, "The Inversion of Class Perspective in Marxian Theory," p. 130.
15 Negri, "Domination and Sabotage," p. 241.
16 Negri, *Marx Beyond Marx*, p. 145.
17 Negri, "Domination and Sabotage," pp. 270–1.
18 Cleaver, "The Inversion of Class Perspective," p. 130.
19 Negri, "Domination and Sabotage," p. 273.
20 Antonio Negri, "Proletarians and the State: Toward a Discussion of Worker's Autonomy and the Historic Compromise (1975)," in *Books for Burning*, pp. 138–42.
21 Negri, "Domination and Sabotage," pp. 253–63.
22 Antonio Negri, "Toward a Critique of the Material Constitution (1977)," in *Books for Burning*, p. 199.
23 See Thoburn, "Autonomous Production?," and Thoburn, *Deleuze, Marx and Politics*.
24 Negri, "Proletarians and the State," p. 152.
25 Negri, "Domination and Sabotage," pp. 236–41.
26 Negri, "Toward a Critique of the Material Constitution," p. 200.
27 Thoburn, "Autonomous Production?," p. 85.
28 Negri explains this as the fact that "the subsumption of society under capital ... is much more fragile than capital itself believes, or than the objectivism of the Marxist epigones ... [sic] is prepared to admit." See Antonio Negri, "A Contribution on Foucault," available at www.generation-online.org/p/fpnegri14.htm (last accessed September 30, 2007).
29 Thoburn, "Autonomous Production?," pp. 90–1.
30 Thoburn, *Deleuze, Marx and Politics*, p. 90. Paolo Virno's description of post-Fordist labor fits with Thoburn's "cramped" reading of politics. For example, Virno reads post-Fordism as the empirical realization of Marx's "Fragment on Machines" but at the same time suggests that it is a pseudo-communist counteractant to the multitude's self-realization, organized by capital. See Paolo Virno, *A Grammar of the Multitude* (New York: Semiotext(e), 2004). As Lotringer suggests, the difference is that Negri posits a "struggle looking for a class" whereas Virno posits a "class looking for a struggle." See Sylvère Lotringer, "We, the Multitude," introduction to Virno, *A Grammar of the Multitude*, pp. 7–19.
31 Lotringer and Marazzi, "The Return of Politics," pp. 16–17.
32 Michael Hardt and Antonio Negri, *Empire* (Cambridge: Harvard University Press, 2000), p. 24.

33 By "outside measure," they mean capital's inability to capture and order labor's productivity. By "beyond measure," they mean labor's constituent power to produce goods out from under the thumb of exchange value. See Hardt and Negri, *Empire*, pp. 353–69.
34 Hardt and Negri, *Multitude*, p. 134.
35 Ibid., p. 222.
36 Ibid., p. 134.
37 Ibid., p. 340.
38 For example, see Michelle Malkin, *Invasion: How America Still Welcomes Terrorists, Criminals and Other Foreign Menaces to Our Shores* (Washington DC: Regnery, 2002).
39 See, for example, Douglas S. Massey, Jorge Durand, and Nolan Malone, *Beyond Smoke and Mirrors* (New York: Russell Sage Foundation, 2002).
40 For an excellent discussion, see Jef Huysmans, *The Politics of Insecurity* (London: Routledge, 2006); or Didier Bigo, "The Möbius Ribbon of Internal and External Security(ies)," in eds. Mathias Albert, David Jacobson, and Yosef Lapid, *Identities, Borders, Orders* (Minneapolis: University of Minnesota Press, 2002), pp. 91–116.
41 Hardt and Negri, *Empire*, p. 397.
42 Ibid., p. 399.
43 For a similar argument, see Kitty Calavita, *Inside the State* (New York: Routledge, 1992).
44 Hardt and Negri, *Multitude*, pp. 333–4.
45 Antonio Negri, *Time for Revolution* (New York: Continuum, 2005), pp. 259–60.
46 Negri writes: "In point of fact, the more we sabotage the state and the more we give expression to the self-valorizing/destructuring nexus, the more the rules governing the development of capital's state-system become ferocious, monstrous, and irrational." See Negri, "Domination and Sabotage," p. 242.
47 Hardt and Negri suggest as much by claiming that sabotage as a form of resistance now has been supplanted by a more "oblique" project of desertion and/or defection. See Hardt and Negri, *Empire*, p. 212. See also Antonio Negri, "Ruptures within Empire: The Power of Exodus," *Theory, Culture and Society* Vol. 19 (2002), pp. 187–94.
48 Hardt and Negri, *Multitude*, pp. 341–47.
49 See Roxanne L. Doty, *Anti-Immigrantism in Western Democracies* (London: Routledge, 2003).
50 See Peter Schuck, *Citizens, Strangers and In-Betweens* (Boulder: Westview Press, 1998), pp. 19–81.
51 Mark Ellis and Richard Wright, "The Balkanization Metaphor in the Analysis of US Immigration," *Annals of the Association of American Geographers* Vol. 88 (1998), pp. 686–98; and Richard Wright and Mark Ellis, "Race, Regions and the Territorial Politics of Immigration in the US," *International Journal of Population Geography* Vol. 6 (2000), pp. 197–211.
52 Karen Tumlin, "Suspect First: How Terrorism Policy is Reshaping Immigration Policy," *California Law Review* Vol. 92 (2004), p. 1175; Karen Engle, "Constructing Good Aliens and Good Citizens: Legitimizing the War on Terror(ism)," *University of Colorado Law Review* Vol. 75 (2004), pp. 59–114; and Julie Farnam, *US Immigration Law under the Threat of Terrorism* (New York: Algora, 2005).
53 See Joseph Nevins, *Operation Gatekeeper* (New York: Routledge, 2002); and Peter Andreas, *Border Games* (Cornell: Cornell University Press, 2000).
54 This was, for example, a key theme during the passage of the 1986 Immigration Reform and Control Act (IRCA), the first in a series of US laws dealing explicitly with undocumented migration. As the influential Hesburgh Commission concluded prior to the passage of IRCA: "As long as undocumented migration flouts US immigration law, its most devastating impact may be the disregard it breeds for other US laws." See US Select Commission on Immigration and Refugee Policy, *US Immigration Policy and the National Interest* (Washington DC: US GPO, 1981).
55 For a critical look at this argument, see Nevins, *Operation Gatekeeper*, pp. 123–49.
56 For more detail on this, see Mathew Coleman, "Between Public and Foreign Policy: US

Immigration Law Reform and the Undocumented Migrant," *Urban Geography*, Vol. 29, No. 1 (2008), pp. 4–28.
57 Mick Dillon, "Sovereignty and Governmentality: From the Problematics of the 'New World Order' to the Ethical Problematic of the World Order," *Alternatives* Vol. 20 (1995), pp. 323–68. Bigo also usefully discusses this as a Möbius ribbon-type landscape of threat in which a general securitization of social change "connects fear of crime, unemployment, foreigners, drug trafficking, terrorism and war." See Bigo, "The Möbius Ribbon of Security(ies)," p. 113.
58 The effect of IIRIRA, in particular, was a sort of scaling up and down of undocumented immigration as a political issue. Bob Jessop describes this trend, albeit in a different context, as the tendency of state elites and practitioners to interiorize foreign policy at the same time as they internationalize domestic policy. See Bob Jessop, "Capitalism and its Future: Remarks on Regulation, Government and Governance," *Review of International Political Economy* Vol. 4 (1997), pp. 561–81. David Campbell describes a similar process by which foreign policy codes percolate to the domestic scale to constitute what he describes as a parallel internal geopolitical inscription of danger. See David Campbell, *Writing Security* (Minneapolis: University of Minnesota Press, 1998).
59 See Didier Bigo, "Security and Immigration: Toward a Critique of the Governmentality of Unease," *Alternatives* Vol. 27 (2002), pp. 63–92.
60 See Susan Mains, "Maintaining National Identity at the Border: Scale, Masculinity and the Policing of Immigration in Southern California," in eds. Andrew Herod and Melissa Wright, *Geographies of Power* (Oxford: Blackwell, 2002), pp. 192–214.
61 Andreas, *Border Games*, pp. 3–14.
62 The current Secure Border Initiative calls for approximately US$5 billion worth of additional fencing, vehicle barriers, sensors, surveillance units, roads and command, control and communications centers along the border with Mexico.
63 Timothy Dunn, *The Militarization of the US-Mexico Border, 1978–1992* (Austin: CMAS, 1996).
64 Deaths along the border have roughly doubled since the mid-1990s. See Karl Eschbach, Jacqueline M. Hagan, and Nestor P. Rodríguez, "Deaths During Undocumented Migration: Trends and Policy Implications in the New Era of Homeland Security," *In Defense of the Alien* Vol. 26 (2003), pp. 37–52; and US GAO, *Illegal Immigration: Border-Crossing Deaths Have Doubled Since 1995; Border Patrol's Efforts to Prevent Death Have Not Been Fully Evaluated, Report GAO-06-70* (Washington DC: GAO, 2006).
65 For example, see Didier Bigo, "Security and Immigration;" See also eds. Didier Bigo and Elizabeth Guild, *Controlling Frontiers* (Aldershot: Ashgate, 2005); Virginie Guiraudon and Gallya Lahav, "A Reappraisal of the State Sovereignty Debate: The Case of Migration Control," *Comparative Political Studies* Vol. 33 (2000), pp. 163–95; and Gallya Lahav and Virginie Guiraudon, "Comparative Perspectives on Border Control: Away from the Border, Outside the State," in eds. Peter Andreas and Timothy Snyder, *The Wall Around the West* (Lanham: Rowman and Littlefield, 2000), pp. 55–77.
66 Daniel Kanstroom, "Deportation, Social Control and Punishment," *Harvard Law Review* Vol. 113 (2000), pp. 1890–1935. In the post-9/11 context, see Theresa Miller, "Blurring the Boundaries Between Immigration and Crime Control After September 11," *Boston College Third World Law Journal* Vol. 25 (2005), pp. 81–124.
67 Terry Coonan, "Dolphins Caught in Congressional Fishnets: Immigration Law's New Aggravated Felons." *Georgetown Immigration Law Journal* Vol. 12 (1998), pp. 589–619; and Mathew Coleman, "Immigration Geopolitics Beyond the Mexico-US Border," *Antipode* Vol. 39 (2007), pp. 54–76.
68 Data from Department of Homeland Security, *2006 Yearbook on Immigration Statistics* (Washington DC: Office of Immigration Statistics), Table 36, and Department of Homeland Security, "Total Apprehensions by SAC Investigations, 1992–2003," Personal communication with Department of Homeland Security Office of Statistics, dated November 20, 2005.
69 Map by Jim DeGrand, Department of Geography, The Ohio State University. Data compiled by author from sources listed in note 68 above.

70 For more on this, see Daniel Booth, "Federalism on ICE: State and Local Enforcement of Federal Immigration Law," *Harvard Journal of Law and Public Policy* Vol. 29 (2006), pp. 1063–83; Mathew Coleman, "A Geopolitics of Engagement: Neoliberalism, the War on Terrorism, and the Reconfiguration of US Immigration Enforcement," *Geopolitics* Vol. 12 (2007), pp. 607–34; and Michael Wishnie, "State and Local Police Enforcement of Immigration Laws," *University of Pennsylvania Journal of Constitutional Law* Vol. 6 (2004), pp. 1084–115.

71 See Lisa M. Seghetti, Stephen R. Viña, and Karma Ester, *Enforcing Immigration Law: The Role of the State and Local Enforcement* (Washington DC: CRS, Library of Congress 2004).

72 Miriam Wells, "The Grassroots Reconfiguration of US Immigration Policy," *International Migration Review* Vol. 38 (2004), pp. 1308–47.

73 This language comes from Sue Roberts, Anna Secor, and Matt Sparke, "Neoliberal Geopolitics," *Antipode* Vol. 5 (2003), pp. 886–97. See also Coleman, "A Geopolitics of Engagement."

74 Apprehensions are not the same as removals. Individuals "removed" from the United States include those "deported" from the interior as well as "excluded" at the border. Although the Department of Homeland Security (DHS) publishes the number of removal cases, it does not differentiate between those deported and those excluded. For that reason, I am using apprehensions (see note 75 below) as a proxy for heightened interior enforcement.

75 Immigration enforcement statistics in the United States are recorded as either pertaining to Border Patrol apprehensions or Investigations apprehensions. The latter are in the interior; the former are at the Mexico-US, Canada-US, and maritime borders. See Department of Homeland Security, *Immigration Enforcement Actions: 2005 Annual Report* (Washington DC: Office of Immigration Statistics, 2006).

76 Department of Homeland Security, *2003 Yearbook on Immigration Statistics* (Washington DC: Office of Immigration Statistics, 2004), Table 39; and US GAO, *Immigration Enforcement: Weaknesses Hinder Employment Verification and Worksite Enforcement Efforts*, Report GAO-06-895T (Washington DC: US GPO, 2006).

77 Indeed, in 1999, the ratio of hours spent on worksite enforcement to other interior investigations (for example, on benefits fraud, criminal investigations, and so on) was 1:10. By 2003, it had dropped to almost 1:40. See GAO, *Immigration Enforcement*, p. 15.

78 See Kanstroom, "Deportation, Social Control, and Punishment."

79 Department of Homeland Security, *Operation Community Shield*, available online at www.ice.gov/pi/investigations/comshield/index.htm (last accessed September 30, 2007).

80 Department of Homeland Security, *Operation Predator*, available online at www.ice.gov/pi/news/factsheets/070607operationpredator.htm (last accessed September 30, 2007).

81 Bigo, "Security and Immigration," p. 81.

82 Hardt and Negri, *Multitude*, p. 138.

83 John A. Agnew, "Sovereignty Regimes: Territoriality and State Authority in Contemporary World Politics," *Annals of the Association of American Geographers* Vol. 95 (2005), pp. 437–61. See also James Ferguson and Akhil Gupta, "Spatializing States: Toward an Ethnography of Neoliberal Governmentality," *American Ethnologist* Vol. 29 (2002), pp. 981–1002.

84 Michel Foucault, *"Society Must Be Defended"* (New York: Picador, 2004).

85 Butler describes this as the re-emergence of sovereignty within the field of governmentality. Judith Butler, *Precarious Life: The Powers of Mourning and Violence* (London: Verso, 2005).

86 Michel Foucault, *Security, Territory, Population* (New York: Palgrave, 2007).

87 Foucault, *"Society Must Be Defended,"* p. 13.

88 Hardt and Negri criticize Giorgio Agamben for his obsession with constituted power. See Hardt and Negri, *Multitude*, p. 364, as well as Cesare Casarino and Antonio Negri, "It's a Powerful Life: A Conversation on Contemporary Philosophy," *Cultural Critique* Vol. 57 (2004), p. 187.

7 The biopolitics of American security policy in the twenty-first century

Julian Reid

Introduction

The final decade of the twentieth century was characterized by vast changes in the international organization of power. The end of the Cold War, the development and strengthening of international governmental organizations, intensive technological innovation, the growth and spread of practices and institutions of liberal democracy, the proliferation of non-governmental organizations (NGOs) and spread of a "global" civil society, the penetration of capitalism into previously non-capitalist societies, and the emergence of new systems of global governance (all subsumed under what came to be known both heroically and pejoratively as globalization) were all hallmarks of the immediate post-Cold War era. These changes challenged most traditional assumptions made by theorists of international relations (IR) as to what constitutes power internationally. At the center of the discipline, liberal conceptions of power that privileged the theorization of forms of interdependence rapidly overtook the traditionally statist orientations of political realism. Beyond the center, poststructuralist accounts of the disseminative and biopolitical character of power relations challenged the emphases upon hegemony and imperialism in both critical theory and classical variants of Marxism. By the end of the last decade of the twentieth-century, there was a prevailing assertion within areas of thought concerned with the international that the world we were living in was defined by either a softening or a complexification of power relations in virtually every area of politics, and that this was challenging the rigidity with which power was theorized in more traditional IR accounts.

Among the many texts that sought to account for these developments, none was more ambitious in scope than Michael Hardt and Antonio Negri's *Empire*. Written at the very end of the 1990s, this volume attempted to detail the emergence of a new global order mediated by a new logic and structure of rule.[1] The global order of the post-Cold War world was, according to the authors of *Empire*, no longer defined by the powers of nation-states, but by supranational organisms. Nor was the international order defined by a division between centers and peripheries mediated by the imposition of imperialist forms of power. Rather, this global order was now characterized by no established power center and no reliance on fixed boundaries, but, instead, by a "decentered and deterritorializing apparatus of rule" that operated within expanding and open frontiers.[2] While Hardt and Negri rather curiously chose to retain the denomination "Empire" for this form of order, they were insistent on its departure from traditional forms of imperialism associated with nation-states. Their

Empire was not to be defined by the existence of any nation-state at its core, least of which would be the United States. Rather, as they expressed it, "no state can today form the center of an imperialistic project."[3] Traditional imperialism itself had been displaced by a newly emergent decentered order, the order of Empire.

In theoretical terms, there were significant implications that were said to follow from this shift. Hardt and Negri's major theoretical claim was that we had witnessed the emergence of a "new form of sovereignty" or power in the global era.[4] Contextualizing the development of political modernity in terms of a struggle between the transcendental apparatus of nation-states and the immanent powers of what they called the multitude, Hardt and Negri were quick to declare the prevalence of the powers of immanence over the apparatuses of transcendence in an era of declining nation-states' power and of increasing mobilization of populations across borders.[5] The story of political modernity was about a gradual realization of biopolitical forms of organization concomitant with the decline of the transcendental nation-state order.[6] Following Michel Foucault, Hardt and Negri argued that the foundational dependence of the modern state on a sovereign capacity to take life gradually had been displaced by an investment in a power to protect and promote life.[7] This was not (as was also not the case for Foucault) a simplistically utopian narrative that they were trying to weave. Rather, they portrayed the gradual dissemination of biopolitical arrangements among the dispositions of subjects as a radically "disutopian" project, one through which transcendence was eliminated in order to realize the greater empowerment of the immanent movement of human beings, while at the same time maintaining unprecedented degrees of domination over them.[8] Thus, the biopolitical can best be understood in Hardt and Negri's context as the residual forms that life assumes once sovereignty renders the labor of immanent power constituent. In this sense, biopolitics is only conceivable in the context of the existence of immanent struggles against the transcendental apparatuses of sovereign power. But biopolitics is not reducible to immanence. Immanent power and biopower can be said to exist in a form of confrontation. Yet, the development of biopolitical modernity also functions as a sign of the productive labor of immanence, and equally of the dual weakening and intensification of modern forms of political sovereignty.[9] As a consequence, Hardt and Negri situated contemporary political struggles in terms of an attempt to wrest back the plane of immanence from its domination and colonization by modern sovereignty. The aim was to release, as they described it, the immanent powers of the multitude from the biopolitical shackles of sovereignty.

There have been few so immediately and yet so transitorily influential texts as *Empire*. With the World Trade Center attacks on September 11, 2001, the US declaration of a "war on terror," and the subsequent invasions by the United States of Afghanistan and Iraq, the global order is now widely said to be fragmenting into a form of organization far more anachronistic than it is innovative. Faced with vital threats to their security, the major nation-states of the Western world, it is argued, are reasserting themselves territorially, militarily, and politically. Among them, the United States has committed itself to a war and a political strategy that have invoked accusations of traditional forms of imperialism.[10] It is also claimed that the postmodern complexities and fluidities of the global order are now being rent asunder by the re-imposition of a form of power and organization enduringly modern: the sovereign, imperialist power of the nation-state, especially that of the United States. The "permanence, eternality, and necessity" that Hardt and Negri attributed to the postmodern global order are thus interpreted by some as fragile now and, perhaps ultimately, obsolete. Consequently, we are witnessing a return to a condition of international politics that some consider to be much more consistent with the prevailing models of the late nineteenth century than with Hardt and Negri's Empire.[11]

In contrast to these assertions, the central line of argument I want to pursue in this chapter is that it is a mistake to construe the war on terror, the invasions of Iraq and Afghanistan, and the broader reassertion of US military and strategic power globally as simple "returns" to imperialism.[12] The 9/11 attacks did initiate some changes in the international organization of power. Yet, they did not foster a power regression. Central to my discussion here is the question of how we understand the relation of sovereign power to biopower in the context of the war on terror. In essence, while there are problems with the argument that Hardt and Negri make regarding the extent to which biopolitical forces were said to exceed the traditional sovereign power of nation-states at the end of the twentieth century, their main observations about the increasingly biopolitical character of international order still ring true. The major weakness with Hardt and Negri's account is their failure to fully theorize the intersections and oscillations between biopower and sovereignty that still constitute the strategy of power pursued in a late-modern context.

But this analytical failure can be remedied by looking at the work of Gilles Deleuze and Felix Guattari, from whom the concept of deterritorialization (relied upon by Hardt and Negri) actually is derived.[13] In turn, by thinking about how deterritorializations effected by biopolitical bodies are intersecting with reterritorializations pursued by sovereign nation states, we can understand the contemporary war on terror in continuity with the forms of development that reshaped the international system during the 1990s. I argue that accounts insistent upon reading contemporary US strategy as a reassertion of a traditional form of imperialism that destroys the complex systems of global governance created during the 1990s are overstated. They neglect the integral logistical and normative roles that biopolitical forces continue to play in the international organization of power today. In addition, such accounts place too great an emphasis on the role and agency of government, and especially on the discursive shift that supposedly has occurred within US foreign policy and in its articulation since the declaration of the war on terror. A closer analysis of how the war on terror is conducted, with a particular focus on the war in Iraq, demonstrates the continuing importance of biopolitical forces in the international constitution of power.

Following from this, I want to think about the consequences of such a reading of the contemporary organization of power for understandings of the potential for critical responses to the war on terror. In interpreting this war, most IR theorists are still largely trapped within the narrow confines of the debate between Hobbesian and Kantian positions.[14] Can the codification of international law and the development of multilateral international institutions posit a solution to the problem of sovereignty? Or does sovereignty always, by necessity, override the potential for a cosmopolitan world order? These are the kinds of parameters that, even with the complex changes presaged by the war on terror, are still being used to frame the terms of the debate within IR theory in the twenty-first century. Attempting to think about the problems in the relations between law and force in such dichotomous terms forges the kind of simplistic characterizations of IR in terms of anarchy or order, characterizations that continue to sustain the age-old dialectic of realism versus liberalism (that remains the motor of IR theory). One of the significant contributions that *Empire* has made to IR theory is to demonstrate the collusion between sovereign and biopolitical forms in the constitution of modern power internationally. The development of international organizations and international law, the codification of human rights, the range of liberal aggressions at work in the onslaught by globalization are all features of forces that can only superficially be distinguished from the modern institutions of sovereign state power.

Thus, there is a continuum between the form of sovereignty with which nation-states (still today) utilize force to breach the law and the modality of sovereignty with which the most narrowly biopolitical account of man is being enforced, often through law, by humanitarian and other generally liberal actors in the world. But this continuity is something that IR theory still struggles to recognize. If we want to resist the reassertion of the form of sovereignty at work today in the context of the war on terror, it is essential that we focus upon this complicity between law and force, or, to put it another way, the complicity between the biopolitical and the sovereign.[15]

The rest of this chapter proceeds as follows. In the first section, I give a brief account of how the war on terror is being interpreted as a reassertion of the sovereign and imperial power of the nation-state. I criticize this account for its over-reliance on the idea of a shift in the discourse of government and foreign policy in the United States, an idea that is used as an explanation for that reassertion. In the second and third sections, I reveal the extent to which the actual deployment of US sovereign power in the context of the war on terror remains conditioned by features that are continuous with the forms of development in the international system that occurred in the 1990s, and that Hardt and Negri identified with the degeneration of the nation-state's sovereign power. In the final section, I offer a reflection on where this analysis leaves us, particularly in terms of thinking about the political legacies of humanist politics, and also in terms of the necessity of avoiding the cheap humanist traps currently being set by thinkers who are concerned with the promotion of global civil society as a response to terror. At the very least, the aim of the last section is to illustrate the extent to which the organization of power in the twenty-first century remains defined by features that emerged in the twentieth and to start to explore the consequences of such a reading for political engagement and critique in the era of the war on terror.

The "return" of imperialism?

Those who assert that we have witnessed a regression in the international organization of power since 9/11 point to the contingencies of the global political order during the 1990s.[16] The end of the Cold War, they argue, bequeathed the United States a preponderance of power internationally. The absence of a symmetrical threat allowed the United States, under the auspices of the Clinton administration, to embark upon a multilateral strategy that involved the cultivation of the very forms of interdependence and connectivity that Hardt and Negri (among others) assumed were definite indicators of a permanent and necessary change in the organization of international politics. The shift in administrative/political power nationally within the United States, coupled with the 9/11 attacks, provided the grounds for a change of direction in US foreign policy, and for the subsequent return to a more traditionally unipolar and (ultimately) imperialist world order.[17] As Michael Cox describes it, the intellectual groundwork for a reassertion of US imperialism had been carried out some years in advance of 9/11. As early as 1997, the neo-conservative think-tank Project for the New American Century had dedicated its work to the reframing of the Republican agenda and was advocating a "restoration of a foreign policy of American leadership" based on "the three M's of American foreign policy: ... Military strength, Morality, and Mastery."[18]

Not only was it the case that the increasingly multilateral character of international politics during the 1990s was perceived to threaten the national interest of the United States, but there was also a sense that a more fundamentally normative commitment to the defense of the international state system was at stake. The war on terror itself has been conceived within the United States as an attempt to defend the very forms of the nation-state and the international state system from incursions and threats shaped or conditioned by globalization. "International terrorism is not dangerous because it can defeat us in a war, but because it can potentially destroy the domestic contract of the state by further undermining its ability to protect its citizens from attack," wrote Audrey Kurth Cronin after 9/11.[19] The type of threat posed by Al-Qaeda as well as by other international terrorist groups appears to have been interpreted by the Republican right in the United States as an advanced expression of the deterritorializing force of globalization. Thus, the war on terror has been articulated within key areas of the US foreign policy establishment as a commitment to the defense of the traditional values and institutions of the nation-state against deterritorializing dangers. The current foreign policy strategy of the United States is still articulated in these terms, that is to say, as an attempt to force a regression within the international system back to an older, more reliable form of order. This is viewed as a return or regression that can secure and reinforce state boundaries against the encroachments and malign insecurities forged through various processes of globalization.

One of the most remarkable features of the current articulation of US foreign policy is the apparently naked commitment to imperialism that the United States seems to display. Throughout much of its history, the United States has been accused of pursuing an imperialist agenda.[20] Still, customarily, US foreign policy decisions have been accompanied by discursive commitments to democratically anti-imperialist ends. But it would nonetheless appear that the current reassertion of American power is avowedly imperialist. "Mastery" has become a positive term of reference in the current US foreign policy lexicon, and the concomitant condition of possibility for "enslavement" is an inferred aim of US strategy. IR theorists are used to dealing with orthodoxies that either discount the role of structural economic or political inequalities within the international system as unimportant (for IR's understanding of how that system functions, something that is typical of the realist perspective) or account for those inequalities, but as contingencies that the system is in the process of overcoming through the development of democratization (this is a traditional liberal internationalist view). In turn, IR scholars have become accustomed to critiques of those orthodox interpretations that demonstrate how essential the production of inequality and unevenness really is to the existence of the international system. Thus, at the turn of the new millennium, it seemed that we were able to witness a puzzling reversal in the order of those debates. Neo-conservative discourses on the international system were revealed as naked in their ambitions about the possibility and pursuit of imperialism while definitively critical accounts of international politics were insisting upon the permanence and necessity of a "post-imperialist" order (à la Hardt and Negri, for example).

But according to some, the current state of world politics has made Hardt and Negri's claims about this necessity of a post-imperialist moment in international politics look naïve. Critical appraisals of the war on terror continually make reference to the neo-conservative discourse as if it were an unproblematically accurate descriptive account of the deployment of US power.[21] Yet, critiques of the war on terror that buy into the regime's own account of US power and claim a return to imperialism ignore the vital roles played in the conduct of the war by agencies, practices, and discourses of biopolitics. The discursive attempts among the Republican right, for example, to qualify US foreign policy in terms of imperialism are, in a certain sense, strangely out-of-sync with the actual deployment of the sovereign power of the United States internationally. After all, the assertion of US sovereignty in the midst of today's war on terror remains conditioned to the continuing roles of institutions, processes, and procedures that Hardt and Negri had identified in the 1990s in the context of a deterritorialization of sovereignty and other advances on the part of biopolitical power. Here, I am thinking chiefly about the roles played in the 1990s by the United Nations and by a whole range of non-governmental actors that adopted as their own strategies the types of power shifts that Hardt and Negri have described and detailed. These transnational agencies and their practices remain crucial today to both the logistical efficacy and the assertion of legitimacy that accompanies the reassertion of US sovereign power.[22] It is fair to say that Hardt and Negri's concept of Empire placed too large an emphasis on the prevalence of biopolitical forms and deterritorialized forces at the expanse of traditional units of sovereign power in international politics. Nevertheless, in order to comprehend the strategy of power at work in the international organization of power today, it is still necessary to pay heed to the role of these transnational institutions and processes. Part of this chapter's goal is to do just this.

Rethinking sovereignty amid the war on terror

There is little doubt that Hardt and Negri's assertions about the degree and necessity of change presented in *Empire* were courageous intellectual endeavors. Again, the apparent return of US sovereign (perhaps imperial) power that seems to have occurred since 9/11 makes it look like the boldness of Hardt and Negri's initial claims is now compromised. Even Negri himself has intimated so.[23] That being said, there were always going to be problems with a form of analysis that, despite Hardt and Negri's repeated attempts to deny it, often reads like a teleological account of political modernity.[24] But, more importantly perhaps, their insistence on highlighting trends that exemplify a prevailing deterritorialization of power over reterritorializing capacities of nation-states, on exploring the immanent powers of a multitude over the formerly transcendent powers of state sovereignty, and on revealing the expansive

132 J. Reid

rather than retractive characteristics of many phenomena in the international system has done an injustice to the traditions of political thought that their own ideas are derived from. Deleuze and Guattari, whose influence hangs heavy over Hardt and Negri's *Empire*, actually provide a more coherent way of approaching the forms of change that Hardt and Negri claimed were operative in the late 1990s. Rather than implying that the forms of deterritorialization provoked by globalization were eternal or even necessary (something that Hardt and Negri's theoretical model intimates), Deleuze and Guattari argued throughout their work that processes of deterritorialization, by necessity, always occur in relation to corollary responses in the form of reterritorialization.[25] The international state system, according to Deleuze and Guattari, oscillates continually between two opposing tendencies that are nonetheless inextricably bound with one another: the schizoid revolutionary tendency; and the paranoid fascist trend. As they describe it:

> The social axiomatic of modern societies is caught between two poles, and is constantly oscillating from one pole to the other. Born of decoding and deterritorialization, on the ruins of the despotic machine, these societies are caught between the Urstaat that they would like to resuscitate as an overcoding and reterritorializing unity, and the unfettered flows that carry them toward an absolute threshold. They recode with all their might, with worldwide dictatorship, local dictators, and an all-powerful police, while decoding—or allowing the decoding of—the fluent quantities of their capital and their populations. They are torn in two directions: archaism and futurism, neoarchaism and ex-futurism, paranoia and schizophrenia. They vacillate between two poles: the paranoiac despotic sign, the sign-signifier of the despot that they try to revive as a unit of code; and the sign-figure of the schizo as a unit of decoded flux, a schiz, a pointsign, or flow-break. They try to hold on to the one, but they pour or flow out through the other. They are continually behind or ahead of themselves.[26]

Deleuze and Guattari's theorization of the necessarily intertwined processes of deterritorialization and reterritorialization provides a more helpful framework to comprehend the apparent reassertion of the sovereign power of the nation-state (the United States above all) today, in the context of what was previously said to be an increasingly decentered global order. For Deleuze and Guattari, there is no predestined certainty committing the international system to a decentered or deterritorialized form of rule, as was argued throughout *Empire*. Rather, we can understand the contemporary moment in the development of the international organization of power as the articulation of this basic oscillation between deterritorializing and reterritorializing forces. The act of reterritorialization, through which the nation-state reasserts its sovereignty and redraws its boundaries in the constitution of "a milieu of interiority" (as Deleuze and Guattari put it), necessarily requires the presence of deterritorializing flows. Indeed, we can only understand the global scope with which the reterritorializing force of sovereign power is being asserted today in relation to the global flows through which the deterritorialization of power took place during the 1990s. The global assertion of state sovereign power (or imperialism sometimes) that is occurring in the context of the war on terror assumes, as its condition of possibility, the existence of spaces, practices, and discourses created by the very bodies that contributed to the deterritorialization of sovereignty in the 1990s. This is an important element of the theorization of power in the war on terror that largely goes ignored in those many IR accounts that emphasize a return to a traditional form of imperialism (through US policies). In spite of discursive commitments that allegedly substantiate a form of imperialist power that revokes any reliance on allies or alliances, champions the national interest at all costs, neglects the relevance of norms, or eschews any sort of moral and ethical underpinning to policy, today's global war on terror is still conditioned by biopolitical flows, agencies, and procedures.

We can start to think about this issue of the continued presence of biopolitical power forms despite imperial appearances concretely in relation to the ongoing war in Iraq. One of the major features of the immediate post-Cold War era was an expansion in the aims and ambitions of the United Nations (and its agencies). In the 1990s, there was a new spirit of optimism about the potential of the international organization to fulfil the humanitarian tasks described in its founding Charter.[27] There was even a widespread belief that the United Nations' newly burgeoning strength and expanded scope were representative of a shift away from an international system predicated on the sovereignty of nation-states and toward a supranational and decentered global order that could empower a truly deterritorialized humanity against the sovereignty of nation-states.[28] One of the most important initiatives of the United Nations in this perspective, after the end of the Cold War, was the imposition of a comprehensive sanctions regime upon the state of Iraq, implemented on humanitarian grounds.[29] The Iraqi state was targeted on the ground that it repressed "the Iraqi civilian population in many parts of Iraq," especially the Kurdish people in the North.[30] Perversely, the maintenance of this sanctions regime throughout the 1990s caused a more generalized humanitarian crisis throughout Iraqi society. This humanitarian effect eventually led to the creation of the UN-mandated oil-for-food program that was supposed to mediate the sale of Iraqi oil in return for economic assistance to Iraq (up until the US invasion in 2003). The oil-for-food program started with the provision of economic and basic humanitarian assistance, but soon turned into an involvement of UN agencies in the entire project of the Iraqi state infrastructure redevelopment.

From its inception in 1995, the oil-for-food program in Iraq expanded gradually beyond an initial emphasis on facilitating the distribution of food and medicine to incorporate by 2002 a crucial dimension of infrastructure rebuilding in a vast array of sectors (food, food handling, health, nutrition, electricity, agriculture and irrigation, education, transport and telecommunication, water and sanitation, housing, settlement rehabilitation, demining, assistance to vulnerable groups, oil industry spare parts and equipment, construction, industry, labor and social affairs, youth and sports, information, culture, religious affairs, justice, finance, and banking).[31] The UN program was regarded as effective insofar as it disciplined the Iraqi state to dedicate funds derived from the oil sale to its population rather than to military investments.[32] To an important degree, the program appeared to represent a biopolitically defined endeavor since it was aimed at an increase in the welfare and well-being of Iraqi people's lives at the expanse of the sovereign will of the Iraqi state.

The US-led war in Iraq in 2003 was widely held to represent a direct challenge to the practice and normative framework underlying the United Nations' involvement there. The humanitarian elements of the UN policy, always hotly contested, were abruptly swept away (defenders of the UN program claimed) by the flagrant pursuit of US national security and economic interests. Consequently, in the run up to the war, we appeared to witness a new and significant split between the United States and the United Nations, and between US goals and the perspectives championed by the broader community of NGOs that were dedicated to fulfilling biopolitical objectives.[33] Yet, the development of the UN oil-for-food program ultimately played a fundamental role in the organization of the US war in Iraq. Indeed, the United States' conduct of the war in 2003 (and beyond) was predicated logistically on the existence of the dense social, political, and economic infrastructures created by the United Nations in Iraq through the oil-for-food program and in the prior context of humanitarian assistance.[34] The adoption of UN Security Council Resolution 1483 in 2003 led to the official establishment of relations between the United Nations and the occupying forces in Iraq and to the transfer of responsibilities for oil-for-food activities to the provisional authorities representing the occupying powers.[35] Indeed, the broader framework of the war and later occupation remained fairly consistent with the development of so-called liberal or humanitarian warfare strategies such as those deployed during the 1990s, strategies in which the United Nations often played a major role. In fact, the Bush administration went to inordinate lengths to secure the support of all sorts of non-governmental and humanitarian actors in advance of the actual conduct of the war. Having established an inter-agency group for the planning of post-war relief and reconstruction in Iraq, the US government then held multilateral and bilateral meetings with NGOs in order to pre-plan the new Iraq reconstruction effort. Financial aid was provided to enable the United Nations High Commissioner for Refugees (UNHCR) and humanitarian agencies to pre-position humanitarian aid. Warehouse spaces were paid for in neighboring Gulf countries to store humanitarian supplies.[36] And strategies of social reconstruction were integrated as fully as possible with the military operations in ways that would be congruous with "best-practice" guidelines developed in previous years by the United Nations itself.[37] Thus, the war in Iraq and its aftermath, in crucial ways, were conceived along biopolitical lines.

We can see that the conduct of the Iraq War was not only defined in the simple terms of a naked expression of sovereign power or imperialism by the United States, an interpretation that has been frequently given in critical analyses. The accounts of verbal sparring between the United States and the rest of the international community prior to and during the war in Iraq draw a thin veil over a thick set of logistical relations that continued to combine the sovereign power of the United States with a whole range of biopolitical actors, bodies, and forces. In spite of the many ways the US use of force in the war on terror does circumvent traditional UN norms and principles, in logistical terms, relations between the United States, the United Nations, and the broader domain of global civil society remain very strong. Thus, contrary to the popular perception that the American state is operating in the world on its own terms,[38] US strategy today remains predicated in important respects on the securing of logistical support from all sorts of biopolitical agencies and institutions, among which the United Nations is of central importance.[39] The claims that, in pursuing a "neo-imperial agenda," the United States is neglecting the need to build coalitions with other states or with multilateral agencies to orchestrate aid and assist in rebuilding failed or war-torn states are wide off the mark.[40] The invasion that took Iraq by storm in the spring of 2003 was a complex amalgam of forces that combined the sovereign power of the United States with the biopower of various deterritorialized actors.

The support of forces of deterritorialization for the US-led war on terror is not merely logistical. It is also born out of a shared normative commitment about the conduct of the war. Throughout the 1990s, those at the forefront of liberal political thought, humanitarian activists, and many NGOs concerned with the pursuit of a humanitarian agenda all lobbied international institutions and states for a more forceful approach to dealing with human rights abuses in places such as Iraq or Afghanistan. Some leading humanitarian thinkers and commentators such as Michael Ignatieff bemoaned the "extraordinary gap between rhetoric and performance" in the human rights policies of Western states.[41] Humanitarians would object to what they perceived were strategic limitations that nation-states imposed upon the forms of militarized intervention that they pursued in the name of human rights. This was a continual feature of the liberal critique of the development of humanitarian war during the 1990s.[42] Liberal critics also objected to the failure of nation-states to pursue humanitarian causes in conflicts that emerged outside the realm of states' material self-interests.[43] Yet, ultimately, when liberal humanitarians targeted specific states for chastisement (Iraq or Afghanistan), or when they demanded a more forceful approach to the issue of human rights abuses, they actually created the normative and discursive conditions for the reassertion of the kind of sovereign (perhaps imperial) power that we witnessed in the US-led wars in Afghanistan and Iraq. Many current critical appraisals of the war in Iraq point to its supposedly "unilateral" character. But these views ignore the vital roles that humanitarian arguments have played in legitimizing the war, and they overlook the continual citation of UN resolutions in support of the war. After all, in waging war on Iraq, the US and British governments were able to make repeated references to the perceived failures of Iraq to implement specific UN Security Council resolutions, particularly Resolutions 678, 687, and 1441 (even though there was no direct authorization from the United Nations for the war in Iraq).[44] The so-called imperial United States was able to draw on an indirect or implied form of authority through its own interpretation of edicts directed at Iraq by the United Nations throughout the 1990s.

Sovereignty and biopolitics in the twenty-first century

What does all this tell us about the international organization of power amid the war on terror? Does the war on terror represent an increasingly unilateral expression of the sovereign power of the United States? How can we understand the ways the sovereign power of states relates to the prevailing powers of biopolitical bodies such as the United Nations, various NGOs, and the broader global civil society? Are those latter forms of power/powerful agencies, so crucial to international developments in the 1990s, now simply on the wane? Are we witnessing the subordination of biopolitical agents and discourses to the returning self-interested strategies of sovereign or even imperialist states, as some claim? And how can we theorize the interrelation and co-development of sovereignty and biopower in the international conditions of the early twenty-first century?

Currently, in IR theory, and as I suggested above, the debate is between conditions of possibility for a global biopolitical order (in which a universalized humanity is supposedly enfranchised) and more traditional structures built around the sovereign power of nation-states. The reassertion of the sovereign power of certain Western states in the war on terror is being interpreted either as an attempt to defend an already existing biopolitically grounded system through exceptional circumstances that require suspension of some of those biopolitical principles that appear to define this system, or as a confirmation of the belief that commitments to the development of global biopolitics (that could challenge state sovereignty) are doomed to fail. Thus, either sovereignty is seen to be tragically dominating the domain of biopolitics, or it is perceived as a current transgression of the ongoing development of biopolitics (perhaps, paradoxically, to better defend the biopolitical order). In any case, as was stated above, Hardt and Negri's prior assertions that biopolitical forms and forces have taken over the responsibility of shaping the global order of Empire from the sovereign nation-state look as if they are facing a tough challenge. Again, in this critical context, it makes much more sense to turn to Deleuze and Guattari's more contingent theorizations of power strategies if one cares to comprehend what is occurring in the contemporary international order.

Deleuze and Guattari pitch the relations between biopolitical and sovereign bodies, or what they call forces of deterritorialization and reterritorialization, in terms of a permanent and agonistic tension that makes it possible to imagine an assertion of one without the necessary rejection of the other. Deterritorialization is, by necessity, inseparable from processes of reterritorialization, Deleuze and Guattari once again argue.[45] Yet, they also compel us to think about relations between forces of de- and re-territorialization, between the sovereign and the biopolitical, in terms of strategy, that is to say, in terms of relations organized in the name, for the development, or for the overall sustenance of the condition of political sovereignty.[46] Forces of deterritorialization are continually being set in motion by a form of sovereignty that operates strategically by recombining and entering into new relations with these forces in an effort to create new political assemblages.[47] Indeed, according to Deleuze and Guattari's line of thinking, it is still important to maintain a distinction between processes of deterritorialization and reterritorialization, on the one hand, and the matter of the constitution of the sovereign and the biopolitical, on the other. We can say that it is only through a subsequent process of reterritorialization that forces of deterritorialization can be made biopolitical. The constitution of biopolitics is what defines the strategy of sovereignty. Its reterritorializations are the tactical effects through which deterritorializing forces are brought back within the realm of sovereign control. Thus, the biopolitical is never to be thought of as a naïve representation of a deterritorializing (or transnational) movement, but, rather, is to be seen as primarily defined by the imprint of an always reterritorializing maneuver.

In this sense, the distinctions that Hardt and Negri draw between forms of deterritorialization and instances of reterritorialization, between the biopolitical and the sovereign, between the immanent and the transcendent, or between a constituent power and a constituted power do not pay sufficient attention to Deleuze and Guattari's original theorization of the way strategies of power operate. Within Deleuze and Guattari's framework, the movement of immanence of power described by Hardt and Negri in the context of globalization or Empire always functions not as a simple opposition to transcendence (of power or political sovereignty), but as a reconstitution or recombination of power/sovereignty. Thus, immanence is haunted by the forms of transcendence that it allegedly seeks to ward off.[48] And the biopolitical today functions as the figuration of such a haunting. When we speak of biopolitics, therefore, we are always speaking about political agencies and practices that seek to reconstitute the issue of political sovereignty. The key institutions and actors that make up Hardt and Negri's account of the biopolitics of Empire (the United Nations, the NGOs, and global civil society) are to be understood in this fashion.[49] They are agencies/institutions that do not just enact a deterritorialization of sovereignty, but, rather, already operate a reterritorialization of deterritorializing flows of immanence in the name of political sovereignty. Still, in this particular analytical context, it remains essential to pose the question of how these strategic relations among immanence, biopolitics, and sovereignty are produced. What precisely is being deterritorialized, and how is reterritorialization by these agencies/institutions enabled? The defining feature of the modern international system has been the conflict between the sovereign powers of the system's constituent states and the development of biopolitical organs or agents generated toward the pursuit of an ethical commitment to a universalized humanity. But the account of humanity provided through the institutionalization of biopolitical practices and through the creation of agencies in charge of promoting and defending the rights of humanity in universal terms is a statically imperial one.[50] By defining humanity in accordance with internationalized laws and norms, and by reducing it to another imperial injunction, biopolitical modernity plays into the hands of modern sovereignty (a more detailed study of this phenomenon of universalized humanity is provided by Kosuke Shimizu's chapter in this volume). Coordinating the global deterritorializations of humanity by way of a concomitant belief in universalization realizes the conditions of possibility for the imposition of a new form of transcendent and sovereign power. Global deterritorializations beget global reterritorializations. The idea and pursuit of a universally coded and legally empowered humanity necessarily invokes the idea and pursuit of a universal state. It is for these very reasons that we cannot make sense of the globality with which the sovereign power of the United States is asserted today other than in the context of a global biopolitics.

Contesting sovereign power

What are the implications of this intimacy between sovereignty and biopolitics for a form of political engagement with the reconstituted international order of the early twenty-first century? How does an illumination of the biopolitical underpinnings of that order help us to think about ways of reshaping it? The argument about the intimacy between sovereignty and the biopolitical suggests not only that we ought to be skeptical about the capacities of biopolitical agencies/institutions to impose normative restraints on the current exercise of American sovereignty, but also that we need to think more carefully about the ways answers to questions regarding what human life is or what it may become under biopolitical regimes are always already constituted by imperial claims about the nature of the human. In the midst of conflicts and wars (against terror) in which we have seen headquarters of the International Committee of the Red Cross deliberately and openly targeted, it is time to recognize the limitations of a humanism that asserts itself transcendentally and imposes itself in a dogmatic style reminiscent of the religious traditions that used to attribute power over nature to God. Some have argued that such a recognition of transcendental humanism's limitations does not need to lead to its rejection. Instead, it may still be interpreted (and used) as a demand for a return to the question of how to enact a humanistic politics that would not fall for a universalization of values or would not attempt to secure (and securitize) those values inside the institutionalized or procedural frameworks relied upon by the contemporary global biopolitical order.[51] In many ways, such a revised humanistic endeavor might consist in instigating a Deleuzean theoretical opening for the purpose of a politics that still seems to inspire Hardt and Negri, and particularly their concept of the multitude (despite Hardt and Negri's failure to grasp fully the Deleuzean insight).[52] But is it possible to pursue a politics that deterritorializes the sovereign power of the state without being reterritorialized by it? Can we deterritorialize humanity away from the sovereignty of states without humanity being made biopolitical (and captured by biopolitical agencies and institutions) in the process?

It is doubtful that this last set of questions can be answered satisfactorily by mobilizing the very resources used by the humanist tradition, something that some critical thinkers (such as Paul Gilroy) have recently attempted to do. Indeed, when humanism is called in to respond to these questions (questions regarding what human life is and what it may become, once again), its conceptual imagination is generally cut off by fear. The subject of diversity of life, of the different forms that human life may take, has always tended to be subordinated to the imperative (driven by fear) of the defense of the forms of life that already exist. "Let us educate our children to give answers ranging from +1 to -1 on a seven point scale; that will ensure the tolerance of variability which alone can incorporate our innate diversity," argued H. J. Eysenck in his classic essay "Humanism and the Future."[53] The security of the human always requires the command of the logistical infrastructures through which a biopolitical account of humanity can be organized and provided. In the process, the very essence of the human—its innate indeterminacy, and its nomadic capacity for movement and variation—is withdrawn from it in the interest of the protection of the dominant norm. Hence, the humanist desire to secure the conditions of possibility of humanity becomes a declaration of war against the fundamental conditions of expression for the human. It is a form of biopolitical war waged upon the possibility of difference in and of itself. And it is a war based on the demarcation or difference between those forms of life that constitute the conditions of survival of a biopolitical account of humanity and those other forms of existence that supposedly do not contribute to those conditions, and, as such, may die or be killed.

In their final major work together, *What Is Philosophy?*, Deleuze and Guattari recognized this problem directly. "Human rights say nothing about the immanent modes of existence of people provided by rights," they wrote.[54] In a context where the idea of the human is used as a destructive imposition and as a ground for violent interventions in processes through which the nomadic potentiality of life itself is being expressed, Deleuze and Guattari argued that we must feel only "the shame of being human" and experience the "ignominy of the possibilities of life that we are offered" within the narrow confines of what we are allowed to be and become biopolitically.[55]

Better to die an animal, they suggested, than to live the ignominy of a biopolitically enfranchised life under a condition of liberal humanity.

Inverting the biopolitical distinction between the human and the animal in this way, or expressing solidarity with the suffering of peoples and subjectivities labelled as animals (a suffering justified by claims about the sovereignty of the human over the animal), is a foundational task for anyone interested in changing the conditions through which the United States has exerted its foreign policy in the early years of the twenty-first century. In spite of all the insistence to the contrary, it is of paramount importance that we pay attention to, and express our solidarity with, the abominable sufferings of those subjected forms of life on which the hubris of claims about the capacity to represent the rights of humanity today rest. Doing this may offer a glimmer of hope for the possibility of a different response to the political problems posed by US foreign and security policies in these difficult times. This would also be a response different in measure from the debased solutions provided by liberal theorists in IR who continue to push their project for a "global civil society" as if it were a viable alternative to salvage liberal and humanist ideas from the wreckages of contemporary imperialism. In the wake of the 9/11 attacks, Mary Kaldor, one of the key proponents of the idea of a global civil society, called for a further extension and strengthening of international humanitarian law.[56] The idea of a global civil society is presented, according to Kaldor, as a direct form of struggle with both the Bush administration and Al-Qaeda in order to "bring the 'inside' of human rights and democracy home."[57] Douglas Kellner, another advocate of the global civil society approach, calls for the establishment of a "global campaign against terrorism" and for a reorientation of the agenda of the "anti-capitalist globalization movement" towards the fight against terrorism, militarism, and war.[58] Along the same line of reasoning, Benjamin Barber argues that the creation of "a just and inclusive world in which all citizens are stakeholders is the first objective of a rational strategy against terrorism."[59] Incredibly, in the context of a war where liberal regimes find themselves pitched against an enemy whose hostility they articulate as an attempt to appropriate and control the terms of the debate over the ontology of the human, liberal dissidence expresses its yearning for yet another incessant pursuit of imperial ideals. In the midst of a sovereign or imperial imposition of liberal humanism (as a preferred strategy to fight terror), so-called dissident voices within liberal societies call forth the specter of an even greater expansion of the central principles of the humanist project. In the midst of a vanishing of the law, their demand is to pursue the law even more rigorously and vigorously. The actions of the enemy are deemed "predominantly the consequence of pathology and yield neither to rational analysis nor understanding,"[60] and, as such, dialogue "is not possible with such groups."[61]

In a larger historical perspective, it is worth recognizing the importance of attempts at politically enabling accounts of humanity under conditions of excess controlled by territorially sovereign nation-states. Yet, here (in the West) and today (at the turn of the twenty-first century), we are witnessing a biopolitical attempt to provide yet another account of human life through a strategy whereby the former and arbitrary form of political sovereignty appeared to be challenged at first (as Hardt and Negri claimed), but later revealed itself as (and turned into) the central source of a newly insidious imperialism. Simultaneously though, this particular biopolitical understanding of human existence is also being challenged by another, radically hostile, interpretation of what human life is and what it may become. Struggling against the sovereign impositions of this biopolitical power, we are witnessing the emergence of an attempt at constituting even another way of politically honoring life. The war on terror is precisely this: a struggle between competing sovereign impositions over the political constitution of life, each of which performs different kinds of injustices vis-à-vis the lives of human beings. Thus, in this critical context, the possibility of constituting another political way of life must still be posed. But it cannot be another identity politics, masquerading itself as *the* authentic humanism, and seeking to overcome resistances or alleged affronts from what it pegs as its others by eliminating or excluding their differences. Nor can it be about converting difference into identity or subordinating the play of difference to some banal code by means of which it could be policed. What it can be, rather, is the politics of a life that does not seek security through identity, nor through the development of a world society (the survival of which would be fostered by the subordination of all values to the value of security itself). It is the possibility of a life lived beyond humanism, security, and the law.

Notes

This chapter draws on some insights from an earlier article (Julian Reid, "The Biopolitics of the War on Terror: A Critique of the 'Return of Imperialism' Thesis in International Relations," *Third World Quarterly*, Vol. 26, No. 2 (2005), pp. 237–52), and from some thoughts first expressed in my book *The Biopolitics of the War on Terror* (Manchester: Manchester University Press, 2006).

1 Michael Hardt and Antonio Negri, *Empire* (Cambridge, MA: Harvard University Press, 2000), p. i.
2 Ibid., p. xii.
3 Ibid., p. xiv.
4 Ibid., p. i.
5 The concept of immanent or "constituent" power is developed in *Labor of Dionysus* and is close to Marx's concept of "living labor." The Foucaultian concept of biopower is only developed in the latter part of Hardt and Negri's *Empire*. The distinction between immanence and biopower remains under-theorized in their work, leading to several lines of critique about their theoretical presentation. For more on such critiques, see Julian Reid, *The Biopolitics of the War on Terror: Life Struggles, Liberal Modernity, and the Defence of Logistical Societies* (Manchester: Manchester University Press, 2006), chapter 6.
6 Ibid., p. 23.
7 Michel Foucault, *The History of Sexuality: Volume 1, An Introduction* (London: Penguin, 1991), pp. 135–59.
8 For a more expansive account of the violence of these processes, see Julian Reid, "War, Liberalism and Modernity: The Biopolitical Provocations of *Empire*," *Cambridge Review of International Affairs*, Vol. 17, No. 1 (2004), pp. 63–79.
9 Hardt and Negri, *Empire*, pp. 83–7. For an elaboration of the concept of disutopia, see their earlier *Labor of Dionysus: A Critique of the State-Form* (Minneapolis: University of Minnesota Press, 1994), pp. 310–13.
10 Ivan Eland, "The Empire Strikes Out: The 'New Imperialism' and Its Fatal Flaws," *Policy Analysis*, Vol. 459 (2002), pp. 1–27.
11 Michael Cox, "The Empire's Back in Town, or America's Imperial Temptation—Again," *Millennium: Journal of International Studies*, Vol. 32, No. 1 (2003), pp 1–29.

12 As, for example, is argued in Tariq Ali, "Re-colonizing Iraq," *New Left Review*, Vol. 21 (2003), pp. 1–19.
13 For an additional account of the problems encountered with Deleuze and Guattari's concept of deterritorialization in Hardt and Negri's theory of immanent power, see Reid, *The Biopolitics of the War on Terror*, chapter 6.
14 See, for example, Robert Kagan, "Power and Weakness," *Policy Review*, Vol. 113 (June–July 2002), pp. 3–28.
15 See also Derek Gregory, "The Black Flag: Guantanamo Bay and the Space of Exception," *Geografiska Annaler, Series B* Vol. 88, No. 4 (2006), pp. 405–27.
16 See Cox, "The Empire's Back in Town," pp. 13–14.
17 David Hastings Dunn, "Myths, Motivations and 'Misunderestimations': The Bush Administration and Iraq," *International Affairs*, Vol. 79, No. 2 (2003), pp. 279–97.
18 See www.newamericancentury.org.
19 Audrey Kurth Cronin, "Rethinking Sovereignty: American Strategy in the Age of Terrorism," *Survival*, Vol. 44, No. 2 (2002), pp. 119–39.
20 The denouncement of the imperialism of US foreign policy can be traced back as far as the formation of the American Anti-Imperialist League in 1899.
21 See, for example, Ronald Bleier, "Invading Iraq: The Road to Perpetual War," *Middle East Policy*, Vol. 9, No. 4 (2002), pp. 35–42; Cox, "The Empire's Back in Town," pp. 13–14; Eland, "The Empire Strikes out," p. 5; and Ali, "Re-colonizing Iraq."
22 See also Marieke de Goede, "Underground Money," *Cultural Critique*, Vol. 65 (Winter 2007), pp.140–63.
23 See "The Imperial Backlash on Empire: Antonio Negri Interviewed by Ida Dominijanni," available at www.16beavergroup.org/mtarchive/archives/000487.php.
24 Hardt and Negri, *Empire*, pp. 51–2.
25 For two excellent and nuanced accounts of Deleuze and Guattari's theorization of the relation of state sovereignty to processes of deterritorialization, see Ronald Bogue, "Apology for Nomadology," *Interventions*, Vol. 6, No. 2 (2004), pp. 169–79; and Ulrike Kistner, "Raison d'Etat: Philosophy of and against the State," *Interventions*, Vol. 6, No. 2 (2004), pp. 242–51.
26 Gilles Deleuze and Felix Guattari, *Anti-Oedipus: Capitalism and Schizophrenia*, (London: Athlone Press, 2000), p. 260.
27 As discussed in Dirk Messner and Franz Nuscheler, "World Politics: Structures and Trends," in eds. Paul Kennedy, Dirk Messner, and Franz Nuschele, *Global Trends and Global Governance* (London: Pluto, 2002), pp. 125–55.
28 See, on this point, Hardt and Negri, *Empire*, pp. 4–6.
29 Abbas Alnasrawi, "Iraq: Economic Sanctions and Consequences, 1990–2000," *Third World Quarterly*, Vol. 22, No. 2 (2001), pp. 205–18.
30 As laid out in Security Council Resolution 688, also discussed in Peter Malanczuk, "The Kurdish Crisis and Allied Intervention in the Aftermath of the Second Gulf War," *European Journal of International Law*, Vol. 2 (1991), pp. 114–32.
31 See www.un.org/Depts/oip/background/fact-sheet.html.
32 See Judith S. Yaphe, "America's War on Iraq: Myths and Opportunities," *Adelphi Papers*, Vol. 354, No. 1 (2003), pp. 23–44.
33 G. John Ikenberry, "America's Imperial Ambition," *Foreign Affairs*, Vol. 81, No. 5 (Sept.–Oct. 2002), pp. 44–60.
34 See Roger MacGinty, "The Pre-War Reconstruction of Iraq," *Third World Quarterly*, Vol. 24, No. 4 (2003), esp. p. 606.
35 See daccessdds.un.org/doc/UNDOC/GEN/N03/368/53/PDF/N0336853.pdf?OpenElement
36 See MacGinty, "The Pre-war Reconstruction of Iraq," p. 606.
37 Ibid., p. 607.
38 See Ikenberry, "America's Imperial Ambition," p. 44.
39 See also Simon Chesterman, *You, the People: The United Nations, Transitional Administration, and State Building* (Oxford: Oxford University Press, 2004), pp. 92–7.

40 Ikenberry, "America's Imperial Ambition," p. 44.
41 Michael Ignatieff, *Virtual War: Kosovo and Beyond* (London: Vintage, 2001), p. 209.
42 See, for, example, Mary Kaldor, *Global Civil Society: An Answer to War* (Cambridge: Polity, 2003), pp. 133–4.
43 Michael Ignatieff, *Virtual War: Kosovo and Beyond*, (London: Vintage, 2001), p. 201.
44 Adam Roberts, "Law and the Use of Force after Iraq," *Survival*, Vol. 45, No. 2 (2003), pp. 31–56.
45 Gilles Deleuze and Felix Guattari, *A Thousand Plateaus* (London: Athlone Press, 1999), p. 509.
46 Ibid., pp. 351–423.
47 See Paul Patton, "Future Politics," in eds. Paul Patton and John Protevi, *Between Deleuze and Derrida* (London: Continuum, 2003), p. 21.
48 See Kistner, "Raison d'Etat," p. 250.
49 Hardt and Negri, *Empire*, pp. 35–7.
50 See Costas Douzinas, "Humanity, Military Humanism, and the New Moral Order," *Economy and Society*, Vol. 32, No. 2 (2003), pp. 159–83.
51 See, for example, Paul Gilroy, *After Empire: Melancholia or Convivial Culture* (London: Routledge, 2004), pp. 13–21.
52 Ibid., pp. 91–2.
53 H. J. Eysenck, "Humanism and the Future," in ed. A. J. Ayer, *The Humanist Outlook* (London: Pemberton Publishing, 1968), pp. 265–77.
54 Gilles Deleuze and Felix Guattari, *What Is Philosophy?* (London: Verso, 1996), p.107.
55 Ibid., p. 107.
56 Kaldor, *Global Civil Society*, p. 156.
57 Ibid., p. 159.
58 Douglas Kellner, "September 11, Social Theory and Democratic Politics," *Theory, Culture & Society*, Vol. 19, No. 4 (2002), p. 158.
59 Benjamin Barber, "The War of All against All: Terror and the Politics of Fear," in ed. Verna V. Gehring, *War after September 11* (New York: Rowman and Littlefield, 2003), p. 88.
60 Ibid., p. 76.
61 Kellner, "September 11, Social Theory and Democratic Politics," p. 158.

8 Human security, governmentality, and sovereignty
A critical examination of contemporary discourses on universalizing humanity

Kosuke Shimizu

Introduction

Is human security progressing or is it in retreat? In 1994, the concept of human security shot through the international relations (IR) discipline like a comet. This concept emerged on the international scene for the first time in the *Human Development Report* published by the United Nations Development Program (UNDP) that year, and it has been frequently mentioned in various texts ever since. Since then, human security has been referred to as an antithesis to the realist approach to world politics that, among other things, advocates the use of legitimate violence by states. Thus, IR scholars have often situated human security in the context of a liberal discursive tradition by arguing that the concept reveals a disposition toward liberal ideals, particularly through its focus on individuals rather than on states or other collective bodies.

To be sure, the concept of human security can be seen as a radical departure from the traditional security discourse that has been exclusively centered on nation-states and inter-state relations. Shifting the emphasis away from states to individual beings has the potential to profoundly influence the theory of IR since this shift can offer a new dimension to the concept of security. However, scholars have also admitted that, as far as the 1994 UNDP report and subsequent documents by the Human Security Commission are concerned, human security is still far from anything concrete in the practice of IR. It is also worth mentioning that an attempt to transfer the international political concern away from nation-states and toward individuals is not new and, in fact, this has been frequently witnessed throughout the history of political thought, for example when classical European philosophies encountered political liberalism in early modernity. Moreover, liberal discourses based on a universalized version of humanism (such as the discourse of human security of late) have also been the object of many political theoretical critiques, for example when Hannah Arendt and E. H. Carr both observed the failure of application of the generalized ideas of the nation-state and liberal democracy into the concrete European political order of the early twentieth century. Thus, it is clear that, in the case of human security discourses, there is a need to critically assess the use and meaning of the concept, particularly since it is so closely tied to liberalism. I argue in this chapter that, if the human security discourse is premised upon the liberal principle of the existence of autonomous individuals, there is a danger associated with this kind of discourse. Indeed, this discourse brings back to the forefront of international political analysis the crucial but unquestioned point of the indispensable role or place of human beings. Yet, at the same time, it maintains a lot of ambiguity about who or what has the power, authority, capacity, or right to name/recognize who the individuals in need of security are.

Michel Foucault's concept of "governmentality" will be useful in this context. Governmentality, as Foucault understands it, is a modern technique of domination and political management that seeks to foster lives rather than take them away. By providing particular forms of knowledge to individuals in modern (liberal) societies, governmentality controls the way people conduct themselves. Thus, one of the most intriguing points in this understanding of modern life is the relationship between the knowledge of the "good life" in society and the issue of socio-political governance. The discourse of human security can be seen to be typical of modern regimes of governmentality in the sense that it sets up a model of liberal contemporary living and provides regular norms, values, and modalities of knowledge to individual lives.

This discursive implementation of preset norms, values, and modalities of knowledge, however, is dangerous and contradictory when these advanced principles of governmentality are combined with the liberal ideal of autonomous and rational individual subjects. It is dangerous and contradictory because, according to this configuration of modern social and political life, the individual subject must constantly develop an internal sense of guilt and responsibility, and, moreover, must harbor resentment toward himself/herself if he or she fails to achieve the required goals set by the existing norms, values, and knowledge modalities. This sense of guilt/resentment can only be alleviated through a redirection of these sentiments (and their expression) towards those (Others) who are even more incomplete or defective vis-à-vis the new normative order. In the case of IR, this redistribution of resentment frequently emerges in the form of genocides or massacres of minorities in civil wars and ethnic conflicts. In some cases, the discourse of human security brings devastating consequences to minorities because it imposes a global way of life, and, as such, it also produces those who do not sufficiently fit the standard (and are abnormal vis-à-vis the dominant normative order).

Thus, the objective of this chapter is to connect the current human security discourse in IR with governmentality principles and practices in the contemporary world by focusing mainly on the liberal assumptions about autonomous individual subjects (and what they must do to become and/or remain autonomous subjects) transplanted inside this newly emerging global and allegedly non-state centered security perspective. The chapter critically investigates the ways in which the human security discourse is generalized and universalized in IR and becomes the basis for newly forming norms, values, and knowledge modalities of global life and living. I suggest that an uncritical application or acceptance of the concept of human security, particularly in the margins of the contemporary global (geo)political and (geo)economic arena, will lead to devastating effects for individual lives in specific contexts.

Governmentality, biopolitics, and disciplinary power

Foucault once argued that government is the art of determining the appropriate "conduct of conduct." The term conduct has two meanings here. One is to "lead" others; the other is "a way of behaving within a more or less open field of possibilities."[1] Thus, the "conduct of conduct" seeks to provide a recipe for steering the behavior of all sorts of human subjects. This principle of government or governance is, according to Foucault, not only institutional, but also and more importantly discursive. It does not refer "only to political structures or to the management of states." Rather, it assigns "the way in which the conduct of individuals or of groups might be directed."[2] This Foucauldian analysis can offer IR scholars unconventional but useful ways of remobilizing the terms "government" or "governance," in the cases of the "government" of children, of souls, of communities, of families, or of the sick, for example.

What holds an important place in this critical governmentality scheme, in the practice of the rationality of government put to the service of the "conduct of conduct," is the idea of the importance of self-regulating individuals. Indeed, Foucault's argument about governmentality is also about the political formation of the self as an individual subject. In his history of modern sexuality, Foucault referred to this politics of government as a matter of biopolitics. Biopolitics is a political form of governance in which power (through its various, disparate institutions and agents) encourages people to live, and thus is somewhat contrary to traditional configurations of (modern) power that, ultimately, are concerned with maintaining their capacity to take away people's lives (to cause death). This biopower, or power over life, is thus embedded in techniques of contemporary knowledge, or sets of knowledge-producing regimes, disciplines, and methods (such as statistics, administration models, systems of regulatory control) in order to maximize the utility or productivity of the population, since individual subjects (collectively taken to be a society's population) are now regarded as a main source of wealth for the nation.[3] This modern form of power over life is no longer overt or repressive. It is carried out, rather, perversely but allegedly productively, often in the name of the protection of the health of the population and its protection from all sorts of contaminants.[4] In this sense, governmentality as a modern technique of power is ubiquitous, unlike the traditional sovereign and centered exercise of power that had to be precise, exceptional, but also overt and forceful.

For Foucault, what is crucial to the understanding of power relations and governmentality in modern society is the interaction between governing techniques and the means or methods of subjectification. Modern power in an era of governmentalization of the "conducts of conduct" turned into a power geared toward generating forces, making them grow, and ordering them, rather than into a form of authority or a monopoly on violence dedicated to impeding live forces, coercing them into submission, or even destroying them.[5] Such a power of governmentality (or a biopolitical power as mentioned above) remains a distinctly contemporary modality of power, one that continues to entail the productive (not just repressive) subjugation of live or free bodies and the control or monitoring of populations through the regulation of ways of life (locally and globally) rather than through constant threats of death.[6] Foucault argued that this form of power over the living has been practiced through a variety of supposedly depoliticized apparatuses or institutions such as schools, universities, hospitals, factories, or prisons. In these sites, a "microphysics of power" has been performed, one that has sought to take care of and organize the most common and mundane aspects of a population's activities. This detailed application of a meticulous productive power of government was famously exemplified in Foucault's study of the disciplinary techniques that invented the modern prison and set up the generalized model of a penitentiary system of criminality and punishment in the West.[7] For Foucault, institutions of knowledge acted as key networks of propagation of governmentalized power and facilitated its penetration throughout society. In this fashion, individuals came to internalize the new norms, values, and principles of the generalized system of power and governmental control. Moreover, traditional sites of power, such as the sovereign state or relations between nation-states, started to replicate this modality of production and governmentalization of power. This shift allowed crucial ideas and practices related to nationalism to be propagated to daily life practices beyond Western societies and the so-called modern world. The logic of power and knowledge of the modern West started to be concerned with the production of individual subjects and their internalization of appropriate techniques designed to help them achieve the "good life," a good life that was more and more perceived in a liberal, global way. Thus, it would become possible for any individual in any society or community to be a potential globally governmentalized subject of the new regimes of modern liberal power and knowledge.

This reinterpretation of modern power as governmentalized or disciplinary power has consequences for the way critical political analysts perceive the role or function of the state. From such a perspective, the state (and its government) is not a cold-blooded monster that programs, codifies, or dominates citizens' lives. Rather, government becomes a "contact point" where techniques of domination from above and techniques of self-control and self-disciplinization come into contact. Government is a series of diverse sites of power where technologies of domination of individuals over others have turned into processes that allow individual subjects to act and operate on themselves, and to integrate narrative or discursive methods of production of subjectivity into institutional structures of organization of life.[8]

At the same time, as Hiroyuki Tosa (among others) has argued, the power of administration of people's lives designed to produce a certain way of life inevitably generates a political domain that exists outside the established norms, or outside of the new legal order. For the norm to be maintained and reproduced, a constant reminder of what is not normal or normative (and what is abnormal, outlawed, or irrational) is required too. Thus, control or coercion is really never completely removed from regimes of governmentalized power. Rather, control is now displaced toward "outside" figures or others whose lives are of little value, at least from the perspective of the self-disciplined global individual subject.[9] Put differently, the power to make some people live simultaneously requires a power to take away other lives. Other lives can be removed, not because of capital punishment, but in the name of a state of exception "outside" (in IR, for example), one that continues to give control to a sovereign or state with a prerogative to exercise coercion or with a right to claim that control of the outside sometimes requires a return to repressive measures inside the nation too. Thus, the exercise of biopower is really not so self-evident or, rather, does not just rely on self-disciplined or self-governmentalized subjects, as Foucault would have it. Instead, biopolitics still demands a certain degree of complicity with the kind of centralized, overt, and arbitrary power that terminates the lives of those who are deemed to be without a right to live. This dual modality of biopolitics is particularly apparent in contemporary IR where many purportedly unclassifiable and unworthy people or lives, such as illegal immigrants, terrorists, or members of "rogue nations," are forcibly dehumanized in the name of a certain liberal democratic power and global order of life. Tosa suggests that the dehumanization of those who are supposedly living outside the global norm or legal order is essential to the contemporary reproduction of a lawful, normative, and normal international "good life," one that follows the dictates of a liberal order and makes it possible.[10] There are many norms and laws that produce this space of global governmentality in the contemporary world. Human security, despite its initial intentions, is a typical case of governmentalized power often deployed in exercises of promotion of a certain world order. Of late, there have been several critiques of the way human security is used and abused for global disciplinary purposes. But before introducing those critical perspectives, it is necessary to outline the concept of human security.

Human security

Although it was never explicitly stated as such, human security was initially devised to tackle the question of those lives that fall outside the law, sovereign justice, or the domain of international life protected by fundamental rights. Once again, the concept of human security first emerged in a *Human Development Report* published by the UNDP in 1994. The contents of this document encouraged a general transformation of the meaning of security from a concept applicable to nation-states and their sovereignty to one that now would be exclusively attached to the life of human beings. In this initial discourse on human security, four key features were introduced: the idea of universality; the notion of interdependence; the emphasis on prevention rather than on intervention; and the question of the centrality of human life.

First, claiming that human security is universal means that unemployment, drug abuse, crime, pollution, or violations of human rights are general common threats to people's lives, irrespective of where they live. Furthermore, this basic document on human security suggests that the threats are actual and expanding worldwide. Proponents of the concept thus contend that there may be differences in the degree of suffering. But the risks are common irrespective of the location of the subjects (hence, they are universal).[11]

The second key characteristic—interdependence—means that issues related to the instability of individual subjects' lives (such as famines, pollutions, drug trafficking, terrorism, social and economic crises, and so on) cannot be limited to and contained inside one country.[12] This explanation is based on the recognition that the threats to people's lives/humanity are interconnected and, in fact, form one huge global system of vulnerability. The transnationality of human security risks further implies that interdependent and global measures are required.

Third, the concept of human security seeks to prioritize prevention over intervention. This signifies that a precautionary pragmatic orientation is likely to dominate human security practices whereby the idea is to reduce the cost of suffering by adopting measures before problems get out of control. The UNDP report uses the example of the HIV/AIDS crisis as a model of prevention, and it argues that the global cost of HIV/AIDS treatments in the 1980s was about US$240 billion. The report claims that, if only a few billions had actually been spent on primary healthcare and family planning education instead, much of the crisis could have been averted.[13]

Finally, the last crucial feature of this initial human security discourse is an emphasis on adopting a human-centric perspective. The fact that human security is described as humanity-centered implies that the concept (and the policies derived from it) will be concerned with maintaining or producing a version of global life measured at the level of both individual beings and populations. Because individual lives and populations are prioritized in this discourse, mainly liberal principles such as freedom of choice, access to market, equality in social opportunity, and so forth will be granted privileged status in devising solutions to the identified problems.[14]

Following the path traced by the UNDP, a Commission on Human Security was later created, with Amartya Sen and Sadako Ogata as co-chairpersons. Almost a decade after the initial UNDP Report, this commission released its final report (in May 2003).[15] The Commission was formed as a response to a request made by the then United Nations' Secretary General, Kofi Annan, at the United Nations' Millennium Summit in September 2000, and it was created with a mandate to address two pressing humanitarian issues: the question of "freedom from fear;" and the issue of "freedom from lack." This emphasis on individual freedoms further exemplifies the fact that the discourse on human security is intricately tied to liberal and universal visions, principles, and practices. The "freedom from fear" and "freedom from lack" slogans were famously coined by US President Franklin D. Roosevelt and presented to the US Congress back in 1941 (with the addition of two other freedoms at the time, "freedom of expression" and "freedom of worship").[16] In 1941, responding to the attacks by "aggressors" or "enemy states" from Europe and Asia, Roosevelt insisted that the future of the free world, and of the United States in particular, was dependent upon these four cornerstone principles of liberal and universal human life.[17]

The two concepts/slogans—"freedom from fear" and "freedom from lack"—mentioned at the beginning of the Commission on Human Security's 2003 Report are followed by more concrete targets that include deepening the understanding of the global general public about the importance of human security by promoting public participation and support, turning the concept of human security into a concrete method of policy planning and implementation in every country, and providing concrete action plans in order to cope with extensive threats against human security worldwide.[18]

In this report, the portion that addresses the relationship between human security and the existing national security of every state in the world community needs to be scrutinized. In this section of the 2003 report, it is argued that human security is helpful and contributes to national state security because of the following reasons. First, human security focuses on the society's population rather than on the state and, as such, it can address more extensive security concerns than traditional national security principles and policies. Second, factors that had never been seriously considered as direct threats to national security are now included in the discourse, thus expanding the domain of security's reach. Third, all sorts of social actors and agents, not just states and their governments, can now be involved in protecting and promoting stability and global peace. And fourth, human security requires transcending the state's foreign policy/national security level of protection and moving towards the empowerment of individual beings, something that, down the line, will be beneficial to the security of every state.

Overall, the comprehensive nature of the concept of human security should lead state policy makers to focus on lives and societies across nations' borders and to move away from traditional state-centered security concerns that far too exclusively are concerned with the protection of national borders. Moreover, unlike conventional understandings of security, the primary subject in question in the human security discourse is not the nation-state. In this discourse, it is assumed that various actors are involved in and concerned with the realization of (human) security so that all sorts of threats that nation-states are unable to deal with (or even recognize) can be addressed. In this sense, human security continues to contribute to traditional security matters. But it also goes beyond them by attaching some importance to the participation in security practices of various agents, including individual beings and non-governmental organizations (NGOs).[19]

Highlighting the participation of individual beings and NGOs also implies that human security is formulated on the basis of some key liberal premises, particularly about individual life. In fact, the 2003 report stipulates, in its early stages, that "human security starts from the recognition that people are the most active participants in determining their well-being."[20] Again, this is a typical liberal assumption: nobody can know or understand a person better than himself/herself. Therefore, human security takes the position that new security practices must support individual beings who are making some efforts to improve their lives.[21] This further entails insisting on the principle of self-determination of people, something that will be further discussed below.

In the UNDP report, human security was divided into seven major areas. These were economic security, food security, health protection, environmental security, individual protection, communal security, and finally political security.[22] Economic security meant achieving a stable basic income for individuals.[23] Food security required states to guarantee a necessary minimum food intake for all people.[24] With health security or protection, the maintenance of a suitable medical system for the prevention and cure of infections and illnesses was a central concern.[25] Environmental security was articulated around the issue of contamination of water and land.[26] Individual protection focused on crime, domestic violence, drug abuse, and instances of suicide.[27] Abolition of discriminatory practices based on race, religion, and ties to family origins was a required condition under communal security. And, finally, political security was associated with the realization of democracy and human rights.[28] Yet, despite this initial division of human security into seven key segments, the concrete program of action on behalf of human security championed by the 1994 report (and reprised in the 2003 document) is organized around two crucial areas of intervention: human development, and peace-building. These two areas roughly correspond to a traditional disciplinary sub-division of IR between international political economic concerns on the one hand, and international security/foreign policy matters on the other. It is towards a more detailed examination of this sub-division of human security that I now turn.

Human development

As mentioned above, in the Commission on Human Security's document, human security is conceptualized by way of expressions such as "freedom from lack" or "freedom from fear." These suggest that "freedom from lack" is directly related to issues of human development and empowerment, whereas "freedom from fear" corresponds to political protection and security. The Commission on Human Security places its discourse in the context of larger human development questions and debates by hinting at the need for a specific program of action/intervention. To resolve poverty, the idea is to make sure that the benefits of economic development will reach the most disadvantaged individuals in all sorts of communities. This further entails achieving economic stability, which in turn depends upon the realization of labor opportunities for everyone. Promoting balance and equity in resource allocation will also benefit people's empowerment. Finally, an adequate degree of governmental intervention during economic or financial crises is also recommended. Overall, these more concrete human development proposals are meant to correspond to the sub-domains of security mentioned above, namely, the economy, food, health, and the environment.

At the same time though, both the UNDP and the Commission reports state that human security, even in its more development- and empowerment-oriented dimensions, is a much narrower concept than human development. This is why the two ideas are not supposed to be similar and a specific discourse on human security is required. What human security provides, in other words, is a filtering and reconsideration of what human development is and why or how it matters. The UNDP claims that human development is about widening the range of people's choices. But human security is also about allowing individual beings to exercise these choices safely and freely.[29] The Commission similarly defines human development as a matter of expansion of people's choices so that only they can determine how to live the lives they most value. But human security complements human development by deliberately focusing on the need to "downside risks" in everyday life.[30] Thus, human security not only seeks to complement human development, it also aims at making it more concrete and less arbitrary (and more individual needs-centered).

A common theme in this branch of the official human security discourse is the protection of weaker people. In order to care for these weaker human beings, the two key reports argue that it is necessary to respect the universal and fundamental concepts of global human rights and basic individual freedoms. These rights and freedoms are taken to be the primary steps towards implementing human security.[31] For this reason, the need to develop internationally concerted efforts to work through and perhaps expand national and international norms, institutional structures, and protection processes is emphasized. Those norms, principles, and institutions of human security as human development, it is further suggested, must be systematic, comprehensive, and preventive.[32]

All in all, the advocated policies and recommended directions for implementation of human security (in the domain of international economic/social development in particular) are clearly reliant upon the idea of democratic participation. Democratic participation is the direct link to people's so-called empowerment, and a prerequisite for development and security. According to the Commission on Human Security report, individual empowerment through democratic forms of participation is the distinguishing feature of human security, one that absolutely differentiates it from traditional understandings of state-based national security, but also from humanitarian action and perhaps from traditional development practices too.[33] Individual empowerment is important because human security insists on people developing their full potential as individual beings within democratic communities. And full development of individuals requires that economic, political, social, and cultural components all together be taken into account. Within democratic societies, encouraging people's capacities to act on their own is crucial. Empowered individuals can demand respect for their human dignity and rights and, if those are violated, they can ask for them to be restored because they have now been made aware of the importance of these (liberal) principles. Equipped with those rights and freedoms, they can create new opportunities for themselves, mostly work opportunities, and they can find their own ways of dealing with all sorts of local or national crises. And finally, empowered individuals can be mobilized to protect or defend the human security of others, for example by coping with food shortages early enough, by preventing famines, or by protesting and publicizing human rights violations by sovereign states.[34] Thus, the slogan of "freedom from lack" at the heart of this universalizing human security narrative is connected to many economic, social, and political practices that are key to liberalism as a political ideology.

Peace-building

In contrast to the development track of human security presented in these two crucial reports, the peace-building domain of action/intervention is meant to overlap considerably with security in a more traditional, national, and state-based sense (which often has been the exclusive security concern of foreign policy/security studies). Unlike human development that aims at preventing social crises and eventually conflict by tackling basic economic, social, and democratic empowerment issues, human security's peace-building track has more to do with conflict resolution, that is to say, with restoring peace and stability after a severe crisis or conflict has already taken place. At the same time though, both branches of the human security discourse cannot be separated from one another with absolute clarity. For example, processes of peace-building or conflict settlement inevitably involve, and are designed on, the basis of the prevention of future disorders or wars. Peace-building aims at eliminating the occurrence of human crises similar to the one that gave rise to the security intervention. Clearly, in the human security discourse, conflict prevention (through development and empowerment) and conflict resolution (through peace-building) are meant to be interdependent.

Still, on the side of the peace-building sub-discourse, the "freedom from fear" image serves as an anchoring point. But the fear that is targeted here is supposed to manifest itself at an individual or communal level, not at the level of the sovereign nation-state and its relations with other nations. Since the targeted threat subject is supposed to be the human being (alone or in a group), drug abuse, rapid increase in crime, traffic accidents, violence in the workplace are problems that are more likely to be singled out as sources of insecurity and potential originators of crises or conflicts. Of special note is the point made by both reports that these individual/communal and local risks are often more severe when it comes to the fate of women and children in society.[35]

Women and children as risk targets are key subjects of human insecurity. The insecurities women and children face often lead to social crises and sometimes require peace-building efforts in specific communal settings, particularly when there are instances of discrimination (against women, ethnic minorities, etc.). Here, violence due to certain traditions or communal conventions, such as female circumcision in some African countries, is emphasized and linked to the likelihood of social disorder. In the case of discrimination on ethnic or racial grounds, situations in Sri Lanka, the former Yugoslavia, Somalia, or Rwanda in the 1990s are often cited.[36] All in all, human security as political security (a direct source of eventual peace-building efforts, according to the reports) is still closely connected to questions of human rights. In this fashion, human rights are mobilized in the human security literature to link issues of human empowerment (as we saw above) with more traditional political security concerns that often continue to involve sovereign states. Thus, the Commission on Human Security report concludes:

> To achieve peace and stability in today's interdependent world, preventing and mitigating the impact of internal violent conflicts are not sufficient. Also important are upholding human rights, pursuing inclusive and equitable development and respecting human dignity and diversity. Equally decisive is to develop the capability of individuals and communities to make informed choices and to act on their own behalf.[37]

In this way, human security allegedly can serve to protect individual rights ("freedom from fear") and promote a good life globally ("freedom from lack"). This is certainly a noble attempt. However, doing so is no easy task, all the more so when ideological assumptions trump practical developments. The next section introduces some critical perspectives that detail the problems that are inherent to the practical deployment of human security.

Aporias of security and humanity

While the human security discourse insists on the importance of individual empowerment (through democracy and economic welfare) and of the respect for human rights, there have been several critiques of this universalizing narrative (even before the human security discourse was fully deployed in the 1990s). These critiques have pointed out the "gap" that becomes discursively established and normalized between the idea of the human (with his/her rights and prerogatives) that seems to come straight out of the Western modern humanist tradition (reworked by liberalism) and the emphasis on the individual subject as a national or citizen of existing sovereign nation-states.[38] This idea that the human subject does matter as an individual entity, but only to the extent that he or she is a participating member (a political citizen) of a recognized sovereign state, captures the purposeful ambivalence of the human security discourse described above, a discourse that, ultimately, is indeed about human rights, but within the context of traditional state-centered national security (i.e., international politics and foreign policy). This sort of critical insight is reminiscent of Arendt's argument about the "rights of men."³⁹ Arendt pointed out that, when universalized and abstract concepts such as human rights are placed in concrete historical political contexts, one becomes more aware of how problematic and arbitrary these ideas and principles actually are. The Declaration of the Rights of Men produced by the French revolutionaries (that stated that the rights of men are inalienable and indispensable to humanity) became crucial to the establishment and later development of modern French national sovereignty (of the sovereign French nation-state). Indeed, only inside the political container that is the sovereign state could those individual rights and liberal freedoms be enjoyed. Only in the context of the sovereign state could the idea of individual empowerment make sense.

Thus, the same essential rights were at once claimed as the inalienable heritage of all humankind *and* as the specific outcome of some national policies and ideologies. A double standard was created whereby nation-states were declared to be subjected to universal laws and principles with regard to human rights (that they had to respect) and completely sovereign and independent, that is to say, bound by no universal law since there could be no power superior to the sovereign state.⁴⁰ The result of this double standard would be devastating for human rights. Arendt argued:

> The practical outcome of this contradiction was that from then on human rights were protected and enforced only as national rights and that the very institution of a state, whose supreme task was to protect and guarantee man his rights as man, as citizen and as national, lost its legal, rational appearance and could be interpreted by the romantics as the nebulous representative of a 'national soul' which through the very fact of its existence was supposed to be beyond or above the law. National sovereignty, accordingly, lost its original connotation of freedom of the people and was being surrounded by a pseudomystical aura of lawless arbitrariness.⁴¹

This contradiction between two principles held sacrosanct, equally dominant, and supposedly compatible created a gap in political practice, at the level of individual lives. This unbridgeable gap between individuals as human beings and individual subjects as citizens or nationals of states would lead to catastrophic results in Europe during the first half of the twentieth century. After World War I, and as the result of the Treaty of Versailles, European states, influenced by US President Woodrow Wilson's humanist liberal vision of a world order where democracy would thrive on the basis of self-determination, attempted to preserve a political status quo by recognizing some individual and communal rights, but still within states. As Arendt argued, this system or vision turned out to be a failure because, instead of Wilson's democratic dream, the downfall of the last remnants of European autocracy made it clear that "Europe had been ruled by a system which had never taken into account or responded to the needs of at least 25 per cent of her (minority) population."⁴² Indeed, not just because rights and self-determination were given to individuals only if they were state citizens or nationals, but also because, effectively, state sovereignty was only granted to some dominant groups inside each nation-state while the rest of the people living there (the so-called minorities) were left with a feeling of betrayal, the new international and allegedly democratic system guaranteed that state prerogatives (or at least the prerogatives of those groups that were in a majority position inside nation-states) would take precedence over the universalization of individual or human security and empowerment. It also did not help that those people who took control of sovereign power inside some of the newly formed states and governments (benefiting from the idea of self-determination) chose to oppress the minorities in their states and sometimes beyond their borders too.[43] Again, the post-World War I system, despite (or rather because of) its claims to universal democracy, humanity, and universalization of principles, did nothing to change the dominant practice of state security.

Here, Arendt's critique of the attempt by European powers to apply a universalizing idea of individual rights within nation-states (and to propagate this model throughout Europe) overlaps with Carr's famous challenge of liberal democracy. He contended that "the view that nineteenth-century liberal democracy was based, not on a balance of forces peculiar to the economic development of the period and the countries concerned, but on *a priori* rational principles which had only to be applied in other contexts to produce similar results, was essentially utopian."[44] Carr maintained that the universal utopianism of Western liberal democracies in the nineteenth century gave rise to a paradoxical situation. While liberal democratic proponents placed a strong emphasis on individual liberty and rights, they ended up causing global ruin, particularly outside Western Europe. As Carr put it: "When the theories of liberal democracy were transplanted, by a purely intellectual process, to a period and to countries whose stage of development and whose practical needs were utterly different from those of Western Europe in the nineteenth century, sterility and disillusionment were the inevitable sequel."[45]

Thus, as both Arendt's and Carr's critiques show, the logic of state-centered national security inevitably takes over, plays with, and abuses the universalizing discourses and practices that seek to champion humanity, human empowerment, or (more recently) human security. Today, the global war on terror, which entails a desire for the global expansion of liberal democracy, is one of the most obvious examples of the continued dominance of the logic of national security. The degrading media coverage in Japan of North Korea is another key example.[46] Both reinforce the perception that the inside is always safer than the outside, or, rather, that only inside secure and sovereign state borders can humanity or human security be guaranteed (with the consequence, of course, that the principle of state sovereignty gets to be reinforced in the process).

This point about sovereignty is significant for the following reasons. First, once so-called universality inside state borders is established and reinforced by those in power, humanism/human security is immediately cut from universalism, or from any attempt at a universal application. Humanity/human security, in a traditional historical humanistic sense, is being co-opted by liberalism and the logic of state sovereignty, and therefore effectively becomes sacrificed. Moreover, in this way, the discourse of universalism (or about a universalizing humanity) can still be mobilized, but only if it is connected to the logic of national security or foreign policy-making in IR. This last trend is very clear in the case of the more recent human security discourses described above. According to Tosa, there is a fundamental contradiction in the current way humanism/human security is formulated. While nation-states often affirm that they promote universal humanism/human security in their policies, they actually devote much of their attention to the production and enforcement of patriotic and national-interest driven strategies, and they draw firm boundaries that seek to demarcate an inside from an outside.[47] In fact, recently a high-ranking Japanese official bluntly recognized the notion of "human security on the basis of the nation-state."[48]

Universality or concrete contexts

There is another reason why we should be concerned with the gap between universality and concrete or specific contexts that is being normalized through human security discourses, and this takes us directly back to Foucault's notions of governmentality and disciplinary power. Once humanity/human security is rendered meaningful only in cases of practices, policies, and ideologies implemented by sovereign nation-states (even if those states are democracies), a political discourse about the human becomes converted into a technical and managerial problem and, as a result, the language of universalizing humanity or human security turns into a series of stereotypical, common, and normative statements. Put differently, people start to lose their own languages/modes of expression about their humanity, about what is human and individual about their lives, as the hegemony of a certain application and interpretation of universalism takes over.

Here, we encounter the most important difficulty with the narratives of human security that have emerged in global settings since the beginning of the last decade. The notion of security and the idea of being able to lead a "safe" or "good" life are displaced from concrete or specific settings and, instead, are replaced by generic, pre-established, and technical meanings that claim to be operative and operational across places and situations (but always within sovereign state structures). These abstract, generalized, and pre-determined meanings also hide the particular state-centered and national power relations that work behind the scenes.

Examples of this universalization of the idea of a "good" or "safe" life have recently been found in Japan's foreign policy. The concept of human security has been closely tied in Japan to the desire to see the Japanese state become a permanent member of the UN Security Council. Japanese government officials involved in the campaign for permanent membership frequently referred to human security, and tried to argue that human security and Japan's constitution have a lot in common. But because of growing strategic ambitions (some of which seemed to stretch beyond the domain of human security), many specialists on Japanese foreign policy expected that Tokyo would have to reduce its contributions to human security projects (and perhaps would attempt to reform its constitution too). But Japan (for the time being anyway) chose instead to give up its claim to become a permanent Security Council member (and thus does not have to sacrifice human security objectives to the benefit of more traditional geopolitical security concerns like those that Security Council powers often display).

Beyond Japan's dilemma over its desire to become a permanent Security Council power, a universalized discourse on human security has become intensely relied upon by Japanese government officials, particularly when they seek to justify the legitimacy of the Japanese government's foreign policy decisions. Democracy, development, self-empowerment, and political-social stability principles, around which the discourse of human security has been shaped, helped to produce new, or reinforce existing, images of otherness and difference, especially vis-à-vis North Korea and in the context of diplomatic relations in North East Asia (recently dominated by the logic of the Six Party Talks). Of late, North Korea has been described in Japan as a country positioned in the margins of the global normative order. By contrast, Japan has presented itself as a rational, law-abiding, norm-respecting, and democratic nation. In fact, in the Japanese media, North Korea has often been reported to be an undemocratic, irrational country that lacks any sense of respect for international norms of human dignity or for basic principles of human (social and political) participation. These reported claims of irrationality or insanity even are the direct result of a public discourse that overemphasizes the gap inside North Korean society between the government elites (that spend massive amounts on military expenditure, especially on missile production) and ordinary citizens who are depicted as starving. This representation of North Korea in terms of a domestic human security gap turns out to be the exact opposite of the image Japan is projecting of itself. Indeed, its purpose is to highlight by contrast Japan's own rationality and its status as a legitimate democratic (state) subject in the international community. On those contrasting grounds (but also, revealingly, through a discourse about values, universal norms, "soft power," or non-traditional security matters), some Japanese chroniclers even argue that Japan would be justified to rearm, perhaps with nuclear weaponry even, in order to now protect global democracy and human security from such a dangerous, irrational, and non-democratic state like North Korea.[49]

This kind of argument is not limited to Japanese media pundits, commentators, or politicians. Indeed, it has also been found in academic circles of late. In Japan today, there are quite a number of academics, political scientists above all, who intentionally or unintentionally provide a similar representation of North Korea in the larger context of human security. For example, Yoichi Hirama, a historian and former professor at the National Defense Academy of Japan, has sought to highlight what he considers to be Koreans' cunning as a general, and racial, trait of character, but also as a direct source of political instability. Hirama goes on to explain that these inherent Korean racial/national features are the reasons why, throughout Korean history, Koreans have always been governed or dominated by other nations.[50] Two other scholars, Toshimitsu Shigemura (a specialist in North Korean politics) and Keitaro Hasegawa (a well-known economist), developed a research project on contemporary North Korea, and they concluded that North Korea is a country that failed to achieve civilized status, something that, in the twenty-first century, they specifically associated with the ideas of democracy and liberal economics.[51] Another academic, Masao Okonogi (a prominent professor of IR), could only describe North Korea in terms of abject poverty and economic stagnation.[52]

What all these analyses share is a presumption that North Korea must be understood by Japan (and Japanese people) in terms of pre-modernity or deviance, notions that can only make sense to the extent that they assume a larger discourse about the global (and the national, for Japan) benefits of human security (and all the modern liberal values that come with it, as we saw above). More crucially, depicting North Korea as backward (socially, morally, politically, and economically) allows Japan to stand out—particularly in the North East Asian setting, once again—as modern, advanced, rational, democratic, global, and, eventually, humanitarian and humane. In other words, what Japan becomes, when contrasted to North Korea, is a perfect model of human security. More than a model, in fact: Japan comes out (thanks to its democracy, its political stability, and the social and economic well-being of its people) as the champion of human security in North East Asia (if not yet its enforcer).

But Japan, as the champion of a new universalized humanity, is not only interested in replicating a rather typical inside/outside, self/other, or us/them dichotomy (but on human security grounds this time). In today's globally and humanly secure IR, there is not just an inside and an outside, a democratic and rational Japan as opposed to a backward, irrational, and undemocratic North Korea, for example. Rather, there are also many "in-betweens" that are trapped by the discourses and practices of human security advocated by certain nation-states. Detainees of the United States at Abu Ghraib or in Guantanamo, deprived of their universally granted rights (as human beings), abandoned by both national and international laws, and vulnerable to endless physical or even sexual traumas, are prime examples of this "in-betweenness" that becomes normalized and productive (for those who preach human security). Discourses of human security do not just create model individual subjects in need of self-empowerment and democratic guarantees and, in contrast, backward, totalitarian, or insane enemies that supposedly reject the movement toward the universalization of human good and welfare (à la North Korea). They also facilitate the implementation of new global (yet very much local and contextual in their applications) regimes of governmentality that make use of what Giorgio Agamben has called "bare life" (or that part of individual life that is constantly open to abuse as a result of the proliferation of zones or states of exception inside a generalized system of universalizing humanity).[53]

The trapped lives "in-between" are not limited to those detainees in US pseudo-military prisons or camps. The people who live in Okinawa can also be understood to be in such a condition of individual "in-betweenness" encouraged, yet also unacknowledged, by the discourse of human security. As is well known, Okinawa is home to several American military bases. The end of the Cold War has not drastically changed the hybrid or "in-between" status of Okinawa and Okinawans. In fact, in the perspective of a growing fear in the United States and in Japan of North East Asian insecurity (both geopolitical and human), the US military bases—or rather, the US military occupation and take-over of Okinawan daily life—continue to be justified. Thus, Okinawan lives today are still "in-between": they are between Japan and the United States; between democracy and occupation; between being able to develop an economy and a way of life that is autonomous or follows its own strategic priorities and an economic and commercial culture that is still primarily designed to serve and tend to US military needs. While not totally other, Okinawa and Okinawans are not completely self-empowered either. And despite the focus of Japan's government on human security in foreign policy, the individual lives of local Okinawans are rarely a matter for concern in Tokyo (perhaps because, from Tokyo's point of view, Okinawa is neither about foreign affairs, nor completely about domestic politics). What primarily preoccupies the Japanese government about Okinawa (which is similar to the US position in a way) is Okinawa's place (or non-place perhaps) in global geopolitically strategic and human security designs, and particularly those that have to do with the possible diplomatic or even military threats coming from China or North Korea. In the larger context of the (human) security confrontations between Japan and North

Korea (and potentially Japan and China too), the individual and communal lives of Okinawans remain stuck inside yet another state of exception.

Conclusion

Human security was originally devised to promote the respect, integrity, and diversity of individual life and communal or social experience, and to protect these principles from the violent and totalizing power of sovereign nation-states. This desire to theorize and implement a universalizing discourse/practice of humanity (through liberal democratic notions and methods mostly) was precisely the reason why some of the initial agents of human security included non-state actors and transnational groups, as the goal was to challenge the traditional (geopolitically determined) security concerns of sovereign states. This was surely a courageous attempt, but perhaps an inherently problematic one, as the work of both Arendt and Carr shows.

Today, however, despite or perhaps because of its universalizing and humanistic prescriptions, the generalized global discourse on human security often ends up providing a convenient point of departure for the creation by states and other international actors (international governmental organizations, for example) of new distinctions between rational and irrational subjects, or between sane or insane forms of life. Moreover, inside the gaps formed by these human security-driven oppositional categories, new non-subjects (neither good, nor evil; neither here, nor there) become trapped inside developing regimes of governmentality that take advantage of many zones of exception in the global human security order and make use of all sorts of bodies, lives, and beings.

But while the dominant discourse about universalizing modalities of humanity detailed in this chapter seems daunting and at times terrifying, the notion of human security in and of itself may not be completely useless. Bringing the individual in the realm of heretofore sovereign states-centered security concerns is potentially a daring and destabilizing effort, a way of challenging the strategic and military interests of nation-states and their governments. Yet, as Arendt and Carr once again reminded us, bringing the individual back in through a mainly liberal (and, in particular, liberal economy-filtered) discourse about universality, humanity, and subjectivity can easily become a way for dominant or hegemonic power (including the power of states and their governments, institutions, agents, or processes) to remobilize allegedly free, developed, empowered, and rational individual subjects for typical geopolitical and security tasks, duties, policies, and ideologies. In the end, beyond international and domestic regimes of normalization of life that take advantage of what is supposedly universal in the idea of human security (but gets to be translated as universal in a particular but dominant political-ideological language, that of liberalism), what may be required is a rediscovery of or a return to what, instead, is human—the preservation of the diversity or plurality of life and the integrity of being, and the recognition of local or specific contexts—about human security.

Notes

1 See Michel Foucault in eds. Hubert Dreyfus and Paul Rabinow, *Michel Foucault:*

Beyond Structuralism and Hermeneutics (Chicago: University of Chicago Press, 1982), pp. 220–1.
2   Ibid., p. 221.
3   Thomas Osborne, "Security and Vitality: Drains, Liberalism and Power in the Nineteenth Century," in eds. Andrew Barry, Thomas Osborne, and Nikolas Rose *Foucault and Political Reason: Liberalism, Neo-liberalism, and Rationalities of Government* (Chicago: University of Chicago Press, 1996), pp.100–1.
4   Saul Newman, *Power and Politics in Poststructuralist Thought: New Theories of the Political* (London: Routledge, 2005), p. 100.
5   Michel Foucault, *The Foucault Reader: An Introduction to Foucault's Thought*, ed. Paul Rabinow (London: Penguin, 1984), p. 259.
6   Wendy Brown, *Regulating Aversion: Tolerance in the Age of Identity and Empire* (Princeton: Princeton University Press, 2006), p. 26.
7   Ibid, p. 26.
8   Graham Burchell, "Liberal Government and Techniques of the Self," in eds. Barry, Osborne, and Rose, *Foucault and Political Reason*, (London: University College London Press, 1996) p. 20.
9   Hiroyuki Tosa, *Anakikaru Gabanansu* (Tokyo: Ochanomizushobo, 2006).
10 Ibid., pp. iii–iv.
11 United Nations Development Program, *Human Development Report* (Oxford: Oxford University Press, 1994), p. 22.
12 Ibid., p. 22.
13 Ibid., pp. 22–3.
14 Ibid., p 23.
15 The Commission on Human Security, *Human Security Now* (2003), available at www.human security-chs.org/finalreport/index.html.
16 See Franklin Delano Roosevelt's Presidential Library and Museum website at www.fdrlibrary.marist.edu/od4frees.html.
17 Ibid., no page given.
18 The Commission on Human Security, p. 153.
19 Ibid., p. 153.
20 Ibid., p. 4.
21 Ibid., p. 4.
22 UNDP, *Human Development Report*, pp. 24–5.
23 Ibid., p. 25.
24 Ibid., p. 27.
25 Ibid., p. 28.
26 Ibid., pp. 28–9.
27 Ibid., pp. 30–1.
28 Ibid., pp. 32–3.
29 Ibid., p. 23.
30 The Commission on Human Security, p. 10.
31 Ibid., p. 11.
32 Ibid.
33 Ibid.
34 Ibid.
35 UNDP, *Human Development Report*, pp. 30–1.
36 Ibid., pp. 31–2.
37 The Commission on Human security, p. 5.
38 Among such critical perspectives are: Gary King and Christopher Murray, "Rethinking Human Security," *Political Science Quarterly*, Vol. 116, No. 4 (2001–02), pp. 585–610; S. Neil MacFarlane and Yuen Foong Khong, *Human Security and the UN: A Critical History* (Bloomington: Indiana University Press, 2006); Jef Huysmans, *The Politics of Insecurity* (London: Routledge, 2006); Karin Fierke, *Critical Approaches to International Security* (Cambridge: Polity, 2007), pp. 144–66; and Mary Kaldor, *Human Security: Reflections on Globalization and Intervention* (Cambridge: Polity, 2007).

39 See Hannah Arendt, *The Origins of Totalitarianism* (New York: Harcourt Brace Jovanovitch, 1973), chapter 9.
40 Ibid., p. 230.
41 Ibid., pp. 230-1.
42 Ibid., p. 271.
43 Hannah Arendt, *The Origins of Totalitarianism* (Japanese version), trans. Michiyoshi Oshima and Kaori Oshima (Tokyo: Misuzushobo, 1981), p. 244.
44 Edward Hallett Carr, *The Twenty Years' Crisis 1919-1939: An Introduction to the Study of International Relations* (Basingstoke: Palgrave, 1981), p. 29.
45 Ibid., p. 29.
46 See, for example, Ishihara Shintaro, "Shojo no Namida," *Ishihara Shintaro* website (2002), available at www.sensenfukoku.net/mailmagazine/no5.html.
47 See Hiroyuki Tosa, *Anzenhosho toiu Gyakusetsu* (Tokyo: Seidosha, 2003), p. 119.
48 Yukio Takasu, "Ningenno Anzenhosho no Shiten ni Tatta Kokuren Kaikaku" (2006), available at www.mofa.go.jp/mofaj/gaiko/hs/presen_060202.html.
49 Terumasa Nakanishi, "Nihonkoku Kakubusono Ketsudan," *Shogun* (April 2003), pp. 22-37.
50 Yoichi Hirama, "Rekishikara Mita Kitachosen wo Meguru KongonoTenkai", in eds. Yoichi Hirama and Yoneyuki Sugita, *Kitachosen wo Meguru Hokuto Ajia no Kokusaikankei To Nihon* (Tokyo: Akashishoten, 2004), pp. 231-58.
51 Toshimitsu Sigemura and Keitaro Hasegawa, *Kitachosen Jikai: Nichibeichu ga Nigiru Gunji Kokusai Kokkano Meiun* (Tokyo: Toyokeizaishinposha, 2004).
52 Masao Okonogi, "Kanrisareta Kiga: Kim Jong-Il/Kitachosen tono Tsukiaikata," *Ushio* (1997), reprinted on the Japan Foundation website and available at nippon.zaidan.info/seikabutsu/2001/00997/contents/00299.htm.
53 Giorgio Agamben, *Homo Sacer: Sovereign Power and Bare Life* (Stanford: Stanford University Press, 1995).

9 The aesthetic emergency of the avian flu affect

Geoffrey Whitehall

> The hunt for security leads to a worldwide civil war which destroys all civil coexistence. In the new situation—created by the end of the classical form of war between sovereign states—security finds its end in globalization: it implies the idea of a new planetary order which is, in fact, the worst of all disorders. But there is yet another danger. Because they require constant reference to a state of exception, measures of security work towards a growing depoliticization of society.
>
> Giorgio Agamben[1]

Introduction

The recent film *Chicken Little* presents an interesting twist on a classic childhood fable. In it, Disney rewrites the story of a chicken that believed the sky was falling when in fact it was not; it was only an acorn. Instead of being a variation on the story about the boy who cried wolf, Disney's new rendition replaces a false claim with a real claim. In the new film, the sky *is* falling. No longer a story about the desensitizing effects of perpetually using fear and hype to motivate people, *Chicken Little* is about the problem of getting people to act on an unlikely catastrophic scenario (an alien invasion). The reversal of a cautionary tale into the story of the End of Days, replacing prudent tales with those of Armageddon, is exemplary of a troubling contemporary trend in the American geopolitical imaginary. To justify a national or international response, this contemporary trend requires *making* something an emergency before it has *become* one. In this chapter, I argue that the avian flu emergency embodies a preemptive paradox that develops an aesthetic/affective mode of governance. This mode of governance engenders obedience and political will by producing strong emotional responses. The danger of the avian flu, in effect, lurks in the affect of its representation. The second section of the chapter explores the character of this affective governance in light of a troubling development. I suggest that a critical shift in contemporary sovereignty occurs in the zone between a preemptive state of emergency and an actual state of emergency. In order to match the aesthetic composition of emergencies like the avian flu, the character of sovereignty shifts. As such, a general internationalized state of exception is replacing nationalized states of exception. The avian flu both illustrates and facilitates the shift from a mode of sovereignty that is organized around "national life" towards a mode of sovereignty that defines itself on the basis of "human life." In the final section, I argue that the preemptive paradox of the avian flu embodies a unique transformative political potential. Intervening in the avian flu's aesthetic composition can contribute to politicizing the real state of emergency because human life and animal life become expressions of the same sovereign exception. The material aesthetic in which the majority of the world's populations (humans, chickens, or otherwise) have become affectively domesticated can be politicized because, in the name of protecting humanity, human life is revealed to be as expendable as poultry life.

The aesthetics of emergency and its affect

Like other contemporary crises in the American geopolitical imaginary, what is fascinating about the avian flu is that, in order to justify a national or international response to the globally mediated *situation room*, it has to be made an emergency even before it becomes one. In a language familiar to both George W. Bush and Tony Blair (and their "first strike" justification for the war in Iraq), Klaus Stohr, Coordinator of the World Health Organization's (WHO) Global Influenza Program, states: "One of the most difficult things to explain to the public after a pandemic would be why we weren't prepared, because there have been enough warnings."[2] Any other decision or discussion appears to be irresponsible. The age has become exemplary of a preemptive state of emergency.

In addition to being a logical problem between the chicken and the egg, the preemptive state of emergency involves aesthetic practices that represent a fact and an interpretation. The distance between a thing and the social language used to describe it cannot be definitively stabilized. Constituting a threat to representation, this gap destabilizes the prevailing ordered of self, community, and world. Securing this gap and smoothing over the aesthetic distance between a thing and its sign (the nation, national interest, or the people) have become the cornerstone of responsible politics (representative democracy, advocacy, recognition). Specifically, the discipline of international relations (IR) seeks to annul and/or contain this stealthy gap in the name of securing the self via the state in the world.[3] In this sense, peace becomes the government-management of change and the pacification of calls for global justice.

In order to decide whether the risks concerning the emergence and spread of the avian flu are warranted, those inspired by traditional approaches to IR might survey the *facts*. In the spirit of empirical approaches to biosecurity, Influenza A is best described as a dynamic virus that is "constantly emerging" because of its ability to mutate.[4] These mutations entail the ability of a virus to recombine hemagluttinin (HA) and neuraminidase (NA) with amazing evolutionary speeds.[5] Although rapidly mutating viruses are natural and harmless to their host wild birds, when a mutation leaps the species barrier (for example, from ducks to chickens), it has made a potentially dangerous "antigenic shift" (a shift that occurs when different virus strains form a new subtype). The fallout of a shift like the H5N1 avian flu virus has been an epidemic across Asia's, Europe's, and Africa's poultry stocks. With the current spread, the avian epidemic has also caused about 163 human deaths since 1997, mostly in the Indonesian archipelago. It is important to note, finally, that a pandemic is different from an epidemic. We are currently in the midst of an epidemic (animal-to-human transmission). A pandemic emerges when H5N1 "reassorts" with a human flu so that human-to-human transmission becomes possible. With this antigenic shift, a pandemic human influenza is born.

However, none of these facts, in themselves, amount to saying that *this* threat will become a pandemic. Hence, the paradox of preemption. The gap (therefore, the threat) persists. Nobody really disputes the potential *risk* of the current epidemic. But nobody can guarantee the facticity of a *dangerous* pandemic emergence. To borrow David Campbell's phrase, "danger is not an objective condition."[6] The next mutation might lead to a deadly pandemic or to a harmless sniffle. It is impossible to know whether it might happen tomorrow, next year, in a decade, or never again.[7] The difference between a representation of risk and actual danger is a question of political aesthetics. How the story is told matters. The facts of the avian flu, as such, are less interesting than the aesthetic practices involved in representing the avian flu as an emergency that requires immediate global action. The practices are political since representing something as an enemy has a transformative effect on the very order that is to be protected from this enemy influence.

In keeping with the desire to understand the implications of the political aesthetics used to represent an event as an emergency before it has become one, it is useful to explore the practices of representation, or what Daniel W. Smith introduces as "aesthetic comprehension."[8] The term "aesthetic comprehension" is drawn from Gilles Deleuze's engagement with the paintings of Francis Bacon and with Immanuel Kant's philosophical exploration of "the role of the imagination (when it is) freed from the legislation of the understanding."[9] Specifically, Bacon's attention to aesthetic comprehension restages the problem of deciding what should count as a sensible part or measure when attempting to understand an event, thing, or composition. The phrase evokes a "lived evaluation"[10] that resides in all practices of understanding. This is slightly different from the important assertion that Roland Bleiker makes in relation to the fall of New York's Twin Towers; namely, that, when faced with a sublime event, artistic creativity fills the void of understanding.[11] Instead, in order to understand any event (not just sublime ones), aesthetic practices are always already involved in processes of practical and pure understanding.[12] Again, they are involved because the gap between a thing and its sign can never be closed; there is always a little sublime in everything.

The textures, tensions, frames, contexts, amplitudes, and durations of a representation also contribute to the affective experience of an event. An affective experience is generally understood to be synonymous with an emotional response. Fear, sadness, and happiness are all affects. However, an attention to affect also emphasizes the somatic intensity that surrounds an emotion.[13] Whereas emotion is a subjective experience, affect is something that is not localized within an individual.[14] Affect might be experienced through the tissues of the mind-body, but it also embodies collective constellations of competing intensities. Panic is as much an individual experience as it is a collective expression of an intense event. A state of becoming panicked can turn into a habit and, sooner or later, become an affective ontology. Manipulating affective intensities by framing certain stories or magnifying particular images can constitute a kind of affective governance (for example, outrage, tolerance, or melancholy). As Brian Massumi explains, "to treat the emotion as separable ... from the activation event from which it affectively sprang is to place it on the level of representation ... It makes it seem comfortably controllable."[15] Affective governance, therefore, is not only the production of fear to *justify* control; it is fear itself. Fear *is* part of affective governance in a preemptive state of emergency.

Understanding the avian flu's affect involves an aesthetic evaluation of the framings and magnitudes of representation. Take as an example the claim that H5N1 has an apocalyptic kill rate (figures range from 52 percent to 70 percent). The figures' magnitude justifies emergency measures because it contains enough tension and texture to cause serious trepidation. However, these rates are composed from "reported" cases and highlight only patients who were sick enough to require having to go to the hospital. In the words of American conservative commentator Michael Fumento, "[w]e know the numerator, but without the denominator [these figures are] useless."[16] The actual number of those who become infected remains unknowable. Nevertheless, the tension resonates because it is set within a narrow ribbon of reported cases. It is a sensible part of the constituted distribution. Regardless of whether truthfulness in statistics is ever achievable, the more salient point is that *how* you frame the story about the avian flu really matters. In particular, the temporal and spatial aesthetics of representation constitute an affective governance of fear that legitimizes emergency action.

In order to justify calling the avian flu an emergency, temporal representations substitute a future unknown (what if it does happen?) with an immediate unknowable (will it happen?). The chief of microbiology at Mount Sinai Hospital in Toronto, Dr Donald Low, for example, repeated this aesthetic refrain: "The question is not *if* it's going to happen, but *when*."[17] In this spirit, news reports are provocatively titled "The Next Pandemic?"[18] or "The Race Against Time."[19] This *waiting* is not an absence of action. Waiting is a verb, an all-encompassing action. The anxiety of waiting builds a governmentally useful vigilance in public health.

Drawing from the most extreme historical examples also lubricates the temporal substitution of the uncertain "if" by the plausible "when," and replaces political judgment with an anxious waiting. Emphasizing the avian flu's temporal representation is organized around the 1918 Spanish flu pandemic that killed 20 to 100 million people around the world, largely because of the conditions created by the brutality of World War I.[20] But it elides the fact that the ominous threshold between epidemic bird flu and pandemic human flu was crossed in 2004.[21] The incident occurred when Pranee Thongchan died from the avian flu virus that she caught from her daughter in Thailand.[22] Although tragic for the family and the community, it has been reported that these shifts regularly happen without resulting in Armageddon. But the repeated reference to the 1918 Spanish flu creates an aesthetic link that heightens the impending sense of doom. The aesthetic link between 1918 and today occurs either through analogy (the H5N1 virus has the same properties as the 1918 variety), or through refrain (pandemics are cyclical, so we are "overdue").

The aesthetic effect of analogizing between contemporary and historical events results in some catastrophic scenarios. At one extreme, some argue that humanity could be facing numbers like those that Reuters has reported (150 million dead people) or those that Michael Osterholm, Director of the Center for Infectious Disease Research and Policy (CIDRAP) and Associate Director of the Department of Homeland Security's National Center for Food Protection and Defense (NCFPD), projects (180 to 360 million dead people).[23] Irwin Redlener, the Director of the National Center for

Disaster Preparedness (NCDP), topped everyone by projecting 1 billion deaths.[24] At the other extreme, WHO estimates that the deaths from the avian flu pandemic are likely to be between 2 million and 7.4 million globally.[25] The huge difference between 1 billion and 2 million is due to extrapolating from the mild pandemic of 1967 that killed 1 million people or, instead, from the deadly pandemic of 1918.

However, both the aesthetic analogy between 2006 and 1918 and the cyclical refrain about an overdue pandemic minimize the doubts that *this* virus will ever become a pandemic. These doubts are justified, for instance, because the analogy between 1918, 1957, 1968, or 1997 and 2003 is based, not on a cyclical phenomenon, but on a random set of events.[26] Only unpredictable "cycles" happen in increments of 39, 11, 29, or 6 years. Therefore, elaborate preparation for a random event is not "responsible." Rather, it is hype. The analogous and cyclical aesthetics of the avian flu emergency is a mode of political representation that generates a (de)mobilizing fear. It is part of what Timothy W. Luke calls, in his chapter in this volume, hype-power.

Although temporality provides the political anticipation and magnitude of the emergency, the spatial aesthetic adds its texture, character, and frame. The daily reporting of virus detection is as much a spatial mapping of an immanent disaster as it is a countdown to doomsday. The updates map a geopolitical trajectory from "here" to "there," and back again. Today, it is country "X;"[27] yesterday, Nigeria; the day before, it was Turkey and Russia. And everything prior to that (Cambodia, Vietnam, Thailand, Hong Kong, and so on) is the so-called Asian source. From this Asian source the virus' cousins are stalking Western civilization and getting closer.[28] In Cold War geopolitical form, the West again is facing the "Coming Plague"[29] and the "Coming Anarchy."[30] Instead of the global other being Communism, Africa, and/or Islam, Asia has now become (to use the title of Mike Davis's alarming book), the "Monster at *our* Door."[31]

The spatial framing is crucial to intensifying fear, since hype is indeed about risks being at *our* door. If the risks were at *their* door, to paraphrase the chilling line from the film *Hotel Rwanda*, people would go back to eating their TV dinners.[32] And, for the most part, people do. The spatial frame gives the political character of the crisis to be faced; it is not only urgent because of its magnitude, but also because of its geography. In other words, it becomes important only because it *could* infect us *here*.

Similarly, locating the *source* in Asia, for instance, puts a specific face on the problem and situates the solution within a geopolitical discourse that seeks to contain the enemy over "there." The critique of spatial frames like those presented in "The Coming Anarchy" remains compelling. As Simon Dalby argues, the "danger of the [threat] from 'there' compromising the safety of 'here' ... never countenances the possibility that the economic affluence 'here' is related to the poverty of 'there'."[33] These encroaching representations, Jorge Fernandez argues, signal a deep anxiety in the Western geopolitical imagination. The fear is that "accelerating cultural and political encounters ... threaten the nation-state's political viability by heightening the likelihood of conflicts."[34] The imagined cosmopolitan geography is thus at risk.

Furthermore, underlying statements made about the *source* of the avian flu—cohabitation with chickens, people eating wild birds—is a geopolitical racism that vilifies other cultures through the aesthetics of hygiene and civilized stratifications (public/private, human/animal).[35] In other words, where threats are localized within *their* dangerous/irresponsible cultural practices (instead of *our* international political economies of modern agribusiness), global poverty and environmental destruction become urgent matters only when they threaten *our* cities, *our* economies, and *our* standards of living.

Given that, in times of emergency, it is "not polite to point fingers" to the root causes of discrimination or exploitation, the avian flu's local contexts have been repackaged by national and international organizations as a universal global threat. The Asian Pacific Economic Cooperation (APEC), for example, elides the specificity of particular challenges (poverty, tuberculosis, tsunamis, or International Monetary Fund (IMF) policies) and, instead, expands the flu's spatial ecumene through a universal warning about global economic disaster. In the 2005 APEC meeting on "Avian and Pandemic Influenza Preparedness and Response," for example, Dr Karen Becker reported: "There is danger *everywhere*. No economy on Earth can afford to ignore this threat [since] interruption of supply chains could leave *us* without essential goods and products, particularly in this day of just-in-time manufacturing."[36] Through this universal spatial representation, the whole world is back to the image of the West's lifeboat, and everything that led to the flood is forgotten.

Attending to the aesthetic representation of the avian flu emergency gives a different context to Stohr's cumulative warnings that "there is no doubt there will be another pandemic,"[37] and that "we are living on borrowed time."[38] The danger exists in WHO's representation of the 10 key facts that *everyone needs to know:*

1 Pandemic influenza *is* different from avian influenza;
2 Influenza pandemics *are* recurring events;
3 The world *may* be on the brink of another pandemic;
4 All countries *will* be affected;
5 Widespread illness *will* occur;
6 Medical supplies *will* be inadequate;
7 Large numbers of death *will* occur;
8 Economic and social disruption *will* be great;
9 Every country *must* be prepared;
10 WHO will alert the world *when* the pandemic threat increases.[39]

In the above list, the use of indicative (factual) verbs ("is," "are," "will occur," and "must be prepared") contrasts with the singular use of a subjunctive (conditional) verb ("may be") and justifies the authority of WHO to decide on the governing protocols for political action ("must" and "when"). Beyond the capacity of any one particular state, an imminent danger has been created out of a transcendental "unknown" by rooting an aesthetic emergency in a substantiated affect of fear. Therefore, everyone must become *prepared* for when/where/how WHO decides it is time to act.

State decision makers and international officials have blurred the boundary between a preemptive state of emergency and an actual state of emergency. This blurring requires transforming the way decisions are made and how sovereignty functions. In the next section, I argue that, in order to match the aesthetic composition of emergencies like the avian flu, an internationalized state of emergency is replacing nationalized states of emergency. This occurs when peace becomes a form of war waged through perpetual humanitarian interventions.

International relations and the state of emergency

The proliferating attention to the term "state of emergency" could be embraced as a confirmation of Walter Benjamin's eighth thesis on history. It reads: "The tradition of the oppressed teaches us that the 'state of emergency' in which we live is not the exception but the rule."[40] History is replete with examples that support this thesis.[41] A state of emergency refers to the proliferating interpretive aesthetic-affective frameworks that normalize human and environmental life. How the avian flu emergency is politically reproduced reveals the degree to which a state of emergency has become a rule of everyday life.

This is not the same thing as saying that the reproduction of a state of emergency coincides with the numerical frequency of events that necessitate emergency powers (the Katrina and Rita hurricanes, the Indonesian tsunami, 9/11). Nor does it reflect what has been called a "culture of fear" in the media.[42] Instead, something more interesting is occurring. The state of emergency is the actualization of a particular view of IR and American foreign policy that defines peace as the constant preparation for war. Giorgio Agamben explains:

> President Bush's decision to refer to himself constantly as the "commander in Chief of the Army" after September 11, 2001 must be considered in the context of this presidential claim to sovereign powers in emergency situations. If, as we have seen, the assumption of this title entails a direct reference to the state of exception, then Bush is attempting to *produce a situation* in which the emergency becomes the rule and the very distinction between peace and war (and between foreign and civil war) becomes impossible.[43]

Instead of saying that Bush's politics lead towards contemporary fascism in America,[44] a more politically important point needs to be developed. What is interesting in the American example is that, from wiretapping US citizens and the suspension of habeas corpus to rendering enemy combatants, and from Iraq to Kosovo and back to Iraq again, US security discourse is embodying a *shift* from national juridical law to international exceptional politics. A nationalized state of emergency has made *an antigenic shift*—to borrow the epidemiological term—to an internationalized state of emergency. This shift pivots around the concept of sovereignty.

Sovereignty is both an epistemological and ontological event. It is a way of becoming organized in the world. In an epistemological sense, sovereignty becomes the means through which some statements come to have legitimacy (for example, "rational," "fact," or "progressive") while others are negated (for example, "emotion," "opinion," or "tradition"). These decisions simultaneously constitute a series of ontological friend/enemy distinctions,[45] oppositions that are constitutive of both the nationalized subject that creates and the nation of subjects that are created.[46] In this sense, sovereignty unfolds "by exercising (the) right to kill, or by refraining from killing."[47] It also includes the more contemporary manifestation of simply "letting die."[48] Sovereignty is simultaneously the decision between who lives and who dies and the qualification of a life worth living. The political problem of sovereignty, therefore, does not lie with the *proper* categorization of this life versus that other life. Instead, the political regime of sovereignty functions in the very act of *categorization* of life.

As such, sovereignty makes a declaration of emergency possible through the act of categorization itself. To modify Carl Schmitt's definition in an important way, sovereignty is *how* the exception is made.[49] It is how a risk becomes a danger, an inside becomes an outside, and a state of peace becomes a state of emergency. Drawing a staunch line between friend and enemy, for example, evokes an aesthetic practice of metaphysical conceit. This conceit, or founding violence, has become normalized as state sovereignty and as a nationalized state of exception.

Returning to my earlier point, an antigenic shift has occurred between the nationalized state of exception and an internationalized state of exception that organizes itself around the proliferation of global emergencies like the avian flu. Michel Foucault identified an "earlier" shift between a classic form of sovereign power and a disciplinary mode of sovereignty where "wars are no longer waged in the name of a sovereign who must be defended; they are waged on behalf of the existence (national life) of everyone; entire populations are mobilized for the purpose of wholesale slaughter in the name of life necessity: massacres have become vital."[50] Another shift is occurring today. Instead of protecting life in national terms (defending citizens), an internationalized state of exception is organized around the protection of humanity.[51] An internationalized clamor of global friend/enemy decisions and normal/abnormal classifications is thus materializing. Whereas a nationalized state of exception emerges through an aesthetic-affective framework of international emergencies, an internationalizing state of exception is now materializing through the proliferation of global emergencies (avian flu, terrorism, financial crises).

The pressing question, however, becomes what form(s) of sovereignty emerge(s) when wars are fought and emergencies contained, not for a national biological population, but, instead, for humanity's biological survival or for human life itself? How is the line drawn in this context? And what type of line can be drawn? When categorization loses its sovereign function, the result is a shift to preemption, responsibility to protect, and the precautionary principle. If this proposition holds, the line between friend and enemy is no longer drawn spatially; the line has become a temporal function. Preemptive governance, as such, is the governing of the future from the standpoint of the future. It pivots on the disappearance of the nationalized individual and the biopolitical emergence of a different ontological face.[52]

Anne Caldwell agues that humanitarian intervention represents a new form of global power called "bio-sovereignty." Her argument pushes beyond Schmitt's hesitancy about creating a political category called humanity. Schmitt had argued that the category "humanity" would negate the defining moment of politics (deciding who is friend and who is enemy).[53] For Caldwell, however, "[a]t least since the end of the cold war, humanity has emerged as a material political group in the same manner that 'the people' became a concrete group with the rise of the representative nation states. What political power represents humanity is less apparent."[54] In other words, new preemptive humanitarian actions constitute the nascent normalization of an international state of exception. She states: "The impossibility of locating sovereignty in a precise territory or group does not signal a collapse of sovereignty, but its transformation."[55] As such, the United Nations and WHO do not check sovereign power; they open up avenues for sovereign transformation, redemption, and rejuvenation (on this point, see also the argument advanced by Julian Reid in his chapter in this volume).

This sovereign transformation, or transformation of sovereignty rather, proceeds in, through, and upon the new materializing body called humanity. Reflecting on Agamben's work, Caldwell argues that "[h]umanity, rather than serving as a limit on sovereignty, appears as its medium and product."[56] In other words, Caldwell explains, "[a]s sovereignty expands beyond the nation state form, it increasingly operates as bio-sovereignty: a form of sovereignty operating according to the logic of exception rather than law, applied to material life rather than juridical life, and moving within a global terrain now almost exclusively bio-political."[57] Pushing Caldwell's definition further, one could say that bio-sovereignty preemptively decides between life and a life unworthy of life in a radically decentralized and highly mobile set of decisions, technologies, networks, and affective constellations.

As such, new preemptive global practices of sovereignty are emerging and becoming recognizable in the name of protecting humanity from the next pandemic. In his opening statement to the APEC Health Task Force, an initiative born out of an earlier SARS scare, Dr Amar Bhat suggests that the "human and economic cost of an uncontained influenza pandemic could be horrifying. We have a humanitarian obligation (as officials and individuals) ... to do our part."[58] Bhat's plea appears innocent. However, we do not know what "doing our part" entails. Who lives, who dies, and who decides, and how, why, and when?

In the midst of an international state of emergency, a new global triage constitutes its own necessity. A centralizing and decentralizing sovereignty becomes an "objective condition."[59] Citing the "lack of international harmony," a permanent global task force is called for to deal with the next pandemic.[60] Such a force would include international agencies like WHO, the United Nations' Food and Agriculture Organization (FAO), and the World Organization for Animal Health (OIE). The task force would need to seamlessly integrate US organizations like the Department of Health and Human Services (HHS), Centers for Disease Control and Prevention (CDC), National Institutes of Health (NIH), and the Food and Drug Administration (FDA). It would also need to incorporate the European equivalents. Other regional organizations like Asia's APEC, the Association of South East Asian Nations (ASEAN), the Asian Resource Foundation (ARF), or the Asian Development Bank (ADB) could not be omitted, nor could Europe's or even Africa's. And we have not even mentioned getting the *local* authorities and the *multinational* pharmaceutical companies to cooperate. A governmental nexus himself, Osterholm declared that "pandemic planning must be on the agenda of every school board, manufacturing plant, investment firm, mortuary, state legislature and food distributor (in the world)."[61] The scope and scale of planning is simply awesome.

What we are witnessing is not a unified global government; instead, this global triage amounts to empowering a monotony of people to make seemingly mundane choices about the characteristics of life.[62] The APEC Health Task Force, for example, convenes to discuss regional and global responses to the avian flu threat and claims to do nothing more extraordinary than have its "members simply share information, lessons, and advice to help facilitate more efficient and effective responses."[63] A typical call to *global action* includes nothing more exciting than claiming that

> specific monitoring of virological, serological and clinical parameters is urgently

needed for people at risk. Also needed are detailed autopsies to characterize the disease, and the subsequent establishment of appropriate animal models to evaluate available intervention strategies. For poultry, bird populations should be actively surveyed for all types of flu viruses, using high-throughput technology; production and distribution systems should be modified; and stricter adherence to contamination measures achieved when there is an outbreak.[64]

However mundane they might sound, these choices will amount to extraordinary circumstances for someone somewhere.

The implications from this global triage are most obvious in the relations between humans, viruses, and birds. In this threat scenario, birds and viruses will be exterminated to save humans. The decisions become more difficult, however, when choosing between human lives. Osterholm has warned that only about 500 million people could be vaccinated, about 14 percent of the world's population. On April 1, 2005, Bush issued an "executive order authorizing the use of quarantines inside the United States and permitting the isolation of international visitors ... if one country implements such orders, others will follow suit."[65] This is no prank. Given the US precedent of not sharing vaccines during the 1976 H1N1 crisis, it is unlikely that *all* humanity will be saved.[66] To the degree that a global biological apartheid does not already exist as the *de jure* norm of IR, there is simply not enough Tamiflu to go around. The global triage will decide how, when, and where to create quarantines, cull populations, establish no-travel zones, and distribute antiviral drugs.[67] If the occasion arises, how will the decision between your life and death be made?

Once again, in the name of humanity, the affluent will likely be saved from the imposed fate of the rest. In order to meet the needs of the rest, the Ontario Health Plan for an Influenza Pandemic (OHPIP) convened a working group of clinicians with expertise in critical care, infectious diseases, medical ethics, military medicine, triage, and disaster management in order to create a critical care triage protocol.[68] Deciding who lives and dies (in the emergency) will depend on your Sequential Organ Failure Assessment (SOFA) score. The triage has "4 main components: inclusion criteria, exclusion criteria, minimum qualifications for survival, and a prioritization tool."[69] Life and death decisions will rest in someone's hands. Backed by a set of guidelines, they will prescribe courses of action as if these were not in themselves ethically, politically, and emotionally contentious propositions.

However, conversations about life and death are much more complicated when the illusion of modern sovereignty slips from the hands of a single individual (the president, or the doctor). Aihwa Ong and Steven Collier call these new ways of deciding, new moments of decision, and new kinds of governance "global assemblages."[70] These global assemblages are constituted by a series of overlapping calls to emergency, demands for preemptive action, and a contemporary episteme that slowly claims the name of "humanity." The result is a new population, a new essence of humanity, and a new appreciation of life called "biovalue."[71] Biology establishes citizenship, rights, and responsibilities. According to this means of valuation, Nikolas Rose explains that biological citizenships "encompass all those citizenship projects that have linked their concepts of citizens to beliefs about the biological existence of Human beings, as individuals, as families and lineages, as communities, as population and race, and as a species."⁷² These linkages occur well before an emergency has begun through a medicalization and pharmaceuticalization of life (with initiatives like the human genome project, stem-cell research, AIDS research, and organ harvesting).⁷³ A biological-technological indistinction emerges in the encoding, recoding, and decoding of contemporary biomedical research.⁷⁴ Eugene Thacker calls this the *optimization of biology*.⁷⁵ Signaling a radical transformation and dislocation of thinking about the future of human life, biological citizenship and biomedical research protect and optimize life by simultaneously minimizing what it can mean.

As the indistinction of biological life becomes possible, the conditions for a preemptive global triage emerge. Human life becomes chicken life through sickness, and chicken life becomes viral life through infection. "What would thus be obtained," Agamben explains, "is neither an animal life nor a human life, but only a life that is separated and excluded from itself—only a bare life."⁷⁶ What emerges, in fact, is *infected life*. In the narrative of the "next pandemic," the same technologies of control, surveillance, containment, vaccination, and extermination will constitute the indistintion between human, chicken, H5N1, and antiviral life. Quarantines and dead zones will be shaped around how life is appreciated through a battlefield triage.

The risk of war, as Carl von Clausewitz presented it, rests in the escalating logic that leads towards total war.⁷⁷ From *a* war to *the* war to end *all* wars, greater and greater applications of violence are justified in the majesty of the objective—saving humanity. Replacing the nuclear shadow of World War II, the twilight of the next pandemic makes civilian casualties managerially expendable. This risk, however, rests as much with peace as it does with war. When overlapping appeals to emergency powers govern everyday life, then, as Stohr warns us, "we are living on borrowed time."⁷⁸ Most of us (now speaking inclusively to chickens and viruses too) are already planned casualties, biomedical collateral damage, in the very war to protect human life.⁷⁹ As such, the living-dead wait in suspended tension between panic and docility, caught between stockpiling Tamiflu and nervously consuming Kentucky Fried Chicken. This global triage, in particular, and emerging preemptive governance in general, are what Benjamin called the "real" state of emergency that is "the monster at the door."⁸⁰

The material aesthetics of resistance

The monstrosity of an internationalized state of emergency with a global triage sounds less menacing when put in the context of the aesthetic-affective governance of the avian flu emergency explored in the first section. The only threat greater than the avian flu emergency, experts warn, is the danger of becoming complacent against an imminent danger. In one of its surveys, the APEC task force reports that the greatest barriers to influenza preparedness are the Ministers' lack of "interest," absence of "funding" and "international collaboration" on surveillance, poor risk communication, and the difficulty of securing vaccine and antiviral supplies.⁸¹ When the barriers to creating a global system of societal controls are mainly motivation, funds, and collaboration, then, it seems completely reasonable that the remedy consists in generating an appropriate aesthetic-affective political will, like panic.

Creating panic amounts to emotional brinkmanship. Any other course of action besides panic appears to be simultaneously irrelevant and suicidal. Emotional brinkmanship eventually turns into the all-encompassing term "preparedness." As if only capable of being represented through a media montage, the US television network ABC released its horrifying made-for-TV movie, "Fatal Contact,"[82] in order to secure the appropriate frenetic mix of hope and despair in the public. The *New York Times*, acknowledging that the use of panic has the potential of replicating Orson Welles's famous "Martian Invasion" performance, warned that its article about preparing "for a Real Outbreak of Avian Flu" (the article's very title) was "not a real article." It was only an "exercise."[83] In fact, Donald McNeil, Jr was only reporting on the CDC's first "fully functional" simulation of an avian emergency. Again, a cinematic aesthetic was employed to represent the news. McNeil, Jr reported that "[l]ike an episode of the television program '24' the drill was supposed to be taking place in real time," and, therefore, resulted in its own "movie-within-the-movie moments."[84] He concluded by recounting the words of Peter Taylor, the man behind the scenes "pulling the strings ... in a little room upstairs known as the Simulation Cell." When asked if the human race survives, "Taylor gave only a hint: the exercise never really ends," revealing the underlying logic of preemptive governance.[85] When Orson Welles, Jack Bauer, and the Wizard of Oz are all mentioned in the same *New York Times* article, this is certainly enough to reassure everyone that everything will work out fine in the end; that is, if we do not all die first.

Identifying the emergence of a troubling trend, Paul Virilio notes that "[n]o one is waiting anymore for the revolution, only for the accident, the breakdown, that will reduce this unbearable chatter to silence."[86] Facing a bio-nano-tech future and looming social-environmental disasters, the slogan of the 1909 Futurist Manifesto, "war is the world's only Hygiene,"[87] ironically unites proponents of a preemptive state of emergency and its most outspoken critics.[88] This paralyzing chatter forces politics into a corner where the only options are to contribute to the state of emergency and/or to dream of a total economic and political collapse of the "real" state of emergency.

This political paralysis combines two aspects of Walter Benjamin's project; the first is embodied in his lament for the Angel of History depicted in Paul Klee's famous painting. Benjamin writes:

> An angel looking as though he is about to move away from something he is fixedly contemplating. His eyes are staring, his mouth open, his wings are spread. This is how one depicts the angel of history. His face turned toward the past. Where we perceive a chain of events, he sees one single catastrophe which keeps piling wreckage upon wreckage and hurls it in front of his feet. The angel would like to stay, awaken the dead, and make whole what has been smashed. But a storm is blowing from paradise; it has got caught in his wings with such violence that the angel can no longer close them. This storm irresistibly propels him into the future to which his back is turned, while the pile of debris before him grows skyward. This storm is what we call progress.[89]

The aesthetic composition of this image is compelling because of the way the viewer is drawn into the diagram of the painting (the edges are darkened and it almost looks like smoke is looming in the background). This tension builds through Klee's childlike bridge between abstraction and realism in the awkward figure of the Angel. Perhaps the fact that this Angel of History looks remarkably like a chicken is inconsequential. However, it allows a further analogy to be made about framing. The same modern aesthetic composition blackmails the Angel and the alarmists who demand that we act responsibly in the face of the avian flu emergency. Together, the new pandemicists and the Angel of History stand *eyes staring, mouth open, and wings spread*, paralyzed, docile, stupefied, and caged with fear.

The second component of this political paralysis, however, is Benjamin's insistence that we overcome the fate of Klee's "angelic chicken." To this end, Benjamin differentiates between a state of emergency and a *real* state of emergency. The "real" state of emergency transforms it into a political struggle that radically reorganizes the material conditions of modern society. Benjamin asserts that

> the tradition of the oppressed teaches us that the 'state of emergency' in which we live is not the exception but the rule. We must attain to a conception of history that is in keeping with this insight. Then we shall clearly realize that it is *our task to bring about a real state of emergency, and this will improve our position in the struggle against Fascism*. One reason why Fascism has a chance is that in the name of progress its opponents treat it as a historical norm ... [90]

Bringing about the real state of emergency is a messianic project of reinvigoration of the political. This occurs in two steps. The first is to politicize the historical norm of the state of emergency already underway. The second is to build a material aesthetic resistance sufficient to this development. It is at the juncture of these two political vectors or steps that the political question of aesthetic composition becomes a critical political resource.

The first vector requires reinvigorating the political that, Agamben argues, "has suffered a lasting eclipse because it has been contained by law."[91] To reinvigorate the political, in this sense, would require re-politicizing the relationship between life and law. Law and its sovereign founding violence would no longer be the constitutive condition of modern life.[92] Instead, politics would occupy the "emptiness"[93] in-between law and life, and become a space for "human action."[94] Politics would become "a counter movement that, working in an inverse direction in law and in life, always seeks to loosen what has been artificially and violently linked."[95] Subverting the very state of emergency that gives law in general or, in this case, global surveillance, its legitimacy and ontological necessity, a creative politics would not attempt to re-impose a normalized sovereign rule of law. Instead, by revealing the political nature of the state of emergency's normalized rule of law, it would politicize the aesthetic-affective boundaries that manage and produce the state of emergency.

Although its development exceeds the scope of this chapter, such a creative politics requires keeping the metaphysical boundaries between human, animal, and viral life open in order to offer the possibility of a new future solidarity.[96] If the avian flu is a form of human governance that requires thinking about other animals as either food, pets, or wild, then politicizing this sovereign exception would engender a "human politics" that would involve developing a different relationship with the animal inside the human and the human inside the animal.[97] Without politically opening the insecurities that constitute humanity, the fate of animals will become the fate of some humans.

The second vector requires affirming political openness while pluralizing the political tactics available. As I argued in the first section of this chapter, the paralyzing force of the avian flu emergency's affective blackmail operates by making an uncertain future a governable resource. In this formulation, fear of the future does not precede the operability of this uncertainty; fear *is* the affective governance of a preemptive state of emergency. That affective governance, or what Massumi calls "activation," is the production of fear itself.[98] In other words, we are not afraid first; fear is the experience of an operation (political control). Citing William James, Massumi explains: "We don't run because we are afraid, we are afraid because we run."[99] Paralysis sets in because the "emergence of emotion preempts action. Actual action has been short-circuited."[100] Political paralysis becomes a habit, a habit of becoming, in which an affective consensus constitutes the political limits of life itself.

In the middle of an affective build up, it is unlikely that a calming call to reevaluate the categories used to frame the problem will break the panic habit. The affect is too great. The ABC drama *Fatal Contact*, for example, represents a total reification of fear.[101] In this TV program, dead bodies are dumped in parking lots, the death toll spirals out of control, and helpless fathers commit suicide in front of their children. In the face of such a representation, docility seems justified. Perhaps the drama would be harmless if the result was only a spike in sales of canned goods and emergency candles. On the other hand, if it bolsters contemporary justifications for fueling proliferating states of emergency, then the aesthetic composition of the pandemic needs to be targeted as a site of political significance.

It is possible to disrupt the aesthetic composition of the avian flu emergency and invite a pluralization of creative political possibilities. This is already underway. For example, the proliferation of political satire is illustrative of a strategy that re-contextualizes the aesthetic comprehension of the avian flu pandemic by employing measures other than the 1918 flu analogy. David Letterman's *Late Show*, the *Colbert Report*, or the *Daily Show with John Stewart*, in particular, have opened up a different way to comprehend the "unavoidable Armageddon." Their satirical accounts of the drama *Fatal Contact*, for instance, have used a different lived evaluation (for example, the Cold War, the Killer Bees, Y2K, or the War on Terror) as an aesthetic measure. Instead of trying to solve the problem of the avian flu, the constitutive relationship between emergency law and life is targeted and opened to political evaluation.

In other words, with a different aesthetic measure, the nature of the emergency and the form of governance could change. For example, the world community is spending US$1.9 billion[102] to confront a potential risk of 2 to 7 million deaths. But what if these funds were directed towards more routine pandemic killers like tuberculosis (8.8 million cases and 2 million dead people a year), malaria (5 billion episodes and over 1 million deaths a year), or AIDS (2.9 million dead people a year and 25 million deaths in total)?[103] Similarly, the US contribution to the global avian flu effort actually diverts funds from existing emergency and preparedness commitments (like the tsunami relief for Southeast Asia, a region where the economic and political vulnerability to avian flu is actually greatest).[104] Such examples show where the line between qualified and unqualified life resides and whom the "international" community cares about most.[105]

When the aesthetic measures shift from mapping migrating birds, human-induced emergencies themselves become a potential cause of future global pandemics since they (like all aspects of globalization) create the very web of interconnections that the avian flu cannot develop on its own. In a chilling tale, for example, we learnt that, in October 2004,

> the American College of Pathologists mailed a collection of mystery microbes prepared by a private lab to almost 5 000 labs in 18 countries for them to test as part of their recertification. The mailing should have been a routine procedure; instead in March 2005 a Canadian lab discovered that the test included a sample of H2N2 flu—a strain that killed 4 four million people worldwide in 1957. H2N2 has not been in circulation since 1968, meaning that hundreds of millions of people lack immunity from it. Had any of the samples leaked or been exposed to the environment, the results could have been devastating. On learning of the error, the WHO called for the immediate destruction of all the test kits.[106]

Repeatedly, the very problems that stalk humanity are created by human attempts to contain the threats they face. The way emergencies are produced and managed constitutes the real emergency. There is a failure to recognize that threats are not isolated from the affective governance that created them.

Similarly, the emergency looks different when the threat of the bird flu has less to do with birds than with the political economy of industrial food production. For instance, an article in the *New Scientist* in January 2004 reported that the source of today's emergency, the 2003 H5N1 super-virus that emerged in Hong Kong, is the result of "a combination of official cover-up and questionable farming practices."[107] Specifically, Chinese growers actually accelerated the evolution of the H5N1 superstrain by using an inactivated virus to immunize their chickens and safeguard industrial scale production.[108] Simply put, if Tyson Foods incarcerates and slaughters 2.2 billion chickens annually, it creates vast amplifiers of viral risks. The expedient way to minimize the avian flu risk, therefore, is not color-coordinating surgical masks or organizing photo opportunities for government officials to eat chicken lunches that *imply* that something "real" is being done. Rather, it involves changing the most basic material relationships that constitute the current "human picture." The industrial production of agriculture needs to be made a political problem if the future of viral infections is to be, not managed, but renegotiated.

Failing to condemn capitalism's "human-induced environmental shocks" and "corporate livestock revolutions"[109] that are actively championed by the World Bank (WB), the IMF and regional organizations like APEC, ASEAN, or the ABD only serves to reproduce a hysterical danger that stands in for political debate. These responses mask the very practices of impoverishment that champion industrial agriculture and economic specialization while reducing culturally specific and traditionally rooted support networks. Modernity panics because its abstract plans cannot be rooted and rehearsed in local historical knowledge practices that create pluralities of well-being.

Conclusion

Instead of reproducing the contemporary theme of Disney's *Chicken Little*, a material aesthetic resistance invokes the political skepticism engendered through the prudent story of *The Boy Who Cried Wolf*. This fable ends with the moral statement that, *even when liars tell the truth, nobody believes them*. The beginning of the fable might prove more instructive, however: it presents a boy who is so bored with his own existence, as if it were as dull as a chicken's, that he decides to entertain himself by crying wolf. In a world where the human-chicken-virus distinction has already collapsed in the singularity of boredom and fear, the call to emergency not only becomes more likely, but also apolitical. Perhaps as appreciations of different degrees of fear develop, a wider affirmation of lived risks will replace the pandemic blackmail of fear. When opened politically, the aesthetic emergency loses its affective weight. In turn, it becomes more palatable to call for sustained social, economic, and environmental transformation.

The irony is that the *expedient and responsible* political response to the avian flu does not involve empowering a global plutocracy to manage every risk as if it were a world-ending danger. It involves changing the way human organization relates to the world in which it is embedded. Simple "conservative" solutions like empowering local food networks or taking responsibility for socio-ecological footprints will do much more to reduce future threats than "utopian" solutions like global surveillance or full spectrum dominance.[110] This is not about avoiding the scale of the avian flu problem. On the contrary, what is required is nothing short of a sustained reorganization of humanity's relationship within its animal and environmental self. What form this aesthetic material affirmation may look like, however, is unknowable because, in each instance, resistance writes its own aesthetic and affective geography.[111] This spread of political possibility might also constitute a world that is viable and resistant to future human-made problems, like the avian flu, or America's global model of industrial food production.

Notes

1. Giorgio Agamben, "Security and Terror," *Theory and Event* Vol. 5, No. 4 (2002), p. 2.
2. Quoted in Mike Davis, *The Monster at Our Door* (New York: The New Press, 2005), p. 139.
3. Richard Ashley, "Living on Borderlines: Man, Poststructuralism, and War," in eds. James Der Derian and Michael J. Shapiro, *International/Intertextual Relations* (Lexington: Lexington Books, 1989), pp. 259–321.
4. Jeffrey Taubenberger and Ann Reid, "Archaevirology: Characterization of the 1918 'Spanish' Influenza Pandemic Virus," in eds. Charles Greenblatt and Mark Spigelman, *Emerging Pathogens: Archaeology, Ecology and Evolution of Infectious Disease* (Oxford: Oxford University Press, 2003), p. 189.
5. Davis, *The Monster at Our Door*, p. 11.
6. David Campbell, *Writing Security: United States Foreign Policy and the Politics of Identity* (Minneapolis: University of Minnesota Press, 1998), p. 1.
7. See also, François Ewald, "Insurance and Risk," in eds. Graham Burchell, Colin Gordon, and Peter Miller, *The Foucault Effect: Studies in Governmentality* (Chicago: Chicago University Press, 1991), p. 199.
8. Daniel W. Smith, "Introduction," in Gilles Deleuze, *Francis Bacon: The Logic of Sensation* (Minneapolis: University of Minnesota Press, 2002), p. xvii.
9. Ibid., p. xvii.
10. Ibid., p. xviii.

11 Roland Bleiker, "Art after 9/11," *Alternatives* Vol. 31, No. 1 (2006), p. 80.
12 See Jacques Rancière, *The Politics of Aesthetics* (New York: Continuum, 2004), pp. 12–19.
13 Brian Massumi, *Parables for the Virtual* (Durham: Duke University Press, 2002), p. 27.
14 Ibid., p. 27.
15 Brian Massumi, "Fear (the Spectrum Said)," *Positions* Vol. 13, No. 1 (2005), p. 39.
16 Michael Fumento, "Fuss and Feathers: Pandemic Panic over the Avian flu," *The Weekly Standard*, November 21, 2005, p. 28.
17 Quoted in Margot Andresen, "Avian Flu: WHO Prepares for the Worst," *Canadian Medical Association Journal* Vol. 170, No. 5 (2004), p. 777.
18 See Canadian Broadcasting Corporation, "The Next Pandemic?," available at www.cbc.ca/news/background/avianflu (last visited on September 4, 2006).
19 Anthony Fauci, "Race Against Time," *Nature*, Vol. 435, May 26, 2005, pp. 423–4.
20 Davis, *The Monster at Our Door*, pp. 124–5.
21 Dr. Klaus Stohr, the head of WHO's H5N1 outbreak response, reports that the 1997 Hong Kong strain did mutate into a form that was transmissible between humans, but because of its relative weakness, it caused few illnesses. See Andresen, "Avian Flu," p. 777.
22 Davis, *The Monster at Our Door*, pp. 4–8.
23 Number quoted in Fumento, "Fuss and Feathers," p. 24.
24 Redlener later clarified that he meant to say 1 billion sick people. See Fumento, "Fuss and Feathers," p. 24.
25 Ibid., p. 29.
26 Ibid.
27 Every day I worked on this chapter I debated whether I should change this country to reflect the current news reports. As such, I will leave it as country "X."
28 One can check out the interactive map showing how the contagion is getting closer at news.bbc.co.uk/1/shared/spl/hi/world/05/bird_flu_map/html/1.stm.
29 Laurie Garrett, *The Coming Plague: Newly Emerging Diseases in a World out of Balance* (New York: Farrar, Straus and Giroux, 1994).
30 Robert D. Kaplan, "The Coming Anarchy," *The Atlantic Monthly*, Vol. 273, No. 2 (February 1994), pp. 44–76.
31 See Davis, *The Monster at Our Door*; my emphasis.
32 See the film *Hotel Rwanda*, dir. Terry George (MGM, 2004).
33 Simon Dalby, "Reading Kaplan's 'Coming Anarchy'," in eds. Gearóid Ó Tuathail, Simon Dalby, and Paul Routledge, *The Geopolitical Reader* (London: Routledge, 1998), p. 199.
34 Jorge Fernandez, "Ebola Takes to the Road," in eds. Jenny Edkins, Véronique Pin-Fat, and Michael J. Shapiro, *Sovereign Lives: Power in Global Politics* (London: Routledge, 2004), p. 192.
35 See Anne McClintock, *Imperial Leather: Race, Gender and Sexuality in the Colonial Conquest* (London: Routledge, 1995), chapters 1 and 5.
36 Karen Becker, "Avian and Influenza Pandemics: A threat to the Asia-pacific Community," available at www.apec.org/apec/documents_reports/health_task_force/2005.html#AI; my emphasis.
37 CNN, "Who Warns of Dire Flu Pandemic," available at www.cnn.com/2004/HEALTH/11/25/birdflu.warning/ (last visited on April 10, 2006).
38 Stohr, quoted in Davis, *The Monster at Our Door*, p. 165.
39 World Health Organization, "Ten Things You Need to Know about Pandemic Influenza," available at www.who.int/csr/disease/influenza/pandemic10things/en/ (last visited on April 10, 2006); my emphasis.
40 Walter Benjamin, "Thesis on the Philosophy of History," in Benjamin, *Illuminations* (New York: Schocken Books: 1968), p. 257.
41 See Mark Neocleous, "The Problem with Normality: Taking Exception to 'Permanent Emergency'," *Alternatives* Vol. 31, No. 2 (2006), pp. 191–213.
42 Barry Glassner, *The Culture of Fear* (New York: Basic Books, 1999).

43 Giorgio Agamben, *State of Exception* (Chicago: University of Chicago Press, 2005), p. 22; my emphasis.
44 This question was debated at the 2006 annual meeting of the American Political Science Association in Washington, DC on a panel titled "Is it Time to Call it Fascism?" The participants unanimously agreed, with certain reservations about historical analogy, that it was in fact time to call the contemporary political scene in the United States fascism.
45 See Carl Schmitt, *The Concept of the Political* (Chicago: University of Chicago Press, 1996), p. 26.
46 For more on this critical line of analysis, see Ashley, "Living on Borderlines," pp. 259–321.
47 Michel Foucault, *The History of Sexuality, Volume I* (New York: Vintage, 1978), p. 136.
48 Nikolas Rose, *The Politics of Life Itself* (Princeton: Princeton University Press, 2007), p. 64.
49 Schmitt states "Sovereign is he who decides on the exception." See Carl Schmitt, *Political Theology* (Chicago: University of Chicago Press, 1985), p. 5.
50 Foucault, *The History of Sexuality, Volume I*, p. 137.
51 See Paul Rabinow, "Midst Anthropology's Problems," in eds. Aihwa Ong and Steven Collier, *Global Assemblages: Technology, Politics and Ethics as Anthropological Problems* (London: Blackwell, 2005), pp. 40–54.
52 Michel Foucault, *The Order of Things* (London: Routledge, 1989).
53 See Schmitt, *The Concept of the Political*.
54 Anne Caldwell, "Bio-Sovereignty and the Emergence of Humanity," *Theory and Event* Vol. 7, No. 2 (2004), pp. 1–2.
55 Ibid., p. 10.
56 Ibid., p. 2.
57 Ibid., p. 3.
58 Amar Bhat, "Remarks by the APEC Health Task Force Chair," available at www.apec.org/apec/documents_reports/health_task_force/2005.html#AI.
59 Agamben, *State of Exception*, p. 29.
60 Ron Fouchier, *et al.*, "Global Task Force for Influenza," *Nature* Vol. 435, May 26, 2005, pp. 419–20.
61 Michael Osterholm, "Preparing for the Next Pandemic," *Foreign Affairs* Vol. 84, No. 4 (July/August 2005), available at www.foreignaffairs.org/20050701faessay84402/michael-t-osterholm/preparing-for-the-next-pandemic.html.
62 To see how this materialized in US military policy under the leadership of Donald Rumsfeld, see Robert D. Kaplan, "Supremacy by Stealth," *The Atlantic Monthly*, Vol. 292, No. 1 (July/August 2003), pp. 66–83.
63 See APEC, "Regional Health Threats," available at www.apec.org/apec/apec_groups/som_special_task_groups/health_task_force/apec_information_on.html.
64 Fouchier *et al.*, "Global Task Force for Influenza," pp. 419–20.
65 Osterholm, "Preparing for the Next Pandemic," no page given.
66 Ibid., no page given.
67 Nelson Schwartz, "Rumsfeld's Growing Stake in Tamiflu," available at money.cnn.com/2005/10/31/news/newsmakers/fortune_rumsfeld/.
68 Michael D. Christian *et al.*, "Development of a Triage Protocol for Critical Care during an Influenza Pandemic," available at www.cmaj.ca/cgi/content/full/175/11/1377 (last accessed on February 2, 2007).
69 Ibid., no page given.
70 See eds. Ong and Collier, *Global Assemblages*.
71 Nikolas Rose and Carlos Novas, "Biological Citizenship," in eds. Ong and Collier, *Global Assemblages*, p. 445.
72 Ibid., p. 440.
73 See Gisli Palsson and Paul Rabinow, "Iceland Controversy: Reflections of the Transnational Virtue," in eds. Ong and Collier, *Global Assemblages*, pp. 91–104; Sarah Franklin, "Stem Cells R Us: Emergent Life Forms and the Global Biological," in eds.

Ong and Collier, *Global Assemblages*, pp. 59–78; Vinh-Kim Nguyen, "Antiretroviral Globalism, Biopolitics, and Therapeutic Citizenship," in eds. Ong and Collier, *Global Assemblages*, pp. 124–44; and Nancy Scheper-Hughes, "The Last Commodity: Post-Human Ethics and the Global Traffic in 'Fresh' Organs," in eds. Ong and Collier, *Global Assemblages*, pp. 145–68.
74 Eugene Thacker, *Biomedia* (Minneapolis: University of Minnesota Press, 2004).
75 Thacker, *Biomedia*, p. 28.
76 Giorgio Agamben, *The Open* (Stanford: Stanford University Press, 2002), p. 38.
77 Carl von Clausewitz, *On War* (Oxford: Oxford University Press, 2007).
78 Stohr, quoted in Davis, *The Monster at Our Door*, p. 165.
79 Agamben, *State of Exception*, p. 86.
80 See Davis, *The Monster at Our Door*, p. 165.
81 APEC, "Results from Survey—Pandemic Influenza and Preparedness: Situation Assessment for APEC and Western Pacific Economies Public Health Emergency Preparedness Training Course," available at www.apec.org/apec/documents_reports/health_task_force/2005.html#AI.
82 See Richard Pearce and Ron McGee, *Fatal Contact: Bird Flu in America*, ABC television network (2006).
83 Douglas McNeil, Jr., "In Daylong Drill, an Agency Tries to Prepare for a Real Outbreak of Avian Flu," *New York Times*, February 1, 2007, p. A14.
84 Ibid.
85 Ibid.
86 Paul Virilio, *Art and Fear* (London: Continuum, 2004), p. 75.
87 Ibid., p. 29.
88 Vancouver-based anti-consumerist magazine *Adbusters* conducted a very interesting thought experiment in the summer of 2004 when it asked its readership to accept an end of the world scenario and then report on life after the end. The hope was that, in those ruminations, people would begin to develop local strategies that could be useful today. Note to the wise: although some reported that anarchy was fun, most lamented not having a garden.
89 Walter Benjamin, "Thesis on the Philosophy of History," p. 257.
90 Ibid., p. 257.
91 Agamben, *State of Exception*, p. 88.
92 Ibid.
93 Agamben, *The Open*, p. 92.
94 Agamben, *State of Exception*, p. 88.
95 Ibid., p. 87.
96 See Geoffrey Whitehall, "Viral Politics: Avian flu, Difference and Contagion," paper presented at the 48th Annual Convention of the International Studies Association (Chicago, IL, 2007); and Geoffrey Whitehall, "Infected Life and Viral Politics: Agamben and the Avian Flu," paper presented at the Canada Research Chair in Sustainability and Culture Conference on the topic of *Nature Matters: Materiality and the More-than-Human in Cultural Studies of the Environment* (Toronto, Canada, 2007).
97 For instance, see ed. Cary Wolfe, *Zoontologies: The Question of the Animal* (Minneapolis: University of Minnesota Press, 2003); and Cary Wolfe, *Animal Rites* (Chicago: Chicago University Press, 2003).
98 Massumi, "Fear (the Spectrum Said)," p. 35.
99 Ibid., p. 36.
100 Ibid., p. 40.
101 See Pearce and McGee, *Fatal Contact* (ABC).
102 See *New York Times*, "Global Effort Attracts $1.9 Billion in Pledges to Battle Bird Flu," January 19, 2006, p. A9.
103 Figures from Osterholm, "Preparing for the Next Pandemic," no page given.
104 *New York Times*, "Global Effort," p. A9.
105 For an equally, if not more, compelling tale of preemptive need, see Steven Lewis, *The Race against Time* (Concord: House of Anansi Press, 2006).

106 Laurie Garrett, "The Next Pandemic?," *Foreign Affairs* Vol. 84, No. 4 (July/August 2005), available at www.foreignaffairs.org/20050701faessay84401/laurie-garrett/the-next-pandemic.html.
107 See Debora Mackenzie, "Bird Flu Outbreak Started a Year Ago," *The New Scientist*, January 28, 2004, available at http://www.newscientist.com/article.ns?id=dn4614
108 Ibid., p. 102.
109 Ibid., p. 8.
110 See *Joint Vision 2020: America's Military; Preparing for Tomorrow*, available at www.dtic.mil/jointvision/jvpub2.htm.
111 Inspired by Chris Connery's comment that "resistance writes its own geography," quoted in Rob Wilson and Arlif Dirlik, *Asia/Pacific as Space of Cultural Production* (Durham: Duke University Press, 1995), p. 6.

10 Over a barrel

Cultural political economy and oil imperialism

Simon Dalby and Matthew Paterson

> How did our oil get under their sands?
> Protest slogan[1]

> A completely new basis for everyday life is required which we can term "conspicuous asceticism," the nemesis of Americanization built on conspicuous consumption ... Any sustainable non-Fascist future will require the development of a popular world view that condemns unnecessary consumption as anti-social behaviour.
> Peter Taylor[2]

Introduction

For many critics of contemporary US geopolitical strategy, the anxieties provoked by US imperialism are directly tied to the material practices that give rise to it in the first place. Geoffrey Whitehall's chapter in this volume concludes by contrasting strategies to deal with avian flu through global surveillance or through agricultural restructuring and localization. If the avian flu is undoubtedly one of those contemporary anxieties produced by material practices, another set of material phenomena related to oil and automobility are even more crucial to the maintenance of US imperialism. As the connections between oil, imperialism, and automobility become clear to many, questions about how these links work have led to protests and debates about consumption and war. But how should we understand and respond to these links? Attempts to deal with this sort of question can be seen in two prominent recent forms of resistance politics that have been organized around intertwined critiques of the Sports-Utility Vehicle (SUV) on the one hand, and oil imperialism on the other.

Our overall aim in this chapter is to suggest that both sets of critiques misunderstand the character of the problematic at hand and, therefore, do not have an appropriate normative vision that could underpin resistance. Specifically, to focus on the SUV alone is to erroneously take a particular type of car as "the problem" when it is in fact the whole complex of automobility that is at the heart of increased oil dependence. At the same time, critics of oil imperialism tend to ignore the social purposes to which oil is being put, principally, the energy to sustain the vast complex of automobility that remains central to the American way of life. As a consequence, dealing with the problems posed by contemporary US imperialism requires us to address the centrality of automobility to contemporary economic and social life. This becomes even clearer when we add climate change, and the political contestations surrounding this matter, into the mix. The contemporary critical debates about the way the United States will develop and deploy its global power in the future center on the possibility of detaching the United States from its oil dependence and thus from both its pressures for geopolitical adventure and its ability to play a part in addressing climate change.

As Timothy W. Luke notes in his chapter in this volume, these criticisms are not limited to activist protestors, but also include established political and economic interests, something that reveals a split in the US ruling bloc between imperialists and the forces most closely associated with the notion of "Empire" (specifically Clintonite neoliberals). Thus, resistance movements face odd dilemmas in their campaigns to end US imperialism or to address climate change. The essential conclusion of this chapter, however, is that whatever path to change emerges, at the heart of anxieties about US power is the basic political question of how we are to live. Will it be as conspicuous consumers or as conspicuous ascetics? Or as drivers of SUVs, hybrid cars, or perhaps as cyclists? Again, similar to Whitehall's conclusion, we suggest that the pursuit of a gentler geopolitics necessarily entails the pursuit of a social transformation away from automobile dependence.

Anti-SUV activism

SUVs and their drivers have come under widespread attack in the US heartland as much as elsewhere since the mid 1990s. Much has been written about the movements and organizations these challenges have generated, and it is not our purpose to go on describing them. Instead, we wish to focus on the character of the arguments advanced by these movements and organizations.[3] Suffice it to say that the anti-SUV challenge has been one of the most prominent forms of public dissident activity in the United States since 9/11, with its contestation of US foreign policy, climate change strategies, corporate power, and American hyper-individualist culture. These kinds of critiques can be placed into at least four dominant lines of argumentation:

- SUVs have led to a rise in oil consumption because of their fuel inefficiency, and to a rise in US import dependence. As such, they have contributed to geopolitical instability since US foreign policy is directed towards securing access to oil, usually in areas of the world that are already unstable.
- The rise in oil consumption associated with SUVs also contributes negatively to climate change, and thus the trend toward SUV buying and driving undermines efforts to reduce CO_2 emissions (something that may have further contributed to Bush's rejection of the Kyoto Protocol).
- SUVs are significantly more dangerous than "conventional" cars (being built from a rigid truck body that does not collapse on impact), and are substantially higher and heavier than regular cars, factors that augment the risk of serious injury or death. While the danger is particularly for pedestrians or people in other cars, SUVs are also more dangerous for those who ride them, in part because of their higher gravity center that facilitates rollover.[4] This critique emphasizes the contradictions in the marketing of SUVs whereby they are often presented as safer than regular cars because they are bigger and stronger.

- The SUV danger is not only about an increase in the material risks that people are exposed to, but also about cultural issues since SUVs represent, reproduce, or intensify a form of aggressive individualism that pits people against each other and erodes social and communal bonds through an association of security with brute force. Thus, security at the individual level is to be understood in irreconcilably antagonistic terms (for *me* to be safer in the "urban jungle," *you* have to be put in danger). SUVs are linked to a generalized cultural malaise: the (re)production of a hyper-individualist and anti-social cultural identity and politics.[5] At times, this ethical/cultural argument takes on a religious tone (as with the well-known "What would Jesus drive?" slogan campaign), but it also has many secular variants.

Despite the final point about the type of society SUV culture promotes, two issues are worth noting about these arguments. First, these critiques engage in an individualization of their targets; campaigns are frequently directed at the individual SUV driver, through a strategy designed to persuade him/her not to buy such huge vehicles and, instead, opt for other, apparently less destructive, cars. Buying a SUV in this activist discourse frequently becomes presented as an act of individual moral failure.[6] Second, these challenging arguments draw a radical distinction between SUVs and other cars, and they also favor a form of individualization at the level of the type of vehicle that is being driven. These two individualizing moves (focusing on the consumer, and targeting the vehicle) are highly problematic because they are not engaged with the larger system of what Canadian activist John Bacher simply calls "petrotyranny."[7]

Taking on the second issue first, the rather straightforward problem with it is that, with much of this critical perspective, the case for operating a radical distinction between SUVs and other cars is pretty thin.[8] Regarding safety matters, SUVs are about 8 percent more dangerous than regular cars. But apart from the fact that this represents a relatively small, if at all significant, risk increase, it only works as a meaningful figure after one has already aggregated the statistics for both SUVs and non-SUVs. In other words, it masks the variation in safety levels between different types of SUV and different types of car. As far as the first issue is concerned, the constitution of an atomistic and aggressive individualism, the SUV merely exemplifies one version of the kind of subjectivity associated with most cars since the invention of the automobile roughly a century ago (or, at least, since the time of the Italian futurists, of Le Corbusier, or of military planners from World War I onwards who all celebrated cars precisely because of their potential for individual violence and domination over others).[9] The cultural meanings of the SUV, both to critics and drivers, are thus drawn from assumptions about domination providing individual security. Being bigger and more powerful means that you can either dominate the road or, if necessary, invade other countries to get your hands on the fuel you need. In both cases, big and powerful is the route to security.

But, for our purposes, it is perhaps with regards to fuel efficiency, and its connection to both oil imperialism and climate change, that the recent SUV critiques become most problematic. Clearly, at the level of the individual vehicle, SUVs are noticeably less fuel-efficient than other cars. But if one wants to explain the pattern of overall oil consumption, it turns out that the variation in the fuel consumption of individual vehicles is relatively insignificant. Peter Newman and Jeffrey Kenworthy have shown that different patterns of city design (notably urban density and mixed patterns of land use combining residential, work, and amenities in close proximity), along with provisions for public transportation infrastructures, do explain much of the variation in overall oil consumption.[10] Put bluntly, oil consumption per capita is much higher in the United States than in the Netherlands (for example), hardly because of Americans' propensity to drive Hummers or Suburbans while the Dutch prefer Golfs, but almost entirely because an overwhelming amount of Dutch people choosing to walk, ride bicycles, or take the train to go to work, school, or shopping whereas Americans do not.

But again, were the argument to stop here, the first problem with the individualism argument of the anti-SUV activists would remain. The appropriate critical or normative response would simply be to get people to walk, ride a bike, or take the bus rather than to drive. Instead, we need to call into question the individualist limits of automobility as a working concept. For it is car driving as an apparently necessary, and often normatively valuable, aspect of daily living that ultimately is at the heart of a continually expanding oil consumption and, thus, of both climate change and oil imperialism as contemporary social problems.

Anti-oil imperialism

Alongside these anti-SUV activist arguments are movements that oppose oil imperialism and argue that geopolitical interventions, either by the United States individually or through some sort of international coalition, should be seen primarily as ways of securing access to and control over energy resources. Such arguments were prevalent during the Gulf War in 1990–91 (not only about the United States/international coalition intervention, but also about the original Iraqi invasion of Kuwait), during the US invasions of Afghanistan in 2001 and Iraq in 2003, and, at times, were discussed in other geopolitical contexts too (for example, NATO's intervention in Kosovo in 1999). Some argue that the pattern of US expansion of military bases across the world is significantly directed towards sustaining the possibility of US interventions in oil-rich regions. Our argument here suggests that, while the basic notion that oil geopolitics has played a very significant role in US military strategy (and in the strategy of some other states such as Iraq, or even China more recently) is certainly persuasive, oil geopolitics claims tend to misrepresent the character of oil imperialism, particularly because they disconnect it from the social purposes and usages to which oil is being put.

Central to the oil imperialism perspective are two fundamentally contradictory assumptions. One the one hand, this type of argumentation implies that wars such as the one in Iraq today are designed to grant favors to certain corporate allies of American politicians (above all), notably those corporate interests tied to the oil sector. Thus, proponents of this view suggest that wars are primarily fought on behalf of Exxon, Halliburton, or other similar firms, precisely to enable them to establish control over energy resources that they can then exploit and commodify through the world markets (also to the relative advantage of the US economy in general).[11] A significant dynamic said to be underlying this scheme is geopolitical/economic competition with oil firms from other states, in the Iraq case, with French or Russian firms (since French and Russian companies had lucrative contracts with Saddam's regime), but increasingly with Chinese firms too. Thus, the US military is being used in an attempt to secure continued domination over the oil market, and to structurally and materially secure capital accumulation in the United States.

Shimshon Bichler and Jonathan Nitzan develop this argument through a notion that they refer to as the "weapondollar-petrodollar complex."[12] They reveal that patterns of military instability in the Middle East are correlated to, and driven by, the interests of both US oil firms and US weapons exporters. All of the major conflicts in the region since 1973 have been preceded by periods when US oil firms performed worse than the Fortune 500 average, but followed by periods when they outperformed that same average. Firms (oil companies above all), in Bichler and Nitzan's view, are principally motivated by the prospect of differential accumulation: to drive capital to themselves to the detriment of other firms, both within their own economic sector, but also across the entire economy. Bichler and Nitzan also believe that these companies' maneuvers have been key to the instability and even conflicts in the Middle East, from the Yom Kippur war in 1973 to the recent US invasion of Iraq.

A second strand of argumentation inside the oil imperialism critical analytical framework has tended to focus on oil prices instead. This view intimates that oil wars (and the oil imperialism for which those wars are fought) are effectively attempts at securing continued low prices necessary to maintain a given pattern of wealth and capital accumulation based on cheap oil. The assumption behind this perspective is that oil producers will collude to increase prices, and that intervention is in effect designed (although the rationale is generally not meant to be made public) to restore "stability" and force producers to once again reduce prices. Most of the recent arguments that have been made about a SUV-oil imperialism linkage fit right in here. For example, Michael Klare's line of reasoning connects interventions during the 1990s to a rise in oil consumption and oil import dependence in the United States (and moves from this point to the emergence of SUVs and to the decline in fuel efficiency).[13] From this analytical standpoint, the increase in oil consumption requires a military intervention to stabilize prices, or at least it favors forces and logics that will promote the idea of an intervention.

The main problem with this argument, as Bichler and Nitzan have persuasively pointed out, is that its central premise is manifestly false. Indeed, the wars that have been fought over oil, right up to the ongoing conflict in Iraq, have not resulted in lower oil prices. Nor have they been preceded by periods of rising oil prices. The present period, since the start of the Iraq War, has been characterized in fact by a dramatic surge in crude oil prices (despite the reintroduction of Iraqi oil onto the world market, widely predicted to facilitate a reduction in prices). Contrary to what the "war to secure low costs" argument supporters believe, the pattern of prices shows that conflicts and disturbances are followed by long periods of high oil prices (after 1973–74, after 1979, after 1990–91, and after 2003). Given the fact that high prices also lead to high profitability rates for the oil industry, this pattern fits instead the explanation given by Bichler and Nitzan that, among the chief beneficiaries of these wars, are the oil companies to whom significant profit accrues. In the Iraq case, the assumption that prices would decline as Iraqi oil would be traded again misses the point that the consequence of the war has been an increase in the oligopolistic control of US firms over the world's oil markets and, thus, their ability to continue to manipulate oil prices to their advantage.

The contradiction between these two views, both of which are prevalent in the oil imperialism critical camp, should be understood as an expression of a more general opposition between accumulation and legitimization in capitalist societies. That is, while accumulation creates pressures for military intervention to support the interests of specific firms and boost conceptions of the national interest, such crude adventurism needs to be legitimized. Of course, one dimension of this legitimization of interventions is to present the wars as being about anything but oil (for example, the creation of a "new world order" or the recognition of the importance of state sovereignty and international law in 1991, the humanitarian crises in Kosovo in the late 1990s, the war against Al-Qaeda in Afghanistan since 2001, and arguments about weapons of mass destruction or human rights abuses in Iraq in 2003). But the implicit assumption that the war would reduce oil prices still constitutes a significant element in the way the wars have been "sold" to the public (and not just to the US public, but across the West too). Crudely put, as it were, while wars are in the interest of oil firms that often drive those wars, they are sold as being about the interests of everyday oil consumers.

In our view, the principal problem with these oil imperialism arguments is the fact that they too (somewhat similar to the anti-SUV critiques) abstract the oil over which the wars are fought and over which countries are occupied and restructured from the social purposes and cultural usages to which oil is being put in the countries where oil consumption mostly takes place. For example, while Bichler and Nitzan present powerful reasons for linking the wars to the interests of oil companies, they still do not focus on the patterns of oil consumption that sustain the power of those firms. Only if one could demonstrate the claim that consumption is entirely driven by the strategies of the firms towards differential accumulation or profit could it then make sense to engage in this sort of abstractionism. For scholars like Klare and others who emphasize the connection between SUV driving and oil-imports dependence, there is an important relationship to oil consumption. But this connection is almost always exclusively focused on the anti-SUV critique and thus falls into the other traps outlined above.[14]

As a consequence, many of the leftist, radical, or green movements that oppose SUVs and/or oil imperialism end up being complicit in the reproduction of not just capitalism per se, but, more precisely, of a specific form of capitalism, one that systemically promotes oil imperialism but also creates a full range of other social crises, and notably climate change. In other words, by failing to identify automobility (and its centrality to both twentieth- and twenty-first-century capitalism) as the main structuring force behind oil imperialism, resistance or opposition movements miss their target and, as such, reduce their chances of being able to (re)shape society towards a more peaceful and more ecologically viable future. The geopolitical anxieties and insecurities related to oil imperialism take on a historically significant dimension for many people on the left in Western industrialized countries because of the key role played by the car industry in the development of the labor movement. Even the designation of Fordism is directly derived from automobile production. This is of course not accidental as cars have been, are, and will continue to be the most important industrial commodity in the global economy. But a political strategy that is limited to increasing wages and benefits for workers without any consideration for either the ecological or the cultural effects of this commodity is bound to perpetuate the geopolitical anxieties/insecurities.

Geopolitics and oil imperialism

There is an important third dimension to this argument about oil and imperialism, one that might be referred to as the geopolitical view. The geopolitical view finesses some of the oil price argument described above by adding a much simpler dimension to the discussion: the idea of access to fuel regardless of financial cost. Much of the official state planning on energy issues is dominated by concerns over security of supply, not just matters of oil price. As Klare suggests, this was key to the so-called Cheney plan during the first George W. Bush administration where security of oil supply was seen as the main impetus for the plan despite all the rhetoric about technical innovation, conservation, or renewable energy research.[15] It is this argument about access to supplies and the necessity to keep them flowing that adds a crucial dimension to the economic discussion about wars and the role of the Gulf region because, in terms of military planning, keeping the Straight of Hormuz open and tankers moving (something that was at the heart of the "re-flagging" exercises of the 1980s) were and still are the rationale for much of the military presence in the region.[16] Ignoring the priority of the state in terms of this strategic mission is to miss the simple but important point that imperial ambition is not just a reflection of narrow corporate interests, although many corporations do benefit from and undoubtedly influence the conduct of military activities (as, once again, Bichler and Nitzan have shown).

Thus, to follow David Harvey's rendition of the question, the focus on Iraq and American involvement there is too narrow. Iraq is symptomatic of a much larger imperial ambition, one that Harvey poses as "whoever controls the Middle East controls the global oil spigot and whoever controls the global oil spigot can control the global economy, at least for the near future."[17] The history of growing American military power in the region, starting with the Carter Doctrine and continuing to the present, is part of the logic of American state power. Seen this way, prior involvement in the 1953 coup in Iran that brought the Shah to power, long-term backing of the house of Saud, and support for Israel are all part of a strategy aimed at gaining influence in the region. More recently, the scope of the ambition among American state and defense planners has increased. This can be read as part of an imperial plan to control the region and to ensure that American companies will continue to do business on favorable terms, but also to guarantee that the geostrategic interests of the American state in controlling the fuel to run the global economy will continue. In Harvey's terms:

> if the US successfully engineers the overthrow of Chavez and Saddam, if it can stabilize or reform an armed-to-the-teeth Saudi regime that is currently based on the shifting sands of authoritarian rule, ... if it can move on ... from Iraq to Iran and consolidate a strategic military presence in the central Asian republics and so dominate Caspian Basin oil reserves, then it might, through firm control of the global oil spigot, hope to keep effective control over the global economy for the next fifty years.[18]

While this was written before the difficulties of running Iraq after the invasion of 2003 became completely apparent, the pattern of aspiration to control matters in all the oil producing states is clear. Iranian attempts, in particular, at resisting this American strategy are a focal point in the struggles over who writes the international rules on access and use of nuclear technology. But the overarching issue here is the nationalist assertion of resistance to American power in the region, a matter that might become much more fraught if attempts to set up a regional oil market in Tehran are successful in the next few years, and especially so if oil were to be traded in euros rather than dollars.

Two crucial points follow from taking the geopolitical view seriously. The first is that the argument about security of supply, and about the American attempt to secure its own energy from abroad by military means, simultaneously gives American decision makers the ability to control aspects of the global economy and serves their own fuel security needs. Dressing up a geopolitical advantage in the rhetoric of national necessity both strengthens the case for military action and confuses opponents whose anti-geopolitical arguments are then depicted as anti-American insofar as they are said to render America vulnerable to disruptions of essential supplies. The second is that the cultural dimension comes into play here as particular patriotic and military tropes play out in the mobilization of nationalist sentiments of support for the troops. Patriotism is an especially powerful cultural force, and the nationalism invoked in the invasion and occupation of Iraq is one dressed up in the defensive anger and aggrieved self-righteousness of the post-9/11 war on terror.[19] American military technology uses large quantities of gasoline and other petroleum-based fuels. Neither Humvees (the ultimate SUV), nor Abrams M1 tanks are exactly fuel-efficient vehicles, and some of the military difficulties encountered by the American occupation forces in Iraq are in ambushes of fuel convoys. So the troops in Iraq are both symbols of the American way of doing things and vulnerable precisely because of the automobility that is one of their great combat advantages.

Oil, automobility, and war

To understand the forms of contemporary geopolitical anxiety better, we need to reconceptualize the automobility-oil imperialism connections. Automobility can be understood to be at the heart of "carboniferous capitalism."[20] Automobility is also a system that links a specific industrial commodity to infrastructure production by states (that hugely subsidize highways, roads, bridges, and other "necessary" economic structures). Automobility is thus central to the reproduction of capitalist societies in the twentieth and twenty-first centuries.[21]

Fordism, in its classic form ("you can have any color you want as long as it is black"), has given way to a more post-Fordist series of production arrangements whereby vehicles are customized to fit individual desires, desires that, in turn, are promoted through advertising campaigns that sell standard vehicles as the epitome of individual prowess or status (further producing the consuming subject by way of numerous tropes about freedom, social standing, conquest over nature, or technical acumen in newly networked capitalist systems).[22] Culturally and politically, contemporary capitalism entails the production of the (auto)mobile subject as one of its central elements. The association of cars with freedom, in particular, is a crucial ideological element in capitalist reproduction, something that can tie people discursively and materially to state imperatives too. This ideological connection can enable the means of accumulation to become the means of legitimization. But this is also always potentially contradictory, and always contingent on the ability (of capitalist industrialists and governments) to discursively present cars as freedom.

Politically, automobility is constituted through an oil/car industry bloc that is able to secure numerous interests and provides core factions in capital-legitimizing states. But this production and consumption system also benefits disproportionately from state activities such as road building, the running of public transports, consistent subsidies to car firms and consumers, and so on. Oil imperialism is only one dimension of this subsidy system whereby the state decides to intervene abroad to ensure uninterrupted supplies of fuel. But, from a socio-technical perspective, the state is also built and dependent on a range of specific technologies that make the whole system sustainable. Crucial here is the oil/internal combustion engine relation that has given rise to a specific pattern of development that has locked Western societies, and increasingly the rest of the world too, into oil dependence.

Many critics now think that this automobility-driven model of economic growth and social organization has reached its limits. Productivity gains are exhausted. The technological model is obsolete. And the costs of urban sprawl, air pollution, and military adventures now mean that the net subsidies of driving are enormous. More importantly, the costs of congestion and the social dysfunctionality that results from the amount of time people spend in their cars suggest that the system is in crisis. Some of this realization also implies that political wedges are increasingly being driven between the oil and the automobile industries as the costs of dealing with automobility's side effects (notably, air pollution) are borne by car firms only (that increasingly, and especially in the wake of the California "zero emissions" legislation, want oil companies to bear some of these costs). These contradictions are greatest in the United States where car dependence is most pronounced. But, simultaneously, the ideological attachments to automobility/cheap oil are the highest there as well. On top of all this, debates about "peak oil," and switches in some energy and petroleum companies (especially non-US ones) away from oil suggest that changes may be in the offing.[23] Ecological modernization, smart growth, and other initiatives looking to use technology innovation to replace fuel and crude power seem to indicate that there is now a potential for a different ecological future.[24]

Thus, oil imperialism can be interpreted as the "last gasp" effort on the part of a bloc of forces representing carboniferous capitalism (the Bush administration, the US oil industry, and the SUV-driving identities and interests). The forces representative of carboniferous capitalism are now faced with a significant challenge from an "ecological modernization" bloc (promoting hybrid technologies or hydrogen fuel systems) that today may even include some individual elements in car companies (like Ford) who are starting to green more than their company's image. Oil imperialism is thus an attempt on the part of carboniferous capitalist interests to secure their share of accumulation and profit while they try to maintain the conditions under which there can be continued consumption of cars and oil. Here, we reconnect with Bichler and Nitzan and their point that accumulation is also about shaping the contours of society.

The discursive codings and modes of legitimization of the car culture in the United States operate increasingly through patriotism/nationalism (as suggested above) and through a security discourse that directly associates SUVs with foreign policy and geopolitical strategy. Hummers are once again the most explicit example of this, but, more generally, this process works through a mimetic system whereby security replicates forceful domination and physical prowess.

This argument inevitably provides ramifications to the discussion about Empire and its relation to imperialism (something that has been developed in several chapters in this volume). As Michael Hardt and Antonio Negri have suggested, with its global modes of consumption, Empire is premised upon strategies of accumulation that do not rely on direct state control.[25] But imperial (or "empirean" perhaps, as Luke puts it in his chapter in this volume) strategies of intervention, in particular in the Gulf region, still rely heavily on state control, and in particular on American military power controlling oil exports from this region. In Harvey's terms again, controlling the "global spigot" is seen as key by imperialists or proponents of Empire who are concerned with maintaining political power by controlling essential fuels for the global economy. This in turn is related to a geopolitical understanding of the world that still assumes the inevitability of state rivalries.[26] Thus, if China is potentially a threat, so the argument suggests, American imperial control over its key energy supplies from the Gulf region will provide a powerful political lever in future crises. It should be noted that, in contrast, the imperial or "empirean" argument intimated by Hardt and Negri is more likely to perceive such state rivalries as a thing of the past (since more traditional imperial strategies are said to be counterproductive to the ultimate success of globalization/Empire).

Thus, what becomes clearer when we reconnect different geopolitical strategies to arguments about modes of consumption is that today's "weapondollar/petrodollar" version of carboniferous capitalism does require imperialism (and vice versa) whereas neoliberal Empire is really not so structurally linked to oil and automobility. This is obvious in the discussion about appropriate strategies for dealing with the Gulf region after the Iraqi insurgencies started to be recognized as a problem for occupying US forces. Traditional realist scholars advocated a political compromise with Iran and encouraged a comprehensive attempt to deal with the instabilities of the region, most obviously through the *Iraq Study Group Report* of late 2006.[27] This report's subsequent rejection by the Bush administration, and the explicit decision to continue the Bush doctrine of directly using military force in Iraq and of pushing for regime change in Iran (by force if necessary) epitomize a neo-Reaganite imperialist policy of direct control over the "oil spigot," but under the guise now of what is called a "long struggle to end tyranny."[28]

Security, consumption, and the future of American power

In his chapter in this volume, Luke provides an overview of arguments about the "hollowness" of US global power. This perspective conjures up an alternative history of security, one that is focused on the social origins, or biopolitical character, of security and insecurity. Alternative understandings of security frequently suggest that the pursuit of security is intimately tied to the recognition of the limits of desires and satisfaction. At the most general level, this alternative view can be seen in various religious movements around the world for whom self-denial is not only a sign of virtue but also provides a sense of freedom from the tyranny of desires or wants. In our current context, the recognition of the limits of material desires can be seen in the debates about the need for a large-scale energy infrastructure as a way to "secure development." These sorts of beliefs are not new, and they were already present in one form or another in the debates between Nehru and Gandhi in relation to Indian independence back in the 1940s, for example, or in Erich Fromm's distinction between "to be" and "to have" (whereby "to have" was said to generate wants, hence insecurities too).[29] In the 1970s, Amory Lovins outlined two different energy paths, or what he called "soft" versus "hard" trajectories. The hard path was premised on centralized technologies for electricity generation, fuel distribution, and high levels of material consumption. This path produces what he called later "brittle power," that is to say, a capacity to exert significant force but that remains dependent on fragile supply networks. The alternative, the soft energy trajectory, offers security through moderate consumption and through decentralized systems of largely renewable energy sources (and thus obviates the need for the military to secure supplies).[30]

Lovins' notion of brittle power overlaps with Luke's description of the hollowness of US contemporary (hype) power. But it also makes clear that this hollowness/brittleness is intimately connected to the character of daily life and to the course of political-economic development prevalent in the United States and globalized from that particular geopolitical center. Luke's discussion of Joseph Nye's "soft power" of the United States suggests that its attractiveness is due to consumption, and especially cars. Our suggestion is that the pursuit of US "soft power," if it is to be understood as an alternative to constant military intervention, is dependent on the pursuit of a "soft energy" path, or the turning away of US daily life and economic strategy from oil and/or automobile dependence. Historically, there has been a contradiction at the heart of the "soft power" strategies deployed by the United States. To the extent that automobility provided a central aspect of America's global seductiveness (by enabling its presentation to the rest of the world during the Cold War as a site of freedom, for example), at the same time, it created increasing pressures for hard imperialist strategies to secure access to and control over oil resources that made automobility possible. Luke quotes Ferguson who states that "Americans themselves lack the imperial cast of mind. They would rather consume than conquer."[31] Ferguson is mistaken, both because consumption is itself imperial (appropriating resources over vast spaces), and because it favors imperialist geopolitical strategies (to control such resources). In the long run, therefore, "soft power" still requires access to "soft energy."

The debates over alternative energy sources prevalent in the 1970s were thoroughly quashed in the Reagan era by the automobile/oil bloc. In part, this was because at that point oil was still used in electricity supply, and solar and wind energy forms were seen as direct competitors to oil. Solar energy was also tainted culturally by its association with the 1960s alternative lifestyles' assaults on the idea of the "American way of life." Imperialists in contemporary US politics explicitly hark back to Reaganism as a foreign policy ideology that emphasizes military power. In the late 1990s, the situation changed significantly (perhaps revealing "the cloudiness of the rearview mirror," as Luke suggests). Oil dependence and its consequences had returned with a vengeance, transforming what for Lovins was only a prophecy or at least a potential worry about future conflicts in the Middle East into a reality.

Today, the socio-political environment that oil interests face is dramatically different from that of the 1970s. Particularly interesting in today's context is the possibility of disentangling oil consumption and, thus, of decoupling the petroleum industry from car manufacturing. Technically, we can now envisage energy efficiency gains that could make a big difference for fuel consumption. It is possible to imagine hybrid cars that could go over 200 miles per gallon.[32] This vision entails design changes though (such as moving from steel to carbon fibers that dramatically reduce weight and improve aerodynamics). With fuel cells, it is also possible to envision a zero carbon emission car, assuming that the electricity supply system to make hydrogen vehicles does not rely on carbon fuels. From this perspective, the automobility-oil imperialism nexus is partly broken. However, until concrete manufacturing and asphalt road technology are replaced with other modes of infrastructure production that are far less energy intensive, the other half of this automobile-carboniferous capitalism complex will remain a potent contributor to climate transformation.

Such technical possibilities are unlikely to be realized without political struggle, precisely because the oil companies, and some of the more stubborn car manufacturers, will resist these developments. At least as important are the discursive-cultural shifts that are needed to legitimize political changes. Of particular relevance in this debate are the shifts in understanding the security dilemma, both at the personal level of daily driving and at the geopolitical level of inter-states relations. At both levels, the dominant trope or image that oil imperialism relies on is to pursue one's security by making others more insecure (by buying a Hummer or by invading Iraq). Bigger, more powerful, heavier supposedly mean safer in both the SUV-driving and Iraq-occupying instances. Lovins' radical vision entailed (and still does) a total rejection of that image/trope, and it replaces it with one for which security is about intelligent thinking, reducing weight or bulk, being stronger but through the use of more flexible materials, and so on. This different view of security and/as technological virtue gets closer to Peter Taylor's vision about conspicuous asceticism that we quoted at the opening of this chapter (although such a future might not even include the private automobile).

The elaboration of these connections between war, imperialism, and automobility is increasingly understood across a wide political spectrum. Even more moderate interpretations of these linkages have been advanced. For example, some of the arguments made by Thomas Friedman in his *New York Times* columns in 2004–05 sought to articulate the fairly common claim (common among mainstream environmental groups like Worldwatch in particular) that the best way to pursue security and democracy in the Middle East is to promote fuel efficiency and the development of fuel cells or hybrid vehicles in the United States.[33] Former US Vice-President Al Gore's many interventions, and even parts of Bush's State of the Union speeches, also affirmed the necessity of rearticulating security matters, particularly given today's anxieties about oil, imperialism, and war. Thus, there is a broad (multi-partisan) view that something needs to change. Security understood as power or domination has downsides that can no longer be overlooked. This view, in varying degrees, is shared by feminist anti-war activists, Bush administration's supporters, and even religious groups that discuss the "What would Jesus drive?" slogan. Indeed, a wide array of politicians, activists, and civil groups sense that automobility, oil, and war are intricately tied together and that this tight relationship is part and parcel of many contemporary social problems. Crucially though, what these various groups do not agree on is how to proceed, what to change, and who should change key aspects of social life. Herein lie the main difficulty and the source of so many contemporary geopolitical anxieties (with regards to oil and war, in particular), as well as the crucial divides over the possibility or not of political change.

One of the consequences of our analysis is to suggest that the sites or means of resistance to oil imperialism can be broadened. As Hosea Jaffe succinctly puts it, "anti-car demonstrations are anti-imperialist."[34] But alongside arguments devised by anti-war activists and various solidarity movements, our study draws attention to the underlying cultural politics and political economy that produce war. And there are at least three possible sites of or goals for an expanded mode of resistance that would target the culture, politics, and economics that make war possible and that would be built loosely around some technological innovations and updated versions of Lovins' "soft energy" path.[35] First, planning for green cities and for the utilization of smart growth that minimizes energy inputs and resource throughputs in urban systems may be able to rebuild an infrastructure for people rather than for cars. This strategy can be placed in the context of a cultural politics of caring as opposed to a social domain where rugged masculinity and assumptions about hostile spaces requiring technological securitizing would prevail. It suggests a softer politics as well, one that is focused on living within ecologies rather than imposing a technological order upon them.

This first site of resistance, in turn, creates a second possibility. It is the possibility to think about activist coalitions among businesses focused on ecological modernization, peace movements, greens, feminists, health groups, numerous leftist organizations, city managers for smart growth, fuel cell supporters, public and alternative transportation lobbies, and many religious groups. All these groups have interests in reducing the pernicious ecological consequences of automobility and in challenging the deleterious effects of road infrastructure construction. For many of these groups, the moral case against war is also a powerful political source of mobilization, one that can challenge the military machismo tied to the technologies deployed in contemporary wars. Likewise, Vancouver-based anti-consumerist magazine *Adbusters*' resistance to the construction of subjectivities centered on private consumption can provide a similar kind of challenge to automobility.

There is a third possibility or site of resistance. This one is based on the idea of an alliance with avid free marketers (such as the Clintonite neoliberal Friedman). The assumption here is that the intervention of military forces to manage the oil business goes against basic neoliberal philosophical principles (whereby the market place should be left alone to set prices and guarantee supplies). Letting supply and demand rule freely rather than using the military to fix matters would lead to ask the question: why securitize oil? A neoliberal would argue that, if it is indeed such a dangerous commodity, then let prices send their own signals rather than turn to the state and its agents to subsidize supply through military budgets, infrastructure write-offs, or convoy protection as was done throughout the 1980s in the Gulf, for example. Going down the path of state interventionism rather than letting the market go free may prompt some neoliberals to ask why military measures are relied upon whereas international regimes or human rights standards are not used to regulate oil exports, or governments and secessionist movements that live off the petroleum-generated wealth. After all, if that strategy has worked for conflict diamonds, why would not it work for oil?[36]

The point here is not to suggest that Friedman and those pursuing a radical resistance politics are part of the same social or political bloc. Rather, if we return to the debate between Empire and imperialism touched on above, Friedman appears to be a representative of Empire rather than imperialism. Thus, the conceptualization of the future of American foreign policy and power as a struggle between a neoconservative imperialism versus a neoliberal Empire can also be overlaid with a distinction between a hard energy path (carboniferous capitalism) and a soft one (ecological modernization). Friedman's approach can certainly be regarded as a cooptation of various radical forces (anti-war and environmentalist, in particular). But it can also be regarded as an opportunity for such forces, since it constitutes a major site in mainstream US politics and culture where the rearticulation of the pursuit of (energy) security takes place. This too suggests the possibility of a mode of international citizenship based on multilateral cooperation in a network of powers rather than a unilateral way of attempting to dominate the international environment.

Conclusion

Climate change possibly provides the central "threat" through which a rearticulation of the oil/energy security debate becomes more widely accepted. As the planetary biosphere undergoes dramatic and unpredictable changes in the coming decades, there is a compelling case for refocusing our attention on the need to produce technologies and infrastructures that make decent living possible. The Clintonite neoliberals have long recognized this (and their manner of responding—as in the marketization of the climate approach they displayed in Kyoto—is clearly consistent with reading contemporary geopolitics as Empire). Even the Bush imperialists are forced to recognize this necessity. Katrina and the destruction of New Orleans made the realization of the threat unavoidable. And the repeated scientific announcements about rapidly changing environments have garnered wide attention. All of this debate, of course, has also spread through society because of Al Gore's *An Inconvenient Truth*, a media/cinematic intervention that has been able to raise popular questions about what really the most important threat to America is.

Reading the future of US power this way suggests that, at its core, is the question of whether a normal life now still includes driving Hummers over long commutes from 4,000 square-foot houses in exurbs to work in buildings that cannot withstand climatic extremes. Put differently, in terms of identity and security, the trajectory of US power will be shaped profoundly by a struggle between competing sets of phenomena of which Americans are supposed to be afraid. Are they more afraid of being enGulfed by another Katrina, of the consequences of continued military operations in the Middle East and Central Asia, or of the imperative to change long-standing daily practices, with their associated economic benefits and social commitments? Which identity with its associated locus of fear will prevail? Both to facilitate the adaptation to whatever new circumstances arise in particular places, and to slow the increase of carbon dioxide in the atmosphere, confronting the most pervasive commodity and simultaneously the most prominent symbol of capitalism is a most necessary task in the new century.

Addressing contemporary geopolitical anxieties thus involves raising the question of how to live. To avoid imperialism requires reshaping daily life amongst over-consuming populations, a profoundly biopolitical project. This is both a call to ethical action and a matter of producing subjects for whom asceticism is not so much conspicuous, but mundane, and for whom the production of their security is about reducing wants and desires for endless commodities, rather than having to exert power over others in order to secure those practicalities of life.

Notes

1 Protestors' slogan at anti-war demonstrations, February 2003.
2 Peter Taylor, *The Way the Modern World Works: World Hegemony to World Impasse* (Chichester: John Wiley, 1996), p. 219.
3 See, for example, David Campbell, "The Biopolitics of Security: Oil Empire and the Sports Utility Vehicle," *American Quarterly*, Vol. 57, No. 3 (2005), pp. 943–72; or Steve Vanderheiden, "Assessing the Case against the SUV," *Environmental Politics*, Vol. 15, No. 1 (2006), pp. 23–40.
4 See Keith Bradsher, *High and Mighty: The Dangerous Rise of the SUV* (New York: Public Affairs, 2002), chapters 7 through 9.
5 One paper drawing on the SUV in this way offers the broad metaphor of the "SUV model of citizenship," thus denoting a highly abstracted, but at the same time expansive, notion of individual rights. See Don Mitchell, "The SUV model of Citizenship: Floating Bubbles, Buffer Zones, and the Rise of the Purely Atomic Individual," *Political Geography*, Vol. 24, No. 1 (2005), pp. 77–100.
6 See Campbell, "The Biopolitics of Security."
7 John Bacher, *Petrotyranny* (Toronto: Dundurn Press & Science for Peace, 2000).
8 See also Vanderheiden, "Assessing the Case against the SUV."
9 See Paul Virilio, *Speed and Politics* (New York: Semiotext(e), 1986); and Matthew Paterson, *Automobile Politics: Ecology and Cultural Political Economy* (Cambridge: Cambridge University Press, 2007), chapter 5.
10 Peter Newman and Jeffrey Kenworthy, *Sustainability and Cities: Overcoming Automobile Dependence* (Washington, DC: Island Press, 1999).
11 This argument is at times complemented with another one that states that, just prior to the 2003 invasion, Saddam Hussein was planning to switch the sale of the oil that Iraq was allowed to export under the oil-for-food program over to euros, something that would have generated significant seigneurage benefits for the European economies at the expense of the United States.
12 Shimshon Bichler and Jonathan Nitzan, "Dominant Capital and New Wars," *Journal of World Systems Research*, Vol. 10, No. 2 (2004), pp. 255–327.
13 Michael Klare, *Blood and Oil: The Dangers and Consequences of America's Growing Dependence on Imported Petroleum* (New York: Metropolitan, 2004).
14 One of the few to make the oil-to-cars imperialism link explicit is Hosea Jaffe. See his *Automobile, Pétrole, Impérialisme* [The Automobile, Oil, and Imperialism] (Lyon: Parangon, 2004).
15 See Michael Klare, "Blood for Oil: The Bush-Cheney Energy Strategy," in eds. Leo Panitch and Colin Leys, *Socialist Register, 2004: The New Imperial Challenge* (New York: Monthly Review Press, 2003), pp. 166–85. For a similar argument, see Linda McQuaig, *It's the Crude, Dude: War, Big Oil, and the Fight for the Planet* (Toronto: Doubleday, 2004).
16 See Andrew Bacevich, *The New American Militarism: How Americans Are Seduced by War* (New York: Oxford University Press, 2005).

17 David Harvey, *The New Imperialism* (Oxford: Oxford University Press, 2003), p. 19.
18 Ibid., pp. 24–5.
19 Anatol Lieven, *America, Right or Wrong: An Anatomy of American Nationalism* (New York: Oxford University Press, 2004).
20 See Lewis Mumford, *Technics and Civilization* (New York: Harcourt Brace, 1934).
21 For a fuller elaboration of automobility as a complex, see Paterson, *Automobile Politics*.
22 This is an argument that we develop in more detail in Matthew Paterson and Simon Dalby, "Empire's Ecological Tyreprints," *Environmental Politics*, Vol. 15, No. 1 (2006), pp. 1–22. More generally, on the emergence of these developments in car production and markets, see David Gartman, *Auto Opium: A Social History of American Automobile Design* (London: Routledge, 1994); or F. C. Deyo, *The Social Reconstruction of the World's Automobile Industry* (London: Macmillan, 1996).
23 James Howard Kunstler, *The Long Emergency: Surviving the End of Oil, Climate Change, and Other Converging Catastrophes of the Twenty-First Century* (New York: Grove, 2005).
24 On ecological modernization and the car industry, see once again Paterson, *Automobile Politics*, chapter 7. On this topic, see also Arthur Mol, *Globalization and Environmental Reform: The Ecological Modernization of the Global Economy* (Cambridge, MA: MIT Press, 1998).
25 Michael Hardt and Antonio Negri, *Empire* (Cambridge, MA: Harvard University Press, 2000).
26 Reiterated in Jakub Grygiel, *Great Powers and Geopolitical Change* (Baltimore: Johns Hopkins University Press, 2006).
27 See *The Iraq Study Group Report: The Way Forward—A New Approach* (New York: Vintage, 2006).
28 See Simon Dalby, "Regions, Strategies, and Empire in the Global War on Terror," *Geopolitics*, Vol. 12, No. 4 (2007), pp. 586–606.
29 See Erich Fromm, *To Have or To Be?* (New York: Harper and Row, 1976).
30 See Amory Lovins, "Energy Strategy: The Road Not Taken," *Foreign Affairs*, Vol. 55 (1976), pp. 65–96; see also Amory Lovins, *Soft Energy Paths: Toward a Durable Peace* (Cambridge: Ballinger, 1977) and Amory Lovins and L. Hunter Lovins, *Brittle Power: Energy Strategy for National Security* (Andover, MA: Brick House, 1982).
31 Niall Ferguson, *Colossus: The Price of America's Empire* (New York: Penguin, 2004), p. 29.
32 See Paul Hawkens, Amory Lovins, and L. Hunter Lovins, *Natural Capitalism: The Next Industrial Revolution* (London: Earthscan, 2000), chapter 2.
33 Lovins has made this argument repeatedly. See, for example, Amory Lovins and L. Hunter Lovins, "Make Fuel Efficiency Our Gulf Strategy," *New York Times*, December 13, 1990, p. A15. Friedman's case is summarized in Thomas L. Friedman, "The Greening of Geopolitics," *New York Times Magazine*, April 15, 2007, pp. 40–51, 67, and 71–2.
34 See Jaffe, *Automobile, Pétrole, Impérialisme*, p. 58.
35 See the numerous materials on Lovins' Rocky Mountain Institute website, available at www.rmi.org.
36 See Philippe Le Billon, *Fuelling War: Natural Resources and Armed Conflict* (Oxford: Routledge/International Institute for Strategic Studies, 2005).

11 Zombie democracy

Patricia Molloy

Introduction: vote or die

In the run-up to the 2004 US federal election, rapper P. Diddy (a.k.a. Sean Combs) drew the ire of conservatives, including African American groups, when his non-profit organization, Citizen Change, launched a three-day "Vote or Die" campaign to appeal to legions of non-registered African American youth in the swing states. For its detractors, the issue was not the push to get Black youth out to vote, but that the slogan itself was a decided effort to "scare and manipulate blacks" into voting for John Kerry. According to the Reverend Jesse Lee Peterson, "[m]ost of these so-called 'disenfranchised' people don't care about the issues. All they know is what they've been told: Bush is evil. Bush hates blacks. He's (Bush) going to bring back the draft and you (blacks) have to vote or you'll die!"[1]

Presumably, if the Black youth vote came out in support of a Republican administration, it would have been because they were more scared of Sean Combs than of the prospect of four more years of George W. Bush. It would seem therefore that, for the Reverend Peterson, the African American population at best holds up to a long-held stereotype and process of infantilization: easily manipulated, willing to believe anything they are told because they know no better in their child-like inability to govern themselves. At worst, they are zombies: lacking the capacity to reason and devoid of consciousness.

While the Reverend may have simultaneously overestimated the power of Hollywood entertainers to influence the American electorate and undermined the political agency of African American youth, a simple Google search of key words "zombies" and "democracy" reveals that Diddy's "Vote or Die" slogan resonates with what many in the blogosphere see as the moribund state of contemporary democracy, especially the violence with which it is spread. Ask anyone in Fallujah.

On the other hand, claims of a nation of passive zombies, whether America or Iraq (in the blogosphere it can be either), may be selling the undead a bit short. Ask Jeff Waugh, whose blog posting of "zombies are people, too" questions cinematic representations such as *Shaun of the Dead* and *From Dusk till Dawn* that feature "no known people or established characters." After all, "if your local milkman can become a zombie, why not your local representative?" Waugh calls for a "realistic cultural representation of the undead in popular culture and entertainment," and looks forward "to a film that depicts the fullness of zombie life, eschewing the traditional discrimination towards zombies."[2] Waugh's desire has already been realized in part in two recent films that I discuss in this chapter: Joe Dante's *Homecoming*, which was part of the Masters of Horror Series aired on Showtime in December 2005 (also screened at the Torino film festival); and the Canadian comedy, *Fido*, directed by Andrew Currie, an audience favorite at the 2006 Toronto International Film Festival that played also at the 2007 Sundance festival before its commercial release. Though neither film features politicians or rock stars as zombies, they both, in their own way, eschew the traditional discrimination towards zombies and call for their full (or at least partial) participation in the mechanisms that (supposedly) define modern democracies including, in the former film, the right to vote and, in the latter, basic human rights and freedom from tyranny. In other words, we are seeing a shift within the cinematic apparatus (more than in conventional wisdom) from passive to active zombies (and, importantly, as we shall see, with a little help from the non-undead too).

My reading of this shift stems from and modifies John Marmysz's theorization of active vs. passive nihilism in George Romero's trilogy of zombie films (*Night of the Living Dead* (1968), *Dawn of the Dead* (1978); and *Day of the Dead* (1985). Taking on mainstream film critics who dismissed Romero's 1968 film as nihilistic, Marmysz argues that that was not only the point but also the strength of the film and its subsequent instalments. A distinction must be made, however, between the normative sense of nihilism as a general sense of negative sentiment and a philosophical understanding of nihilism as a doctrine of nothingness, an "extreme form of skepticism which holds that any genuine knowledge of the world, whether it be moral, scientific, metaphysical, political or theological is impossible."[3] Within the philosophical understanding, especially Camus' and Nietzsche's, a further distinction is drawn between passive and active nihilism wherein the passive nihilist (indicative of a decline in spiritual power) is unable to act or even react to the uncertainties of the world and withdraws rather than engages with its absurdity. An active nihilist, on the other hand, chooses action and creation over passivity and withdrawal, sees freedom where the passive nihilist recognizes only meaninglessness, and possesses a creative energy and power to not only face but also confront the world with a sense of purpose. In this regard, the active nihilist is somewhat of a hero.[4]

In Marmysz's analysis, we see a struggle between the impulses of passive and active nihilism over the course of Romero's trilogy, with passive nihilism ultimately triumphing over the active kind, often with "apocalyptic consequences." To this end, Romero's films serve as a warning against passivity.[5] This is not to say that the human characters within the films do not have their moments of active resistance to the descent into moral chaos wrought by a zombie takeover of the world. Indeed, Marmysz spends a great deal of time tracing a progression from passive to active nihilism exhibited by the central characters within the films, most notably an evolutionary shift from weakness to strength on the part of Romero's female characters. The zombies, however, remain in the camp of passivity. They are "a kind of revolutionary force of predators without a revolutionary program," and possessing a drive for predation with no actual biological purpose. As Marmysz explains:

> They appear and attack without explanation or reason, violating taken for granted principles of sufficient cause and rationality. Because of this, they are especially

threatening to the surviving human beings. Enemies such as Nazis or Communists are comprehensible in terms of their historical backgrounds, economic interests, religious, political or philosophical beliefs. But these zombies are a new breed of enemy in that they do not operate according to the same underlying motivations human beings share in common. They are a nihilistic enemy which, as lifeless, spiritless automatons, exemplify the epitome of passive nihilism.[6]

Joe Dante's and Andrew Currie's zombies, by contrast, are threatening *because* they have sufficient cause and rationality along with a revolutionary program. In Dante's *Homecoming* the just cause is an overthrow of an unjust US administration that catapulted men into a war not of their choosing, whereas *Fido*'s zombies are an indentured class of servants and menial laborers who revolt against a corporatized security society operating on an ethos of containment and consumption. Neither film, I should qualify, is the first to suggest that the zombie is not a wholly unsympathetic figure and may indeed exhibit or express signs of rational intelligence and consciously felt emotion that may warrant the viewer's ethical consideration of their treatment. This much has been implicit within Romero's later films themselves, particularly his most recent offering *Land of the Dead* in 2005, in which the zombie character Big Daddy is more fleshed out, so to speak, and more sympathetic than many of the non-undead characters.[7] What interests me with *Homecoming* and *Fido* is how they extend, develop and make more pronounced the notion of zombie rights and freedoms at a precise moment when those rights and freedoms are denied a goodly proportion of the (so-called) "living," those whose lives might better be described as precarious given the current war on terror.[8] This would and must include soldiers returning from Iraq and Afghanistan or refusing to go at all, civilians within those same countries, terror suspects both at home and abroad, Palestinians, those imprisoned at Guantanamo Bay, and those who survived Abu Ghraib. It is to the above films, and the new democratic possibilities they initiate in supplanting the Bush administration's politics of death with a politics of love beyond the sovereign and violent space of nations, that I now turn.

Vote first, die later: Dante's *Homecoming*

When *Homecoming* screened at the Torino Film Festival, it was greeted with a five-minute standing ovation. When it aired in the United States on Showtime, horror fan sites and IMDB message boards registered a markedly different response. Indeed, Dante got "Dixie Chicked." Horror films are often political allegories.[9] But, with *Homecoming*, Dante ups the ante with a biting satire of the invasion of Iraq and its resultant slaughter of US troops. And while critics responded overwhelmingly in favor of Dante's reworking of the B-movie zombie genre into an anti-war black comedy, for many horror fans, *Homecoming* is "biased" and Dante is anti-American, if not downright communist.[10]

In the opening scene, we meet our human protagonists, a man and a woman, driving frantically in the night when their car slams into "one of them": a walking one-armed corpse on a crutch, dressed in tattered army fatigues, which causes the vehicle to veer off the road. As they get out of the car (something you should never do in a horror film), a truck stops and more of "them" advance on the harried couple. The woman, Jane, takes a shotgun out of the trunk and tells her companion, David, that there is also a semiautomatic (obviously, they are prepared). He utters that it is no use, but she takes aim and screams that she's not giving in to "a bunch of crippled [she shoots], stinkin' [she shoots again], maggot infested, brain-dead zombie dissidents." Jane continues to fire away—at their legs, as they cannot be killed, only slowed down. "Come on and get it, come on you pussies, bring it on!" As she continues to shoot we see that she's wearing a large red and white political campaign button bearing the words "four more years." David, utterly resigned to his fate, says that it is all his fault, "the whole damned thing." He takes a gun and fires, not at the zombies, but at her.

The story then flashes back to four weeks earlier, with David providing a voice-over narration to how it all began the night he met "her." David Murch is a "political consultant" (spin doctor) to the current Republican administration who first meets the leggy blonde Jane Cleaver, author of "How the Radical Left Took Over Cable TV," on a political affairs television talk show, *Marty Clark Live*. (That Jane is an Ann Coulter look-and-spew-alike, and Marty Clark an obvious nod to Larry King, should please our blogger Jeff Waugh who wants more "famous people" in zombie flicks.) The year is 2008, it is three weeks before the federal election, and the Republicans' campaign slogan is "Stay the Course 08." The president goes unnamed (though his voice bears a remarkable resemblance to Bush). The country is at war. But Iraq is not mentioned. The topic for the evening's telecast is political dissent with footage of anti-war protesters who Jane describes as "men with breasts and women with armpit hair." The pivotal moment for both the scene and the horror that is about to unfold occurs when a "former Gold Star mom" named Janet Hofstader appears via video. Mrs Hofstader's son Gordon had been killed in the "current engagement," and Marty asks her to tell her story about why she heckled the president. Quite simply, she wanted to know why her son died:

> Mrs Hofstader: They said there was a threat but the weapons of mass destruction weren't there. The nuclear threat wasn't there.
>
> David: Mrs Hofstader, I honor you. I had a brother who gave his life in Vietnam. If I had one wish [he pauses and almost weeps] … I would wish for your son to come back, because he would tell us all how important a struggle it is to protect this country.
>
> Mrs Hofstader: Frankly, sir I don't think you know my son at all … [and she is cut off].[11]

After the show, David and Jane go for martinis. She suggests that the President should incorporate David's "wish" into his campaign speech. While next engaged in some friendly S&M with Jane, David gets a call from Kurt Rand (Karl Rove), the president's campaign advisor, and the plan is put in motion. We then see David and Jane munching on post-coital popcorn while watching the president's speech in which he repeats "because if they could come back I think I know what they would say."

"He was wrong about that," goes David's subsequent voice-over, "dead wrong," as the camera shifts to rows of flag-draped coffins at the Dover Air Force Base where, by Pentagon decree (in the "real" Iraq War), no cameras are allowed and the president refuses to appear. But it is not a dissident camera-wielding civilian causing the noise that startles the (live) soldier guarding the coffins (from the media). It is, rather, the corpses of the fallen rising from their coffins and, in a particularly compelling image, casting off the Stars and Stripes that shroud them. Indeed, not only are these soldiers, as we shall see, refusing to stay dead, they are also refusing the denial, the veiling and containment of their very deaths.[12]

There are worse things than having war veterans return from the dead, of course. For one thing, they cannot be (re)killed—that had already been tried. Unlike "real" zombies, these cannot be killed with a shot to the head. This, for Rand, could solve the recruitment problem. "If we can keep dead GIs in the field, it's the answer to our prayers." When David asks why he thought they came back, Rand's response is: "Could be for the disability benefits." But no, our most reliable narrator informs us that "we found out what they wanted, and coincidentally, how to kill them." With the election only weeks away, advance polling stations are now set up across the country. We see a dead soldier lumber into one and point to the sign indicating that he is here to vote. Clearly dead (the polling booth assistant recognizes him), he nonetheless has proper ID (his dog tags) and is permitted to vote. Upon exiting the booth, he keels over dead, really dead this time. In somewhat of a reversal of P. Diddy's "Vote or Die" campaign, it is now vote *and* die.

News that "resurrected soldiers" are appearing all over the country is initially framed by media pundits as a sign from God—and with patriotic fervor. Discussing the issue on *Marty Clark Live,* Jane remarks: "Not even death will stop their march for freedom." But their death also poses a legal conundrum: Do they have the right to vote? Jane asks: "Are these soldiers legally dead? Is undead the same as dead?" This of course is as much a *philosophical* as a legal question. Indeed, just what constitutes a zombie has been a preoccupation of philosophical thought since the 1970s.[13] For philosophers of mind especially, the zombie is the figure *par excellence* for examining fundamental questions of consciousness and reason, and the mind/body distinction.[14] Philosophers of mind, however, do not concern themselves with zombies in the undead sense more commonly associated with Hollywood films and pop culture phenomena. Rather, "philosophy zombies" are you and I in all physical respects, but have no conscious or subjective experience (*qualia*).

But it is the Hollywood zombie that interests me here, insofar as its representation raises the ethical considerations that govern life and death—were this distinction so easy. For, in Derridean terms, the zombie epitomizes the undecidability of any logical distinction between life and death. "Having both states, it has neither." Indeed, "[z]ombies are cinematic inscriptions of the failure of the 'life/death' opposition. They show where classificatory order breaks down: they mark the limits of order."[15] Perhaps, then, if we follow Terry Pratchett's *Discworld* series of books, zombies might be better categorized as "differently alive,"[16] a liminal state of being that equally describes the precarious existence of those governed by the war on terror. But although the zombie may not be fully contained in death, the manner in which Dante's soldiers died accords them a status not ordinarily granted even to the living. Referring to Robert Bunton, the first of the undead to cast a ballot, Jane offers that "this man is a hero who died fighting for his country. Who's going to inform him he doesn't have the right to vote?"

While it was clear that they did want, and expect, to vote, it soon becomes apparent that the soldiers' campaign extends beyond the mere assertion of their democratic rights and freedoms. They begin to speak out against the logic of the war that got them killed in the first place, and they use the media to do it. Says one dead soldier: "I've seen men killed, women and children get killed for a lie. I was killed for a lie. We will vote for anyone who ends this evil war."

This marks a turning point in the film, and the election campaign, as well as the evolutionary progression of the zombie. For these zombies disrupt the passive/active binary that, in Marmysz's analysis, defines the human/zombie distinction: not only are they active nihilists, but they are activ*ist* ones. For one film critic, Dante transforms the classical zombie movie paradigm that began with Romero's "return of the repressed, into the return of the *suppressed*: political dissent and public disapproval of the Bush government's handling of, well, everything."[17] To this end, Dante's zombie soldiers resemble the undead in medieval folklore more than Hollywood cinema. Indeed, it was commonly held in the Middle Ages that the souls of the dead could return to earth and haunt the living. In France in particular, *les revenants* were thought to rise from the dead to avenge a crime committed against them, usually a murder.[18] However inadvertently summoned by David Murch, Dante's soldiers are *conjured* to (re)appear to avenge their own murder by haunting more than hunting those responsible. There is, in other words, a sense of the spectral surrounding the zombie soldier that signals a call for a justice that is not yet there. In *Specters of Marx*, Derrida writes that, when we speak of the ghost/specter, it is in the very name of justice. As he puts it:

> It is necessary to speak *of the* ghost, indeed *to the* ghost and *with* it, from the moment that no ethics, no politics, whether revolutionary or not, seems possible and thinkable and *just* that does not recognize in its principle the respect for those others who are no longer or for those others who are not yet there, presently living, whether they are already dead or not yet born.[19]

For Derrida, the logic of haunting, or "hauntology," lies in the specter's state of repetition—its ability to appear, disappear and reappear. The specter, he argues, is always a *revenant*. "One cannot control its comings and goings because it *begins by coming back*."[20] It becomes important, therefore, to conceive of Dante's soldiers less in traditional zombie terms as corpses that *reanimate* (for no express purpose) and more as *revenants* (with a civic purpose). I make this qualification because, in *Homecoming*, not all the soldiers come back, but only those who are seeking to avenge their wrongful deaths in "this evil war" by voting the president out of office. The rest, as David Murch rightly observes, are at peace and have no need to return.

Back to the film: the president, meanwhile, has slipped in the polls, as the zombies gain increasing public support following their prior mentioned media appearance. And how could they *not* elicit sympathy when, as Rand puts it, "they're looking all shot up." With this realization, the advisors' task is now to counter-spin their previous position. Back on *Marty Clark Live*, Marty announces that the government has declared the zombies (now held in an internment camp) as a public health threat until further tests are done. When he questions Jane about whether she thinks their rights are being violated, she now asserts that they are "turncoats and traitors" who possess no higher brain function. The same (Jerry Falwellesque) Christian-right Reverend who originally revered the soldiers as a "sign of God" now proclaims that "the bowels of hell have opened" as these "demons, satanic-spawn devils walk among us," and "we must beg God's forgiveness." And for David, well aware that the zombies are in the right, the solution is to ignore them—in other words, "treat them like real vets"—and just let them vote.

But the challenge now is to find a spokeszombie willing to support the Republican campaign. "It's a tough sell," as Jane sneers, "look at all these soldiers who support our president by staying dead." So they have to coerce one into reading a scripted statement on Marty Clark's show, preferably one already in the media spotlight, and who better than Gordon Hofstader, the dead son of the woman who had previously heckled the president. The plan backfires, however, as Gordon attacks Rand and smashes his head to a pulp (though he does not eat his brains). Later, on our favorite political affairs show, Marty plays footage of the "formerly deceased soldiers" in internment camps and accuses the Republicans of deliberately keeping them away from the voting booths. There is also a burgeoning liberal backlash on the internet with one blogger questioning the validity of David's claim that his brother died in Vietnam.[21]

There is little choice now but to concede defeat and let the dead soldiers vote. "So we gave POTUS a pitch. They voted, I made sure they did. And their voices were heard, they were finally at peace." Well, not quite. In true American electoral fashion, the Ohio and Florida counts are rigged. An astounded David and an elated Jane leave the television studio, but then Jane gets word that mayhem has broken out at Arlington Cemetery. They are *all* coming back now: vets from Korea, Vietnam, even World War II. Why? David explains in a voiceover: "We said we'd count their votes, but we didn't. We lied. What were they going to do? Well, they did what soldiers always do: they called for reinforcements."

The film now shifts back to the opening scene with our added wisdom of why David shoots Jane in the head. He also attempts to shoot himself, but is out of bullets. One of the zombies lumbers up to him: "You're the one who called us back. You said we'd have a voice. But you betrayed us." David, thinking he has reached his own logical conclusion, says to "do what you gotta do." But the soldier instead asks him for his help: "Join us. We're looking for a few good men." At this point, David's dead brother Phillip steps up and, after a brief reunion, congratulates his brother for having done his best. "I'd be proud to fight beside you," he says, and he snaps his brother's neck (this, it should be noted, is the only time in the film that a zombie kills a human in order to turn him into one of them). The film's final scene is an image of the White House that fades into a montage of zombie soldiers against the backdrop of the American flag. While "America the Beautiful" plays in the background we hear David's final voiceover:

> The government continues, in exile. But Washington, DC, is ours. We're here to stay, all across this country, an army of one million who laid down our lives to defend this land. But know this truth. Our lives are precious and if you ever again send our brothers and sisters to give their lives for a needless pointless lie, then we guarantee that you will see the true face of war—the face of hell.

Dante's *Homecoming* lasts 59 minutes and was shot in 10 days. And while the director clearly plays with the look and feel of the B-movie zombie genre, it is precisely this: a play with a sub-genre of horror cinema. One would think, given the horror that war is, that there would be more celluloid offerings that merge "the horror film" with "the anti-war film." What makes *Homecoming* unique is that, unlike most zombie films, it is not an allegory of or a metaphor for "the human condition" or the larger "social order." Dante's zombie soldiers do not stand in for something else or represent anything other than what they are: dead soldiers. They could, however, become the spokespeople for the growing numbers of *living* US soldiers who, in refusing to deploy or re-deploy to Bush's "needless pointless lie" of the Iraq War, are haunting the soul and conscience of the Nation.[22]

All you need is love

While, as noted above, the overtly anti-war horror film is a rarity, there has been a surge of late in horror films with a highly visible US military presence, from direct-to-DVD low budget zombie flicks like *Dead and Deader*, to larger blockbuster fare including *The Hills Have Eyes 2* or the artier *28 Weeks Later*. At the same time, the current climate of zombie mania has also seen a move to a decidedly lighter sub-genre: the zombie comedy, a.k.a., the "zomedy" or "zom com." And while the British comedy-satire *Shaun of the Dead* is attributed with ushering in the zombie comedy genre, a steady flow of "zom coms" are rapidly emerging from Canada for some reason, including Andrew Currie's *Fido*.[23]

Within film and popular culture, the zombie is placed on the lowest rung of the evolutionary ladder of the undead, well below your ordinary vampire. While both seek sustenance from the bodies of the living, bloodsuckers, it seems, are more palatable to the general public than flesh-eating ghouls. For Jane Caputi, the key distinction between zombies and vampires is twofold. First, the vampire is an intensely individuated being whereas zombies form a mass of interchangeable, ordinary ghouls. Moreover, "the disturbance at the heart of the vampire myth is one of emotion, sexuality, desire. The ghouls, however, show no emotion whatsoever, only the hunger for flesh."[24] While, as previously noted, there are individual exceptions within Romero's films, Dante's soldiers break almost every rule in the zombie book. They speak, have individual identities, use reason, and they emote. To be sure, they even love their mothers.[25]

For philosophers of mind, reason is a precondition for emotion. One has to be a rational, conscious, and self-aware being to feel love, as love requires subjective felt experience. It might not require a great deal of intelligence to love someone (if any at all, as is often the case), but it demands a higher level of consciousness beyond being merely cognizant of your surroundings (the sort of limited consciousness that typifies the zombie). This again raises questions for ethical philosophy in terms of a hierarchy that is being placed on life or, rather, on undeath. Is it ethical for humans to kill vampires and zombies to begin with? Under what circumstances and under whose authority can the undead be legitimately killed such that it is not homicide? These questions are matters of the exercise of sovereign decision with which I have dealt extensively elsewhere (regarding vampires and werewolves) and will not reiterate here.[26] What interests me in the context of this chapter is the (equally sovereign) distinction between vampires and zombies, and the latter's ethical treatment while "differently alive," insofar as this treatment typifies the differently alive who may not be zombies but still are subjected to the geopolitical conditions of Bush's "war *of* terror" (as Borat better puts it).

Similar to Caputi, Richard Greene and K. Silem Mohammad note that vampires are conscious and rational whereas zombies "are barely classifiable at all; the individual zombie is often only one unit in a larger collective organism which operates outside most conventional definitions of 'intelligence,' let alone ethical awareness." Thus, "plunging a stake into the vampire's heart generally pricks the conscience more than that of shooting a zombie in the brain."[27] Unless, of course, the zombie in question is a rational and conscious being who loves his mother—or, in the case of *Fido*, a lonely little boy.

A boy and his ... zombie?

During the Questions and Answers session following the *Fido* screening at the Toronto film festival, one audience member quipped: "It's *Shaun of the Dead* meets *Far From Heaven*." The latter film, directed by Todd Haynes (2002), recreates in glorious technicolor the settings of Douglas Sirk's 1950s melodramas, and Currie's film is likewise set in a 1950s-esque universe wherein a façade of emotional restraint barely conceals an underlying simmering paranoia. While *Fido* is clearly a send-up of American Cold War fear of a communist takeover and presumed inevitability of nuclear war, an indictment of 1950s discourse and practices of "threat containment" (but with zombies replacing the commies), it is also, as Currie himself has acknowledged, a comment on the Bush administration's Homeland Security agenda in the wake of 9/11.[28] But for many reviewers, *Fido* is a film about love, and the desire to be loved. Ultimately, the tale that *Fido* tells is at once a satirical take on America's love of security (both historic and contemporary),[29] and a heartfelt and universal story about the security of love, with the 1950s nuclear family central to both.

A common device in the typical zombie film is an exposition of the possible causes of the zombie takeover *du jour* in the form of a background radio or television news broadcast (which just as often fuels public confusion if not panic). *Fido*'s opening scene has great fun with this convention in adding a corporate twist, or twisted corporation if you will. With a nod to the opening of *Day of the Dead*, *Fido* begins with what first appears to be a black-and-white newsreel providing the background of the great Zombie Wars (the Earth passed through a cloud of radioactive "space particles" that caused the dead to rise) and how they were won: "But then, in our darkest hour: a saviour—ZomCon!"

The film is, we discover, a corporate promotional vehicle being shown to an elementary school class visited by the Willard division of ZomCon's new head of security, Mr Bottoms. We learn from the film that it was ZomCon's founder who first discovered how to kill a zombie by destroying its brain, and thus the war was won. It was ZomCon that subsequently designed the "perimeter fence" to enclose towns across "this great land" and keep the remaining zombies out. However, "even within the fence danger lurks." Traces of radiation remained, and it soon became apparent that anyone who died would become a zombie. The ZomCon solution? The "domestication collar" that keeps the new zombie in check with a red light indicating that its desire for human flesh has been contained, thus making the zombie "as gentle as a household pet." Should the light go off, you merely call ZomCon and they'll come and "take care of your zombie problem, large or small" (accompanied by an image of a child zombie on a leash struggling against the collar). The film continues:

> Thanks to ZomCon, we can all become productive members of society, even after we die. Or, for those who can afford it: a ZomCon funeral which comes with a head coffin guaranteeing you a burial you won't come back from. Your tax dollars allow ZomCon new ways to protect our homeland from the zombie threat, giving us more time to relax and be with our families. So thank you ZomCon for winning the Zombie Wars and building a company for tomorrow that gives us a safer future today. ZomCon: A better life through containment!

This idea of safety through containment can only succeed if there is a measure of insecurity and fear to begin with, in an environment where, for example, old people are treated with suspicion (they might die at any moment), the legal age to own a gun is 12, and "outdoor education" constitutes target practice with children shooting at zombie cut-outs. But sitting in the back row of the classroom is little Timmy Robinson who upsets both his teacher and Mr Bottoms with the philosophical query of whether zombies are dead or alive. The life/death opposition of the zombie seems unproblematically clear to everyone in this picture-perfect town, except Timmy. They have death insurance as opposed to life insurance, the latest issue of *Death* rather than *Life* Magazine is Mr Robinson's bedtime reading. A good "life" nonetheless it is in Willard and in the greater "homeland." Prisons are obsolete since now anyone who messes with the law (or ZomCon's social order) is thrown into the "wild zone," outside the security fences where zombies roam unfettered, and uncollared. Moreover, the zombie threat is not only contained, but also works to benefit middle-class citizens, and the economy, through the provision of cheap, and docile, menial laborers. Zombies pick up the trash, mow the lawns, deliver the milk and newspapers (though with not terribly great aim); they work as crossing guards and as domesticated servants. As film critic Manohla Dargis put it, here "zombies don't feast on the living, they serve them."[30] And everybody who is anybody seems to own at least one. Except for the Robinsons.

But two things happen that disrupt this tightly contained, but perhaps not so secure alter-universe. Mr Bottoms, the aforementioned new head of security at ZomCon, moves across the street from the Robinsons, and Mrs Robinson finally acquires a zombie—much to the chagrin of her husband, Bill, who has had a life-long fear of the creatures. But Bill also fears his wife, Helen, and reluctantly agrees to keep the zombie. Timmy is at first ambivalent about the presence of a "stupid zombie" in the house and the status it will bestow upon his mother. He is also an achingly lonely little boy who is bullied at school and ignored, when not treated with disdain and disappointment, by his father who prefers to play golf than with him. His mother, although kindly, seems oblivious to her son's pain. "Honey, please don't play baseball by yourself. It makes you look lonely."

Lacking the companionship and love from the living, Timmy comes to bond with the undead. When the zombie protects Timmy from some bullies in the park, he realizes he has a friend and names him Fido. However, in a mishap involving the crotchety old Mrs Henderson, Fido's collar becomes temporarily disabled and he, well, eats her. When Timmy sneaks out late at night to bury her, in an effort to protect his beloved pet, he discovers that she has reanimated. He decapitates and buries her unaware that she has already been munching on living flesh and that a zombie outbreak is underway. Meanwhile, Helen Robinson, equally ignored and neglected by her husband, has also grown fond of Fido. She dresses him up in one of her husband's suits and tenderly cuts his hair before taking him on a family Sunday drive (to a funeral, which is an obsession for Bill). She serves him cold drinks, throws him furtive glances, flirts with him (and he with her), and one evening, when in the mood for romance, she dances openly and seductively with Fido in order to get her husband's attention.

Helen also comes to trust Fido with her son's life. One day, when Timmy takes Fido for a walk in the country, they encounter the bullies who tie both of them to a tree, taunting Timmy that Mr Bottoms is going to send his entire family to the wild zone. One of the bullies inadvertently causes Fido's collar to malfunction, once again, and Fido kills him. But even with his collar disabled, Fido has no designs on Timmy's flesh. Unable to free Timmy (rigor mortis hampers one's ability to untie a knot), Fido shuts the bullies in a shed and goes to fetch Timmy's mother (after promising not to eat her). When Helen arrives, she shoots the now zombified bully who has escaped from the shed and is about to kill Timmy. With Fido's help, Helen shuts them both back in the shed and sets it ablaze.[31]

But the demise of the bullies comes not before they have been questioned by Mr Bottoms, who then implicates both Fido and Timmy in Mrs Henderson's disappearance. Bottoms warns Bill that Helen may be getting a little too attached to her zombie, which is "never a good idea." When Timmy's bloody baseball is eventually found in the park near Mrs Henderson's body, Timmy wakes to see Fido being hauled off in a ZomCon truck. Mr Bottoms places the blame for Mrs Henderson's death squarely upon Timmy, warning him that he can indeed send his family to the wild zone. "Yes sir," Bottoms says to Bill, "the problem is all about containment." What exactly he means by this becomes evident the next day when the newspaper headline reads that Mrs Henderson had been killed by the bullies. ZomCon's strategy of containment, in other words, also extends to the control of the media.

In what follows, Helen tries to console her forlorn son by telling him that she loved Fido too, but not, she clarifies, in the way their next door neighbor, Mr Theopolis (a former Zomcon employee), loves his zombie Tammy.[32] Indeed, the exact nature of Mr Theopolis's relationship with his young, nubile, and scantily clad zombie is cause for much neighborhood gossip. Helen redirects the conversation away from Fido and her feelings for him "as a friend" to the topic of Timmy's father and how he does love them but is afraid to show it. Bill Robinson is the epitome of 1950s nuclear sensibility and its post-September 11 reincarnation. Consumed by a paranoid fear of death and dying (at the hands of an evil enemy Other), Bill's obsessive drive for safety and security renders him unable to simply live, let alone love.[33] When a visibly pregnant Helen finally breaks the news to him (he is so oblivious that he did not notice), his response is at first denial, followed by panic: "I'm afraid that with my salary I just can't afford another funeral." Bill later insists to Helen that he is not a bad father (his own father tried to eat him when he was a child) and that he is in fact a much better father to Timmy than his own had been to him. In his own stilted and awkward way, Bill tries to connect with Timmy over the loss of Fido, but what is revealed instead is the depth of his own "psychic numbing":

> Bill: You 'feel things' when you're a kid. You have to get over that.
>
> Timmy: What?
>
> Bill: Feelings. Being alive is what counts. [He hands him a gun]. I know you're not supposed to have a handgun until you're 12.

Bill does, in the end, get another opportunity to demonstrate he is good father, which, again, is manifest in his wielding a gun. As it turns out, Fido is alive and has been put to work in the ZomCon factory. Mr Theopolis, having been fired from ZomCon (over his relationship with Tammy as rumor has it), is more than willing to help, and he, Tammy, and Timmy set out to rescue Fido.

Mr Theopolis gains permission to enter ZomCon by pretending he is taking Tammy in for a "tune-up." Once inside, he provides a distraction by releasing the collar of one of the zombies also in line for servicing. During the commotion, Timmy slips into the factory, but Tammy is shot—in the head, which clearly anguishes both Mr Theopolis and the audience. Timmy spots Fido, but Mr Bottoms grabs Timmy first, drags him outside to the perimeter fence to show him the wild zone, and throws him into it. By this point, Helen and Bill have arrived. Helen demands that Bill give her the rifle, but, insisting that he is a good father (because he has bought Timmy a head coffin), he runs into the building. Bill finds Fido and together they approach Mr Bottoms outside while the zombies in the wild zone are advancing on Timmy. In the ensuing mayhem, Bill lunges at Bottoms. They fight over the rifle, but Mr Bottoms shoots Bill with a pistol at the same moment that Timmy frees himself from the wild zone and grabs the rifle. Timmy disables Fido's collar with the instruction to "get him, boy." And so Fido kills Mr Bottoms, the zombies burst through the wild zone's gate, and shots ring out. The family escapes with Mr Theopolis and the wounded Tammy as the battle rages on.

The final scene takes place after some time, Bill's funeral (complete with head coffin) has passed, and the surviving Robinsons are having a backyard party. In a reversal of the living/undead and male/female relationships we have seen thus far, Mr Theopolis is now serving a recovered Tammy, decked out in a floral print dress and hat, and tells her that she is the only Tammy for him.[34] Helen tends to the new baby while Timmy plays catch with Fido who is also sporting fancy new duds. When the Bottoms family arrives, daughter Cindy is leading her father, dressed not in his usual suit but in a ZomCon worker's uniform, by a leash. Bottoms and Fido glare and grunt at each other. Fido takes a long drag off a cigarette, reaches into the baby carriage and strokes the baby's face, grunting happily, while Helen watches and smiles.

Conclusion: walking with zombies

It may seem, on the surface, that the zombie theme is all that *Homecoming* and *Fido* have in common. As discussed earlier, for his detractors, Dante's politics are too overt, and the tone of his film too biased and disrespectful of soldiers. Dante's is indeed an angry film, yet not without humor. For some critics, on the other hand, *Fido* is too light with its sweetness and charm obscuring its politics. For Dargis, Currie's film does not push the master/slave allegory far enough. "They set up a divide between the light-skinned humans and dark-skinned zombies that they never fully engage, shying away from anything heavy or dangerously downbeat .... It won't make you bleed, just howl."[35]

What binds these respective "feel bad" and "feel good" films, however, is the notion of resistance to sovereign power that is a necessary precondition for a more just and democratic future, indeed, for a democracy that is just—for the living and the dead, by way of the fluid space of undeath in-between. There are, as both films indicate, states of being that are worse than undeath. I am not suggesting here that we should strive to be more like zombies or that we are always already zombies, but rather, that we can learn a little from the undead about how to "live" and to love, and that this in itself, as I shall elaborate, does constitute a politics.

First, to briefly recap, I have argued in this chapter that both *Homecoming* and *Fido* reconfigure the Hollywood zombie as a being that possesses, rather than lacks, faculties of reason, intelligence and emotion. Marmysz's theorization of active versus passive nihilism in George Romero's original trilogy of zombie films has been useful in this regard, and I extended the analysis to representations of the undead (rather than the living) in more recent North American cinema. Unlike traditional Hollywood zombies, the zombies in *Homecoming* and *Fido* have a purpose beyond primal instinct. To be sure, they have, as I put it, a revolutionary program. In *Homecoming*, this program is to vote out of office the administration that sent soldiers to die in a war justified by lies and public deception. Drawing on Derrida, I described Dante's zombie soldiers as spectral: they have come back to haunt the nation's guilty conscience in order to keep the state in check.

In *Fido*, however, while there is still a sense of spectral haunting that shames the living into purposive action, there is no state to speak of (or against), as all functions typically ascribed to a sovereign state have been usurped by a corporation, ZomCon (short for Zombie Containment), whose scientific research and innovative technologies led to victory in the Zombie Wars. Lest the reader forget, as stated in ZomCon's propaganda film, tax dollars go directly into the company's coffers in exchange for protection and security from the zombie threat. ZomCon owns the patent on the "domestication collars" and manages the (zombie) labor force, controls the media and the prison system (the wild zones), and extends influence over the education system and the military itself. There are no army or soldiers here, only "ZomCon cadets."[36] Even funerals fall under the dictates of ZomCon. ZomCon, in short, rules. That is to say, it is sovereign in a biopolitical sense: presiding over every aspect of life, death, and undeath. ZomCon decides who gets to be undead in the first place, which is a simple matter of socioeconomic class as we learn that only 10 percent of the citizens can afford a proper funeral (complete with a ZomCon manufactured head coffin). The rest have little choice but to become zombies, as they are literally sentenced to undeath and servitude to the more affluent. In containing the zombie threat by exploiting their labor, ZomCon controls economic production as well as the production of social life and social relations. Thus, ZomCon has not only built an empire, it is Empire itself. As theorized by Michael Hardt and Antonio Negri, "in Empire capital and sovereignty tend to overlap completely."[37]

The good news is that the sovereign relation between ruler and the ruled is on increasingly shaky ground despite its seemingly firm geopolitical grip in the current war on terror. For Hardt and Negri, resistance is not futile but quite possible when what they term "the multitude" challenges the accepted truths of sovereignty as *the one* that rules.[38] More inclusive and expansive than prior (and totalizing) concepts of "the people," "proletariat" or "the working class," the multitude is a global network of internal differences, comprised of "different cultures, races, genders, and sexual orientations; different forms of labor; different ways of living; different views of the world; and different desires."[39] Despite, or perhaps because of its internal and multiple differences, only the multitude, when acting for what it has in common, can restore and rescue democracy from its current incantation of "security" and ensure a democratic life for all, wherein democracy is "the rule of everyone by everyone."[40] This vision of democracy that only the multitude can realize is not only a challenge, but also a threat to the entire tradition of sovereign rule. "Rather than a political body with one that commands and others that obey, the multitude is *living flesh* that rules itself."[41]

Written in the context of a post-September 11 global war on terror, Hardt and Negri's theorization of the potential emancipatory politics of the multitude bears much in common with the democratic possibilities envisioned by zombies in the films I have been discussing. There is, obviously, one important distinction that must be made. The multitude that I, and these films, speak of includes not just living, but dead and undead flesh. As evidenced in *Homecoming*, we must act in common with the dead in order to resist a political order that does not just send young men and women to die for a lie, but also send them *to kill* in the name of that lie. What we see in both *Homecoming* and *Fido* are cooperative and collaborative alliances between the living and the dead that resist both sovereign rule (be it state or corporate) and the exploitation of Others. In *Homecoming*, the zombie soldiers have the support of the living public as well as the media in their bid for the right to vote and in their opposition to the war, and they also find an eventual ally in David Murch, the spin-doctor with a conscience. And in *Fido*, the living population of Willard comes to realize that it has more in common with the undead than it originally thought, and recognizes that real "security" comes from a respect for the differently alive as they take on the corporate entity that contains them.

This vision, then, of a just and democratic life for all replaces a politics of security (amongst and within nation-states) with a politics of love (across the differences of social subjects). It was Timmy and Helen Robinson's love for Fido and his for them, and Mr Theopolis's realization that Tammy is a being with genuine feelings and not an object of sexual exploitation, that lead to the happy alliance between the living and the undead that we see at the end of *Fido*. It was David's love for his dead brother, the wish he made on national TV, that conjured the dead soldiers to rise in *Homecoming*. And it was David's brother's love that turned David into a zombie to fight in their revolution.

For Hardt and Negri, in order to realize love as a political concept, love must be wrestled away from its modern confinement in the couple or the nuclear family and returned instead to its premodern (Christian and Judaic) conception "as a political act which constructs the multitude."[42] Whilst the acts of love we see in both films are, to a certain extent, within the nuclear family and couples, they also reach across varying states of consciousness and life/death. But whereas David Murch had to die, or rather, to become undead in order to collaborate with the zombie soldiers, the human protagonists in *Fido* remain very much alive, more "alive" than they have ever been in fact, in standing beside the undead. In the end, ZomCon has not been totally defeated, as Fido and Tammy remain in their domestication collars. This, in fact, is important. As I remarked earlier, the object is not for the living to become more like zombies or that "the zombies are us." At the same time, we should not wish the zombies to return to their living state and become more like "us." In remaining zombies, Fido and Tammy retain their distinctiveness *as* zombies and show that the multitude is possible. *Fido*'s happy ending, therefore, does not obscure but rather solidifies its politics. For, as a politics that only the multitude makes possible, "[l]ove means precisely that our expansive encounters and continuous collaborations bring us joy."[43]

Finally, it appears through watching these two films that there is a disconnect between the conventional wisdom of the larger popular cultural understanding of zombies as constituting the "mindless masses" (be those "masses" the voting public/s or mall-going consumers) and what we might term new zombie cinema, such that the metaphor of "zombie" for all that is bad or wrong with the world might no longer be useful.[44] For we see in these films a reconstituted figure of the zombie: one with emotions, reason, as well as a civic purpose to resist the exploitation and oppression of Others. We also see in these films the hypocrisy of waging war(s) in the guise of spreading "democracy," as well as challenges to the denial, containment, and concealment of death itself. A zombie democracy would ultimately work in a larger spectral sense of haunting and shaming those of us in guilty nations (the United States, Canada, the United Kingdom, etc.) into a collective responsibility against a (geo)politics of death and towards a politics of love. Perhaps, rather than dressing up as and walking *like* "zombies" through various cities on Buy Nothing Day or in Toronto's annual Zombie Walk, or even in anti-war demonstrations, we ought to walk *with* zombies and, to give the last word to Waugh, "share the fullness of zombie life."

Notes

1 See "Black Group Slams 'P. Diddy' Voter Drive; Charging 'Vote or Die' Campaign with Scaring Blacks," available at www.sixshot.com.
2 See www.bethesignal.org/blog/2006/11/02/zombies-are-people-too/
3 John A. Marmysz, "From *Night* to *Day*: Nihilism and the Walking Dead," *Film and Philosophy*, Vol. 3 (1996), p. 138.
4 Ibid., p. 139.
5 Ibid., p. 143. Jane Caputi defines the extreme passivity exhibited by Barbara, the female lead in *Night of the Living Dead*, and the ghouls themselves (the word zombie is never uttered in the film) as a "psychic numbing" characteristic of nuclear-age films, regardless of whether the films make an explicit reference to nuclear war or technology or not. See Jane Caputi, "Psychic Numbing, Radical Futurelessness, and Sexual Violence in the Nuclear Film," in ed. Nancy Anisfeld, *The Nightmare Considered: Critical Essays on Nuclear War Literature* (Bowling Green: Bowling Green University Press, 1991).
6 Marmysz, "From *Night* to *Day*," p. 140.
7 Marmysz's article was published well before Romero's last film. Nonetheless, we can trace in the original trilogy a progression of zombie consciousness, memory, intelligence and emotion. The experiments conducted on captured zombies in the third film, *Day of the Dead*, raise ethical concerns amongst some of the medical personnel, and the lead zombie

character Bub develops a clear emotional attachment for his "trainer," Dr ("Frankenstein") Logan. Bub, in fact, comes off as more human than the nasty military leader, Captain Rhodes, to the extent that we cheer him on at the end when he kills Rhodes.
8 Judith Butler, *Precarious Life: The Powers of Mourning and Violence* (New York: Routledge, 2004).
9 For an excellent analysis of the social and political themes in Romero's films, see Michael Ryan and Douglas Kellner, *Camera Politica: The Politics and Ideology of Contemporary Hollywood Film* (Bloomington: Indiana University Press, 1988), pp. 179–82.
10 See the customer reviews for the DVD release on Amazon.com that can be filtered by "loved it" or "hated it." However, the strongest negative criticisms that followed the episode's initial airing on Showtime appeared on the imdb.com message boards.
11 Dante explains in several interviews that the film was in production when Cindy Sheehan began her anti-war campaign. Any resemblance to her is thus coincidental and only a stroke of luck.
12 When interviewed about the overt anti-Bush and anti-Iraq War message of the film, Dante commented that, while for legal reasons he could not directly name "Bush" or "Iraq," the imagery in the movie speaks for itself. "It's just, these are the images. I mean, when you see those coffins, which is a sight that's generally been withheld from us, there's a gravity to it." See Mark Peranson, "Dante's Inferno: The Necessary Satire of *Homecoming*," *Cinema Scope*, No. 25, available at www.cinema-scope.com/cs25/int_peranson_dante.htm.
13 The first to attribute the term "zombie" to the unconscious or soulless state of physical existence was Robert Kirk in "Zombies vs. Materialists," *Aristotelian Society Supplement*, Vol. 48 (1974), pp. 135–52.
14 See the special issue on zombies in the *Journal of Consciousness Studies*, Vol. 2, No. 4 (1995). See also Edward Ingrim, "The Mark of Zombie," *Philosophy Now* (Dec. 2000–Jan. 2001), no page given. For an overview of the question of zombies in philosophy, see the *Stanford Encyclopedia of Philosophy* (available at www.plato.stanford.edu/entries/zombies). On the further distinction between "philosophy zombies," "Hollywood zombies," and "Haitian voodoo zombies," see David Chalmer's website at www.consc.net/zombies.html.
15 Jeff Collins and Bill Mayblin, *Introducing Derrida* (Cambridge: Totem Books, 2006), pp. 19–23.
16 In *Discworld*, claimed by Wikipedia to be one of the few fictions in which zombies retain all their memories and cognitive functions, the character of Reginald Shoe forms an undead support group with the slogan "Undead, yes! Unperson, no!" See www.wikipedia.org.wiki/zombie.
17 Peranson, "Dante's Inferno," no page given.
18 See wikipedia.org.wiki/zombie.
19 This includes the ghosts of those already or not yet dead from wars and other forms of violence, extermination, capitalist imperialism, and totalitarianism. See Jacques Derrida, *Specters of Marx* (New York: Routledge, 1994), p. xix.
20 Ibid., p. 11.
21 We later learn that David's brother was actually killed by David himself in an accidental shooting when he was a child. David later repressed the memory.
22 The US Army did not meet its recruiting quotas for May and June 2007, months in which numbers are usually up due to students graduating from high school. Moreover, the numbers of desertions have been steadily increasing with 3,196 soldiers deserting in 2006 compared to 2,543 in 2005, and 2,357 in 2004. The number of deserters seeking refugee status in Canada also increased. See Ian Urbina, "As Loved Ones Fight On, War Doubts Rise," *New York Times*, July 15, 2007, available at www.nytimes.com, no page given. On those seeking refugee status in Canada, see www.resisters.ca.
23 The others are Carl Bessai's *Severed*, C. J. Hutchinson's *Denizens of the Dead*, and Eliza Kephart's *Graveyard Alive: A Zombie Nurse in Love*. See Stephen Cole, "Bring out the Undead," *The Globe and Mail*, March 15, 2007, p. A2.
24 Caputi, "Psychic Numbing," p. 61.

25 In the scene in which Gordon Hofstader's mother is being pressured to coax her son into signing a statement supporting the war, she tells him over the phone that she loves him. "I love you Mom," he replies.
26 See Patricia Molloy, "Demon Diasporas: Confronting the Other and the Other Worldly in *Buffy the Vampire Slayer* and *Angel*," in ed. Jutta Weldes, *To Seek Out New Worlds: Science Fiction and World Politics* (New York: Palgrave, 2003), pp. 99–121; and "Perpetual Flight: The Terror of Biology and Biology of Terror in the *Ginger Snaps* Trilogy," in *Jump Cut: A Review of Contemporary Media*, Vol. 49 (Spring 2007), available at www.ejumpcut.org.
27 Richard Greene and K. Silem Mohammad, "(Un)dead (Un)certainties," in eds. Greene and Mohammad, *The Undead and Philosophy: Chicken Soup for the Soulless* (Chicago: Open Court Publishing, 2006), p. xvi.
28 Curiously, none of the American film reviewers seem to have noticed the Eisenhower/Bush era connection. See Geoff Pevere, "'Fido': Adorably Gory," *Toronto Star*, March 16, 2007 (available at www.thestar.com), and Cole, "Bring out the Undead." Cole's article is based on an interview with Currie who discussed the ten-year evolution of the film. Cole writes, "After 9/11, homeland security became an important theme in the film, and [Henry] Czerny's obsessed zombie hunter developed the strained affability of President Bush." See Cole, "Bring out the Undead," p. A2.
29 For an analysis of how the Department of Homeland Security policy is a reprise of the Cold War era's Federal Civil Defense Administration, see Keven Ruby, "Don't Panic! Civil Defense and the Management of (In)Security in the Nuclear Age," mimeo, paper presented at the International Studies Association annual meeting, San Diego, CA, March 2006.
30 Manohla Dargis, "Hard to Find Good Help? Not in This Little Town," *New York Times*, June 15, 2007, available at www.nytimes.com, no page given.
31 The question of whether it is ethical for a human to kill a zombie is answered by Helen herself when she says to Timmy: "They're zombies and they were going to kill you, so I had to kill them. But I want you to know that in no way should this be considered normal or right." She then proceeds to torch the shed.
32 As they are possessions, zombies are not ordinarily given names. This is brought up in another dinner table discussion in the Robinson household.
33 Currie readily acknowledged his debt to Sirk's 1950s melodramas at both the Q&A session in Toronto and in various interviews, stating that the forbidden love between Helen and Fido is modeled upon the wealthy Jane Wyman's infatuation with her younger gardener, played by Rock Hudson, in Sirk's *All That Heaven Allows*. Zombie movies, for Currie, "are a good fit with Sirk because both kind of get at the same thing ... which is fear of living is a kind of death. Though he's dead, Fido is really more alive than either Timmy's dad or Mr. Bottoms." Quoted in Cole, "Bring out the Undead," p. A2.
34 When Mr Theopolis tries to gain admission to the ZomCon "containment center," ostensibly for Tammy's tune-up, he remarks to the guard that zombies are replaceable, something which clearly hurts Tammy's feelings (that zombies are not supposed to have) and that Mr Theopolis finds funny.
35 Dargis, "Hard to Find Good Help?," no page given.
36 The boys who bully Timmy are ZomCon cadets.
37 Michael Hardt and Antonio Negri, *Multitude: War and Democracy in the Age of Empire* (New York: Penguin, 2004), p. 334.
38 Ibid., p. 100.
39 Ibid., p. xiv.
40 Ibid., p. 100.
41 Ibid.
42 Ibid., p. 351.
43 Ibid.
44 Thanks to Henry Taylor for raising this point.

Index

24 (TV program) 1, 11, 75–9, 102

Abu Ghraib 61, 76, 84, 86n40, 92, 199; photos of 68, 71, 73, 75, 78–80, 83
Adorno, Theodor 78
aesthetics 96, 162–5; of control 93
affect 13–14, 161–4, 166–9, 171, 173–4, 176
Afghanistan 14, 26, 28, 30, 55, 57, 75–6, 79, 81, 127–8, 135, 184, 186, 199
Agamben, Giorgio 8, 9, 93–4, 157, 161, 167, 169, 171, 173
Al-Qaeda 26, 44, 55, 130, 139, 186
Algeria 10, 56–65, 67–9, 78, 82
American Interest 3, 7, 102
American South 46–7
Anti-Drug Abuse Act 115
Antonelli, Paola 93–7, 99
anxiety 2, 7, 11–14, 89–90, 98, 118, 163–6, 173–4, 188, 207
Arendt, Hannah 8, 10, 11, 13, 57, 63–7, 143, 153–4, 158
Armitage, Richard 7, 102
Asian Pacific Economic Cooperation (APEC) 166, 169, 171, 174
assemblage 5, 136; global 170
Aussaresses, Paul 59–61
automobility 14, 181, 184, 186, 188–93
autonomia (autonomy) 12, 108–10, 112, 121
avian flu 13, 28–9, 161–9, 171–6, 181
Baghdad 26, 29–30, 55
Barber, Benjamin 139
bare life 8, 93–4, 157, 171
Bauman, Zygmunt 2, 5, 89, 96
Benjamin, Walter 167, 171–3
Bichler, Shimshon 185–7, 189
Bilmes, Linda 6
bio-sovereignty 168–9
biopolitics 3, 8, 11–14, 24–7, 30, 38–9, 42, 88, 100, 113–15, 120, 126–9, 133–40, 144–6, 168, 190, 195, 209

Bix, Herbert P. 81
Blair, Tony 162
body politic 35–6, 40, 42–4, 47, 66
border 88, 92, 108, 111–13, 118–20, 125n74, 125n75, 149, 154; and militarization 114–17; US–Mexico 12, 115
Botero, Fernando 79–80
Bremmer, Jan 41
Brown, Gordon 102
Buchanan, Pat 76, 82
Building on Progress (report) 102
Burroughs, William 90–1, 93
Bush, George W. 2, 5–6, 28–9, 31, 47, 54–5, 65, 67, 71–2, 76–7, 80–2, 162, 167, 170, 182, 187, 190, 192, 194, 197, 200, 202, 204–5
Butler, Judith 73, 75, 84

Caldwell, Anne 168–9
Campbell, David 4, 124n58, 163
Caputi, Jane 204–5
carboniferous capitalism 14, 188–90, 192, 194
Carr, E.H. 13, 154, 158
casualties 39, 81, 171
Center for Infectious Disease Research (CIDRAP) 164
Centers for Disease Control and Prevention (CDC) 169, 172
Cheney, Dick 79, 83, 187
Chertoff, Michael 76
Chicken Little 161, 176
Children of Men 2, 89, 92
chronopolitics 75–7, 84
climate change 3–4, 7, 27, 34, 88–9, 102, 182–4, 186, 194
Cold War 1, 4, 18–19, 31, 45, 49, 65, 83, 90, 96, 126, 129, 165, 174, 191, 209
Colomina, Beatriz 89–90
Combs, Sean (P. Diddy) 197

Commission on Human Security 148, 150, 152
conspicuous asceticism 181, 192
containment 171, 199, 201, 205–7, 211
control society 11–12, 88–95, 99–100, 102–4
Crime Scene Investigation (CSI) 92
critical geopolitics 3, 9, 107, 112–14
critical pedagogy 77–8, 84
Currie, Andrew 198–9, 204–5, 209

Dalby, Simon 4, 165
Dante, Joe 15, 198–9, 201–4, 208–9
Dargis, Manohla 206, 209
Davis, Mike 165
Day of the Dead 198, 205
De Gaulle, Charles 56, 62
Debrix, François 73
Deleuze, Gilles 9, 11, 88, 90–6, 100–1, 108, 128, 132, 136, 138, 163
democracy 45, 55–7, 66–8, 81, 139, 143, 152–7, 192, 197, 209–11
Der Derian, James 4, 9
Derrida, Jacques 102, 202, 209
Dershowitz, Alan 61, 82
Design and the Elastic Mind 1–2
deterritorialization 76, 114, 119, 126, 128, 130–3, 135–8
Dick, Philip K. 88, 93
discipline 6, 39, 56, 90, 96, 101, 112, 133, 145–6
discourse 5, 10, 13, 25, 30, 73–4, 82, 112, 129, 131, 143–4, 147–52, 154–8, 167, 190, 205; and activism 183; and geopolitics 165; and identity 107; political 43, 46, 155
Dorfman, Ariel 78–9
Dunne, Anthony 89

ecological modernization 189, 193–4
Empire 2, 12–13, 20, 107–8, 118–20, 126–8, 131, 136–7, 182, 190, 194; as "empirean" order 22–31, 190, 209
Elshtain, Jean Bethke 35
epidemic 47, 162–3; as pandemic 164
ethnic politics 36–9, 42–3, 152; American 45–8
extraordinary rendition 49, 55, 67, 75, 79

Falk, Richard 3
fear: politics of 2, 4, 9, 14, 41, 66, 84, 102–3, 138, 161, 167, 174, 176, 194, 206; *see also* anxiety
Federal Emergency Planning Agency (FEMA) 26
Ferguson, Charles 83–4

Ferguson, Niall 19–20, 28, 30, 191
Fernandez, Jorge 165
Fido 15, 198–9, 204–11
Fordism 186, 188
Foucault, Michel 9, 12, 26, 40, 82, 88, 90–1, 108, 119–21, 127, 144–6, 155, 168
freedom from fear 148, 150–2
freedom from lack 148, 150–2
Friedman, Thomas 81, 192–4
Fukuyama, Francis 3–4, 7, 9, 25, 27

Geneva Conventions 54, 63, 69n33, 77, 79
ghosts 44, 79, 202
Ghosts of Abu Ghraib 75, 79
Gibson, William 89
Giroux, Henry 78
global civil society 12–13, 126, 129, 134–5
global governance 24, 126, 128
global triage 169–71
globalization 12, 24–6, 126, 129–30, 132, 139, 161, 175
Global War on Terror (GWOT) *see* war on terror
Gore, Al 2, 4, 102, 192, 194
governmentality 9, 13–14, 25–6, 67, 144–5, 147, 155, 157–8
Graseck, Susan 80
Gray, John 6
Guantanamo Bay 68, 75–6, 81, 157, 199
Guantanamo: Honor Bound to Defend Freedom 74, 79
Guattari, Felix 128, 132, 136, 138
Gulf War 184

Habermas, Jürgen 2, 103
Hanson, Victor Davis 41
Hardt, Michael 2, 9, 12, 24–5, 27, 67, 99, 107–8, 110–13, 118–21, 126–32, 13–40, 190, 209–10
Harvey, David 187, 190
haunting 15, 44, 137, 202–4, 209, 211
Heritage Foundation 76
Hoffmann, Stanley 3
Homecoming 15, 198–204, 208–10
Homeland Security 26, 29, 68, 76, 96, 103, 118, 125n74, 164, 205
Horne, Alistair 57–8, 60–3
horror films 198–200, 204
Hotel Rwanda 165
human development 149–51
Human Development Report 143, 147
Human Rights First 74, 77
human security 13, 143–58
humanism 129, 138–40, 143, 152–4, 158
Hurricane Katrina 4, 8, 10, 18, 28–9, 167, 194

hype-power 8, 9, 18–19, 21–25, 27–31, 88, 101, 165, 191
hyper-power 2, 4, 8–10, 15n2, 18–24, 27, 29–31, 56

Illegal Immigration Reform and Immigrant Responsibility Act (IIRIRA) 114, 116–17, 124n58
imperial citizen 11, 57, 65–8
imperialism 12, 18, 21–2, 28, 126–9, 131–3, 139, 190, 194–5; American 28, 83, 130–1, 134, 181–2; and oil 14, 181, 183–9, 192–3
individualism 183–4
industrial food production 175–6
infected life 171
Iraq 14, 28, 30–1, 44–5, 55–8, 60, 68, 75, 77, 81–2, 128, 133–5, 167, 184–7, 190, 192, 199
Iraq War 5, 19, 31, 47, 49, 55–6, 58, 66, 68, 71, 73–4, 80, 127–8, 133–5, 162, 185, 190, 197, 199–200, 204; films 83; news coverage of 74
Iran 27, 29, 44, 55, 58, 187–8, 190
Israel 9, 90, 187
Israel lobby 5

Japan 28, 72, 74, 81, 154–8
Johnson, Chalmers 24

Kandahar 18
Kaplan, Robert D. 6, 9, 24
Karbala 18
Kellner, Douglas 73, 139
Kennedy, John F. 46
Kennedy, Paul 19
Kennedy, Rory 79
Klare, Michael 185–7
Klee, Paul 172–3
Klein, Naomi 2, 81
Kolko, Gabriel 20
Korean War 24, 45, 49
Kosovo 167, 186
Kuwait 30, 47, 184
Kyoto Protocol 182

Lagouranis, Tony 77–8
Lebanon 90
legitimacy 10–11, 38, 43–5, 54–7, 62–5, 67–8, 74, 119, 131, 155
Loewen, James W. 73–4
"long war" 19, 31
love 204–7, 210; of country 39, 76; politics of 199, 209–11
Lovins, Amory 191–3
Luban, David 61

Luke, Timothy W. 4, 14

Marmysz, John 198, 202, 209
Marx, Karl 108, 140n5
Massumi, Brian 163, 174
Mayer, Jane 76
Mearsheimer, John 2, 5–7
Mitterrand, François 59
Morgenthau, Hans 6, 17n32
multitude 2, 24–7, 111–12, 118–21, 127, 131, 138, 210–11

national identity 10, 35–40, 44–6, 48
National Liberation Front (FLN) 59, 62
Negri, Antonio 2, 9, 12, 24–5, 27, 67, 99, 107–13, 118–21, 126–32, 136–40, 190, 209–10
neo-conservatism 5–6, 12, 55, 130–1
Night of the Living Dead 198
nihilism 198–9, 202, 209
Nitzan, Jonathan 185–7, 189
No End in Sight 83–4
Nordstrom, Carolyn 100
North Korea 23, 29, 154–8
Nye, Joseph 7, 14, 20–1, 102, 191

Obama, Barack 17n34
Okinawa 157–8
Ontario Health Plan for an Influenza Pandemic (OHPIP) 170
ontopolitics 10, 34–45, 47
operaismo (workerism) 108–9
Operation Community Shield 118
Operation Predator 118
Organisation Armée Secrète (OAS) 62, 65
Osterholm, Michael 164, 169–70

panic 13–14, 48, 163, 171–2, 174
peace-building 149, 151–2
Pentagon 22, 24, 46–8
pharmakon/pharmakos 10, 35–6, 39–44
pharmacotic violence and war 10–11, 14–15, 34–45, 47–9, 101
political economy 4, 21, 111, 175, 193
political identity 72–3, 107, 115, 146, 188, 194
preemption 72, 163, 168
Primetime Torture 74, 77–8
Project for the New American Century 130
Promise to the Dead 75

Raby, Fiona 89
Red Cross 69n33, 138
refusal of the state 108, 111, 118, 120
refusal of work 108–10, 112
Rejali, Darius 81–2

Rendition 75, 79
resistance 2, 18, 78, 99–101, 171, 173, 176, 181–2, 193–4, 198, 209–10
reterritorialization 128, 131–2, 136–8
Road to Guantanamo 75, 79
Romero, George 198–9, 202, 204, 209
Rumsfeld, Donald 19
Russia 20, 44, 184

SAFE: Design Takes on Risk 14, 88–90, 93–9, 103
Salan, Raoul 62, 65
Sartre, Jean-Paul 62
scapegoating 10, 12, 35–6, 38, 40–1, 43–5, 48–9
Schmitt, Carl 57, 63, 168
Scott, A.O. 71
securitization 39–40, 112, 119, 121, 193; of migration 108, 112, 114, 120
self-valorization 109–12
September 11, 2001 (9/11) 1, 20, 44, 47–8, 73, 76, 78, 91, 127–9, 207, 210; aftermath of 2–3, 5, 8–10, 31, 49, 54–5, 67, 76, 78–80, 93, 102–3, 130–1, 139, 167, 182, 188, 204
Shaun of the Dead 197, 204–5
Shaviro, Steven 93
Sinclair, Cameron 93
smart power 7–9, 12, 14, 17n47, 102
Smith, Anthony 45
Smith, Daniel 163
South Korea 28
Southland Tales 1–2, 102
sovereignty 4, 12, 18, 24, 26, 43, 112, 119, 121, 127–9, 131–9, 147, 153–4, 161, 166–70, 209–10
Spanish flu 164
specters *see* ghosts
Sports-Utility Vehicles (SUVs) 14, 96, 182–3, 185, 188, 190, 192; activism against 182–4; critiques of 181, 183, 186
state of emergency 11, 13, 29, 93, 95, 161–76
state of exception 8, 13, 146, 158, 161, 167–8
Stiglitz, Joseph 6
Stohr, Klaus 162, 166, 171
superpower 19, 24, 57, 65–8
Syria 29, 55, 58

Taleb, Nassim Nicholas 4
Taxi to the Dark Side 75, 79, 83

Taylor, Peter 181
Teitgen, Paul-Henri 54, 60–2
The Battle of Algiers 58–9, 75, 78
The Torture Question 75
Tipton Three 81
torture 11, 42, 48, 54–64, 67, 71–2, 74–84
Tosa, Hiroyuki 146–7, 154
tsunami 167
undocumented migration 112–15, 120, 123n54
United Nations 12, 26, 59, 131, 133–5, 137, 148, 168
United Nations Development Program (UNDP) 143, 147–50
US immigration law 113–16, 118, 123n54; and aggravated felony 115, 118; and interior immigration enforcement 115–20; and worksite enforcement 118, 125n77

vampires 204–5
Vietnam War 6, 24, 47–9, 83, 203; and education 71, 73–4
Virilio, Paul 18, 25, 30, 76, 98, 172

Walt, Stephen 2, 5–7
war: American 18–9, 24, 34, 36, 45–9, 77–8, 133, 199, 203–4; and anti-war activism 56, 65–6, 74, 81, 192–4, 199–200, 204, 211; biopolitical 138–40, 168; just 51n20; of attrition 54–63; over oil 184–6, 193; regenerative function of 10, 34–7; relative 27, 30–1; total 171; veterans 199, 203; visual 72–5
war on terror 5, 7, 10–13, 25, 29, 47, 54–6, 67–8, 71–6, 83–4, 91, 107, 127–36, 188, 199, 210
Weizman, Eyal 9
white Southerners *see* American South
Wolin, Sheldon 11, 57, 65–6
World Health Organization (WHO) 13, 26, 162, 165–6, 168–9
World Trade Center, the 73, 114, 127
World War I 44, 47–9, 153–4, 164, 183
World War II 18–19, 47–9, 56, 58, 60, 65, 74–5, 91, 171, 203
World War III 1, 31

Yelavich, Susan 97–8

Zizek, Slavoj 77, 81
zombies 15, 197–211

eBooks – at www.eBookstore.tandf.co.uk

A library at your fingertips!

eBooks are electronic versions of printed books. You can store them on your PC/laptop or browse them online.

They have advantages for anyone needing rapid access to a wide variety of published, copyright information.

eBooks can help your research by enabling you to bookmark chapters, annotate text and use instant searches to find specific words or phrases. Several eBook files would fit on even a small laptop or PDA.

NEW: Save money by eSubscribing: cheap, online access to any eBook for as long as you need it.

Annual subscription packages

We now offer special low-cost bulk subscriptions to packages of eBooks in certain subject areas. These are available to libraries or to individuals.

For more information please contact webmaster.ebooks@tandf.co.uk

We're continually developing the eBook concept, so keep up to date by visiting the website.

www.eBookstore.tandf.co.uk